# DATE DUE

| | | | |
|---|---|---|---|
| NO 2 0 '96 | | | |
| NO 2 6 '99 | | | |
| DE 6 '99 | | | |
| | | | |
| | | | |
| | | | |
| | | | |
| | | | |
| | | | |
| | | | |
| | | | |
| | | | |
| | | | |
| | | | |
| | | | |
| | | | |
| | | | |
| | | | |

DEMCO 38-296

ALSO BY ALAN BRINKLEY

*Voices of Protest:*
*Huey Long, Father Coughlin, and the Great Depression*

*The Unfinished Nation:*
*A Concise History of the American People*

# The End of Reform

# The End of Reform

## New Deal Liberalism in Recession and War

# Alan Brinkley

*Alfred A. Knopf   New York   1995*

THIS IS A BORZOI BOOK
PUBLISHED BY ALFRED A. KNOPF, INC.

Library of Congress Cataloging-in-Publication Data
Brinkley, Alan.
The end of reform: New Deal liberalism in recession and war/
by Alan Brinkley.—
1st ed.
p.    cm.
Includes bibliographical references and index.
ISBN 0-394-53573-1
1. New Deal, 1933–1939. 2. Liberalism—United States—History—20th
century.
3. United States—Politics and government—1933–1945.
I. Title.
E806.B747 1995
973.917—dc20        94-21478
CIP

Manufactured in the United States of America

First Edition

*To my parents*

*Liberalism*
*p. 8*

#2

# Contents

# Acknowledgments

One of the few advantages of taking as long to write a book as I have taken to write this one is that it has given me the chance to benefit from the generosity of many people. I am grateful to the John Simon Guggenheim Foundation and to Harvard University for financial support for my first year of research on this project; and to the Woodrow Wilson Center, the National Humanities Center, and the Freedom Forum Center for Media Studies at Columbia University—stimulating and supportive intellectual environments in which I did much of the writing. I am grateful as well to the staffs of the many archives I visited in connection with this project. A complete list of these libraries appears at the end of this book, but I want to offer particular thanks to the archivists of the Manuscripts Division of the Library of Congress, the National Archives, and the Franklin D. Roosevelt Presidential Library in Hyde Park, all of whom cheerfully accommodated voluminous and at times arcane requests.

I owe special thanks to Daniel Aaron, Brian Balogh, Robert Cuff, Frank Freidel, Gary Gerstle, Hugh Heclo, Arnold Hirsch, Michael Lacey, Bradford Lee, William E. Leuchtenburg, Nelson Lichtenstein, Richard L. McCormick, Michael McGerr, Michael Sandel, Judith Shklar, and Sam Bass Warner—all of whom read and commented on my work at one or another stage of its progress. Robert Dallek, Charles B. Forcey, Steven Gillon, Ira Katznelson, Mark Leff, James T. Patterson, Roy Rosenzweig, and Theda Skocpol read the entire manuscript in its penultimate form. I benefited enormously from their advice, even if I was at times unable to do it justice. Ashbel Green was, as always, a patient, supportive, and perceptive editor.

I was fortunate in having the help of skilled research assistants at almost every point along the way. I am grateful to, among others,

Matthew Brogan, Vincent Chang, Charles B. Forcey, Simon Frankel, Caroline Fredrickson, David Goldberg, Richard Greenwald, Yanek Mieczkowski, Francesca Morgan, Edward Rogers, Thaddeus Russell, William Storey, and Evan Williams.

My wife, Evangeline Morphos, brought her considerable gifts as an editor and literary critic to bear on this manuscript and showed me how to make some of my arguments more comprehensible to readers outside the academic world. More important, she, and our daughter, Elly, have enriched my life in ways far beyond my capacity to express.

*Alan Brinkley*

# The End of Reform

# Introduction

# The Concept of
# New Deal Liberalism

EVEN FRANKLIN ROOSEVELT must ultimately have realized, looking back on the frustrations of his second term as president, that by the
end of 1937 the active phase of the New Deal had largely come to an end.
There were, to be sure, occasional initiatives and occasional triumphs in
the years that followed, some of real importance. On the whole, however,
the Roosevelt administration in those years no longer had the political
capital—and at times, it seemed, no longer the political will—to sustain
a program of reform in any way comparable to its earlier efforts. The
result was a political stalemate that continued into and beyond World
War II.

Yet if the New Deal developed only modestly as a program after 1937,
it continued to develop as an idea. Indeed, it was in the late 1930s and the
war years, even more than in the earlier and more dynamic period of
activism and accomplishment, that what a later generation came to know
as "New Deal liberalism" assumed its mature and lasting form—a form
related to, yet substantially different from, the cluster of ideas that had
shaped the earlier stages of the Roosevelt administration.

This redefinition of New Deal thought occurred slowly and at times
almost imperceptibly, so much so that in 1945, when the transformation
was well advanced, relatively few liberals were fully aware that it had
even occurred. The new liberalism was not the result of a blinding
revelation or a sudden decision. It emerged, rather, from innumerable
small adaptations that gradually but decisively accumulated. It emerged
because by the late 1930s it had become evident that the concrete
achievements of the New Deal had ceased to bear any clear relation to
the ideological rationales that had supported their creation, and thus that
liberals needed new rationales to explain and justify them. It emerged
because the recession of 1937, the changing political climate of the late

1930s, and the experience of World War II substantially altered the environment in which liberals thought and acted.

Above all, it developed because, as in all eras, political ideas were constantly interacting with, and adapting to, larger changes in the social, economic, and cultural landscape. Even without fully realizing it, liberals in the 1930s were reshaping their convictions in response to the realities of the world they knew. It was a world of increasing urbanization; a world in which independent merchants, family farmers, and small entrepreneurs, whose interests had inspired earlier generations of reform, were rapidly losing their dominance in American economic life; a world in which large-scale bureaucracies were becoming ever more dominant and in which it was becoming increasingly difficult to imagine an alternative to them. It was a world in which workers, farmers, consumers, and others were mobilizing and becoming powerful interest groups capable of influencing public policy and political discourse. Most of all, perhaps, it was a world in which both the idea and the reality of mass consumption were becoming central to American culture and to the American economy, gradually supplanting production as the principal focus of popular hopes and commitment. In an economy driven by consumer spending, and in a culture increasingly dominated by dreams of consumption, it is not surprising that political thought began to reflect consumer-oriented assumptions as well.

The new liberalism that evolved in response to this changing world wrapped itself in the mantle of the New Deal, but bore only a partial resemblance to the ideas that had shaped the original New Deal. It was more coherent, less diverse, and on the whole less challenging to the existing structure of corporate capitalism than some of the ideas it supplanted. For at least twenty years after the end of World War II, it dominated liberal thought and liberal action. To some extent, battered and reviled as it has become, it remains near the center of American political life still. How and why it emerged is the subject of this book.

WHAT MOST CLEARLY characterized the intellectual landscape of the first years of the New Deal was an exceptionally wide range of approaches to reform. Some were rooted in the progressive philosophies of the first decades of the twentieth century, others in the experience of World War I, still others in some of the generally unsuccessful reform initiatives of the 1920s.[1] Observers at the time and since have commented on the seeming chaos of New Deal policy and the apparent absence of any coherent rationale for it all. Alvin Hansen, the eminent economist who was himself an important figure in the later New Deal, answered a question in 1940 about the "basic principle of the New Deal" by saying, "I really do not know what the basic principle of the New Deal is. I know from my experience in the government that there are as many conflicting opinions among the people in Washington under this administration as we have in the country at large." Fifteen years later, the historian Richard Hofstadter called the New Deal a "chaos of experimentation"—virtually bereft of ideology except perhaps for a vague general commitment to pragmatic change.[2]

In fact, the early New Deal was awash in ideas—ideas of significant range and diversity (at least by American standards), but ones that somehow managed for a time to coexist. One broad assumption was particularly important to the early New Deal notion of reform, just as it had been of special importance to most American reformers since early in the twentieth century: the assumption that the nation's greatest problems were rooted in the structure of modern industrial capitalism and that it was the mission of government to deal somehow with the flaws in that structure. Like the progressives before them, few New Dealers were genuinely hostile to capitalism. But they were not uncritical defenders. The belief that something was wrong with capitalism and that government should find a way to repair it was, therefore, a central element of liberal thought throughout much of the 1930s.

Among the most important manifestations of this critique was a preoccupation with the issue of concentrated economic power, the problem of "monopoly." It produced a variety of approaches to economic policy that competed with (and often frustrated) one another in the first years of the Depression. Both inside and outside government, there were important voices advocating a decentralization of economic power, "anti-monopolists" who envisioned a frontal assault on "bigness" and concentration in the corporate world and who often called as well for policies that would redistribute wealth and income. There were advocates of centralized economic planning, who wished to curb the power of corporations by greatly increasing the managerial power of government and who sought to create an effective state apparatus closely involved in the day-to-day workings of the economy. There were (as there had been at least since World War I) supporters of the vaguely corporatist concept of business "associationalism," who advocated cartelistic arrangements within major industries to curb the destabilizing impact of competition—arrangements in which the government would play a modest, largely uncoercive role.[3] On the edges of liberal economic thought were more radical ideas: the conviction that the Depression had revealed the obsolescence of capitalism and the need for a fundamentally new system. Few New Dealers embraced such beliefs; but given their own preoccupation with the structure of capitalism, most found them less alien and threatening than would later generations of liberals.[4] All these approaches had some effect on policy; none of them prevailed.

Alongside this concern with the structure of the economy, other legacies of past reform crusades and other responses to the problems of the 1930s were shaping the early New Deal. The search for a way to end the Depression was, of course, the most immediate and compelling challenge facing the administration in its first four years. But the desire for economic recovery led New Dealers in many different directions. There were efforts to stabilize particular sectors of the economy or particular regions. Two of the administration's most important and successful initiatives were agricultural reform and regional planning (embodied most notably in the Agricultural Adjustment Administration and the Tennessee Valley Authority).[5] One of the New Deal's most significant ventures was its substantial investment in what we now call "infrastructure" projects, most of them in the South and the West: roads, bridges, dams, irrigation and hydroelectric projects, rural electrification, and others, which together helped lay the groundwork for substantial economic growth and expansion in these regions after the war.[6] New Dealers worked as well to create government-sponsored social welfare and social insurance programs; to enact protective legislation for labor; to promote public power development; and to advance conservation. There were even vaguely utopian schemes, such visionary experiments as creating new cooperative communities. In the heady atmosphere of those early years, it often seemed that no dream was too extravagant, no proposal too outlandish, that almost anything was possible.

The intellectual life of the early New Deal, in short, was unusually diverse and fluid. The nation's problems were serious enough, the political possibilities great enough, to permit the coexistence of many different prescriptions for government's response.

A decade later, in 1945, the ideology of American liberalism looked strikingly different. The critique of modern capitalism that had been so important in the early 1930s (and, indeed, for several decades before that) was largely gone, or at least so attenuated as to be of little more than rhetorical significance. In its place was a set of liberal ideas essentially reconciled to the existing structure of the economy and committed to using the state to compensate for capitalism's inevitable flaws—a philosophy that signaled, implicitly at least, a resolution of some of the most divisive political controversies of the industrial era.

At the heart of the "New Deal liberalism" of these later years were many of the impulses that had been present but not yet pre-eminent within liberal thought in the 1930s, most notably the commitment to retaining and expanding the institutions of the welfare state. But equally vital was a set of beliefs about the role of government in the economy that were rhetorically familiar but substantively new. Liberals in the 1940s still talked about fighting monopoly, about economic cooperation, and most of all about planning (a term that had for some taken on an almost religious significance). But the familiar language of reform was describing a significantly altered approach to reform. When liberals spoke now of government's responsibility to protect the health of the industrial world, they defined that responsibility less as a commitment to restructure the economy than as an effort to stabilize it and help it to grow. They were no longer much concerned about controlling or punishing "plutocrats" and "economic royalists," an impulse central to New Deal rhetoric in the mid-1930s. Instead, they spoke of their commitment to providing a healthy environment in which the corporate world could flourish and in which the economy could sustain "full employment."

Fiscal policy—the getting and spending of money by the federal government—had become the focus of liberal hopes for the economy; "planning" now meant an Olympian manipulation of macroeconomic levers, not direct intervention in the day-to-day affairs of the corporate world. Keynesianism was the label Americans ultimately assigned to this new approach. But even before the ideas of John Maynard Keynes had won a large audience in the United States, important elements of Keynesianism—most of all, the idea that the state could manage the economy without managing the institutions of the economy—had already begun to emerge as important elements of liberal thought.[7]

This reconstruction of New Deal liberalism was the product of two overlapping periods of adjustment. In the first, the late 1930s, influential liberals—responding in part to the political and economic crisis produced by the recession of 1937—sought to make sense of the achievements of Roosevelt's first term and to create an agenda for the future. The result was a confused and contentious process of adjustment during which many liberals repudiated (at least implicitly) some of the impulses that had been prominent in the early New Deal and haltingly embraced new assumptions. The outbreak of World War II found this process of adaptation far from complete, and the war itself produced a second, and more decisive, period of change. The wartime experience muted liberal hostility to capitalism and the corporate world. It challenged the commitment of liberals to a powerful, centralized state and turned their efforts into less direct, less confrontational channels. And it helped legitimize both Keynesian fiscal policies and the idea of expanded social welfare commitments.

The story of the New Deal, then, is not simply the story of the important legislative and administrative accomplishments of the presidency of Franklin D. Roosevelt. It is also a story of ideological adaptation: the story of how a broad community of New Dealers and their liberal allies made choices among a wide range of policy prescriptions, and how in the process they helped define an agenda for future liberal efforts. It is the story of how they helped bring to a close a long period of "reform" and replace it with a new, and different, liberal order.

Hence the title of this book. *The End of Reform* refers in part to a conventional, and generally correct, view of the New Deal in the period from 1937 to 1945. The New Deal did, in fact, largely come to an end in those years as an active force for reform; its growing political weaknesses left it unable to match, or even approach, the great liberal achievements of its first term. But the title also refers to a less visible and less familiar story—the movement of liberalism itself away from one tradition and toward another.

ANYONE PROPOSING to write in the 1990s about liberalism and the state must come to terms with vigorous debates over the meaning of both concepts. In particular, it is necessary to explain how one proposes to use that versatile and controversial term "liberal."

Liberalism is not, as some scholars in the 1940s and 1950s maintained, the only important political tradition in America.[8] It has always coexisted, and often competed, with alternative traditions and movements in a diverse ideological world. But liberalism has been near the center of American political and intellectual life since the beginning of the republic. And it has itself been a broad and changing set of beliefs, difficult if not impossible to define with any real precision. All liberals claim to believe in personal liberty, human progress, and the pursuit of rational self-interest by individuals as the basis of a free society. But there is considerable, often intense, disagreement among them over what those ideas mean. In the twentieth century alone, the word "liberalism" has designated at least three very different concepts of progress and freedom.[9]

At the beginning of the century, and for many decades previously, "liberalism" generally referred to a belief in economic freedom and strictly limited government. This laissez-faire liberalism is often described today as "conservatism," but it was, in fact, a challenge to an earlier nineteenth-century conservatism rooted in the protection of tradition and fixed social hierarchies. Laissez-faire liberalism envisioned a fluid, changing society in which the state would not protect existing patterns of wealth and privilege, in which individuals could pursue their goals freely and advance in accordance with their own merits and achievements.[10]

In practice, of course, laissez-faire liberals did not create a genuinely fluid, open society. Ambitious entrepreneurs decried state interference when it constrained them, but they welcomed, even demanded, government assistance when it was of use to them. Nor were the capitalist champions of laissez-faire genuinely committed to an open competition for wealth and power. They lobbied for protection from foreign competition through tariffs; they struggled to escape domestic competition by creating pools, cartels, holding companies, and trusts; and they often benefited from government intervention in protecting themselves from challenges from their own workers.[11] But the "liberal" idea—however inadequately it described social reality—became a potent justification for a rapidly expanding capitalist world, and for a notion of individual freedom that was becoming increasingly important within that world.

Beginning early in the twentieth century, a competing form of liberalism emerged: a "reform" liberalism, skeptical of laissez-faire claims that an unrestricted social and economic marketplace would produce a just and open society. Reform liberals (most of whom at first called themselves progressives) embraced so many different goals that historians have at times despaired of establishing any definition at all of the concept of "progressivism" or "reform." But among the ways in which progressives distinguished themselves from laissez-faire liberals was their belief in the interconnectedness of society, and thus in the need to protect individuals, communities, and the government itself from excessive corporate power, the need to ensure the citizenry a basic level of subsistence and dignity, usually through some form of state intervention.[12]

The New Deal emerged out of this diverse and conflicted tradition of reform, attached the word "liberalism" to it,[13] and set about transforming it. New Dealers had little interest in the moral aspects of progressive reform; they generally avoided issues of race, ethnicity, family, gender, and personal behavior—in part because they feared the cultural and political battles such issues had produced in the 1920s, battles that had done great damage to the Democratic party and ones many liberals had come to interpret as a form of popular irrationality. And they were not much committed to political reform either; the Roosevelt administration rarely challenged, and indeed did much to buttress, the power of bosses and machines, and never made the assault on political corruption as central to its self-definition as earlier generations of reformers had done. But the New Deal did embrace (and indeed defined itself by) other concerns of progressive reformers. Above all (and unsurprisingly in the midst of the greatest economic crisis in American history), it embraced the conviction that government must play an active role in the economy. "I am not for a return to that definition of liberty under which for many years a free people were gradually regimented into the service [of capital]," Franklin Roosevelt once said. Liberalism, he argued, "is plain English for a changed concept of the duty and responsibility of government toward economic life."[14]

In the aftermath of the New Deal, and partly as a result of it, a third form of liberalism emerged—one that has now dominated much of American political life for several generations. This new liberalism has focused less on the broad needs of the nation and the modern economy than on increasing the rights and freedoms of individuals and social groups. It has sought to extend civil rights to minorities, women, and others previously excluded from the mainstream of American life. It has also attempted to expand the notion of personal liberty and individual freedom for everyone. Rights-based liberalism has embraced some of the issues that were of importance to earlier reformers—among them the commitment to generous programs of social insurance and public welfare. But there has been little room within rights-based liberalism for the broad efforts to reshape the capitalist economy that concerned previous generations of reformers.[15]

The later years of the New Deal were an important moment of transition between the reform liberalism of the first third of the twentieth century and the rights-based liberalism that succeeded it. In those years, a large and influential group of people in and around the Roosevelt administration—people who considered themselves liberals—attempted to redefine liberalism in relation to what they considered the central issues of their time. New Dealers had by then long since rejected the classical laissez-faire liberalism of the nineteenth century and had worked strenuously to give their own, very different meaning to the word. They were not yet particularly concerned with (or, at first, even much aware of) the rights-based liberalism that would become central to the postwar era. They differed on many things, but most began with the assumption that Roosevelt had expressed early in his presidency: that liberalism meant a commitment to reform, and in particular to using government to deal in some way with the problems of the modern economy—its structure, its performance, and the distribution of power within it. Most agreed that the state must play an important role in the solution of such problems.

But in dealing with the questions they considered important—questions of political economy—liberals of the late 1930s and 1940s gradually changed both the questions they were asking and the answers they were providing. Ultimately, New Dealers so transformed their vision of political economy that it no longer bore much direct relation to the progressive traditions that had originally informed their efforts. As a result, the New Deal was at once the culmination of and the end to a long tradition of reform—and the beginning of a new and very different liberal era.

SCHOLARLY DISCUSSIONS of political economy inevitably intersect with an important debate over the character of the state and its role in shaping public action. And since much of this book deals with the inner workings of the state and its relationship to various other communities, it seems appropriate to explain the ways in which it does and does not relate to that debate. A large body of scholarship, much of it the product of the 1960s and 1970s, has attempted to portray the state as an agent of social and political forces external to it. Public policy, scholars assumed, was a response to popular movements, interest groups, political coalitions, party structures, or corporate elites. The state itself was an essentially reactive vehicle through which individuals and groups largely outside government pursued their ends.[16]

In the last decade or so, another group of scholars has challenged this "society-centered" approach, offering instead what they call a "state-centered" (or, more recently, "polity-centered") theory of public action. The state and the institutions surrounding it, they argue, are themselves crucial factors in determining the outcome of political struggles, indeed often more influential than social forces or the efforts of popular interest groups. Eric Nordlinger, one of the early theorists of the "state-centered" approach, wrote in 1981 (somewhat more starkly than would most later scholars):

> ... the preferences of the state are at least as important as those of civil society in accounting for what the democratic state does and does not do; the democratic state is not only frequently autonomous insofar as it regularly acts upon its preferences, but also markedly autonomous in doing so even when its preferences diverge from the demands of the most powerful groups in civil society.[17]

Historians of the Roosevelt years have tended, not always wittingly, to align themselves with those who see the state as highly autonomous. Some have portrayed the New Deal as a triumph of enlightened, progressive leaders—Franklin Roosevelt first among them—who used the political opportunities created by the Great Depression to shatter an existing orthodoxy and create a new, more democratic distribution of power.[18] Others see the New Deal as the triumph of essentially conservative leaders who understood better than most capitalists did themselves what was necessary to preserve existing patterns of power and wealth; they reshaped the state to make it an effective and essentially unthreatening ally of corporate power.[19] Both supporters and critics have, more often than not, portrayed the New Deal as the product of impulses and initiatives within the government (and within the Roosevelt administration). Some scholars in the 1960s, and others more recently, have challenged these implicit assumptions of state autonomy during the New Deal by demonstrating the direct and decisive influence of corporate leaders in shaping policies in the 1930s. But even these scholars tend to portray the state in the 1930s as a relatively rarefied world, dominated by a small group of intersecting elites.[20]

I began my work on the character of liberalism and the state convinced that the state-centered approach to policy was inadequate to explain the New Deal—that an examination of the way in which liberals and others defined and articulated their aims would reveal the influence of a much broader array of social and political forces than some earlier accounts had suggested. I still believe that. The history of the New Deal is replete with evidence of how outside forces shape the behavior of the state. Some of the New Deal's most important achievements were to a large degree a direct result of the influence of those outside forces. Agrarian dissent and powerful farm organizations were important to the creation of New Deal agricultural policies. The rank-and-file labor activism of 1934 and beyond was vital to the passage of the Wagner Act of 1935 and to government initiatives affecting labor relations in subsequent years. The apparent strength of the Long, Coughlin, Townsend, and other popular movements affected the Roosevelt administration's decisions to propose such measures as Social Security and progressive taxation in 1935. And the influence of social workers, women's organizations, and reform activists helped shape the character of the New Deal welfare state.[21] More evidence that social movements and cultural forces outside the state often shape government action comes from the more recent past. The civil rights movement, the antiwar movement, feminism, the environmental movement, the right-to-life and pro-choice movements, the gay and lesbian civil rights movement, and many others have had substantial, often direct, effects on public policy.

And yet there remain public questions that exist within a more contained and exclusive political sphere, a sphere the clamor of popular protest and the power of social movements do not penetrate as often or as effectively. Among them are the questions that dominate this book—questions of political economy, the questions that preoccupied liberals in the later years of the New Deal and that, for many of them, represented the essence of liberalism. Debates on these issues were not confined to the state itself, and it was not institutional factors alone that determined their outcomes. But they did exist largely within a world of elites—intersecting networks of liberal policymakers, journalists, scholars, and intellectuals, both inside and outside government. It was a world overwhelmingly dominated by white middle-class men, most of whom were insulated—by position or temperament or both—from many of the pressures and claims of popular politics and social movements. Women, minorities, and working-class people became part of their deliberations from time to time, but they rarely shaped the direction or tenor of the conversation decisively.

That is not to say that the network of elites who dominated the debates over political economy existed in a cultural or social vacuum. They responded directly and self-consciously to external events—to the recession of 1937, to the rise of totalitarianism in Europe, to the experiences of World War II, and to the ebb and flow of liberal political fortunes within the electorate and within Congress. They responded to other, competing elites—most notably to the courts and to elements of the corporate world.

Above all, they responded to broad social processes, even if they were not always fully aware of how they were doing so. One of the defining features of the later years of the New Deal was the way in which liberals of all kinds adjusted to large changes in their world; the way in which the trajectory of their own ideas came to mirror the trajectory of the larger culture. In particular, liberals responded to the transformation of the United States from a producer-oriented to a consumer-oriented society, and they developed a set of ideas that reflected that transformation. Understanding liberal ideas and actions requires, therefore, not just consideration of political elites and their institutional milieu, but consideration as well of the often elusive connections between the elite world of politics and the state, and the larger world of which politicians and intellectuals are a part and to which they, like everyone else, respond.

·  ·  ·

I BEGAN this book in part because it seemed to me that there was an important missing chapter in the history of the New Deal and modern liberalism. I wanted to explore some aspects of political and intellectual life in the late 1930s and early 1940s, a period that had attracted relatively little attention from scholars of political economy and political thought. And I wanted to explain why "New Deal liberalism" as postwar America knew it looked so different from the ideas that had characterized much of the New Deal itself.[22]

Still, I would be less than frank if I did not concede that this project also emerged in part as a response to more contemporary political questions. I began this book in the heyday of the "Reagan Revolution," a moment of defeat and disarray from which American liberals have yet fully to recover. I complete it in the midst of a weak and floundering liberal revival. As I tried to understand why modern American liberalism had proved to be a so much weaker and more vulnerable force than almost anyone would have imagined a generation ago, my thoughts turned to the process by which liberalism assumed its modern form in the last years of the New Deal. And as I looked further, I found that process—a process of adjustment and redefinition in the face of failures and frustrations—similar in many ways to the process by which many liberals in our own time have attempted to change themselves during their long years in the wilderness.

This book tells the story of one effort to transform liberalism in response to the demands of a new and challenging time. Another such effort is still in progress.

*Chapter One*

# The Crisis of
# New Deal Liberalism

FRANKLIN ROOSEVELT spent election night 1936 sitting in his mother's dining room in Hyde Park, New York, surrounded by charts, graphs, and teletype machines bringing news of his remarkable triumph. "It looks as though this sweep has carried every single section of the country," he told the jubilant crowd of local Democrats who gathered on the front lawn late in the evening, while inside his adviser Tommy Corcoran entertained the President's friends, family, and political allies by playing the accordion.[1]

In the immediate aftermath of his unprecedented victory—60.8 percent of the popular vote, 523 of 531 electoral votes, decisive Democratic majorities in both houses of Congress—the President spoke modestly of his plans. As he prepared to board a train back to Washington a few days after the election, he told well-wishers at the Hyde Park station, "Now I'm going back . . . to do what they call balance the Budget and fulfill the first promise of the campaign." James A. Farley, chairman of the Democratic National Committee, told reporters, "No individual and no corporation that is on the level with the people has any cause to dread Mr. Roosevelt's second term. . . . Nobody on our side of the fence has any thought of reprisal or oppression."[2]

Others, however, were less restrained. To the large community of committed activists who had supported the President in 1936—the men and women who called themselves "progressive," "New Dealers," or, more often, "liberals"—the results of the 1936 election were nothing less than epochal. They were not just a vindication of Franklin Roosevelt and his party. They were a vindication of liberalism. More specifically, the electorate had provided an affirmation of the identification of most liberals with a strong and active federal government. "It was the greatest revolution in our political history," gloated the *New Republic*. Heywood

Broun, writing in the *Nation*, could "see no interpretation of the returns which does not suggest that the people of America want the President to proceed along progressive or liberal lines." Others wrote of the "blank check" the voters had given the administration, the mandate "to improve the status of working men and women," to "keep up the New Deal," to be "as liberal and progressive as possible." The political writer Max Lerner attributed the election results to "progressives" having "massed their forces behind President Roosevelt with an undreamed of success. . . . Mr. Roosevelt is now, as never before, a colossus bestriding the American world."[3]

Roosevelt's second inaugural address—delivered in an icy rain before a crowd largely hidden beneath black umbrellas—expressed the boldest of such hopes. The most renowned passage of the address was Roosevelt's famous litany of social problems, culminating in his description of "one-third of a nation ill-housed, ill-clad, ill-nourished." The most important and ultimately the most controversial portions, however, dealt not with the people but with the state. The speech celebrated the New Deal's rejection of the old individualistic orthodoxies: "We refuse to leave the problems of our common welfare to be solved by the winds of chance and the hurricanes of disaster." And it called explicitly for a major expansion of the power of government: "Nearly all of us recognize that as intricacies of human relationships increase, so power to govern them must also increase. . . . [W]e have undertaken to erect on the old foundations a more enduring structure for the better use of future generations. . . . and in so doing, we are fashioning an instrument of unimagined power for the establishment of a morally better world."[4]

The statements of the liberal magazines and the rain-spattered pages of Roosevelt's address recorded an optimism that was difficult to sustain even a few months later. In January there were heady predictions of great victories to come, naive talk of what one journalist called "no opposition worth mentioning."[5] By the end of the year, liberals were expressing bafflement at the New Deal's rapid demise. How had an administration that had always displayed such sure political instincts blundered so egregiously at the moment of its greatest triumph? Why had a mandate that had seemed so unequivocal twelve months earlier proved powerless to stop the resurgence of conservative opposition?

In fact, the New Deal's problems were less paradoxical than most contemporaries believed. The political crises of 1937 occurred not in spite of, but to a great extent precisely because of, the "mandate" of November 1936—and because of the way the President and his liberal allies misinterpreted that mandate. Liberals liked to believe that the President's triumph represented widespread popular support for a significant expansion of state (and executive) power, even if they themselves had widely varying ideas about how that expansion should proceed. But many voters (and many legislators) had supported the New Deal for other reasons: because it seemed to have alleviated the Depression; because they had benefited from its relief and welfare programs; because the President himself had so effectively conveyed an image of strength and compassion (and had, like many popular leaders, attracted the support of voters who liked him more than they liked his policies). As on other occasions both before and after the Great Depression, much of the American electorate welcomed (even expected) assistance from government in solving their own problems but nonetheless remained skeptical of state power and particularly of efforts to expand and concentrate it.

Many New Dealers believed, too, that the 1936 election had not only produced great Democratic majorities but had transformed the party as a whole into a bastion of liberalism, that conservatives would now be on the defensive and largely powerless. But the very scope of the Democratic triumph had, in fact, helped revive the historic divisions within the party. The President's allies were no longer intimidated by the crisis they had faced in 1933. Powerful liberal factions were, therefore, now less inclined to follow the President's (often cautious) lead and were more committed to pursuing their own interests and goals. Conservatives in Congress, by contrast, saw the 1936 election returns as a warning. Southerners and westerners, in particular, feared that Roosevelt would attempt to use his landslide to promote "dictatorship" and "radicalism." They girded themselves to resist both.[6]

In the weeks after the 1937 inaugural, members of the administration launched a series of initiatives designed to translate into legislation what they believed to be their popular mandate. Their efforts encountered unexpectedly intense opposition. Support for Franklin Roosevelt was not the same, either within Congress or among the public, as support for a liberal vision of a powerful state. By choosing to believe otherwise, the administration had propelled itself into crisis. Much of the New Deal's subsequent history consisted of efforts to extricate itself from that crisis. Out of those efforts would emerge the beginnings of a new pattern of liberal thought.

THE ADMINISTRATION'S most conspicuous initiatives in 1937 were efforts to remodel the government itself. Faced during his first term with what he considered systematic obstacles to his goals, armed now with a great popular mandate, Roosevelt set out to change the institutions that had stymied him. In quick succession, he introduced legislation to reform the Supreme Court and to reorganize the federal bureaucracy. Both proposals became intensely controversial. Both, in the end, foundered.

Roosevelt's plan to reshape the Supreme Court was born of anxiety and frustration. Liberals had been afraid of the Court since the beginning of the New Deal, aware that many of its members were conservatives appointed by Republican presidents. (Roosevelt had no opportunity to appoint a justice in his first term.) And in the spring of 1935, after two years of deceptive judicial calm, the Court confirmed the administration's worst fears. Among the first signs of danger was a decision invalidating the Railroad Retirement Act of 1934, which had established pensions for railway workers and whose demise seemed to threaten virtually all social security legislation. Then, on a single day in late May, the Court delivered three decisions hostile to the New Deal, the most important of which— *Schechter Poultry Co.* v. *United States*—invalidated the central elements of the National Industrial Recovery Act of 1933, the cornerstone of the New Deal's original economic program.

That the *Schechter* decision created such alarm in the administration was mildly ironic, for the NRA by 1935 was a woeful failure, even a political embarrassment; many liberals (including, it seems likely, Roosevelt himself) were quietly relieved to see it die. But the Court's reasoning in the case, based on a very narrow interpretation of the Constitution's interstate commerce clause, not only doomed the decrepit NRA but seemed to threaten other New Deal legislation as well. The President reacted sharply, telling reporters during a long and rambling press conference in the Oval Office: "The implications of this decision are much more important than almost certainly any decision of my lifetime or yours, more important than any decision probably since the Dred Scott case. . . . The big issue is this: Does this decision mean that the United States Government has no control over any economic problem?" A few moments later, as he riffled through the pages of the *Schechter* decision, he observed: "We have been relegated to the horse-and-buggy definition of interstate commerce."[7]

Roosevelt took no action against the Court for nearly two years, both because he did not yet have a viable plan for doing so and because he was reluctant to move before the 1936 election. The problem, in the meantime, grew more severe. In January 1936, the Court (in *United States* v. *Butler*) struck down the Agricultural Adjustment Act of 1933, destroying the original foundations of New Deal farm policy and forcing a reformation of it that many feared would also fall victim to the Court. Other decisions followed in which the Justices seemed to establish precedents that would allow them, perhaps require them, to rule against the administration on additional cases soon to come before them: cases involving, among other things, the TVA, the National Labor Relations Act, and Social Security. For more than a year, amid mounting fears that what remained of the New Deal was in imminent danger, there were covert discussions in the White House and the Justice Department of the "Court problem." Late in 1936, emboldened by the magnitude of his reelection victory, the President finally settled on a plan.[8]

Roosevelt said nothing explicit about his intentions in his 1937 inaugural address; but there were enigmatic passages in the speech, largely unnoticed at the time, that suggested his preoccupation with the issue: "The essential democracy of our Nation and the safety of our people depend not upon the absence of power, but upon lodging it with those whom the people can change or continue at stated intervals." And a blunter comment: "The Constitution of 1789 did not make our democracy impotent."[9] Two weeks later, on February 5, he proposed legislation to reform the Supreme Court. The "Court-packing plan," as critics quickly and pejoratively named it, would have given the President the power to appoint an additional Justice to the Supreme Court whenever a sitting Justice failed to retire within six months of his seventieth birthday; since the Justices in 1937 were as a group unusually aged, passage of the bill would have allowed Roosevelt to name six new members immediately. (The bill would also have permitted him to name additional judges to lower federal courts on the same grounds.)

The President's motives were obvious: to shift the balance of the Court decisively in his favor. But his explanation was deliberately deceptive. His message to Congress and his accompanying public statements said virtually nothing about ideology and spoke instead about "congestion," "delays," "overcrowded dockets," and "insufficient personnel with which to meet a growing and more complex business." This would be legislation, Roosevelt claimed, to improve the efficiency of the courts. Only weeks later, after the opposition had begun to coalesce, did the President begin to speak openly of his real intentions: to bring to the judiciary younger men "with a present-day sense of the Constitution."[10]

In one sense, at least, the Court-packing plan was a considerable success. Within weeks of the bill's introduction (and almost certainly in response to it), the Supreme Court began prudently to change course by upholding New Deal measures that months earlier it seemed prepared to invalidate. In May, a conservative justice, Willis Van Devanter, retired, giving Roosevelt the opportunity to name a sympathetic replacement,

Senator Hugo Black of Alabama. The appointment consolidated the new pro-administration majority. The danger that a hostile judiciary would dismantle the New Deal and thwart all future progress had disappeared. Simply by proposing to reform the Court, the President had accelerated something close to a revolution in constitutional law—a movement away from fixed principles and toward a more fluid view of the Constitution, a movement already in progress before 1937.[11] By the time the bill actually came to a vote, it was largely redundant.

Politically, however, the Court-packing plan did deep and lasting damage. Although there had been considerable popular hostility toward many conservative judicial decisions, Roosevelt's frontal attack on the Court (and his obviously insincere explanation of his purposes) struck even many of his admirers as dangerous and duplicitous. In attempting to bend the Court to his will through extraordinary measures, he seemed to be challenging the constitutional separation of powers and giving credence to the charges of "dictatorship" that had been surfacing intermittently since 1933. The historian James Truslow Adams expressed a growing popular fear in a radio address in March 1937. "The question," he said,

> is of the freedom of that Court which in the last resort is the sole bulwark of our personal liberties. . . . If a President tries to take away our freedom of speech, if a Congress takes away our property unlawfully, if a State legislature, as in the recent case of Louisiana under the dictatorship of Huey Long, takes away the freedom of the press, who is to save us except the Courts?

By the middle of the summer, congressional sentiment had turned decisively against the plan; and the rapidly emerging conservative coalition, which would do so much to frustrate the administration for the next eight years, had gained substantial strength as a result. "Only last November, Mr. Roosevelt was elected by 11,000,000 votes," the *New Republic* noted. "Both friends and enemies agreed that he had come to hold greater effective political power than any other man in our history. Now, incredible as it seems, he may have to accept partial defeat from a Congress that he was supposed to own, body, votes and soul."[12]

At a moment when critics of the administration felt timid and insecure, Roosevelt had given them the confidence to strike at him. When Congress finally defeated the proposal in July 1937, the New Deal absorbed a humiliating defeat from which it never fully recovered. In the process, the battle destroyed the image of invulnerability that had been among the President's greatest political strengths.[13]

. . .

THE COURT-PACKING battle overshadowed another, nearly simultaneous political controversy: a fight over reorganization of the executive
branch of the federal government. But the nature of the reorganization
proposal, and more important the nature of the opposition to it, illustrated as vividly as the Court fight how large the obstacles were to liberal
visions of a more powerful state.

On the surface, the executive reorganization plan seemed an uncontroversial measure—a natural outgrowth of successful progressive efforts
to reshape state and municipal governments earlier in the century. Two
Republican presidents—William Howard Taft and Herbert Hoover—
had previously endorsed the general concept of executive reorganization,
arguing that it would contribute to governmental efficiency and economy.
The administrative expansion of the first years of the New Deal—the
proliferation of new offices and agencies—made the case for reorganization seem even more compelling, as did the President's frustration (shared
by most of his predecessors and all his successors) at the difficulty of
getting the bureaucracy to do what he wanted. In the spring of 1936,
therefore, Roosevelt appointed a Committee on Administrative Management to recommend reforms.[14]

The committee's report, delivered to Roosevelt shortly after the 1936
election, reflected the progressive inclinations of its three principal authors: Luther Gulick, Charles Merriam, and Louis Brownlow (the chairman), all of whom had been active in municipal reform efforts and all of
whom believed strongly in the efficacy of administrative action. In the
past, they argued, courts, parties, and legislatures, not the executive
branch, had generally charted policy in the American government. But in
the twentieth century, with its more urgent challenges, there was a need
to find more effective and reliable ways for the state to exercise power.
"Administrative agencies and activities are moving to the front all over
the world more rapidly and powerfully than judicial or representative
bodies," Merriam wrote some years later.[15] The Brownlow report sought
to advance that process.

Among its recommendations were proposals to expand the White
House staff, to move the Bureau of the Budget out of the Treasury
Department and into the White House, to give the President more
control over the civil service, to limit the autonomy of the independent
regulatory commissions, and to create a powerful planning mechanism
within the executive branch. All these measures were designed to
strengthen the President's control of his own administration. But they
were also intended to expand the power of the executive at the expense

of the legislature. The report said nothing about abridging congressional prerogatives, but an unspoken assumption behind its recommendations was that an improved administrative structure would free the executive branch from at least some of the obstacles to action that the slow and cumbersome legislative process had traditionally created. Rather than seek passage of new statutes, creative administrators could make extensive new uses of existing laws, even uses Congress had not foreseen.[16]

Roosevelt gave no indication that he shared this expansive view of reorganization. He was aware, no doubt, that expressing such a view would increase conservative opposition to the legislation. But there is little to suggest that, even in private, he considered the measure as important as its framers did. His own public defense of the proposal always stressed the "efficient and economical conduct of governmental operations." Even some of his liberal supporters seemed to agree that the plan would have a relatively modest impact.[17]

But the President's critics sensed danger. And when the administration introduced its Court-packing scheme only a few weeks after sending the Brownlow report to Congress, conservatives began to see the two measures as part of a single plan; together, they constituted a program to strengthen the presidency by emasculating the other branches of government.[18] Critics attacked executive reorganization with much the same language they used in attacking judicial reorganization; it was evidence of Roosevelt's "dictatorial ambitions."

In the spring of 1938 (by which time Congress had still taken no action on the proposal), events in Europe—Nazi Germany's annexation of Austria (the *Anschluss*) most prominently—had added a new element to the debate: the supposed parallels between the designs of Roosevelt and those of totalitarian leaders. "We have just witnessed, in Europe, what happens when one man is permitted too much power—Hitler in Austria," one opponent wrote. Another, more friendly observer warned the President that there was a growing popular tendency "to unconsciously group four names, Hitler, Stalin, Mussolini and Roosevelt." After months of nearly hysterical attacks by, among others, Father Charles Coughlin and William Randolph Hearst, after a surprising popular outcry that culminated in large anti-reorganization rallies in New York and Washington, and after some members of the administration itself (in agencies threatened by the proposed reorganization) began mobilizing opposition, even the President seemed to draw back from the bill. On April 8, 1938, the House of Representatives defeated the proposal by eight votes. The 204 opponents included 108 Democrats.[19]

Roosevelt introduced a second, much milder reorganization bill in

1939, a bill so emasculated that it moved quickly and easily through Congress. But this modest victory could not heal the wounds of the earlier defeat. The death of the Brownlow plan was both a reflection and a cause of the New Deal's political torpor—not so much because executive reorganization itself was crucial to liberal hopes as because the battle over the plan revealed the magnitude of both popular and congressional opposition to the liberal vision of a strengthened state. That vision, seemingly vindicated by the 1936 election, was proving much more difficult to promote than its defenders had anticipated. The administration's critics, far from cowed by their electoral defeats, were proving both obdurate and effective. Even the New Deal's friends seemed unreliable.

The defeat of the reorganization bill was "the most important event since 1932 . . . more important, even, than the defeat of the Supreme Court plan," wrote T.R.B. of the *New Republic* (somewhat hyperbolically) in April 1938. "Twelve months ago such a vote would have been unthinkable. The wounds it has created in the liberal bloc cannot be easily healed." The administration was, in short, already experiencing dangerous political difficulties when it encountered another crisis, before which all the others paled: an unexpected economic collapse.[20]

THE ADMINISTRATION'S greatest political asset in 1937 was its presumed success in restoring the economy to health. As the year began, many New Dealers were boasting that the Depression was over—a sentiment much of the public seemed eager to share. But events soon delivered a fatal blow to that assumption. Beginning in late summer, and accelerating in the fall, the economy experienced one of the most rapid downturns in its history, a slide that exceeded in severity (although not in longevity) the collapse of 1929–1930. The much vaunted "New Deal recovery" suddenly gave way to the "Roosevelt recession."

The 1937 recession came as a surprise to most Americans, and to most New Dealers. Yet it was not wholly unanticipated. Several liberal journalists had expressed skepticism when reports of the "end of the Depression" began to proliferate. The columnist George Soule, for example, wrote in March 1937: "Now that . . . factories are noisy again . . . people ask questions about how long good fortune is going to last, whether we shall have another boom and whether it will be followed by another crash." Some members of the administration were likewise pessimistic. Leon Henderson of the Commerce Department circulated a memorandum (also in March) describing the current prosperity as uncomfortably similar to that of 1929, arguing that prices were rising too rapidly, and predicting that "unless firm action is taken, [there] will come the race between purchasing power . . . and inflated prices,—a losing race since purchasing power can not keep up." There were similar warnings of inadequate purchasing power a month later from Marriner S. Eccles, chairman of the Federal Reserve Board, and Lauchlin Currie, one of his assistants, both of whom insisted that the recovery was not yet stable and could easily be derailed.[21]

Even the pessimists, however, were restrained in their warnings; they foresaw neither the severity nor the imminence of the coming collapse. Currie's bleakest warnings spoke only of "a mild business recession"; by late September, he had retreated even from that modest prediction and was forecasting a "broad recovery." Eccles once warned of "another 1929," but in 1940, not 1937. Even Henderson wrote relief administrator Harry Hopkins late in August and cautiously predicted "a new burst of vigor in recovery."[22] In any case, vague forebodings could not compete with the wave of optimism that was sweeping both the government and much of the business community in 1937. Almost every economic index—personal incomes, wholesale prices, industrial production, corporate profits, employment—showed marked gains over the levels of four years earlier. The steel industry, which had been operating at only 47 percent of capacity in 1935, was at 80 percent by the beginning of 1937. Construction expenditures were 200 percent higher than they had been two years earlier. National income, which had dropped as low as $43 billion in 1932, had climbed back to over $70 billion. Only in a few areas did the economic statistics show levels of activity matching (let alone exceeding) those of 1929. But the optimists were not making comparisons to the boom years. They were measuring 1937 against 1932 and 1933; and by that standard, the gains were impressive.[23]

"Railroads put on extra trains," Business Week wrote in midsummer. "Mountain and seashore hotels packed them in. That is 1937's July Fourth story. And to business it brings hope, faith, and clarity. . . . Over the next six months, barring an unexpected catastrophe . . . , business should get better." Two months later, the journal remained optimistic: "Business is good. This fall it will be better." A series of economic setbacks over the summer failed to dampen the public cheerfulness. Newsweek shrugged off a mild downturn in the second quarter, noting that it was much less severe than expected and writing exuberantly of the "brisk pace" of the "recovery van." An unusually volatile stock market in August gave way to rising prices again in September.[24] But the most vivid illustration of confidence in the economy came from the administration itself. For in the spring of 1937, Franklin Roosevelt decided to balance the federal budget.

In the twelve years of his presidency, Franklin Roosevelt never brought a budget into balance.[25] But through most of those years, he continued to believe in the importance of eliminating deficits and rarely stopped trying to do so. Roosevelt's harsh attacks on Herbert Hoover in 1932 for extravagant spending have often been dismissed either as campaign demagoguery or as reflections of an orthodoxy he subsequently abandoned. In fact, Roosevelt was always serious about balancing the budget. Even in 1936, he was clearly uncomfortable with the deficits he had been accumulating for over three years. Throughout the campaign, he spoke defensively about the federal budget and denounced "fiscal recklessness." Now that the country had "turned the corner," he assured his audiences, "federal revenues are increasing; emergency expenditures are decreasing. A balanced budget is on the way." Within months of his reelection, he decided to make good on that promise.[26]

There seemed to be compelling reasons for doing so in early 1937. The administration was eager to believe the emergency was over—that the New Deal had, as two Treasury Department officials wrote early in 1937, "licked the great depression." The President, at least, clung fervently to that conviction despite the persistence of high unemployment, the absence of significant new private investment, and the continuing sluggishness of several major industries. Such confidence, however misplaced, made a reduction of federal expenditures seem possible.[27]

The expected political benefits of producing a balanced budget, and the expected costs of failing to do so, made spending reductions seem desirable. Even many members of the administration who did not believe deficits were economically dangerous considered them a political rebuke to the New Deal. The deficits (and the spending programs that had produced them) were symbols of the economic "emergency." The best way to prove that the emergency was over was to eliminate those symbols. The President himself had frequently suggested that progress toward a balanced budget would be the best measure of the administration's success. In his 1936 annual message to Congress, for example, he had said: "We are justified in our present confidence. Restoration of the national income, which shows continuing gains for the third successive year, supports the normal and logical policies under which agriculture and industry are returning to full activity. Under these policies we approach a balance of the national budget." Balancing the budget, in short, would mark the triumph of the New Deal.[28]

Above all, perhaps, budget reductions seemed necessary because of growing signs of inflation. Wholesale prices had risen by more than a third in the first four years of the New Deal and by more than 7 percent in 1936 alone. Consumer credit had more than tripled in two years. The prospect of inflation was, as always, alarming to investors, creditors, and financiers—and to their many allies in government. But it was also alarming to Roosevelt, and many others, for different reasons: because rising prices were disturbing to consumers and thus politically damaging to leaders who did nothing to hold them down.

Particularly ominous was the rapid flow of gold and other capital out of Europe and into the United States—the result of nervous foreign investors fleeing their own unstable regimes in search of security in America. To reduce the inflationary pressures of this "refugee capital," the Treasury Department late in 1936 began "sterilizing" gold—putting newly purchased specie in an "inactive" account rather than using it to increase the money supply. At roughly the same time, the Federal Reserve Board raised the reserve requirements for member banks by a stiff 50 percent; it raised them again, by a third, early in 1937. The banking system still had substantial available cash despite the new requirements, and the Board insisted that "credit conditions will continue to be easy." But clearly the focus of concern was shifting from deflation to inflation.

Throughout the spring, Roosevelt spoke intermittently about "the present hazard of undue advances in prices," the "upward" [price] spiral which is at least a danger flag." The proper response to the danger, he insisted, was for the government itself to restrain its spending. Even many liberals agreed. "An unbalanced budget in a period of rapidly rising prices," the *Nation* warned in April 1937, "is the surest path to an uncontrolled inflation." Still, the elimination of the deficit might not have become a central item on the administration's agenda without the tenacious and at times ferocious efforts of Secretary of the Treasury Henry Morgenthau.[29]

Morgenthau seemed an unlikely leader of a bureaucratic battle and an even less likely successful one. He was lightly regarded by most of his colleagues in the administration, who tended to dismiss him as a passive and befuddled sycophant and who watched his consistently inept performance in Cabinet meetings and other public forums with a mixture of amusement and contempt.[30] Few considered Morgenthau intellectually equipped for his position. He had no academic training in economics; indeed, he had been an indifferent and unhappy student and had dropped out of Cornell without graduating. He had little experience in business or finance; he had refused to join his wealthy father in the family real estate business and had spent most of his adult life as a gentleman apple farmer.

He owed his public prominence largely to an accident of geography:

He was a neighbor of Franklin Roosevelt in Dutchess County, New York. The two men had become friends in 1915, and Morgenthau spent most of the next thirty years serving Roosevelt's purposes. Passed over in 1933 for the position he most coveted, secretary of agriculture, he stumbled into the Treasury Department almost accidentally in November of that year. Roosevelt asked him to fill in temporarily for Secretary William Woodin, who was on leave of absence because of illness. Several months later, when it became clear that Woodin would not return (he died in May 1934), Morgenthau officially succeeded him. He served as secretary of the treasury for eleven and a half years, longer than anyone but Albert Gallatin.[31]

Why Morgenthau developed so intense, even obsessive, a commitment to a balanced budget is difficult to explain. He was, to be sure, the Cabinet officer with direct responsibility for fiscal policy; the Budget Bureau was housed in the Treasury Department until it moved to the White House in 1939. Moreover, he was surrounded by the department's professional economists and civil servants, people long committed to fiscal orthodoxy—so much so that such orthodoxy became known in the 1930s (in America as in England) as the "Treasury view." Yet Morgenthau displayed a level of passion on this issue that seemed to reflect something more than the traditional inclinations of his office. The battle to balance the budget became, for him, something intensely personal: a test of his relationship with the President and of his stature within the government. Lifelong insecurities that made him indecisive and ineffectual in other contexts seemed to strengthen his resolve on this issue.[32]

Like the President himself, and like most other members of the administration, Morgenthau had accepted the need for deficits during the first years of the New Deal because he recognized the importance of assisting the unemployed and propping up the sagging economy. But also like Roosevelt, he had never wavered in his belief that the administration should balance the budget as soon as conditions made it possible to do so. By the end of 1936, he was convinced that the moment had arrived, that it was time (to use Morgenthau's own unfortunate metaphor) "to strip off the bandages, throw away the crutches" and see if the economy "could stand on its own two feet." Shortly after the election, he began an intense, if largely private, campaign to win a promise from the President to eliminate the deficit by 1938. Roosevelt was clearly sympathetic. In his budget message to Congress in January 1937, he made a direct connection between achieving recovery and eliminating the deficit; a balanced budget, he said, would be the culmination of the New Deal's four-year battle "to restore a successful economic life to the country." Federally-funded relief programs had been necessary during the "emergency," but it was now time for private industry to step in and "give employment to persons now receiving government help."[33]

Others in the administration—among them Marriner Eccles—argued vigorously that reductions in federal spending were premature, that the economy was not yet healthy enough to be able to absorb a major drop in government support. (Eccles also insisted that the budget could be balanced without cuts, through the growth in revenues that a sustained recovery would produce.)[34] But Roosevelt sided with Morgenthau. "I wish you'd heard the President talk about balancing the budget to Eccles," Morgenthau gloated early in April. "If he'd only say publicly what he told him, it would be marvelous." A few weeks later, Roosevelt obliged. In a message to Congress on April 20, 1937, he called for "eliminating or deferring all expenditures not absolutely necessary" so as "to eliminate this deficit during the coming fiscal year." That meant substantial reductions in the budgets of the "emergency" programs: the Works Progress Administration, the Public Works Administration, and others. Morgenthau was ecstatic: "The President gave me . . . everything that I asked for. . . . It was a long hard trying fight but certainly at some time during the weeks that I argued with him he must have come to the conclusion that if he wants his Administration to go forward with his reform program he must have a sound financial foundation."[35]

Disaster followed.

THE ECONOMIC CRISIS of 1937, which began six months after the budget decisions, had ominous similarities to its 1929 counterpart—most visibly in the behavior of the stock market, which collapsed in a great wave of panic selling in mid-October. By the end of 1937, stock prices had fallen by more than a third from their peak in August; by the following spring, the Dow Jones Industrial Average had dropped by 48 percent, achieving in seven months a decline that had taken more than a year in 1929 and 1930. "Yesterday the 1929 panic was really repeated with more to come," Adolf A. Berle (a member of Roosevelt's original "brain trust") confided to his diary in October, in the aftermath of a day that many traders compared to the "Black Tuesday" of eight years before. "The stock market people," Berle added, "are most bewildered and frightened."[36]

But the more disturbing similarity to 1929 was that the collapse of the financial markets in 1937 was only the most dramatic sign of a much broader economic decline. Just as eight years before, there had been clear, if largely ignored, signs of erosion in key economic indicators over the summer. And just as in 1929, the decline of production and employment accelerated dramatically in the fall. "It is now plain that business is dropping as well as the market," Berle noted. "In other words, we are in for a rather bad winter." By the end of that winter, industrial production had dropped by more than 40 percent; corporate profits had fallen by 78 percent; four million more workers had swelled the already large unemployment rolls; the national income had slipped by 13 percent from its post-1929 peak of the previous summer. As striking as the extent of the erosion was that it occurred so quickly, much more rapidly than the collapse of 1929–1930. "In several particulars," *Time* noted late in November, "the Recession is more remarkable than the Depression. It is remarkable because the 35% plummet from last summer's high is the swiftest decline in the history of U.S. business and finance."[37]

Roosevelt's initial reaction to this devastating setback was a forced optimism that resembled denial. "I have been around the country and know conditions are good," he told the Cabinet in October. "Everything will work out if we just sit tight and keep quiet." Even four months later, with conditions significantly worse, he assured James Farley that "things will be all right." And while he avoided public statements minimizing the problem (fearful of comparisons to the Hoover of 1930 and 1931), he tried in subtle ways to suggest that this crisis was not as grave as the earlier one; among other things, he insisted on describing it as a "recession," to distinguish it from the more ominous term "depression."[38]

At other moments, however, Roosevelt was clearly nervous. ("The White House has the jitters," Henry Morgenthau noted in his diary after a telephone conversation with the President in October.) That was partly because the people around him were encouraging him to worry. Indeed, the collapse created an anxiety within the government that at times verged on panic. Morgenthau himself wrote the President a few days after the stock market collapse: "I have had to come to the conclusion that we are headed right into another depression. . . . This cruel process has already begun." At the Federal Reserve Board, there were similar expressions of alarm: "This country again faces a very serious business and financial crisis," the board's Fiscal and Monetary Advisory Committee warned. "To put it bluntly, we face another major depression. . . . Plants are closing down every day. Thousands and thousands of industrial workers are being laid off every day. Forward orders are being cancelled. . . . Prices are falling. . . . Such movements gather their own momentum, and feed upon themselves."[39]

And always, behind both the strained optimism and the panicky warnings, there was the one great fear: the fear that this crisis, like the 1929 crisis, might move beyond the administration's control; the fear that the New Deal, so triumphantly vindicated only a year before, might end in failure. The recession was already an economic disaster. It threatened to become a political catastrophe as well. The President "is greatly disturbed over the business and economic situation and doesn't know quite which way to turn," Secretary of the Interior Harold Ickes confided to his diary in November. "He is plainly worried." Four months later, Ickes offered an even gloomier assessment: "It looks to me as if all the courage has oozed out of the President. He has let things drift. There is no fight and no leadership."[40] Representative Maury Maverick of Texas gave public voice to the same fear. "Now we Democrats have to admit that we are floundering," Maverick told his colleagues in the House. "We have pulled all the rabbits out of the hat, and there are no more rabbits. . . . We are a confused, bewildered group of people, and we are not delivering the goods. The Democratic administration is getting down to the condition in which Mr. Hoover found himself."[41]

That was the forbidden image that began slowly to creep into the consciousness of New Dealers as 1937 drew to a close: the image of exhaustion and paralysis; the image of an administration devoid of ideas; the image of a presidency that might (as Secretary of Agriculture Henry A. Wallace privately feared) "end like Hoover's." There was a faint note of desperation in the calls for action that were emanating from every corner of the administration. Economists from several agencies collaborated on a report to the President that concluded: "There is little reason to expect a 'natural' upturn in the near future. The recession *could* be severe and prolonged if government does not intervene." From every corner of the administration, from the Congress, from the liberal press, and from much of the public, a clamor was arising for a decisive presidential response to the new crisis.[42]

But what kind of response? On that, even liberals were unable to agree. There were several very different explanations of what had caused the recession, each of which suggested a different approach to ending it. And there were several very different interpretations of the New Deal itself: of what its important accomplishments had been and what its lessons for subsequent efforts should be. It was one thing to talk, as almost all liberals did, about the importance of reinvigorating the New Deal. It was quite another to define what the New Deal was. And so for American liberals, the bleak winter of 1937–1938 produced not just a severe recession, but an intense ideological struggle—a struggle among different conceptions of the economy, among different views of the state, and among different conceptions of the political traditions from which contemporary liberalism had emerged. It was a struggle to define the soul of the New Deal.

# Chapter Two

# "An Ordered
# Economic World"

ALMOST EXACTLY TEN YEARS after the stock market collapse that
marked the beginning of the 1937 recession, Henry Morgenthau published
an article in a popular magazine explaining (and justifying) his own
response to the crisis. "I was convinced," he wrote, "that the only way out
was through restoring business confidence. . . . I felt that private investors
would not risk their capital when economic conditions were uncertain."[1]
Perhaps without realizing it, Morgenthau was allying himself with one of
the several competing interpretations of the causes of the recession. The
idea that the economy had collapsed because of the failure of business to
invest had a broad following in 1937 and continued to attract support from
historians and economists many years later; it also helped sustain several
visions of the course the government should follow in combatting the
recession.

The key to any stable recovery, the argument went, was an expansion
of production through new investment. But in the years preceding the
1937 recession, despite deceptive signs of economic vigor, there had been
very little new investment. What investment there was dropped off
quickly in the fall of 1937. And the reason, according to Morgenthau and
many others, was a decline in "business confidence."[2]

That private investment had remained sluggish throughout the years
of the "New Deal recovery" is hardly open to question. Indeed, the
productive capacities of American industry increased almost not at all
through the entire decade of the 1930s. Investments in plant and equipment totaled nearly $60 billion in the 1930s, but almost all of that ($55
billion, or 92 percent) represented replacement of existing facilities. Even
in the first half of 1937, the Depression-era peak, capital was flowing into
new investment at barely a third of the highest rate of the 1920s.[3]

Many conservative critics of the New Deal, unsurprisingly, blamed
what they considered the "anti-business" policies and rhetoric of the

administration. "What are the factors that have brought about this change?" asked Winthrop Aldrich, chairman of Chase National Bank, speaking of the 1937 collapse. "I think the answer is clearly and definitely to be found in the cumulative effect of a variety of governmental policies." Among them were the "punitive" tax provisions that targeted profits from investments; unreasonable restrictions on speculative investment by the Securities and Exchange Commission; the Wagner Act and other legislation that encouraged labor unrest and raised labor costs; the regulatory initiatives that limited corporate freedom of action; the growing federal deficits and the threat of inflation they created; and a general atmosphere of government hostility toward the corporate world, a "class war" that was pushing business "back into its shell." Hence, conservative capitalists claimed, investors were uncertain, defensive, and threatened. They were unwilling to take risks, unwilling to invest. "Business men I know," a financier wrote SEC Commissioner William Douglas, "are so puzzled as to what course to follow, they are marking time, much of it in the garden, on the seashore or on the golf links." The solution, Aldrich and like-minded people argued, was to dismantle the "anti-business" elements of the New Deal and restore the kind of state to which they had become accustomed, one that at times assisted but seldom restricted private enterprise.[4]

But it was not only capitalist foes of the New Deal who worried about the problem of inadequate investment as they considered the 1937 recession. Many supporters of the administration also believed that the proper government response to the recession—indeed, the proper government role in the economy at any time—was to encourage investment. That meant, to be sure, avoiding confrontational policies that pitted government against business and eroded investor confidence. "I have consistently thought," Adolf Berle once wrote, "that you could not have a government perpetually at war with its economic machinery."[5] But, much more important, it also meant taking positive steps to create a stable economic environment conducive to growth. Rather than scaling back state efforts to reform the economy, as business critics demanded, such liberals wanted a substantial, in some respects even radical, increase in the government's commitment to creating economic harmony and order. The best way to create "business confidence" and encourage more investment, they argued, was to create a stable concert of interests among the state, business, and labor—an effort, often described as "associationalism" or (less charitably) "corporatism." It was an approach with many antecedents, including—most powerfully—the first years of the New Deal.

· · ·

ONE PLACE IN the government where the more conservative version of the "business confidence" argument had important defenders was the Treasury Department. The need to reassure investors had been one of the principal arguments of Henry Morgenthau and his advisers in the summer of 1937 when they persuaded the President to cut federal expenditures so as to balance the budget. And the arrival of a recession only strengthened the Treasury view of the nature of the economic problem.[6] The administration, Morgenthau and his allies believed, had not yet done enough to reassure the business community; only reaffirming the commitment to a balanced budget could revive investment and save the recovery.

Memoranda flew around the Treasury Department late in 1937 assessing the outlook of the business community. Businessmen were, according to economist Wayne Taylor, "in a state of stagnation, if not panic." They were worried about the labor situation. They were concerned about the "present tax structure, in particular the undistributed profits tax, and the capital gains tax." And they were afraid above all that the government lacked "the courage to curtail subsidies and what they consider unnecessary expenditures." If the administration tried to fight the recession with "excessive spending" or by "monkeying with the dollar," businessmen feared, the result would be a disastrous inflation.[7]

Morgenthau, who feared the same thing, urged the President at a November 4 Cabinet meeting to offer public reassurances that "we are going to continue on a capitalistic basis," that the government had a commitment to fiscal responsibility, that it did not intend to supplant the private sector as the principal agent of investment. When Roosevelt complained sourly that he had already told them that "again and again," Morgenthau pressed the attack: "All right, Mr. President, tell them for the fifteenth time . . . because . . . that's what they want to know." Postmaster General James Farley chimed in: "What about telling them that you are going to reduce the cost of Government? . . . That's what people are interested in."[8]

Roosevelt's grudging acquiescence ("All right, Jim," he told Farley, "I will turn on the old record") encouraged Morgenthau to launch his own efforts to placate the business community. On November 10 (against the counsel of some of his advisers) Morgenthau delivered a speech to a meeting of the National Academy of Political Science in New York—a group dominated (despite its academic-sounding name) by conservative businessmen and financiers. Morgenthau had been working on the speech feverishly, even obsessively, for months and considered it one of the most important of his career. Originally it was to have been a proud tribute to the economic successes of the New Deal (among them the anticipated balanced budget in 1938); but now, in light of the recession, it became an attempt to instill confidence in suspicious capitalists. There were some people in the administration, Morgenthau conceded, who contended "that another great [public] spending program is desirable to ward off the risk of another business depression." But the President and his most important advisers, he assured his audience, believed otherwise. The administration intended "to foster the full application of the driving force of private capital. We want to see capital go into the productive channels of private industry. . . . We believe that one of the most important ways of achieving these ends at this time is to continue programs toward a balance of the Federal budget."[9]

Morgenthau's rigid economic orthodoxy, even in the face of one of the New Deal's severest crises, reflected his own timid, constricted view of economics. But it reflected, too, the larger poverty of thought plaguing almost everyone engaged in considering economic policy in the 1930s. Not many New Dealers were as cautious as Morgenthau, although some— including, at times, the President—were. But even the most optimistic liberals often had difficulty conceiving of alternatives to traditional, investment-centered solutions to economic problems. Evidence of that came from, among other places, those New Dealers arguing for associational arrangements as a solution to the challenge of the recession.

THOSE WHO PROMOTED the associational approach to economic reform in 1937 were much less concerned than Morgenthau was about protecting capitalists from government. To them, the greater challenge was protecting the business world from excessive competition. The most serious problems facing modern economies, advocates of this approach contended, were the conflict and instability of a chaotic marketplace: destructive rivalries within industries, destabilizing clashes between capital and labor, disastrous swings in the business cycle prompted in part by the desperate gambles capitalists took to gain advantages in precarious markets. Competition, so highly valued by some liberals, seemed to others an obstacle to economic stability. "We are resolved to recognize openly," Rexford G. Tugwell, a member of Roosevelt's original "brains trust," wrote in 1933, "that competition in most of its forms is wasteful and costly. . . . Unrestricted individual competition is the death, not the life of trade."[10]

The desire to limit competition was, for many, part of a much larger vision: the dream of using the state to create a more ordered economy. Like Europeans developing a rationale for corporatist experiments in managing industrial economies, some Americans yearned for political arrangements that could produce social and economic harmony. At times, that dream could take on an almost mystical quality, reminiscent of such earlier utopian visions as Fourierism and Edward Bellamy's Nationalism. Some Catholics referred to the teachings of Saint Thomas Aquinas and called for a modern equivalent of the "organic" economies of medieval societies. Other visionaries rallied to the Technocracy movement, which was based loosely on the teachings of Thorstein Veblen and which advocated replacing the existing price system with a centrally administered market run by trained engineers.[11]

For most reformers, however, the inspirations were more prosaic. They looked with particular admiration at the War Industries Board of World War I, the first real effort to form a partnership among business, government, and labor on behalf of a larger national goal. In reality, the WIB had been a hastily cobbled-together expedient, which had accelerated war production only by effectively suspending the antitrust laws and allowing large firms to dominate their industries. But according to subsequent mythology, the wartime experiment had been a brief and glorious moment of economic harmony, in which business, government, and labor cooperated effectively on behalf of the larger economic good.[12] Among the most effective promoters of that myth was the durable Bernard Baruch, who had served as the WIB's chairman and who spent much of his long subsequent career attempting to teach the nation the lessons of his experience. "Many businessmen have experienced during the war," he later wrote,

> the tremendous advantages, both to themselves and to the general public, of combination, of cooperation and common action, with their natural competitors. . . . [T]he experience of the War Industries Board points to the desirability of investing some Government agency . . . with constructive as well as inquisitorial powers—an agency whose duty it should be to encourage, under strict Government supervision, such cooperation and coordination in industry as should tend to increase production, eliminate waste, conserve natural resources, improve the quality of products, promote efficiency in operation, and thus reduce costs to the ultimate consumer.[13]

There were many such encomia to the work of the WIB in the years after the Armistice. Grosvenor B. Clarkson, who had directed the Council of National Defense during the war and had developed a great admiration for Baruch and his works in the process, incorporated such "lessons" into a massive semi-official history of war mobilization published in 1923:

> If we had a Government business manager with a free hand to run the business side of Government, as free as Baruch had in the War Industries Board, we should have a successful Government of business. . . . It is little wonder that the men who dealt with the industries of a nation, binned and labeled, replenished and drawn on at will for the purposes of war, and its train of consequences, meditated with a sort of intellectual contempt on the huge hit-and-miss confusion of peace-time industry, with its perpetual cycle of surfeit and dearth and its eternal attempt at adjustment after the event. From their meditations arose dreams of an ordered economic world.[14]

Such dreams survived and even gained strength in the 1920s. Among their most effective promoters was Secretary of Commerce Herbert Hoover, who had headed the Food Administration during World War I and who spent much of his subsequent public career trying to develop similar cooperative arrangements in other areas of the economy. Throughout the 1920s, Hoover encouraged and at times actively orchestrated the creation of trade associations (hence the term "associationalism"). He exhorted individual firms to cooperate with one another to advance the interests of their industries. By the end of the decade, a growing number of economists and corporate leaders were calling for even more ambitious experiments; and during the first years of the Depression, their calls grew louder. Industrial partnerships, they contended, should allow businessmen to do more than attend conferences and share general information. They should enable industries to avoid destructive competition through joint pricing and production agreements; they should, in effect, permit businessmen to form cartels and fix prices.[15]

As the Depression deepened, such calls grew more insistent. Charles Stevenson, a management engineer and a prominent trade association figure, made the business case for "the rationalization of our economic life" in a 1932 pamphlet with the desperate title *The Way Out*. Competition, he claimed, was the bogey that had produced "the tremendously excessive productive capacity from which our industries now suffer" and that had "driven prices of most of our commodities below production cost." Americans were, he argued, "being crucified on the cross of competition." The solution was a suspension of the antitrust laws to allow each industry "the right to form a firm organization and to govern and control itself." That must include giving the majority within any industry "the right of compulsion" over a recalcitrant minority.[16]

In the meantime Gerard Swope of General Electric, who had served on the War Industries Board, was generating support well beyond the corporate world for a proposal outlined in his 1931 book *The Swope Plan*. He too proposed suspending enforcement of the antitrust laws to allow members of trade associations to cooperate in adjusting "production to consumption," in other words to form cartels. In return, industries would submit to a modest level of federal supervision and would guarantee their workers such benefits as workman's compensation, life and disability insurance, pension plans, and unemployment insurance. The plan ( which some came to call "Swopism") would enable business "to go forward decisively instead of fearsomely."[17]

Calls for "rationalization" of the marketplace were coming from other quarters as well: from progressive academics enamored of the idea of "planning," from public administrators eager to enhance their own calling, from politicians groping for solutions to the greatest crisis of their age. An important document in many such deliberations was a 1932 study by two scholars at Columbia University: Adolf Berle, a professor of law, and Gardiner C. Means, an economist. (Both would later become significant figures in the New Deal.) In *The Modern Corporation and Private Property*, they challenged the traditional veneration of individual entrepreneurs, small enterprises, and vigorous competition. America, they argued, was in "the throes of a revolution in our institutions of private property." The result was that "the individual owner was steadily being lost in the creation of a series of huge industrial oligarchies." Corporations were no longer "private" institutions in any meaningful sense of the term; ownership, dispersed among thousands of stockholders, had been divorced from control, which was now lodged in the hands of professional managers. This process was, if not inevitable, at least so far advanced as to be irreversible.

Like the trade association theorists, Berle and Means hoped to rationalize economic life by replacing the chaos of individual, competitive decision-making with a system governed by a larger intelligence. Unlike the devotees of the Swope plan, however, they envisioned a major public role in the process. They too spoke of industrial "partnerships," but partnerships far more inclusive and more accountable to the state than the more limited prescriptions of the associationalists. The power of the great economic organizations, they argued, should be funneled into the service of "the paramount interests of the community"—a community defined not as a collection of individual firms within an industry (the trade association view), but as all those affected by the workings of corporate organizations (capital, labor, consumers, and government). "It is conceivable," they wrote, "indeed it seems almost essential if the corporate system is to survive,—that the 'control' of the great corporations should develop into a purely neutral technocracy, balancing a variety of claims by various groups in the community and assigning to each a portion of the income stream on the basis of public policy rather than private cupidity."[18]

Only months after publication of the book, Berle became a member of the original Roosevelt "brains trust," joining other academics with similar visions of creating a harmonious economy. Raymond Moley, another member of this first circle of advisers, liked to talk about the "concert of interests" that an active and enlightened government could promote. Rexford Tugwell called for a centralized state planning mechanism that would remove instability and uncertainty from the economy. Berle, Tugwell, and other planners envisioned a much more important role for the state in any new economic order than did Gerard Swope and his allies. But they shared Swope's belief in the centrality of investment to hopes for recovery, his fear of unfettered competition, and his faith in the value of predictability, stability, and order in the industrial economy.[19]

Roosevelt himself embraced no single concept of political economy, but at times in his 1932 campaign (and at times before), he had expressed enthusiasm for the broad vision of economic rationalization that the business planners and state planners seemed to share. In his first months in office, he helped give life to that dream—in the form of the National Recovery Administration, the keystone of the early New Deal's effort to reform the industrial economy.[20] Optimism was high, in the beginning, that the experiment would indeed produce a true "concert of interests." Hugh Johnson, the NRA's first director, envisioned such dramatic results that he told Secretary of Labor Frances Perkins in 1933: "When this crisis is over and we have the recovery program started, there won't be any need for a Department of Labor or a Department of Commerce."[21] But the brief and troubled life of the NRA revealed that the conflict between the trade association and public planning approaches to rationalization was more troubling than it had at first appeared. The National Industrial Recovery Act of 1933 did not so much resolve that tension as incorporate it into the new institution it was creating.

The NRA established "code authorities" (not unlike trade associations) in major industries and allowed manufacturers to agree on common pricing and production policies without fear of antitrust prosecution. In exchange, firms were required to recognize and bargain with labor unions and submit to a vaguely defined level of government supervision of their agreements. Within a year, the experiment was in turmoil. Consumers complained that industries were inflating prices artificially and that the government was not playing a strong enough role in policing the agreements. Labor organizations complained that wages were not rising and that employers were not bargaining in good faith, or were not bargaining at all. Small businessmen complained that large manufacturers were controlling the codes and using them to enhance their dominance, and that the collective bargaining requirements threatened their ability to compete with bigger firms.[22]

To some, the entire experiment raised uncomfortable images of the corporatist economic policies of fascist Italy, which in 1933 had many American admirers. (Hugh Johnson once startled Frances Perkins by giving her a copy of Raffaello Viglione's *The Corporate State*, a sympathetic description of Mussolini's regime.)[23] To others (including a presidential commission appointed to examine the NRA's performance), the problem was incompetence in the administration of the program and incoherence in its results. "Instead of an economic order," one critic charged, "there are nebulae of economic planets."[24] In the meantime, the industrial economy—although it halted its downward spiral—did not improve enough in the first two years of the New Deal to persuade industrialists that the achievements of the NRA were worth the price they were paying for them. By the time the Supreme Court invalidated the experiment in 1935, support for the NRA had substantially eroded, even within the New Deal itself.[25]

BUT THREE YEARS later, as the government cast about for a response to the 1937–1938 recession, there was considerable interest in renewed efforts to limit competition and "harmonize" the economy. A few New Dealers continued to lobby for making the federal government itself a powerful planning mechanism, capable of orchestrating corporate policies on prices, wages, and investments (or, in the language of a later era, "micro-managing" the economy). But such sentiments, widespread though never decisive five years before, survived in 1938 only in a few corners of the administration—most notably among some of Rexford Tugwell's former colleagues in the Agriculture Department, who called, as one contemporary critic put it, for "the central planning of industrial activity, budgeting each year's national production and assigning it by quotas to individual producers." By 1938, with Tugwell gone from the administration and conservative opposition to the New Deal growing, what the *Nation* called the "exponents of centralized, nation-wide planning" were no longer either numerous or influential.[26]

There was, however, notable interest still in reviving something like the NRA, some system of cooperative partnerships in which the government would play a significant but less decisive role. Although Roosevelt never made a serious effort to resurrect the NRA after the *Schechter* decision, he gave frequent indications of a continuing affection for the concept. Even years later, he spoke warmly of the NRA staff as "trail blazers in a new approach to stability in business and industry" who had "pointed the way to a new economic order which I am sure will be fully realized in years to come." His reluctance to abandon the NRA approach altogether was evident in, among other things, his appointment in September 1935 of a Coordinator for Industrial Cooperation, whose job, according to *Newsweek*, was "to induce industry and labor to do voluntarily what the NRA [had] made them do."[27]

Roosevelt's choice for this new (and unpaid) position was George L. Berry, president of the American Federation of Labor's typographers' union and a former NRA administrator. Berry was deeply committed to the idea of cooperation among capital, labor, and government. He was also a flamboyant self-promoter determined to make his unpromising new office into a major force in the administration.[28] He created a group he called the Council for Industrial Progress and, through it, organized an ill-fated conference of businessmen, trade union leaders, and consumer representatives in December 1935. The meeting produced such acrimony that many of the corporate executives stormed out. A second conclave a year later was less rancorous, but scarcely more fruitful. Berry persisted. In mid-1937, he was promoting a scheme for the creation of a National Economic Board through which competing economic groups might come together "to understand the inescapable community of interest" among them.[29]

Berry was appointed to a vacant Tennessee seat in the United States Senate later in 1937, and his attention shifted elsewhere. But the desire to create a "community of interest" survived in other quarters. Particularly influential on behalf of such visions was the Commerce Department's Business Advisory Council, a committee of businessmen established in 1933 in connection with the birth of the NRA, through the efforts of Gerard Swope and railroad executive Henry I. Harriman.[30] Secretary of Commerce Daniel Roper managed to keep it alive (if at times only barely) after the collapse of the NRA in 1935. The Council had no statutory authority. Its members were unpaid advisers to the government, not real officials, and they only occasionally acted in concert. But by early 1938, they had forged relationships with some important figures in the administration and had won at least a hearing for their ideas. One of those ideas was stabilizing markets by limiting the effects of competition. Another was promoting a more cooperative relationship between business and government.[31]

The Business Advisory Council did not, of course, speak for all, or even most, American businessmen. Even its own membership was diverse and, on some issues at least, divided. Among its most influential figures, however, were representatives of some of the nation's largest and most powerful industrial and financial firms. Unlike the heads of smaller firms and members of more precarious industries, who generally opposed any government "interference" in their operations and who particularly detested New Deal labor legislation, some BAC leaders represented large, capital-intensive firms with international interests—firms in which keeping labor peace was often more important than controlling labor costs; firms that needed assistance from (and protection by) the state as they attempted to expand their activities overseas. Several of these executives went on to become major figures in the Roosevelt administration and in Democratic politics; most accepted and some even applauded many New Deal reforms. In the process, they articulated the outlines of what some historians have called "corporate liberalism."[32]

To be sure, most BAC members were as hostile as other businessmen to what they considered the more extreme "anti-business" policies of the New Deal: to the Wagner Act, which contained what they thought were dangerously radical provisions that could require corporations to bargain with unions and require workers to join them; to the "very high" corporate taxes they considered the New Deal to have levied on them; to the perennial federal budget deficits, which they feared undermined "business confidence"; and to the "demagogic" anti-business rhetoric that had suffused the 1936 campaign and resurfaced periodically thereafter.[33] But they did not oppose everything. Many members of the BAC accepted the less coercive collective bargaining agreements embodied in section 7(a) of the 1933 National Industrial Recovery Act and (despite their distaste for the more forceful Wagner Act) endorsed an extension of those agreements after the nullification of the original law. Most supported the "wages and hours" bill that was making its way through Congress in 1937 and that would eventually become the Fair Labor Standards Act of 1938; it established a national minimum wage and limited the hours an employee could be required to work before receiving overtime pay. (The wages and hours bill, some major industrialists believed, would improve their own competitive position against low-wage small businesses, especially in the South.) Many "corporate liberals" conceded the value of federal regulation of the securities markets, federal insurance of bank deposits, and other financial reforms.[34]

Above all, most BAC members hoped to build a permanent partnership between business and government, a hope the recession of 1937 greatly strengthened. Conservative businessmen insisted that only a complete withdrawal of government from the private sector would give investors the confidence to invest. But to the members of the BAC, a secure and stable economic environment was only possible with government support. A revived effort along the lines of the NRA, the Council argued, was the best route to "the reinvestment of profits on a large scale." Robert Wood Johnson, one of the leading "liberals" on the BAC, showered his friends in the administration with calls for new conferences that would bring together "leaders of labor, agriculture, and business" to form a "tri-party agreement." Roper funneled BAC reports to the White House calling for "cooperation as a basis for lasting industrial recovery" and for the "use of certain features of the N.R.A., voluntary approach in the relationship of private industry to public controls." Such commitments led the BAC to serve with growing frequency as a forum for the leading New Deal defender of the "NRA approach" in the late 1930s: Donald Richberg.[35]

LIKE MANY men and women who became major figures in the New Deal, Richberg had come into politics through the progressive reform battles of the early twentieth century. He began his adult life as a Chicago lawyer who hated practicing law and as an aspiring poet and essayist who only rarely found outlets for his work. In 1905, at the age of twenty-four, he took a few tentative steps into politics and soon found himself entirely immersed in the world of reform. Suddenly the law was no longer drudgery; it had been transformed, in the words of one biographer, "from a petty service for private interests into a service enhanced by the public interest."[36] Richberg continued to write, but his subjects became less literary and more political; for the rest of his life, his essays, poetry, and songs—always more notable for enthusiasm than originality—served as vehicles for promoting his reform ideas.[37]

Richberg was a warrior in the Progressive party campaign of 1912; formed a legal partnership in Chicago with another Bull Mooser, Harold

Ickes; and worked in several crusades against utilities magnates. After World War I, he became one of the nation's leading labor lawyers, a counsel to the railroad unions, and one of the drafters of the 1926 Railway Labor Act, which created new mechanisms for mediating railroad labor disputes. Such experiences convinced him of the importance of cooperation between labor and capital in industrial relations. By the end of the decade, that conviction was growing into a vision of a larger concert of economic interest, "a machinery of cooperative power, whereby men may work together to enrich and make more satisfying their individual lives."[38]

A Republican for most of his life, Richberg quickly lost patience with what he considered the passivity and intellectual bankruptcy of the Hoover administration. So it was natural, perhaps, that in 1932 he committed himself early to the candidacy of Franklin D. Roosevelt, the distant cousin of Richberg's first great political hero. Richberg became (in his own words) an "associate member"[39] of Roosevelt's campaign "brains trust"; and although he was disappointed after the election in his quest for a Cabinet appointment in the new administration, he responded to the urging of Raymond Moley in the spring of 1933 and worked with Hugh Johnson on the drafting of the National Industrial Recovery Act.[40]

Richberg was a logical choice. Not only would his long association with organized labor help win political support for the bill, but only months earlier he had himself advanced a plan for "Self Government in Industry," in which he had called for "industrial councils composed of representatives of managers, investors and workers" along with a "national council composed of similar representatives of all essential industries." Speaking before the Senate Finance Committee in February 1933, he said: "We have reached a stage in the development of human affairs where it has become intolerable to have our primitive capitalistic system operated by selfish individualists engaged in ruthless competition. . . . A planned control of the great essential industries is essential."[41] After passage of the NIRA in June, he became general counsel to the NRA. As the embattled Hugh Johnson was being eased out of the agency in the fall of 1934, Richberg expanded his own role within the agency and ultimately became its last chairman.[42]

Some considered him a representative of labor when he joined the NRA in 1933, but Richberg himself had other ideas. He would be an impartial arbiter of contending interests, a leader who would transcend parochial demands and defend a larger public good. As his sense of his own importance grew, he became convinced at times that the fate of the entire Roosevelt administration, if not of the nation, depended on his success in doing so. That meant, among other things, proving his independence from organized labor; and in 1935, he broke publicly with the AFL over the NRA code for the automobile industry, which Richberg had helped draft and which labor, with considerable justification, considered hostile to its interests. United Mine Workers president John L. Lewis and others attacked him as a "traitor." Richberg responded almost regally: "The charge that I am a 'traitor to organized labor' amounts to the demand that as a public official I should put subservience to the policies of a particular labor organization, above loyalty to the Government and to my conception of the public interest."[43]

By late 1934, perhaps partly in response to the invective labor leaders were directing toward him, Richberg was demonstrating increasing sympathy for and identification with the business community and its aims. The NRA proved, he came to believe, that the corporate world could be receptive to responsible economic reforms in an environment of business-government cooperation. Gerard Swope was only one of many corporate leaders who decided that he "was coming more and more into favor with the business interests." Felix Frankfurter, Harold Ickes, and other New Dealers less enamored of the ideal of cooperation concluded about the same time that Richberg was "a dangerous man for the Administration."[44]

After the demise of the NRA in 1935, Richberg practiced law in Washington while remaining active in the Democratic Party and, on occasion, within the inner circles of the administration. Among other things, he helped draft both the 1936 Democratic platform and the President's message proposing the court-packing plan. Above all, he remained for the next three years the leading public spokesman for reviving the "ideals" of the NRA. In the meantime, his ties to the business world continued to grow stronger. By 1938, he was contemplating joining the Business Advisory Council and was writing glowingly to the White House about the "more liberal attitude manifested in business organizations that have hitherto been quite reactionary."[45]

Almost all of those with pronounced ideas about public policy considered the recession of 1937 a vindication of their own beliefs and an indictment of those who had thwarted their realization. Richberg was no exception. While others used the crisis to reinforce their calls for stronger attacks on monopoly, Richberg spoke passionately about preserving and extending "our carefully built and workable cooperative machinery."[46] "The philosophy of the N.R.A. was wholly consistent with the New Deal," he wrote the President in the spring of 1938. "The philosophy of the fanatic trust busters, with their hostility to all large enterprise, their assumption that cooperation is always a cloak for monopolistic conspiracy—this philosophy is wholly inconsistent with the New Deal." America, he claimed, had been "living in a state of industrial warfare," a condition to which the New Deal had at times unwisely contributed. What the nation needed now was an end to the conflict and a search for "peaceful, democratic cooperation."[47]

Richberg's increasing visibility in early 1938 reflected not only his own energy and ambition but the degree to which some liberals remained enchanted by the cooperative vision and were sympathetic, if not to the details of Richberg's proposals, at least to his general aims.[48] Adolf Berle complained constantly in early 1938 about how irresponsible New Dealers were engaging in a "campaign of bitterness" and driving a wedge between government and business; he urged instead a "campaign to form production committees" and a harmonizing of economic interests.[49] Tugwell and Moley shared this dismay and even years later lamented the New Deal's failure to grasp the logic behind the drive for economic order. "In his thoughtful moments," Tugwell wrote, "[Roosevelt] understood the momentum of collectivism; but he pulled back from the sacrifices implied in acceptance."[50]

Even some New Dealers who supported anti-monopoly efforts seemed drawn at times to the associational ideal. Agriculture Secretary Henry Wallace, for one, spoke glowingly early in 1938 of "the possibility of combining into a truly harmonious whole all the prerequisites to the good life."[51] The economist Mordecai Ezekiel, Wallace's colleague in the Agriculture Department, was promoting what he called an "Industrial Expansion" program that would bring business, labor, agriculture, and government together in "councils" to supervise "programmed industrial operation" and "planned production."[52] And SEC chairman Jerome Frank, despite his close ties to liberals in other camps, never lost his affection for the ideas behind the NRA. "Far more can be done by intelligent cooperation between government, the components of industry, the suppliers of the materials, the purchasers of the materials, labor and the consumer, than we have anywhere as yet canvassed," he told a congressional committee in 1939. He urged a thorough examination of the NRA, "so as to learn by its mistakes" and to revive its "virtues."[53]

The dream of an "ordered economic world," a dream as old as the industrial economy itself, retained considerable luster in the dark winter of recession. But it gradually became evident that support for the economic strategies associated with that dream was much thinner than Richberg liked to believe.

.   .   .

"THERE  ARE  TWO quite different approaches to the problem of
making the American economy work reasonably well," the economist
Gardiner Means wrote in 1939. "Some people think of the problem as one
which can be solved by dealing with one situation after another.... Other
people believe that the problem ... can be solved only on the basis which
envisages the economy as a whole as a single operating machine." The first
solution Means described dismissively as the "piecemeal" approach, the
second (which he favored), as the "unitary" approach. That he found it
necessary to make that distinction suggests how conscious those who
believed in rationalization of the economy were of opposition to their
hopes.[54]

The dream of an ordered economic world was, in the late New Deal
as throughout its long history, alluring to almost all liberals in the abstract.
There were few reformers who did not make at least occasional rhetorical
references to the ideal of harmony, few who were not at times entranced
by the vision of a comprehensive economic "solution" that would forge
a smoothly functioning whole out of the clashing parts of modern capitalism. Translating that dream into practice, however, seemed usually to
involve placing restrictions on competition—either through comprehensive public planning or, more often, through private cartelization—a
prospect that inspired considerably less enthusiasm.

For most liberals, therefore, the dream of economic harmony was by
the late 1930s little more than a hazy vision, quickly and decisively
repudiated whenever it threatened to take concrete form. That was
evident in many ways, but nowhere more clearly than in the retrospec-
tive view most New Dealers took of the National Recovery Administration. Richberg, members of the Business Advisory Council, and even
Roosevelt himself might view the NRA as a noble experiment worthy of
emulation. But far more liberals viewed it as a terrible mistake—the
"N.R.A. disaster," the "NRA of evil memory"—that should never be
attempted again.[55]

Indeed, many critics interpreted the NRA's failures as proof of the
bankruptcy of the associational ideal that Swope, Richberg, and others
were still attempting to promote. The NRA, its opponents complained,
"gave employers the opportunity to raise prices and restrict production ...
and so encouraged monopolistic practices that interfered with the very
object sought—more abundance." It had "hindered recovery instead of
helping it." It had proved that "whenever business men are allowed to
come together to 'cooperate,' the result is almost inevitably an effort to
get more profits by some form of price-raising." It was "merely the trust
sugar-coated," which had "pinned a policeman's badge" on monopolies.

"What big business has previously done in the name of 'cooperation,'" one administration official warned late in 1937, "is too well remembered for us to commit ourselves to it again."[56]

Many interpreted the failure of the NRA in even broader terms: as evidence of the impossibility of imposing any centralized planning—whether by business or by government—on the economy. Most liberals continued in the late 1930s to support the idea of "planning," indeed to embrace it with almost religious veneration. But their disillusionment with the NRA encouraged them to think of planning in something less than genuinely comprehensive terms, indeed to look with considerable hostility upon proposals for imposing order on the industrial economy. The NRA, one critic wrote, was one of the "impetuous grandiosities of the 1933 period." It had collapsed, Assistant Attorney General Thurman Arnold argued, for the same reason that all economic "master plans" must collapse—because it could have succeeded only through a "vast extension of state control," an extension that Americans would not (and should not) contemplate. Henry Wallace, writing earlier, argued that "there is something wooden and inhuman about the government interfering in a definite, precise way with the details of our private and business lives. It suggests a time of war with generals and captains telling every individual what he must do each day and hour."[57]

Economic harmony may have had an abstract appeal, but few liberals were able to conceive of any workable mechanism for achieving it. Indeed, most considered such mechanisms not only unworkable but perilous. Hence, the real legacy of the NRA experiment, and of the decades-long effort to produce an "ordered economic world" that had preceded it, was not a vision of industrial cooperation. It was a heightened awareness of the obstacles to that vision. And the most important responses to the 1937 recession, therefore, came from people who advocated a very different role for the state in the nation's economic life.

# Chapter Three

# The "New Dealers" and the Regulatory Impulse

THE CABINET MEETING of November 6, 1937, was, unsurprisingly, dominated by efforts to explain the economic downturn that had begun so suddenly and unexpectedly over the previous several weeks. In the midst of an inconclusive discussion, during which Henry Morgenthau and James Farley argued strenuously for the need to "reassure business," the President offered his own, perhaps impulsive, interpretation of the crisis: "Organized wealth, which has controlled the Government so far, seizes this opportunity to decide whether it is to continue to control the Government or not." A few minutes later, as the meeting broke up, Harold Ickes showed Roosevelt a note he had scrawled on a memo pad while listening to the conversation: "This looks to me like the same kind of fight that Jackson made against the United States Bank except that big capital is occupying at this time the role of the bank." The President read it, looked up, and said: "That's right."[1]

Roosevelt returned to that idea intermittently from the beginning of the recession to its end: the idea that the crisis was somehow the work of a selfish and vengeful corporate community and that the solution, therefore, was to bring that community to heel. Nor were Roosevelt and Ickes alone in embracing such assumptions. The recession reinvigorated a recently dormant, but deeply rooted, concern among many liberals throughout the administration and beyond about the dangers of monopoly power; and out of that concern emerged a distinctive interpretation of the causes of the recession. The problem, such liberals argued, was not "business confidence," not (as many businessmen claimed) the reluctance of manufacturers to invest because of the uncertain economic and political climate. The problem was that monopolistic interests had used their power to raise prices artificially while keeping costs and wages low. "Were monopolies responsible for this price rise which crippled workable relationships in the American economy?" New Deal economist Leon

Henderson asked early in 1938. "My answer is emphatically yes. I believe the unbalance in prices was touched off by the monopolistic prices."[2]

The "monopoly power" explanation of the recession, like the "business confidence" explanation with which it competed, had at least some basis in economic reality. Prices did rise rapidly after 1934, and particularly rapidly in the months before the October 1937 collapse. In several key areas of the economy, moreover (among them transportation, home appliances, and above all construction), the high-price structure showed significant rigidity, suggesting a relative absence of competition and the influence of monopoly practices. Clearly some prices were rising less in response to the natural working of the market than to the decisions of a few powerful organizations.[3]

But the appeal of the argument had less to do with its economic salience (about which most economists at the time and since have been generally skeptical) than with its ideological appeal. It reflected its proponents' already deep suspicion of the culture of big business. And it strengthened their longstanding commitment to increase public control of it by constructing a potent and vigorous regulatory state. By late 1937 and early 1938, these anti-monopolists had become the most visible faction within the administration: a large and, for the moment, highly conspicuous circle of men and women who considered themselves, and were considered by others, the "liberal crowd."[4]


SOME MEMBERS of this circle had been part of the administration almost from the beginning, a few of them in important positions. But the recession greatly increased both their influence and their visibility, moving them as a group from the periphery to the center. That, at least, was the point of a story recounted by the columnists Joseph Alsop and Robert Kintner late in 1938, when the power of the "liberal crowd" seemed at its highest. On a summer evening in 1936, they reported, several advisers had joined Roosevelt for dinner at the White House to work on his acceptance speech for the approaching Democratic convention. Among them were Raymond Moley, a leader of the original New Deal "brains trust," and Thomas G. Corcoran ("Tommy the Cork"), widely considered the leader of the new one. In the course of the meal, several guests had begun teasing Moley (perhaps not entirely good-naturedly) about his ties to "rich friends." Roosevelt, apparently, had joined in the kidding. Moley, who was already feeling an estrangement from the President and his policies that would within a year make him an outspoken critic of the New Deal, had taken offense, and a bitter argument had followed. A breach was emerging between the President and Moley. It brought to a close a personal and political association that had been important to both for nearly a decade. "On that troubled evening," Alsop and Kintner claimed, "Tom Corcoran's presence at the White House was the sign that these new men, the New Dealers, would soon take over."[5]

Relations between Moley and Roosevelt had already been deteriorating for some time, and it seems unlikely that a dinner table spat was a decisive factor in precipitating the rift. But that Alsop and Kintner chose to recount the incident in 1938 is evidence of what had by then become a widespread public assumption about the Roosevelt administration: that power within it was moving from one group of reformers to another. The original brains trust—Moley, Adolf Berle, Rexford Tugwell, and others—had largely dispersed. In its place was emerging a new generation of liberals, younger for the most part, highly aggressive, and different in both outlook and goals. The term "New Dealers," originally a general label referring to all members of the administration, was becoming in popular parlance a reference to this group alone.[6]

Alsop and Kintner considerably exaggerated the influence of the "New Dealers," just as earlier commentators had occasionally exaggerated the influence of the "brains trust." Corcoran and his allies did not "take over" the New Deal in 1937, and their power within it lasted only briefly in any case. But however limited their ultimate influence, these liberals were for a time a powerful collective presence in the administration and in American politics, articulating and promoting a vision of government significantly different not only from that of the original "brains trust," but also from those of many other liberal politicians and thinkers in 1938.

That the "New Dealers" acquired a clear identity as a group was a result in part of their identification with Felix Frankfurter, the politically energetic Harvard Law School professor who—as friend and confidant of Franklin Roosevelt—was a major recruiting officer for the administration. He became as a result something like a patron saint to liberals in Washington.

He had first befriended the future President during World War I, when Roosevelt was assistant secretary of the navy and Frankfurter chairman of the War Labor Policies Board. As Roosevelt's political fortunes rose in the late 1920s, the friendship revived. And by the time of the 1932 election, the outlines of their relationship were well established. Roosevelt was the reverent student, expressing gratitude for the wisdom he was receiving from a superior intellect; Frankfurter, he once said, had "more ideas per minute than any man of my acquaintance." Frankfurter was the loyal and adoring courtier, showering the great man with advice and sycophantic praise. ("I wish the whole people could see you as I see you—," he once wrote, "your patience, your generosity, your unflagging zeal for the kind of society for which this nation was avowedly established.") Frankfurter took quiet pleasure in small signs of intimacy. He was, for example, one of the few people who always addressed Roosevelt—in writing at least—by his first name, although unlike other intimates he generally shortened it to "Frank."

As with most such relationships, there was artifice on both sides. Roosevelt respected Frankfurter, but followed his counsel no more than that of many other advisers, and then only when it suited his own purposes. Frankfurter, in turn, was devoted to Roosevelt, but less selflessly than he liked to pretend; he used the relationship openly (and some believed shamelessly) to expand his influence in Washington—and, ultimately, to secure an appointment to the Supreme Court.[7]

Frankfurter could exercise influence most effectively, he discovered, by channeling young colleagues and protégés into important positions in the new administration. Major law firms, he wrote in 1936, annually "recruit their lower ranks from the best men of the graduating classes of the leading law schools. From such recruits the government could hope to develop at least a portion into permanent public servants." The article was clearly self-serving; by the time it was published Frankfurter had already pillaged the "leading law schools" of both students and faculty members to fill dozens of significant posts within the New Deal—not always to the delight of more traditionally political figures in the administration. George Peek, the first administrator of the Agricultural Adjustment Administration and by 1937 a disillusioned critic of the New Deal, expressed the alarm many older reformers felt at the arrival of this new breed. "A plague of young lawyers settled on Washington," he wrote in a bitter 1936 memoir of his years in the New Deal. "They all claimed to be friends of somebody or other, and mostly of Jerome Frank [general counsel to the AAA] and Felix Frankfurter. They floated airily into offices, took desks, asked for papers, and found no end of things to be busy about." Peek described them as "boys with their hair ablaze." To Frankfurter, they were "public servants of higher grade."[8]

Perhaps the most important Frankfurter protégé in Washington was Thomas Corcoran, widely and to some degree correctly considered the leader of the "New Dealers." He became, in the end, an early example of what later became a familiar political type: the powerful Washington insider whose position depended on a carefully cultivated network of friends and allies throughout the bureaucracy—and whose influence continued for many decades after his formal government service ended.

Corcoran was born in Rhode Island in 1900 into an affluent, teetotaling, self-consciously "lace-curtain" Irish family, which looked with some contempt on the "cheap" political activities of what one of Corcoran's uncles called the "damned Shanty Irish." He clearly did not absorb his family's dislike of politics; but in his youth, at least, he shared something of their distaste for "politicians" and ultimately brought to his own public career a conviction that, while elected officials were necessary to a democracy, the best sources of public wisdom were intelligent, highly educated, selfless administrators like (he chose to believe) himself.

Corcoran attended Brown University, graduated as valedictorian, and moved on to Harvard Law School. There he distinguished himself academically again, became an editor of the law review, and—along with other exceptionally bright young men—attracted (and prudently reciprocated) Frankfurter's attention. In 1926, when he was leaving Cambridge, Frankfurter secured him a clerkship with Justice Oliver Wendell Holmes. His year at the Supreme Court left him with a deep reverence for Holmes and a passion for the work of government, both of which he retained for the rest of his life.[9]

After five years practicing law on Wall Street (during which time he made and lost a small fortune in the stock market, watched his family's modest wealth all but vanish, and developed an enduring bitterness toward what he considered the lassitude and insensitivity of Herbert Hoover), he returned to Washington in March 1932 to work for the Reconstruction Finance Corporation. The new agency would, he hoped, be the beginning of vigorous federal efforts to revive the industrial economy. But he chafed at his own relatively minor role at the RFC, tried unsuccessfully to expand it, and became quickly disillusioned with what he considered the halting, stingy lending habits of the agency, which seemed to Corcoran perfectly to epitomize the "tired and desperate" character of the administration as a whole. "Goddam—I hate Hoover," he wrote Frankfurter that summer. About Roosevelt, he did not yet know what to feel.[10]

A few months later, however, he was a member of Roosevelt's administration and, almost from the beginning, an important figure within it, even though he never held a major official position. Until he left the government in 1940, he remained (with only one brief interruption) where he had started under Hoover, on the RFC staff.[11] But from that inconspicuous post, Corcoran developed a remarkable network of influence. During the first three years of the New Deal, at least, that was largely a result of his closeness to Frankfurter. The two men were in almost constant communication. When Corcoran neglected on occasion to send full reports of his activities to Cambridge, he could expect a chiding note; "I know you are busy as hell, but what of it?"[12] Frankfurter traveled to Washington two or three times a month. "He would see Roosevelt," recalled Joseph Rauh, another of Frankfurter's New Deal protégés, "and then he would see Tom." When Frankfurter received a request for assistance from the President, more often than not he directed it to Corcoran. Among other things, he recruited Corcoran to help draft the legislation that created the Securities and Exchange Commission in 1933 and, two years later, the controversial Public Utilities Holding Company bill (the so-called "death sentence," designed to break up utilities monopolies). Corcoran's own fame and influence grew quickly in the mid-1930s, but he seemed always to recognize how crucial the relationship with Frankfurter was to his own power. "When Felix walked in the door," Rauh noted, "there wasn't any question who was boss."[13]

Corcoran, however, gradually established a significant power base of his own, by virtue of his energy, his intellect, his personal charm, and his own success in recruiting bright young men (from Harvard Law School and elsewhere) for important posts in the administration. He was a jovial, garrulous man who attracted friends easily and almost always made himself the center of attention. Informal photographs of him from the 1930s (and indeed from throughout his long life) often show him in the middle of things, smiling broadly at the camera, his arms around the shoulders of companions. "Tom was the leader of the group," recalled Frank Watson, one of a number of young, unmarried New Dealers who lived with Corcoran for a time in what became known as the "little red house" in Georgetown. (It was, in fact, the three-story brick mansion on R Street that Ulysses S. Grant had used as a summer home.) Corcoran was a born entertainer who loved playing the piano or accordion and singing, and he considered it his responsibility to enliven any party, even if it was not his own. "Tom wanted everybody to be happy," Watson recalled, "and he kept his eye on everybody. He was an all-engrossing personality."[14]

Corcoran's relationship with the President was the subject of much speculation. Roosevelt clearly liked him and enjoyed his company. He also admired Corcoran's skills as a writer and came increasingly to rely on him to put a "lilt" in his speeches; Corcoran was, for example, one of the principal draftsmen of the President's dramatic 1936 acceptance speech in Philadelphia. Whether Corcoran often shaped Roosevelt's positions on policy in any fundamental way is less clear, but there is little to suggest that he ever exercised anything like the influence over the President that friends and enemies alike believed he did. Corcoran, however, did nothing to discourage such a belief; indeed, he traded openly and at times somewhat dishonestly on the widespread assumption that he was acting as the President's agent.[15]

Corcoran's friend Harold Ickes worried that this growing prominence would increase Corcoran's vulnerability to attacks from ideological opponents both within and outside the administration, attacks he would not have the political or bureaucratic authority to withstand. And, indeed, Corcoran was developing powerful enemies who considered him a dangerous radical or a brazen opportunist or both. Adolf Berle described Corcoran in his diary as "fundamentally an ambitious politician" who had "very little else in his head." Even the usually generous Eleanor Roosevelt had grave reservations about what she considered his excessive ambition and erratic judgment. For a time, however, Corcoran's intelligence and his political skills allowed him to withstand his attackers. And by the end of 1937, he stood at the center of a growing network of liberals in Washington—an increasingly self-conscious group whose members considered themselves something of a vanguard pressing for a revived and more aggressive New Deal.[16]

Corcoran's closest ally and confidant, the man with whom his name would forever be linked, was Benjamin V. Cohen. A brilliant young lawyer from Chicago, Cohen, like Corcoran, had attracted Frankfurter's notice at Harvard Law School and had, as a result, eventually found his way into government. Also like Corcoran, he exercised a much greater influence in Washington than his relatively inconspicuous positions (associate general counsel to the Public Works Administration in 1933–1934 and counsel to the Interior Department's National Public Power Committee from 1934 to 1941) suggested. Cohen was six years older than Corcoran, and probably the brighter of the two. But in many respects he was the junior partner in the relationship. A shy, gentle man uncomfortable in social situations, and a Jew justifiably fearful that anti-Semitism might derail his career at any moment, he relied on Corcoran for advancement, protection, and emotional support. His calm, reasoned demeanor often served to balance Corcoran's occasionally impulsive instincts. His loyalty was unwavering. When Corcoran broke with their mentor, Frankfurter, in 1939, Cohen did so too. After Corcoran married his secretary, Peggy Dowd, in 1940, Cohen—a lifelong bachelor—made himself a virtual member of the family and remained so for more than three decades.

Through the first years of the New Deal, Cohen and Corcoran ("Ben and Tom," as they were known throughout the administration) worked together almost constantly—on the 1933 securities bill, on the 1935 utilities bill, drafting Roosevelt's 1936 campaign speeches. And when the recession of 1937 propelled the "New Dealers" to greater prominence within the administration, they came for a time, in the popular mind at least, to personify the change in direction. They were, one reporter noted that November, "a shadowy, fantastic team entirely unique . . . in the annals of American government." They exercised, said another, "more influence at the White House and, through the White House, are more of a force throughout the entire reaches of the government than any pair of statesmen in Washington."[17]

BUT THE LIBERAL NETWORK taking shape in the late 1930s extended well beyond Corcoran and Cohen, even beyond the other young lawyers they and Frankfurter recruited for the administration. By the beginning of 1938, it was a loose and sprawling alliance of seemingly like-minded people situated in important secondary (and at times primary) positions throughout the departments and agencies. It included James Landis, William O. Douglas, Robert Jackson, Thurman Arnold, Leon Henderson, Jerome Frank, Mordecai Ezekiel, Isidor Lubin, as well as many other, still younger lawyers and economists scattered inconspicuously but strategically through the bureaucracy. Harry Hopkins, the man who was soon to become the President's most important adviser, was their ally at times (although his serious health problems in the late 1930s and his preoccupation with international issues thereafter limited his role in their efforts).[18] Secretary of the Interior Harold Ickes was their principal supporter (and according to some, including Ickes himself, the "only New Dealer") in the Cabinet.[19] Secretary of Agriculture Henry Wallace, too cautious to commit himself openly to any one faction (and almost constantly at odds with the dyspeptic Ickes), was nevertheless an occasional defender as well.[20] They had close ties to the leading liberal journals, principally the *New Republic* and the *Nation*, and to such liberal writers and editors as Bruce Bliven, Freda Kirchwey, George Soule, Stuart Chase, Max Lerner, and Archibald MacLeish. And despite their vague mistrust of elected politicians and their mild contempt for legislators, they had allies in Congress too: senators Hugo Black of Alabama, Claude Pepper of Florida, Lewis Schwellenbach of Washington, and Harry Truman of Missouri; Representatives Maury Maverick of Texas and Jerry Voorhis of California; and others who were generally, though not invariably, sympathetic to their goals.[21]

No formal ties united this group, and its members did not speak with a single voice. They were, rather, linked to one another through an informal pattern of friendships and intellectual associations. Groups of them gathered in restaurants for weekly dinners to talk, one said, about "pending legislation or some current economic controversy." They held private meetings on Sunday afternoons to discuss the contours of administration policy. They attended dinner parties at one another's homes, often to meet with a visiting journalist or scholar sympathetic to their aims. They passed books and articles back and forth. They sent each other frequent letters offering encouragement and advice.[22]

The most important sources of comity, however, were not social connections but shared beliefs. And chief among those beliefs, in the recession winter of 1937–1938, was the conviction that government must exercise an increased level of authority over the structure and behavior of private capitalist institutions. The "New Dealers" expressed such assumptions particularly clearly in the way they interpreted the 1937 collapse: in their lack of patience with those who talked of the need to restore "business confidence" and those who continued to urge a cooperative "partnership" between industry and the state; in their insistence that the recession was a result of unregulated monopoly power in the marketplace. Corporate interests, they believed, had colluded to suppress competition and create what liberals liked to call "administered prices,"[23] choking off what had otherwise been a healthy recovery. The problem was not, as some associationalists argued, that the New Deal had gone too far in regulating the behavior of capitalist institutions. It was that the New Deal had not gone far enough.

Some "New Dealers" offered an even more disturbing explanation for the recession, which revealed how deep the antagonism toward corporate power could sometimes run. The recent collapse, they claimed, was the result of a "capital strike," a deliberate effort by some of the nation's most powerful monopolies to sabotage the recovery so as to undermine the New Deal. Roosevelt himself, angered and frustrated by the latest downturn in the economy's fortunes, seemed at times privately to sympathize with this view. He once went so far as to order the FBI (on the basis of an unsubstantiated letter from a hotel waiter in Chicago about a dinner-table conversation among railroad executives he claimed to have overheard) to look into the possibility of a criminal conspiracy.[24] But Roosevelt never expressed such suspicions publicly. That task fell to two prominent administration liberals: Harold Ickes and Robert Jackson.

Ickes, a combative anti-monopolist by both temperament and conviction, seemed genuinely to believe that the recession was part of a business conspiracy to undermine the administration. "I do not think that we will get anywhere trying to conciliate business," he confided to his diary that fall. "Big business wants all or nothing." The November 4 Cabinet meeting, at which the President had seemed to agree with Ickes's claim that "big capital" was at war with the government, encouraged him to speak out publicly.[25] Armed with that vague presidential assent and fortified with encouragement from Corcoran, Cohen, and others, he delivered a belligerent speech over NBC radio on December 30, 1937, blaming the recession on the reactionary power of the "Sixty Families." (He had borrowed the phrase from a recent book by Ferdinand Lundberg describing the domination of the United States by "a hierarchy of its sixty richest families" which constituted "the living center of the modern industrial oligarchy which dominates the United States.") Ickes spoke of the "irreconcilable conflict" between "the power of money and the power of the democratic instinct"; of the danger of a "big-business Fascist America—an enslaved America"; and of the nation's "first general sit-down strike—not of labor—not of the American people—but of the sixty families and of . . . capital." Had it come four days earlier, it would have been the bitterest attack on private wealth and corporate power ever to have come from the New Deal.[26]

But Ickes had already been outdone by Robert Jackson. Jackson in late 1937 was head of the antitrust division of the Justice Department and soon to become, in quick succession, solicitor general, attorney general, and associate justice of the Supreme Court. He was also, at that moment, widely regarded as one of Roosevelt's particular favorites. He had accompanied the President on a well-publicized fishing trip a few months earlier, and there was speculation that Roosevelt was trying to position him to run for governor of New York in 1938 and perhaps for president two years later.[27] So he attracted special attention when, in two speeches in late December, he gave direct and explicit expression to the theory of a "capital strike."

His addresses—one over the Mutual radio network on December 26, the second before the American Political Science Association in Philadelphia December 29—were in large measure collective efforts, carefully orchestrated by a small circle of New Dealers working closely together. Corcoran and Cohen helped write the speeches; Leon Henderson (who a month earlier had circulated a stinging memorandum accusing banks and corporations of "acting in concert" to produce the recession) contributed economic ideas. But the addresses also reflected Jackson's own private convictions, which were in many ways more genuinely antimonopolist than those of his colleagues.

In both speeches, Jackson painted a dismal picture of a nation in which individuals had lost the ability to control their futures, in which young men and women finishing school had no place to go "except to start at the bottom of an impossibly long ladder of a few great corporations dominated by America's 60 families." He went on to level more specific accusations. "Certain groups of big business," he warned, "have now seized upon a recession in our prosperity to 'liquidate the New Deal' and to throw off all governmental interference with their incorporated initiative." The monopolists claimed that the recession was a result of unreasonable labor demands, but in truth the excesses came from the capitalists themselves. It was, he said a "strike of capital . . . a general strike—the first general strike in America—a strike against the government—a strike to coerce political action."[28]

These strident December speeches were widely interpreted—by the press, by much of the administration, and by Ickes and Jackson themselves—as (in Ickes's words) "a barrage behind which the President could make an advance against big business."[29] And a few weeks later, the President himself addressed the monopoly issue in his annual message to Congress. Roosevelt was relatively restrained on the issue of a corporate conspiracy, referring elliptically to "selfish suspension of the employment of capital" and making no direct accusations of a "strike." But on the general subject of monopoly, his rhetoric was pointed. There were "problems affecting business," he said, that give "food for grave thought about the future. Generically such problems arise out of the concentration of economic control to the detriment of the body politic—control of other people's money, other people's labor, other people's lives." Existing laws governing monopoly, he argued, "undoubtedly require reconstruction," and he would be delivering a special message to Congress on the subject in the near future.[30] With that, the President signaled the beginning of a brief period in which anti-monopoly sentiment was to achieve an ascendancy within the New Deal that it had never had before and would never achieve again.


BUT OF WHAT, it should be asked, did this anti-monopoly sentiment now consist? The rhetoric was suffused with the traditional stuff of antitrust crusades: animus toward concentrated power and commitment to the interests of the common people. Beneath the familiar language, however, lay several quite different positions on both the means by which an antitrust campaign should be waged and the ends such a campaign should serve.

One important strain of antitrust sentiment in the late 1930s did indeed reflect traditional ideas about monopoly, in particular the idea that large concentrations of power were intrinsically dangerous. Many antimonopolists (among them Supreme Court Justice Louis Brandeis, whose 1914 book *Other People's Money* had been an influential statement of anti-monopolistic ideas, and whose title phrase Roosevelt had echoed in his message to Congress) had long argued that big organizations were bad almost by definition. That was in part because they were economically inefficient; human capacities were unsuited to managing a colossus effectively. But the more serious problem was not economic; it was social, cultural, even moral. "Bigness" was a threat not just to prosperity but, more important, to freedom.[31]

This attitude toward monopoly had deep roots both in American history and in contemporary popular politics. For as long as large-scale economic organizations and great concentrations of wealth had existed in America, they had produced fear and resentment among workers, farmers, artisans, small merchants and entrepreneurs, and many others. Such sentiments had helped spawn the Greenback movement, the Grange, the Knights of Labor, and, most significant, the populist movement of the 1890s. They had fueled major elements of progressive reform in the early twentieth century and had played a vital role in attracting support to the American Socialist party. They had given rise to anti–chain store movements in the South and Midwest, and challenges to utilities, railroads, landlords, and bosses throughout the United States. And in the 1930s, they had helped create some of the most important challenges to the New Deal: Huey Long's Share-Our-Wealth Movement, Father Charles Coughlin's National Union for Social Justice, Milo Reno's Farmers' Holiday Association, Floyd Olson's Farmer-Labor party in Minnesota, the La Follettes' Progressive party in Wisconsin, and many others. One reason, therefore, why anti-monopoly ideas received so much attention from politicians, government officials, and opinion leaders in the 1930s—and one reason why the rhetoric of anti-monopoly survived even among some who were uncommitted to its substance—was the existence (and continuing visibility) throughout the United States of so much popular hostility to economic concentration.

Within the realm of national policymaking, traditional anti-monopoly sentiments were associated especially closely with progressives from the West and Midwest (regions with strong populist traditions)—men such as Representatives Wright Patman and Maury Maverick, and Speaker Sam Rayburn, all of Texas; and Senators William Borah of Idaho, Joseph C. O'Mahoney of Wyoming, James E. Murray of Montana, at times Robert M. La Follette, Jr., of Wisconsin, and George W. Norris of Nebraska. "When we see the wonderful power of combined wealth and monopoly," Norris wrote in 1939 (in a private letter explaining why he would quietly support Roosevelt for a third term in 1940),

> the combination of that monopoly with special privilege and their terrible influence and power in controlling and influencing conventions, I say, we cannot afford to take that chance [of leaving the choice of a presidential candidate up to an open Democratic convention]. . . . I have long been a member of the Republican Party, but

with humiliation and regret I have to admit that most of the leaders of that party are under the control and domination of special privilege and organized monopoly, and I do not look for any relief in that direction.

That kind of populist resentment—which saw monopoly as a source of both economic injustice and profound political corruption—had been at the heart of anti-monopoly reform efforts for half a century. Within the New Deal, it found its most powerful voice in Robert Jackson.[32]

In 1944, Jackson wrote (but wisely did not publish) an autobiography whose sprawling narrative offers a revealing picture of the origins and nature of his anti-monopoly sentiments. Jackson's childhood in upstate New York was, as he mawkishly described it, an agrarian idyll, set in a "socially classless" world of independent yeomen and self-reliant communities. Such communities were "truly and deeply democratic, democratic in an economic and social as well as in a political sense . . . the nearest Paradise that most of us ever know." But that way of life, he lamented, "has largely disappeared," subsumed into the new, urban, industrial world and crushed by the power of great economic combinations. "Whether democracy can survive in this atmosphere," he warned, "I leave others to say."[33]

That Jackson's concerns were more moral than economic became clear in, among other things, his discussion of the threat of "chain stores" (a popular target of traditional anti-monopolists). In an exchange of letters with advertising executive Bruce Barton in 1937, Jackson admitted that chain stores were often efficient establishments, providing lower prices to consumers than local merchants. His opposition to them, he said, was "not economic so much as it is a social objection. The question is whether we have paid too much for these economies." For there was a "distinct value" in having "old friends who ran the several stores and performed their important functions in the community." Large combinations, he insisted, robbed individuals of their feeling of connection to their society and to the system of private enterprise; they were a source of powerlessness and alienation. "We are a proud people, raised on the doctrines of equality found in the Declaration of Independence," he said early in 1938 (in a radio debate with Wendell Willkie). "We do not like to be bossed too much. . . . We do not like to have any one man or corporation own the town."[34]

Such rhetoric tied the anti-monopoly crusade of 1938 to the language of Brandeis and Woodrow Wilson, and to the much broader traditions of populism and republicanism. Monopoly choked off opportunities for ordinary people to launch their own businesses. It denied workers the ability to control the conditions under which they labored. It threatened the ability of citizens to manage their own destinies. Fighting concentrated economic power was a way of fighting for what Saul Nelson, a New Deal economist, called "the maintenance of the freedom of individual opportunity and the encouragement of small independent businesses." It was a fight for the integrity of communities and the survival of the small producer. The problem was not the abuse of concentrated power; it was the existence of that power. "The monster is a menace not because of the way he acts," Nelson wrote, "but simply because he is too large." The purpose of an assault on bigness was not literally to restore the arcadian world Jackson remembered from his youth; all but a few anti-monopolists realized that was impossible. But the goal was nevertheless to reduce the size of economic units—to break up, rather than regulate, monopolies. "There is no practical way on earth to regulate the economic oligarchy of autocratic, self-constituted and self-perpetuating groups," Jackson insisted.[35]

This approach to the problem of monopoly rested almost as much on resistance to the idea of a powerful state as on fear of powerful private interests. The power of government was necessary to break up combinations and remove obstacles to competition, anti-monopolists conceded; but beyond that, government should do as little as possible. "The theory of the Antitrust Laws," Jackson wrote in 1937, "is to avoid government regulation by letting business men *regulate each other* through the processes of competition. . . . The failure of competition might bring about government control and it is important that American business men realize that the breaking down of competition means the beginning of government control."[36] Antitrust efforts, in short, were a way for government to fight its own tendencies toward bigness as well as those of industry; they were a way to avoid creating an economy in which (as Jackson warned) a few men might attempt to "operate the whole business life of the United States from a government office building." They were a way to escape what *Fortune* magazine described as the looming danger of "an order in which the powers of Government are *not* limited; in which the right to risk-and-profit is *not* clear; and in which the making, the selling, and even the buying of the products of the biggest show in history are all mysteriously directed from above." The struggle against monopoly was a struggle for the preservation of individual freedom— both freedom from monopoly power and freedom from the state.[37]

.   .   .

NEARLY EVERYONE concerned about the monopoly question in the late 1930s paid obeisance at times to these traditional populist sentiments. But among most of the New Dealers who were attempting to define a course for the administration in 1937 and 1938, the vision of an antitrust campaign was in fact very different. To them, the problem of monopoly was not primarily moral, social, or cultural. It was economic. "As the factory system of organization has come to dominate the country," Gardiner Means argued in the mid-1930s, "a significant part of economic organization has been transferred from the market to [corporate] administration." The result was "administered prices"—prices determined not by the marketplace (whose effectiveness, Means claimed, may have been "entirely destroyed . . . as an overall economic coordination") but by large combinations. Corporate leaders, in short, were thwarting competition, defeating the market, and hence inflating prices. By doing so, they were reducing consumption and choking off recovery.[38]

The proper approach to monopoly, therefore, was not to oppose bigness for its own sake. On the contrary, most liberals argued, large-scale enterprises brought welcome efficiencies to economic life; to talk of abolishing them was nostalgic nonsense. "It is ridiculous to speak of breaking up 'big business,'" the ardent New Dealer Maury Maverick wrote in 1939. "We need big business. We need monopolies. . . . To talk of returning to arts and crafts is not only romantic, it is impossible." The task was, rather, to identify those business practices that limited competition and stop them.[39]

This definition of the problem reflected two significant departures from the traditional anti-monopoly stance. First, it suggested a very different role for government than the relatively limited one envisioned by the traditionalists. To most New Dealers, the idea that the government could ensure competition simply by stepping into the marketplace occasionally to break up a large combination was naive and even dangerous. Controlling monopoly, they believed, required a strong and constant public presence in the private economy, an elaborate system of regulation that would enable the state to monitor corporate behavior continuously and, when necessary, to change it. Antitrust efforts would not be an alternative to the growth of a regulatory state; they would be part of that growth.

Indeed, among many "New Dealers" in the late 1930s there was a remarkable enthusiasm for the idea of enhancing the regulatory powers of the federal government, an enthusiasm based in part on the earlier accomplishments of the New Deal itself. Before 1933, only two federal agencies had exercised important regulatory powers: the Interstate Commerce Commission and the Federal Trade Commission. By the end of the

1930s, there were four major new agencies: the Securities and Exchange Commission, the Federal Communications Commission, the National Labor Relations Board, and the Civil Aeronautics Authority (later the Civil Aeronautics Board), as well as innumerable smaller mechanisms exercising more limited regulatory authority. The powers of the ICC and the FTC had also been significantly enhanced. This increase in public control over corporate institutions was, many liberals believed, the principal achievement of the New Deal, the legacy upon which future efforts should build.[40] The task facing liberals, SEC chairman William Douglas wrote in 1938, was "to battle for control of the present government so its various parts may be kept alive as vital forces of democracy."[41]

Such liberals had a precise idea about the shape those organizations should assume. A modern state, they believed, required the proliferation of independent executive agencies and expert administrators, insulated as far as possible from political pressures. In particular, it required a bureaucracy insulated from the legislature. Congress was cumbersome and fragmented; legislators were, on the whole, provincial and hopelessly politicized. Only in the executive branch (indeed, some believed, only in the independent regulatory agencies) was it possible for trained administrators to work effectively and disinterestedly on behalf of the public interest.[42]

There was an unrecognized irony in this enthusiasm for an expanded regulatory state. On the one hand, the "New Dealers" had a view of what government could hope to achieve that was in many ways more modest than those of some earlier reformers. There was, they realized, no "master plan" by which capitalism would become a just, stable, self-regulating system, and no cooperative or associative scheme that would create a smoothly functioning, ordered, harmonious whole out of the economy's clashing parts. No antitrust strategy could create a small-scale, decentralized economy free from the influence of large combinations. The state could not, liberals had come to believe, in any fundamental way "solve" the problems of the economy.[43] But the very limits of their ultimate ambitions made their vision of government more aggressive and assertive than that of many of their progressive predecessors. The inevitability of constant conflict and instability in a modern capitalist economy was all the more reason for government to become an active regulatory force.[44]

James Landis's *The Administrative Process*, a 1938 meditation on the author's experiences in the Securities and Exchange Commission, attempted to explain that apparent contradiction. "It is not without reason," he wrote, "that a nation which believes profoundly in the efficacy of the profit motive is at the same time doubtful as to the eugenic possibilities of breeding supermen to direct the inordinately complex affairs of the larger branches of private industry." But the impossibility of finding "supermen" to manage the economy was not, Landis believed, a reason to retreat from state activism. It was a reason to expand the federal bureaucracy, to substitute for the unattainable "super manager" the massed expertise of hundreds of trained administrators. "If the administrative process is to fill the need for expertness," he wrote, "the number of our administrative authorities must increase. . . . Efficiency in the processes of governmental regulation is best served by the creation of more rather than less agencies."[45]

There was also another way in which this new definition of the monopoly problem departed from older antitrust ideas. Anti-monopolists emerging from the populist-republican tradition had worried about small businessmen threatened by predatory combinations; about local merchants challenged by the "chain stores"; about independent farmers battling the railroads and the processors; about workers losing their autonomy to large corporate employers. To them, the antitrust laws were above all vehicles for the defense of economic freedom, for the protection of small producers. But the "New Dealer" anti-monopolists were worried principally about consumers. Decades of rising living standards before the Depression had persuaded them that "mass consumption is the basis of the American standard of living." A decade of Depression had persuaded them that the problem of the economy now was the problem of inadequate consumption far more than of insufficient production. Protecting "freedom of individual opportunity"—defending the rights of small producers—was a nice ideal in the abstract, but it was not the goal of the moment. The important thing was to ensure that prices went down and consumption went up.[46]

In this, the "New Dealers" were, without fully realizing it, already moving toward a vision of economic life, and of the role of government within it, significantly different from the liberal visions of the past. They were allying themselves with a set of assumptions that was gaining credence among professional economists, social theorists, and even some important administrators. And they were paving the way for a fusion of the anti-monopoly tradition with a new and very different political impulse, which would transform and ultimately eviscerate that tradition.

## Chapter Four

# Spending and Consumption

AMONG THOSE deeply alarmed by the American recession in the winter of 1937–1938 was the British economist John Maynard Keynes, to whom the success of the New Deal had long seemed important for reasons beyond its impact on the United States. Four years earlier, near the end of Roosevelt's first year in office, he had expressed his hopes, and his fears, in an open letter to the President published in the *New York Times*:

> You have made yourself the Trustee for those in every country who seek to mend the evils of our condition by reasoned experiment within the framework of the existing social system. If you fail, rational change will be gravely prejudiced throughout the world, leaving orthodoxy and revolution to fight it out. But if you succeed, new and bolder methods will be tried everywhere, and we may date the first chapter of a new economic era from your accession to office.[1]

In February 1938, Keynes was beginning to fear that Roosevelt might indeed fail, largely because he was not taking the danger of the new recession seriously enough. "I am terrified," he wrote the President, "lest progressive causes in all the democratic countries should suffer injury, because you have taken too lightly the risk to their prestige which would result from a failure measured in terms of immediate prosperity." The proper response to the crisis, Keynes argued, was to take immediate measures to stimulate consumption. The President was deluding himself if he thought he could turn the economy around by focusing on the capital markets. The revival of investment was important, "but not so important as the revival of sources of demand." And the best route to such a revival was an increase in government spending. He urged Roosevelt to put "most of your eggs in this basket."[2]

A few years later, Keynes's ideas and admonitions would resonate throughout the capitalist world. But in early 1938 he remained, in the United States at least, a relatively minor influence both on public policy and on liberal thought. Even some economists who would later become Keynes's champions had expressed irritation and bewilderment at his great (but dense and difficult) 1936 work, *The General Theory of Employment, Interest and Money*. And although Keynesian ideas had by 1938 established a foothold in the economics departments of a few universities, there was not yet anything that could truly be called a "Keynesian school" in America.[3]

If Keynes's influence remained modest in academia, it was even slighter in government. His work did have well-placed defenders in strategic corners of the Roosevelt administration, but even they generally balanced their support for Keynesian fiscal policies with more traditional concerns about government solvency, inflation, and investor confidence. The President himself, meanwhile, seemed generally to hold Keynes in light regard. He had had an apparently cordial meeting with the economist in 1934 and had made appropriately complimentary remarks about him to Felix Frankfurter and other American admirers of Keynes. At other times, however, he spoke of Keynes with condescension, even contempt.[4]

But while Keynes's own influence in America was relatively limited, in the winter of 1937–38 a set of ideas closely related to his own was emerging from other sources and was slowly gathering substantial support both within the administration itself and in the larger liberal community. These ideas formed the basis of an explanation for the 1937 recession, and of a prescription for ending it, that differed significantly from both the "business confidence" and the "monopoly power" approaches.[5]

The foundations of what would eventually become known as the "Keynesian approach" were two broad assumptions about the economy, neither of them entirely new, but both of them gaining strength and offering powerful challenges to traditional economic notions. One was the belief that consumption, not investment, was now the principal engine driving the industrial economy and hence the principal social goal toward which public efforts should be directed. The other was the conviction that public spending was the best vehicle for fighting recession and economic stagnation. The two ideas had emerged separately, but by the late 1930s they were becoming fused.

· · ·

THE BELIEF THAT consumption was the engine driving the economy, and hence a positive social good, was largely new to the industrial age. In all previous eras, scarcity had been the normal condition of civilization, and societies had been preoccupied with the problems of production— the challenge of creating enough wealth to satisfy mankind's minimal needs. The assumption of scarcity had shaped ideas about economic life and ideas about the role of government within it; it had elevated the values of thrift, restraint, and self-denial to central places in Western culture. But by the beginning of the twentieth century, these traditional assumptions were beginning to erode. For the rise of modern industrialism had introduced to the world a possibility that had once seemed unthinkable: that economies could create enough wealth to satisfy not only the needs but the desires of all.[6]

The assumption of scarcity, and the related ambivalence about consumption, never vanished altogether from western social thought. But new ideas based on the expectation of abundance had begun to emerge as early as the mid-nineteenth century. In the industrial world, such theories maintained, the problems of production need no longer preoccupy mankind. Those problems had been solved; industrialization had given society the power to produce enough for all. Civilization's new goal must be consumption. The task of economics (and, some argued, of politics) was to ensure that the fruits of the new affluence were widely enough distributed to satisfy the basic needs of the population. The task of culture was to persuade the population that increased consumption was not only economically possible, but morally and socially valuable.

Simon Patten, a controversial, German-educated economist at the University of Pennsylvania, was among the first important spokesmen for such ideas in the United States. Early in his life, influenced by the agricultural abundance he saw around him as he grew up in the American Midwest, Patten concluded that poverty was obsolete and unnecessary in the modern world. He went on to become (in the words of his student Rexford Tugwell) "a prophet of prosperity and progress." "The development of human society," Patten wrote in 1896, "has gradually eliminated from the environment the sources of pain." No longer was scarcity mankind's principal concern. Instead, he argued, "we are now in the transition stage from this pain economy to a pleasure economy." The principal goal of such an economy should be "an abundance of economic goods and the pursuit of pleasure." Central to that world would be the legitimation and enhancement of consumption.[7]

The new abundance, Patten claimed, made it necessary for society to change its traditional notions about wealth and poverty. People were no longer poor because economies were unable to produce enough goods to satisfy everyone's needs. They were poor because the economy did not distribute its abundance sufficiently widely. Governments, by acting to raise mass purchasing power, could eliminate poverty reasonably quickly.[8] But simply eliminating poverty (which Patten described as merely "a lack of resources") was not the greatest challenge facing modern societies. The deeper problem was "misery" (a pervasive disaffection, the belief that life is "a burden" and "not worth living").

Misery was not, as some social critics argued both at the time and later, primarily a result of the separation of individuals from the productive process, workers' loss of control over the workplace, or the growth of monopoly power. It was, Patten suggested, a result of the failure of individuals to seize control of their lives as consumers and to experience the joys that consumption could bring them. "The primary task of education," he wrote, was to make the citizen aware of the life of pleasure the industrial world had created "and to arouse him to participation in it through the common use of enormous units like the amusements and recreations of parks, theatres, 'Coney Islands,' department stores," and other attractions. Solving problems, therefore, did not require creating new patterns of capital ownership or control. It required steady increases in purchasing power and the education of wage earners in proper patterns of consumption. In industrial society, he argued, there must be a change in social values, a recognition that indulgence was a greater social good than abstinence, that "the non-saver is now a higher type of man than the saver."[9]

When Patten died in 1922, his ideas had as yet found little support. Even in the 1920s—the "New Era" of apparently boundless economic growth—faith in abundance and commitment to consumption expanded slowly and haltingly in both the academic and the industrial world. Thorstein Veblen made the notion of consumption nearly as central to his work as it was to Patten's, but never awarded it the largely positive connotations Patten had promoted. Veblen was at best ambivalent about the social value of consumption and argued primarily for reforms of the production process. A few influential economists such as Tugwell and Wesley Mitchell cited the importance of consumption in their professional writings, but they seldom made the idea as focal to their work as Patten had made it to his.[10] Some leaders of industry called on American capitalism to focus more of its energies on the creation of consumer goods, the market for which would drive the economy to greater heights; and some embraced the idea of a "high wage economy" as the best route to stimulating demand. But the dominant impulse through much of the business world was to search for ways to keep prices high and wages low.[11]

In politics and in popular culture, however, the idea that consumption was both important and valuable did make substantial strides. Reform movements designed to educate and protect the "consumer," which had made their first appearance in the nineteenth century, proliferated rapidly and had by the 1920s become a significant social and political force. American women had long been the principal force behind these consumer movements; and now, in part by exercising their new power as half the electorate, they helped propel them to new levels of influence. The burgeoning advertising industry spearheaded a broad commercial effort to make consumption seem a positive cultural good: to legitimize the consumer appetites about which many people had once felt uneasy and to make material comfort a measure of self-worth.[12]

Most of all, perhaps, the rising interest in consumption reflected the realities of an economy moving—if slowly and haltingly—into a new age, where consumer spending was rising and production of consumer goods increasing. In the 1920s, in particular, national income rose dramatically· and however unevenly distributed, the increase helped produce a sharp rise in consumer spending (an increase of over 33 percent between 1921 and 1929) that had a particular impact on emerging consumer-oriented industries such as processed foods and home appliances. Where once the driving forces behind the American economy had been such basic capital projects as building canals, roads, and railroads, in the twentieth century growth depended increasingly on purchases of consumer goods by an increasingly affluent public with expanding leisure time and rising material aspirations.[13]

Together, these developments suggest a basic change in the way many Americans were perceiving themselves and their society. In the 1920s, as in all eras, everyone was both a producer and a consumer. But while in the past the individual's role as a producer had generally seemed the more important, now the way men and women functioned as consumers was gaining in relative significance. This shift had implications, in turn, for how Americans thought about the role of the state in their economic life. Traditionally, those who had attempted to define such a role had looked primarily for ways in which government could promote or regulate production. Now, increasingly, such people were beginning to think—even if still tentatively and uncertainly—about what government could do to stimulate consumer demand.

That shift was evident in the way many Americans interpreted the Great Depression. It was self-evident that the United States had enough productive power—that it could grow enough food and manufacture enough goods—to supply the nation's needs; the greatest problem facing both agriculture and industry in the first years of the crisis was not scarcity, but surplus. Much of America's productive power lay idle, creating the seeming paradox of "poverty in the midst of plenty." Businessmen themselves, and many others, tended to speak of "overproduction." But a growing number of liberals began as early as 1932 to emphasize a single and, in their view, irrefutable explanation: "underconsumption." "The effective limit upon production," Wesley Mitchell wrote in *Recent Social Trends*, a 1932 report commissioned by the Hoover administration, "is the limit of what the markets will absorb at profitable prices, and this limit is set by the purchasing power of would-be consumers." The nation's "capacity to produce goods changes faster than our capacity to purchase."[14] "Since we have the technical capacity to produce enough for everyone," George Soule wrote in 1932, "everyone ought to have a large enough income to buy what he needs." "High wages" and "mass purchasing power" should be the principal aims of economic policy.[15]

One of the most energetic early popularizers of the "underconsumption" interpretation of the Great Depression was Stuart Chase, a prolific journalist, amateur economist, and disciple of Veblen. Chase had spent much of the 1920s exposing corporate plots to defraud consumers, and so it was natural, perhaps, that in attempting to explain the economic collapse, he would turn to an explanation that emphasized consumption. "We have left the economy of scarcity behind and entered the economy of abundance," he wrote in a 1932 book presciently titled *A New Deal*. Elsewhere, he argued: "It is not so much *overproduction* as *underconsumption* which is the appalling fact. . . . Millions of tons of additional material could readily be marketed if purchasing power were available. Alas, purchasing power is not available."[16]

Such arguments found a receptive audience among many of the men and women gathering around Franklin Roosevelt in 1932 and 1933, as well as with the new President himself, who seemed to endorse the concept of underconsumption in the most important speech of his 1932 presidential campaign, the Commonwealth Club Address in San Francisco. "Our industrial plant is built," he said.

> Our task now is not discovery or exploitation of natural resources, or necessarily producing more goods. It is the soberer, less dramatic business of administering resources and plants already in hand, of seeking to reestablish foreign markets for our surplus production, of meeting the problem of underconsumption, of adjusting production to consumption, of distributing wealth and products more equitably, of adapting existing economic organizations to the service of the people.[17]

In the early years of the Roosevelt administration, this interest in consumption found greater reflection in rhetoric than in performance. New Dealers used the language of consumption to justify some of their early economic policies; but most of their initiatives were addressed largely to the problems of producers and some—most notably the National Recovery Administration—ultimately worked to the detriment of consumers.[18] Leon Henderson might write in 1936 that the New Deal's principal achievement lay in increasing "mass purchasing power. . . . For when farmers and laborers, that is consumers, have funds to spend, the merchants do more business, factories receive large orders, and soon find themselves compelled to add new equipment and so the spiral of recovery is set into high gear."[19] And Soule might write in March 1937 that New Deal spending provided "a striking illustration of the fact that so-called capital goods industries may be stimulated more by the renewed purchasing power of individual consumers than by new investments on the part of business."[20] But such statements were to a large degree more expressions of hope than accurate assessments of reality. Few New Deal programs were designed with such larger aims explicitly in mind.

That the commitment to consumption remained to large degree rhetorical did not mean that it was unimportant. The rhetoric itself was becoming an active political force, promoting a vision of economic life significantly different from the traditional view. Orthodox economics accepted as a truism that consumption was essential to economic life, but it did not accept that it was central to that life, that it was the principal force in creating economic growth. The challenge to orthodoxy, then, was the argument that consumption was relatively more important to the success of the economy than investment; that consumption drove production and not the other way around; that increased consumption, not increased saving, was the best route to prosperity and growth.

The policy implications of such assumptions, however, were not immediately clear in the 1930s. Many advocates of consumption believed that the best way to promote their goals was to organize consumers as a coherent interest group, able to act in much the same way as organized business and labor in promoting their interests. They advocated legislation to protect consumers from misrepresentation and fraud. They insisted on the inclusion of a Consumers' Advisory Board within the National Recovery Administration. They called for the creation of a new, Cabinet-level Department of the Consumer. They promoted "consumer education," worked to create "consumer cooperatives," and made generally unsuccessful attempts to organize consumer strikes and boycotts.[21]

But the rhetoric of consumption spread well beyond the "consumer movement." As the concept of the "consumer" gained resonance in American politics, it became the basis of an almost universal political language; supporters of nearly every approach to public policy used the language of consumption to justify (or at least rationalize) their efforts. Antitrust champions explained their initiatives in part in terms of the benefits they offered consumers. Planning advocates claimed that rationalizing the production process would stimulate demand and benefit consumers. In short, the "underconsumption" explanation of the Great Depression did not by itself dictate any single public response to the crisis. And so, for a time at least, the idea that society should promote mass consumption did not necessarily produce a commitment to using through government fiscal policy to achieve that goal.

JUST AS BELIEF IN CONSUMPTION did not always connect linked to a belief in public spending, the commitment to spending had not always (or even usually) been part of a commitment to promoting consumption. Indeed through most of American history, what government spending there was—and there was often a great deal—had usually been intended not to promote consumption but to augment private investment and to create an infrastructure for the expansion of production. Efforts to use government largesse to spur development stretched back to Alexander Hamilton's Report on Manufactures, to Henry Clay's American System, and to the federal subsidies and land grants which assisted railroad construction in the mid- and late nineteenth century. In the first decades of the twentieth century, government investment in dams, bridges, highways, and other public facilities had increased dramatically, particularly at the state and local levels.

Many of the early spending projects of the New Deal reflected this traditional emphasis on public contributions to economic development of particular regions and industries—what some have called "state capitalism." The projects of the NRA's Public Works Administration were mostly major infrastructure ventures, whose contributions to mass purchasing power were largely indirect and inadvertent. The Tennessee Valley Authority, one of the New Deal's proudest achievements, fit securely into the tradition of regional development, even if it used unconventional tools for doing so. The Reconstruction Finance Corporation, created near the end of the Hoover administration, remained during the New Deal one of the most important dispensers of public funds; under the leadership of the Texas banker Jesse H. Jones, it was an important source of capital for great infrastructure projects in the South and the

West—seldom for relief efforts, jobs programs, or other efforts that would contribute directly to demand.[22]

The New Deal engaged in other kinds of spending too, of course. It appropriated money for relief and jobs programs. It financed public works projects designed explicitly to create employment and augment purchasing power, not to enhance the nation's productive capacities. It constructed, through the Social Security Act of 1935, what eventually became a broad system of welfare and social insurance. In the process, the federal government accumulated what were, by contemporary standards, significant deficits. (The federal government's $3.5 billion deficit in 1936 was then the largest in American peacetime history—by a considerable margin.) And those deficits were in fact stimulating economic growth, not by augmenting investment, but by increasing mass purchasing power.[23]

Yet as late as the beginning of 1937, there was still only a dim recognition among most New Dealers that public spending could be a valuable tool for its own sake, as the inconsistencies in the administration's own fiscal efforts made clear. Almost every inflationary policy was accompanied by some deflationary measure. The early relief programs coincided with the Economy Act, which cut government salaries and reduced payments to veterans. The administration consistently opposed early payment of veterans' bonuses as excessively inflationary; indeed, the President made a rare personal appearance before Congress in 1935 to justify his veto of a bill providing for such payments.[24] And what may have been the New Deal's single most important contribution to the creation of the modern welfare state—the Social Security System—was, in the 1930s at least, also one of its most deflationary achievements. In the last years of the Depression, the taxes financing the Social Security System were taking far more purchasing power out of the economy than the system's benefits (most of which were as yet reaching relatively few people) were putting back in. In 1936 and 1937, the system removed from the economy at least $2 billion more than it contributed. "The law as it now stands operates unnecessarily to accentuate any tendency otherwise present toward deflation," the economist Alvin Hansen wrote in 1938. "Plainly, the Act operates to reduce the total consumption expenditures of the general mass of the population." And Social Security was not alone in causing such reductions. Other regressive taxes (many levied by state governments) helped offset the inflationary effects of the New Deal's agricultural and jobs programs.[25] The New Deal was promoting recovery through deficit financing, but haltingly, penuriously, and largely inadvertently, as the unintended result of policies designed to achieve other ends.[26]

· · ·

SLOWLY, HOWEVER, the idea that public spending could be a vehicle for increasing mass purchasing power, that government deficits might be not a necessary evil but a public good, was gaining a foothold—if not among academic and policy elites, then in grass-roots politics and popular discourse. Labor organizations and advocates for the unemployed had been making demands for government spending on public works in times of economic contraction since at least the 1870s. Those demands had mostly taken the form of requests for local government to augment inadequate systems of poor relief. But in 1893, when Jacob S. Coxey led his "army" of the unemployed to Washington to demand federal public-works programs as an antidote to the depression of that time, the idea of federal spending as a route to prosperity began to gain ground. By the beginning of World War I, workers and their unions in many parts of the country were calling for national public-works programs to compensate for swings in the business cycle, or, as a Massachusetts labor newspaper argued in 1923, to act "as a balance wheel for business." Some were also proposing a system of national unemployment insurance that would, they believed, help accomplish the same purpose. Public spending, they suggested, would not only help those who received government jobs or insurance payments; it would aid the economy as a whole by increasing purchasing power.[27]

In the early years of the Great Depression, popular pressure for public spending increased rapidly and dramatically. State and local governments, staggering under demands for relief that had overwhelmed their own financial and administrative resources, put enormous pressure on the federal government to step in with relief and public-works programs of its own. The thousands of World War I veterans who formed the Bonus Army in 1932 and marched on Washington to demand early payment of the bonus Congress had promised them justified their campaign at times by citing the benefits to the entire economy of this potential economic stimulus. Organizations of the unemployed—never very large but at times visible and influential—kept alive calls for unemployment insurance and federal job creation through public-works spending, as did many labor unions hoping to restore jobs for their members. By 1935, Huey Long, Francis Townsend, and other dissident leaders were leading substantial national or local movements demanding, among other things, massive government spending and income redistribution programs to restore economic growth.[28]

Seldom did grass-roots activists or local leaders articulate a coherent "underconsumptionist" rationale for public spending; but they helped create a social and political climate that made policymakers more willing to consider such a rationale when it finally did emerge. Of considerable importance in helping it emerge were the efforts of two men who, although they had no professional standing as economists or political theorists, were among the first Americans to state clearly the argument for public spending as a solution to underconsumption: William Trufant Foster and Waddill Catchings.

FOSTER, A FORMER COLLEGE PRESIDENT, and Catchings, an industrialist and financier, began collaborating in the early 1920s in the promotion of what were, initially, relatively familiar economic ideas. Their first book, *Money*, was a fairly conventional monetarist explanation of the nation's economic problems, arguing that the supply and stability of the currency were the key to prosperity.[29] The book received little attention when it appeared in 1923. So two years later they tried again, with *Profits*, which might have gone similarly unnoticed had not the dust jacket contained an announcement that the authors would award a prize of five thousand dollars "for the best adverse criticism" of their argument, and had not the argument been both unconventional and provocative. *Profits* discussed many of the same monetary questions that had dominated *Money*, but it introduced a concept new to their work: the idea of underconsumption. "Why," they asked in their preface, "is it impossible for the people, as consumers, to acquire and enjoy all the commodities which, as producers, they are perfectly able and willing to make?" Their answer to that question became the basis of all their future work.[30]

Buoyed by the attention their publicity gimmick brought them (and perhaps stung by the nearly five hundred critiques they received from economists, businessmen, and financiers), Foster and Catchings republished their arguments twice in the next two years: in *Business Without a Buyer* in 1927, and a year later in an idiosyncratic volume with the alluring title, *The Road to Plenty*. The 1928 book took the form of a Pullman-car conversation in which a few enlightened men convince their obtuse traveling companions that there are relatively simple solutions to problems that had once seemed intractable. In format, it resembled William H. Harvey's classic free-silver tract of 1894, *Coin's Financial School*. In substance, however, it was very different. It outlined a plan for the federal government to solve the problem of underconsumption through public spending.[31]

Publicizers and popularizers they may have been, but Foster and

Catchings were also daring theorists, challenging some of the most sacred orthodoxies of their time. Indeed, it was emblematic of the poverty of formal economic theory in the 1930s that "amateurs" were among the first to articulate a set of ideas which a decade later would be central to professional economics. Anticipating Keynes by nearly a decade, they were launching a direct attack on one of the basic underpinnings of classical economics: Say's Law of Markets. Say's Law maintained that consumption was a simple and automatic result of production; that the costs of producing goods inevitably created purchasing power and hence demand for those goods. Foster and Catchings argued that "classical economics is wrong." Consumption does not automatically follow production. Private and corporate savings, inequitable distributions of income, artificially high prices, and other factors could, and often did, restrict aggregate buying power. "As industry increases its output, it does not, for any length of time, proportionately increase its payments to the people," they maintained. "There is nothing in ordinary business financing which automatically brings about the right adjustment." Society had failed to recognize a central economic truth: "consumption regulates production." Underconsumption was the result of that failure. The "chief remedy" was "adequate consumer income."[32]

One way to achieve that remedy was for consumers themselves to spend more, to avoid the "wasteful thrift" that had helped production outrun consumption in the late 1920s. "At least three million of the unemployed are in that plight because consumers have saved too much," Foster and Catchings wrote in 1931.[33] But increased consumer spending could not happen by itself, at least not in sufficient quantity to solve the nation's problems; even in the 1920s, too many consumers had no money to spend because of inadequate distribution of income. The other avenue to "full employment" and "better standards of living" was government spending. The economic growth of the 1920s, they correctly argued, had been sustained in large part by state and local expenditures for public works. But such contributions to buying power had been inadequate and largely inadvertent. Future government spending policies must reflect greater care—"infinite pains and . . . the aid of far better statistics"—to ensure that government would be "putting more money into consumers' hands when business is falling off, and less money when inflation is under way."[34]

Foster and Catchings liked to portray themselves as voices crying in the wilderness, but they were not without allies. Even before their books appeared, the idea of what would soon be known as "counter-cyclical" government spending had begun to receive some tentative official support (even if without Foster and Catchings's emphasis on consumption). The Wilson administration, for example, had accelerated spending on public works during the recession of 1920 to combat unemployment; and during the succeeding Harding administration a President's Conference on Unemployment, which convened in Washington in 1921 under the sponsorship of Secretary of Commerce Herbert Hoover, endorsed those policies and urged their repetition in similar emergencies in the future. Hoover himself argued throughout the 1920s for a government policy of holding some public works projects in reserve, to be activated and funded in the event of an economic emergency; and although by the end of his own presidency he had largely lost faith in this approach, he attempted at times to use public spending as an antidote to deflation in the first years of the Depression, even if never in sufficient amounts to have a major impact.[35]

In the early years of the New Deal, most liberals defended the administration's spending programs in terms of the benefits the programs offered particular groups (farmers, homeowners, the unemployed) or in terms of the stimulus they provided production. But there were a few voices even then, both within the government and beyond it, who lauded such efforts for their aggregate effects and for what they did for consumers in general. The economists John M. Clark and Arthur Gayer, consultants to the New Deal's National Planning Board, made a case for countercyclical planning of public works expenditures in 1934 and 1935, as did the Yale economist James Harvey Rogers, another regular adviser to the administration. Such spending, Clark argued, could be an "antidote to oversaving" and could "increase general purchasing power in order to offset the decrease due to industrial contraction."[36]

Such notions still appeared fanciful to most of their contemporaries and to the President himself (who had once written in the margin of Foster and Catchings's *The Road to Plenty*: "Too good to be true—You can't get something for nothing").[37] But there was one arm of the federal government where the importance of consumption and the value of deficit spending were the object of considerable attention: the Federal Reserve Board. Beginning in 1934, when Marriner S. Eccles was named its chairman, the board became the center of "Keynesian" thinking in the administration. At first, however, it was not Keynes himself who persuaded Eccles to embrace the idea of deficit spending as a route to recovery. It was Foster and Catchings, whom he had read and admired while working as a banker in Utah.

.   .   .

THAT MARRINER ECCLES was to become the government's most powerful spokesman for "liberal economics" in the mid-1930s would not have been easy to predict even a few years earlier. For throughout the first forty years of his life, he had embraced the conservative economic beliefs of his wealthy and successful family and of the Mormon business community of which he was, from an early age, a prominent and influential member.

Eccles's father, David, migrated to Utah from Scotland when he was still a young boy. David's own father had embraced Mormonism in 1842 after an encounter with American missionaries; twenty years later, blind and impoverished, he borrowed money from the Perpetual Emigration Fund of the Mormon Church and moved his family to the "land of the Saints." In the American West, young David Eccles parlayed early successes in the lumber business into a substantial business empire, which came to include sawmills, coal mines, banks, sugar companies, railroads, power plants, resorts, and a construction company that eventually became one of the world's largest. David Eccles was not a particularly devout Mormon, but he did embrace several important tenets of the faith. He "tithed" annually, which made him, as one of the wealthiest Mormons in America, a major benefactor of the church. He was also a polygamist.[38]

Married to a woman in Ogden, Utah, with whom he would eventually have twelve children, he took an additional wife in nearby Logan in 1885, despite federal laws (then being enforced with increasing severity) against "plural" marriages. Marriner, born in 1890, was the first child of this "second family," which came to include four sons and five daughters (bringing the total of David Eccles's offspring to twenty-one).[39] Apparently disappointed in his sons by his first wife, the senior Eccles devoted considerable energy to raising the male members of his new family. (Neither he nor his wives seemed to consider the education of their daughters to be of any great importance.) In particular, he tried to instill in his sons both the piety and the parsimony he believed had been the keys to his own success. Young Marriner learned from his father to avoid debt at all costs, to save whenever possible, and to work unceasingly. "School, work, and little play filled the years," he recalled of his childhood.[40]

Marriner was by most accounts the brightest of his father's sons. But his formal education (in Mormon schools) ended when he was nineteen. Except for a two-year mission in Scotland, during which Eccles diligently proselytized and during which he met the woman who would later become his wife, he spent most of his youth working in one or another of his father's businesses.

In 1912, David Eccles, sixty-three years old, died suddenly of a heart attack. "The news left me numb with shock," Marriner later recalled.[41] It also left him, as the oldest (and only adult) child of the second family, responsible for its portion of his father's estate—approximately $1.6 million. Resisting pressures from his half-brothers to combine his inheritance with theirs, he created his own investment company and soon became president of one bank and director of several others. The next two decades brought him almost unbroken success; and by 1930 Marriner Eccles was, as his father had been, one of the wealthiest and most powerful men in Utah, indeed in the American West, with far-flung interests in banking, hotels, lumber, dairy products, sugar, railroads, coal, utilities, and construction. Aggressive, outspoken, even autocratic in style, he quickly surpassed his half-brothers (with several of whom he had a bitter falling-out), absorbed most of the family businesses, and inherited the friendship and loyalty of his father's colleagues.[42]

Marriner was like his father in other ways as well. David Eccles, his son later recalled, "had built his works by himself, owned many of them outright, and ran them all in a direct and personal way. He saw no reason why other men could not or should not re-create themselves in his image, providing, of course, they were left free to use their wits and will without governmental interference. All this I, too, believed, until the fortieth year of my life." Marriner was an avid Republican and a fervent supporter of Herbert Hoover throughout the 1920s. He spoke frequently at business meetings and other public events on behalf of conservative, orthodox economic ideas.[43]

The Great Depression shook, but did not topple, the Eccles family empire. It did, however, shatter Marriner's faith in laissez-faire economic doctrine. "It became apparent to me, as a capitalist," he recalled in his memoir, "that if I . . . resisted any change designed to benefit all the people, I could be consumed by the poisons of social lag that I had helped create. . . . I was brought face to face with this proposition: that the only way we could get out of the depression was through government action in placing purchasing power in the hands of people who were in need of it."[44] Eccles came to that conclusion slowly: through his distaste for the harsh credit policies he was forced to adopt to save his banks from collapse ("Seeking individual salvation," he wrote, "we were contributing to collective ruin"), through his despair at the inability of local governments or of private institutions such as the Mormon Church to meet even minimal social needs, and through his careful reading, beginning in 1931, of Foster and Catchings.[45]

The first clear statement of his new convictions came in a June 1932 speech to the Utah State Bankers Convention. "The depression in our own country," he told his conservative audience, "was primarily brought about by our capital accumulation getting out of balance in relationship to our consumption ability. Our depression was not brought about as a result of extravagance. . . . The difficulty is that we were not sufficiently extravagant." The problem, then, was the "failure to be able to use the superabundance of wealth which we have been able to produce." The problem was underconsumption.[46]

Eccles's unorthodox views slowly brought him to the attention of the emerging New Dealers in the East. In February 1933, he was one of several hundred businessmen invited to testify before the Senate Finance Committee on current economic problems. "When it came my turn," he recalled, "I challenged all that had been said up to that point and was practically alone in doing so." Specifically, he laid out a program of monetary expansion and deficit spending, which would, he promised, end the Depression by increasing mass purchasing power. A day later, he was in New York for a meeting with Rexford Tugwell (arranged by Stuart Chase, whom Eccles had met in Salt Lake City a few weeks before). There he repeated his diagnosis of the crisis and his prescription for its cure. Tugwell expressed surprise to hear such "radicalism" from a banker but seemed otherwise unimpressed. The meeting, Eccles concluded, was "fruitless."[47]

Back in Utah, he watched with mounting despair as the New Deal moved, first, to reduce federal expenditures and then to cartelize major industries through the National Recovery Administration, which he believed only worsened an already disastrous deflationary spiral. "The NRA has been launched on the premise that the nation is suffering from overproduction," he complained publicly. "This is false. What appears to be overproduction is, at bottom, a nation-wide case of underconsumption due to the absence among tens of millions of Americans of the effective purchasing power that would enable them to buy the things they desperately need."[48]

By the end of 1933, when the modest "New Deal recovery" of the spring seemed to be collapsing, influential New Dealers—among them Tugwell, Ezekiel, and Wallace—began to take a renewed interest in Eccles's ideas. In February 1934, they brought him to Washington as a special assistant to Treasury Secretary Henry Morgenthau on "monetary and credit matters." Nine months later, Roosevelt named him to succeed Eugene Black as governor (or, as it is now known, chairman) of the Federal Reserve Board.[49]

Eccles brought to his new post the same bluntness and abrasiveness that had characterized his business dealings for years past and that would antagonize his political opponents (and even some of his allies) for years to come. He was constantly at odds with Carter Glass, the powerful chairman of the Senate Finance Committee, whom Eccles made almost no effort to conciliate. His once warm relationship with Henry Morgenthau rapidly deteriorated, less because of the significant policy differences between the two men than because Eccles made no concessions to Morgenthau's vanity and his almost morbid personal sensitivity. He also, apparently, brought with him to Washington something of the westerner's distrust of the East. Even late in life, after nearly two decades at the centers of power, he still referred to himself occasionally as a modern "Joseph" striking out at the "Egypt" of the eastern establishment (and of the New York financial world in particular). At one point in 1935, when told that powerful financial interests would drop their opposition to his confirmation if he abandoned some of his own demands for reform, Eccles replied to the bearer of the message, "You can tell your banker friends to go to hell."[50]

But Eccles was also a shrewd politician, who understood where power lay and how to seize it. He had made the strengthening of the Federal Reserve Board a condition of his appointment. The board, he argued, had been reduced almost to impotence during the preceding decades as power had flowed increasingly away from Washington and to the regional Federal Reserve Banks (particularly the bank in New York). He spent his first months in his new position working to promote new banking legislation, which the administration (in response to his demands) had agreed to introduce. The result was the Banking Act of 1935, passed over the opposition of most leading financiers and only after a protracted struggle with Glass. It reconstituted the board itself and its committees, strengthened its ability to conduct open-market operations, allowed it to raise and lower reserve requirements more easily, and otherwise contributed to a centralization of power over monetary policy.[51]

But while monetary policy was Eccles's charge, it was not his only, or even his principal, concern. From the beginning of his years in Washington, he was at least as interested in promoting his views on federal fiscal policy, and he missed few opportunities to do so.[52] Even as he struggled to reconstitute the Federal Reserve Board and solidify his own authority within it, he was reaching out to other corners of the administration, and to the White House itself, in his effort to legitimize the idea of counter-cyclical deficit spending as a solution to the Great Depression.

For more than four years, he sustained that effort with a striking single-mindedness. Eccles measured almost every New Deal initiative by one standard alone: the degree to which it contributed to mass purchasing power. He applauded the creation of the Works Progress Administration in 1935, but complained that it spent too little money, and spent it too selectively, to be truly effective. "The safest policy is the boldest policy," he wrote the President early in 1935. "A piecemeal program is doomed to failure *unless the national income is increased.*"[53] Throughout 1936 and 1937, he fought against the growing pressure from Morgenthau and the Treasury Department to reduce expenditures. "A reversion to deflationary methods of balancing the budget which were tried with disastrous results by the last Republican administration would imperil the recovery now in progress," he warned in 1936. It would "lead to a new wave of deflation and reverse the processes of recovery thus far set in motion."[54]

Eccles promoted deficit spending not only because he considered it an antidote to deflation. It was also, he believed, an alternative to other, less palatable forms of government intervention in the economy. Like Foster and Catchings, Eccles considered fiscal policy a "safe" approach to solving economic problems, without the dangerously statist features of other, more intrusive methods. "The inherent instability of capitalism may be corrected by conscious and deliberate use of . . . compensatory instruments," he told a group of Boston businessmen in 1935. "If they are not established or if they are not successful in achieving economic stability, as surely as I am standing here, you will not have *compensatory* but direct controls in every important sphere of economic activity."[55]

For several years, Eccles fought a lonely and generally losing battle, his message voiced in what seemed to him "a soundproof room," unheard beyond the narrow circle of allies he managed to draw to his cause. During his months in the Treasury Department, all his advice to the President had to be funneled through Henry Morgenthau, who served as an effective "muffler" of views that diverged from his own, as Eccles's clearly did. Even after he moved to the Federal Reserve Board and established direct access to Roosevelt, he had to struggle against the powerful array of forces pushing the administration toward fiscal orthodoxy, and against the President's own continuing discomfort with the idea of deficit spending. Eccles's strenuous protests against the spending cuts of the spring of 1937 were to no avail.[56]

Eccles considered the recession of 1937–1938 both a major disaster ("The New Deal and all it stands for is in danger of being discredited," he wrote) and a vindication of his own arguments. Early in 1938, he reminded Roosevelt of his warnings "that we could have a really serious depression and that the chances of a 'natural' upturn were remote. Events since then have only served to confirm this feeling." The administration's effort to speed recovery by placating business had "borne no fruits either in dollar terms or in goodwill." Increasing the money supply (a solution largely within Eccles's own grasp) was not the answer either. "The problem is not now and never has been a shortage of money," he insisted. The problem was that the money there was had not found its way into the right hands, that too much was going into savings and not enough was working to stimulate mass consumption.[57]

Even more strenuously than before, he promoted federal spending on a massive scale as the best, perhaps the only, solution. In memoranda, meetings, policy statements, and speech drafts, he bombarded the White House with proposals for major new expenditures on public works, for large-scale loans to homeowners and small businessmen, for increases in relief, and for a refinancing of Social Security to reduce its deflationary effects. "The Federal Government," he observed, "is making a negligible contribution to community buying power in comparison with 1934–1935." It was crucial that the administration "give assurance that while private spending is diminishing, we can't diminish public expenditures at the same time."[58]

WHILE THE RECESSION did little to alter Eccles's already well-developed views, it did a great deal to increase his influence. By the beginning of 1938, he found himself suddenly at the center of an expanding circle of liberals—both inside the administration and without—who considered the deflationary monetary and fiscal policies of 1937 (including some of the actions of Eccles's own board in raising interest rates) a leading cause of the recession. The government, they argued (as George Soule wrote in November), "has now stopped priming the pump and is instead taking some water out of the spout." The solution, they insisted, was stimulating consumption through public spending.[59]

One of Eccles's most important allies was Leon Henderson, serving then as economic adviser to Secretary of Commerce Harry Hopkins (even though he had no more than undergraduate training in economics). Henderson, like Eccles, had long ago dismissed Say's Law—the doctrine that "production creates its own purchasing power"—as "the bunk." And like Eccles, he supported government policies that would focus on stimulating demand rather than investment. Henderson did not share Eccles's belief that public spending was the only, or even the most important, vehicle for promoting demand. Nor did he share Eccles's fear of direct state intervention in the private sector. He was a strenuous advocate of antitrust efforts, a consistent critic of "administered prices," and a leading champion of forms of planning that would include at least some state role in basic decisions about production and prices in major industries. But Henderson believed, too, that "the deficit in purchasing power" was the central problem facing the American economy and hence that fiscal policy had an important role to play in the policy mix—not as an alternative to other, more interventionist policies (as Eccles liked to argue), but as a complement to them. The arrival of the recession in 1937 served greatly to strengthen his conviction. New Deal spending programs, he argued, had made important contributions to the recovery of 1934–1935, but even at their height they had been inadequate. Now, after the cutbacks of 1937, the government was making almost no contributions to purchasing power at all. The best response to the recession, therefore, was a massive, indeed unprecedented increase in public spending. For, he asked, "how can you prime a pump with an eye-dropper?"[60]

Henderson was important to the spending forces for several reasons. Even in an administration that prided itself on its "brain power," Henderson was considered exceptionally brilliant; his imprimatur gave the spending argument an intellectual respectability (and his writing gave it an articulate rationale) that Eccles alone could not provide. Henderson was also better connected than Eccles to the inner circles of the New Deal. He was close to Hopkins, who was rapidly emerging as the President's most trusted adviser. And he was friendly with the "New Dealers" who clustered around Frankfurter and Corcoran, liberals who were primarily interested in more interventionist forms of economic policy such as antitrust campaigns and regulation. Henderson helped persuade them to support Eccles's spending proposals as well.[61] Hopkins, Corcoran, Frankfurter, Harold Ickes, Henry Wallace, Ben Cohen, William O. Douglas, Isidor Lubin, Mordecai Ezekiel, and others were all at least temporary converts to the spending argument by early 1938.[62]

But pressure for increased spending was soon emerging from other quarters as well: from many quarters of the labor movement (especially within the CIO); from farm organizations (and from the small-producer-oriented National Farmers' Union in particular); from dissident consumer advocates in grass-roots organizations throughout the country. Spending arguments were coming too from such administration conservatives as Jesse Jones and James Farley, who (like Eccles) saw a fiscal response to the recession as an acceptable alternative to other, less palatable reforms;[63] from members of Congress such as Robert Wagner and Robert La Follette, who had long championed the interests of consumers and who had strongly opposed the budget cuts of the previous year;[64] and from the leading liberal journals, which had paid scant attention to fiscal

policy in the past but which by 1938 were championing increased spending as if it had been a cornerstone of liberal ideology for years. " 'Confidence' on the part of business men," the *New Republic* editorialized, "is
a hundred times less important than money in the pocket of the average
citizen with which to buy." Roosevelt had seemed to understand that
lesson in 1934 and 1935, when he had contributed large amounts to mass
purchasing power through deficit spending. "If he has now forgotten the
lesson, it must be taught him again."[65]

Even one year earlier, the spending argument had enjoyed scant
intellectual legitimacy and little political support in national politics. By
the spring of 1938, as a result of the new sense of urgency the recession
had produced, it was poised to compete on at least equal terms with
other, more established ideas of political economy.

*Chapter Five*

# The Struggle
# for a Program

WHILE DIAGNOSES of the recession and proposals for curing it were quick to emerge in the last months of 1937, agreement on an actual treatment came painfully slowly. That was partly because of the uneasy balance of forces inside the administration as different factions promoting different courses of action rose and fell, without any one establishing clear primacy. But it was also because of the inconsistency and ambivalence with which the factions themselves (and the individuals who composed them) viewed their own positions. The battle for a policy was not only a struggle among groups and individuals, but within them.

NOWHERE WAS the combination of vacillation and eclecticism that characterized New Deal policy in these months clearer than in the behavior of Franklin Roosevelt himself. Even some of his most loyal subordinates became distraught at his apparent inconsistency and his prolonged reluctance to move. The President "has acted like a beaten man," Harold Ickes recorded in his diary, and his liberal advisers were growing "disgusted" with his "lack of aggressive leadership." Henry Morgenthau claimed to be "terrifically shocked that the President . . . can't call for Plan A or Plan B or Plan C. . . . The President should have certain plans. He's got nothing." And Felix Frankfurter pleaded with Roosevelt to let the public hear "at firsthand and from your own lips, that *you* are not panicky . . . that you have a well-defined direction toward objectives to which you will adhere."[1]

Roosevelt may not have been "panicky," but neither did he have a "well-defined direction." Already shaken by the political reverses of the spring and summer, he now seemed bewildered by the recession and by the conflicting advice he was receiving on how to respond to it. For nearly six months, as the pleas for a clear and unambiguous response grew more strident, the President remained mired in what seemed an agony of indecision: flirting intermittently with first one, then another course of action without fully endorsing any. The special session of Congress that convened in November 1937 became an illustration of his uncertainty.

Roosevelt had summoned the special session on October 12 (a week before the stock market's "Black Tuesday") to consider "important legislation which my recent trip [a speaking tour in the West] . . . convinces me the American people immediately need." In fact, that legislation was nothing more than unfinished business from the previous session—a new farm bill, legislation establishing a minimum wage and a limitation on working hours, the executive reorganization plan, and a proposal for seven regional planning projects (better known as "seven little TVAs")—all of which could just as easily have waited for the beginning of the regular term in January. The real reason for the special session, apparently, was the President's desire to capitalize quickly on the enthusiastic public response to his recent travels.[2]

By the time Congress convened on November 15, the economic situation was rapidly deteriorating. But while Roosevelt noted in his opening message that "since your adjournment in August there has been a marked recession in industrial production," he had no new measures to propose for dealing with it. The agenda remained what it had been a month earlier, "a warmed-up assortment," James MacGregor Burns has written, that served as "a measure of his inability to decide on a basic economic program."[3]

The session was a fiasco. Congress made significant progress on only one piece of legislation: a farm bill so eviscerated by amendments that many members wondered "whether it is going to be worth passing or not." The prospects for the executive reorganization plan remained cloudy; the "seven little TVAs" measure received almost no attention; and the wages and hours bill floundered under attacks from southern members (who opposed the elimination of regional wage differentials) and the AFL (which feared that the proposed administrative structure would invade its prerogatives and favor the rival CIO). In the meantime, conservatives of both parties tried to use the session—and the disillusionment with the administration that they believed the recession had produced—to consolidate their opposition to the New Deal. "The fight on Roosevelt's leadership is to be renewed with increased vigor in the special session," Senator Burton Wheeler of Montana confided to the publisher Frank Knox en route to Washington. "What we have to do," Senator Josiah Bailey of North Carolina wrote at about the same time, "is to preserve if we can the Democratic Party against [the President's] effort to make it the Roosevelt Party." Congressional conservatives not only spurned the President's legislative agenda; they drafted one of their own, an anti–New Deal "manifesto," as the press described it, that called for repealing corporate taxes, reducing government spending, and eliminating such federal "interference" in private industry as government protection of organized labor. The conservatives' proposals made no more progress than the President's.[4]

The dismal results of the special session, and the added evidence it provided of political problems to come, did nothing to bolster Roosevelt's sagging spirits as 1937 came to a close. His colleagues in the administration noticed an unusual testiness in the President's response to suggestions and complaints; reporters observed a rise in his always high sensitivity to press criticism; even his vacation companions were struck by his low spirits. Roosevelt tried to escape his problems early in December by taking a fishing cruise through Florida's Dry Tortugas. Joining him were Harry Hopkins, Harold Ickes, and his new favorite, Robert Jackson. There were fishing and late-night poker games. There were also occasional shipboard discussions of the recession and the monopoly problem, leading Jackson, at least, to hope that the President was ready to act. Most of the others, however, were struck by Roosevelt's listlessness (partly a result of a painfully infected jaw) and his apparent pessimism. "I was a good deal worried about the President on this trip," Ickes wrote shortly after their return to Washington. "He didn't seem at all like himself. . . . [A] remark . . . to the effect that he was going to let Congress alone to find out whether or not it could run the Government without his help might mean a general retreat all along the line."[5]

THE PRESIDENT DID little to allay such fears in the first months of 1938, during which he made another of his periodic efforts to conciliate the leaders of business and finance—a policy that critics from both left and right labeled "appeasement." It was a woeful failure. But it suggested how alluring the dream of a harmonious economy—the dream that had produced the NRA—remained to a substantial group of New Dealers, among them Roosevelt himself.

Roosevelt gave hints of his interest in pursuing conciliation in the first days of 1938. His formal message to the new Congress early in January contained a muted call for cooperation between business and government and a statement that "only a small minority [of businessmen] have displayed poor citizenship."[6] In a press conference the next day, the President was similarly tantalizing. "Don't write the story that I am advocating the immediate reenactment of NRA," he told reporters. But his subsequent remarks made clear that he continued to hope for something very much like the NRA. It was "perfectly legitimate," he said, for industry heads to meet together "with the Government" and try "honestly to find out what the needs are going to be for the next six months or a year, so they won't overproduce." His words alarmed those who had hoped for an aggressive campaign against monopoly. "Listening to him was a horrendous experience," the *New Republic*'s T.R.B. observed. "With each word the possibility of administrative action against monopoly dwindled."[7] But the same statements were gratifying to the still considerable group of planners and associationalists connected with the administration, many of whom had feared that the strident Jackson and Ickes speeches a few days before had reflected the President's real intentions.[8]

Over the next several weeks, the administration embarked on what seemed to be a serious campaign to placate (or "appease") the business community and satisfy the advocates of economic harmony. The indefatigable Donald Richberg, his hopes for an NRA revival suddenly buoyed, argued yet again for "greater cooperation within industry and between industry and government." Policies to foster such cooperation, he insisted, were "the true side of the New Deal." On January 11, Richberg ushered a group of industrialists to a meeting with the President and concluded from Roosevelt's cordiality and apparent interest "that machinery for cooperative ventures might develop out of the conference."[9]

Adolf Berle was even more energetic. Early in January, he met privately with several financial leaders to work out terms for a "grand truce" between the administration and the private sector. Together with Thomas W. Lamont of the House of Morgan, he assembled an "advisory committee" consisting of Lamont himself, Owen Young of General Electric, Philip Murray and John L. Lewis of the CIO, and others. The group met first at the Century Association in New York with Berle and Rexford Tugwell, whose commitment to "planning" and scornful view of competition remained as strong as ever. On January 14, they visited Roosevelt in Washington for a private meeting. It seemed to go well. Owen Young proposed that the group submit, without publicity, a series of proposals for fighting the recession. The President agreed. "The country has never confronted a situation where the need for good will and cooperation among groups of industry and labor and agencies of government has been clearer," the committee subsequently wrote the President. "You will, we hope, command us if you consider that even in slightest measure we can serve the situation."[10]

Over the next several weeks, Roosevelt held more such meetings:

with the Commerce Department's Business Advisory Council, with representatives of the automobile industry, and others. "I think we are clearing the atmosphere very, very well," the President told reporters. "We are trying to see things from a national point of view, and we are making very distinct progress."[11] Berle was elated. "The President came out for the Advisory Council yesterday in talking to the Roper Committee," he recorded in his diary January 20. "So it seems we are there." A few days later, he noted: "We are getting forward with the Lamont-Lewis-Young arrangement for an Advisory Committee. The President seems to think well of it."[12]

But the enthusiasm was short-lived. Both the liberal and the business press expressed open cynicism about the appeasement effort, and (after an apparently malign leak from someone in the White House) there was particular criticism of the new and previously unpublicized "advisory committee," which the New York Times columnist Arthur Krock described as "Mr. Berle's economic zoo." There was open hostility from the left wing of the CIO. And in Washington, Berle noted, "there has been no end of a split . . . over our maneuvers with Lewis and Lamont. Corcoran and Cohen think their position is threatened and have started a row." Unsettled by the public controversy, Young and Lamont withdrew from the group, which for all intents and purposes then ceased to exist.[13]

Even more damaging to the "appeasement" campaign was a disastrous peacemaking conference for small businessmen, which Secretary of Commerce Daniel Roper hosted in Washington in early February. Like the earlier meetings, this one was designed to give executives the opportunity to air their views and hear the administration's proposals. Unlike the others, it produced only acrimony and ill will. Delegates battled for access to the podium, shouted down speakers urging conciliation, passed a series of resolutions condemning the New Deal, and at one point became embroiled in a brawl so ugly that the police had to be called to keep the peace. Roosevelt hastily distanced himself from the imbroglio and refused to respond when reporters asked him about future efforts to placate small business.[14]

The small-business meeting was emblematic of one of the false assumptions underlying the entire "appeasement" effort—and, indeed, the larger drive for an associational economy of which that effort was a part. Richberg, Roper, and apparently Roosevelt himself seemed to believe that the "business world" was a single coherent entity capable of reaching a collective decision on its relationship to government. They acted as if a few major industrialists and financiers (in this case Lamont,

Lewis, and Young) could speak for, and to some degree control the behavior of, a large part of the corporate world. There may have been a time when such assumptions had at least some validity—when J. P. Morgan, John D. Rockefeller, and a few others could make an "arrangement" with the government and ensure the compliance of most of their colleagues in finance and industry—but if so, that time had long since passed. The corporate world had great centers of power, to be sure, and there were reasons for political leaders to try to placate them, as they often did. But there was no central leadership of that world and, indeed, no real community of interests that any central leadership could represent. The gulf between the interests of small businesses and large-scale firms was only one of many divisions that made a genuine "accord" with capital a virtual impossibility.

By the end of February, the "appeasement" campaign was a shambles. Berle and Richberg were fuming privately about how the "Corcoran crowd" had "sabotaged" their efforts. Business leaders (and the business press) were deriding the entire affair as a "con," designed to promote cooptation, not cooperation. Anti-monopolists were expressing relief that the unwelcome experiment had failed. "Appeasement is out the window," the columnist Raymond Clapper wrote in March. "We can forget it because it was all a dream on the part of a few people who thought recovery [as opposed to reform] was the most urgent need of the moment."[15] Opinions differed as to whether Roosevelt had been sincere in his effort to conciliate business or whether the entire affair had been "mere window dressing," designed (as Henry Morgenthau concluded) to permit the administration "to wait to see what happens this spring."[16] In either case, the failure of the campaign served to underscore the absence of any coherent policy for confronting the recession.

EVEN WHILE ENGAGED in these ill-fated "appeasement" efforts, Roosevelt continued to give at least faint signs of interest in anti-monopoly initiatives. His annual message to Congress in January 1938 had Brandeisian overtones in its discussion of "other people's money, other people's labor, other people's lives." It concluded that the "work undertaken by Andrew Jackson and Woodrow Wilson is not finished yet." A few weeks later, the President gave a Jackson Day address that included a ringing tribute to Jackson's attack on the Bank of the United States; he described that battle as "part and parcel of the struggles . . . of those who have lived in all the generations that have followed."[17]

Anti-monopolists in the administration drew what comfort they could from such statements, but they were hardly the decisive signs of support for which many liberals were waiting. The passage in the annual message was buried deep in a text that emphasized other things, and it struck many observers as a perfunctory afterthought (or, equally likely, a result of the President's relative inattention to a speech crafted by many hands); the Jackson Day speech contained only generalities, no indication of support for any course of action. Ickes had hoped that the "Sixty Families" and "capital strike" speeches he and Jackson had given in December 1937 would prod Roosevelt to move on the monopoly issue. He was dismayed when the President, during a January Cabinet meeting, complimented him not for the substance of his speech but for the effect it had had in encouraging businessmen to attend the "appeasement" conferences; and he was even more dismayed by the "abysmal silence" of every other Cabinet member. "I anticipate that practically everyone else there . . . feels that we ought to be conciliatory with business," he lamented.[18] A few weeks later (irritated at being kept waiting for a scheduled appointment with the President while Roosevelt conferred with a steel executive "for a solid hour"), Ickes complained that "after letting Jackson and me stick our necks out with our antimonopoly speeches, [the President] is pulling petals off the daisy with representatives of big business."[19]

For a time, spirits seemed to sag among other "New Dealers" as well while they waited for some sign of presidential favor. Corcoran and Cohen talked bravely of maintaining links among members of the "liberal crowd"—"just so they may touch each other and feel that it is not too desperately lonely in the front line trenches"—and proposed "an unending series of little dinners and five o'clock drinks." But they were at a loss as to who could host such affairs. (Corcoran wrote Frankfurter that he and Cohen "can't afford it with all the other drains. Can you find me some angel or choir of angels?")[20] Particularly discouraging was the sudden absence of Harry Hopkins, whom many liberals considered their best pipeline to the President. Hopkins underwent surgery at the Mayo Clinic for stomach cancer in December 1937 (only months after his wife had died of nearly the same thing) and remained largely removed from the policy debates during the first months of the new year.[21]

Despite these discouragements, two separate proposals for dealing with the monopoly problem began to gather considerable support in the early months of 1938. One emerged from the Senate, where a group of western and midwestern progressives—among them William Borah of Idaho, Gerald Nye of North Dakota, Robert La Follette of Wisconsin, and Joseph O'Mahoney of Wyoming—were losing patience with the administration and promoting a proposal of their own: legislation to create (in the words of O'Mahoney, its chief sponsor) "a national system of licenses and charters for corporations engaged in commerce among the states." Anti-monopolists had railed for decades against the licensing of corporations at the state level. State governments lacked the authority to control corporate behavior, since only the federal government could regulate interstate commerce. Hence, they argued, the power of incorporation should reside in Washington, where it could be used to establish uniform standards for the size and behavior of corporations. "National charters" would also end the practice by which (as O'Mahoney explained it) "a few states [most prominently Delaware and New Jersey], in order to invite the revenue which is derived from corporation fees, have made it possible for ambitious men to create interstate corporations under charters which give them unrestrained power to do as they please." Federal incorporation was appealing, too, because it offered a way to curb monopoly power without requiring a major expansion of government. "The result of a wise system of federal charters," O'Mahoney insisted, "would be to set business free from government domination and to set the people free from both the danger of monopoly on the one hand and of the totalitarian state upon the other."[22]

There was little enthusiasm for the federal incorporation plan among the "liberal crowd" in and around the administration. Establishing fixed standards for corporate organization and behavior was not the solution to the problem of monopoly, they believed; the real need was for a system of public administration capable of monitoring business activity and, when necessary, intervening to change it. At the same time, however, liberals recognized that there was still inadequate political support (in Congress or elsewhere) for an aggressive anti-monopoly policy of the sort they envisioned. Their task, as they saw it, was to find a vehicle with which to build such support; and gradually they came to believe that an appropriate vehicle would be a dramatic public investigation of the monopoly problem.[23]

The idea of "a broad inquiry into the present status of competition" had surfaced intermittently for several years before it became an anti-monopoly rallying cry. Leon Henderson proposed such a study in 1935 and was still promoting the idea when the recession arrived. In August 1937, Isidor Lubin, the commissioner of labor statistics, tried unsuccessfully to persuade the White House "to appoint a small group [consisting of Lubin, Henderson, Robert Jackson, Benjamin Cohen, and Herman Oliphant] to prepare a *confidential* report . . . on the extent of monopolistic control in the United States and the effectiveness of competition in assuring reasonable prices to the American public." Their report, he evidently hoped, might spur a broader and more public investigation of monopoly.[24]

By early 1938, the concept of an investigation was gathering wide support and (perhaps equally important) sparking little opposition. Anti-monopolists of every stripe saw in the proposed inquiry a vehicle for advancing their own views. Borah, O'Mahoney, and other western progressives in the Senate hoped an investigation would generate popular hostility to corporate "bigness" in the same way the 1913 Pujo Committee (whose investigations had formed the basis of Louis Brandeis's anti-monopoly tract *Other People's Money*) had done. Wright Patman, a Texas congressman known for his hostility to "concentrated economic power," championed the idea of an investigation because he thought it might lead to an attack on the "feudalistic chain store system." Representatives of consumer organizations envisioned public exposure of collusive practices that raised prices in such areas as insurance and the building trades. And the "New Dealers" in the administration (including Thurman Arnold, the new head of the Antitrust Division of the Justice Department) hoped to build support for revisions of patent, banking, and antitrust laws that would enhance federal regulatory powers.[25] The proposal was attracting support from areas of the private sector as well. Many small businessmen hoped an investigation would generate public sympathy for their difficulties in finding financing in a "monopolistic" credit market. Members of the Commerce Department's Business Advisory Council and other defenders of large corporate interests considered the proposal less threatening than the federal incorporation bill and saw the investigation as a relatively painless way to satisfy their critics.[26]

The idea of a monopoly inquiry was, in short, a proposal that appealed to many and antagonized few. In the first months of 1938, it gathered momentum.

BACKERS OF PUBLIC spending as an antidote to the recession were somewhat less conspicuous but at least equally energetic in the early months of 1938. Henry Morgenthau and his orthodox colleagues in the Treasury Department continued to insist that a balanced budget was a necessary precondition for recovery, but they were finding themselves increasingly isolated. The concept of public spending was attracting at least some support from almost every ideological camp. Advocates of conciliating the business community—from conservatives such as James Farley and Jesse Jones to planning advocates such as Adolf Berle—considered spending a way to forestall what they considered the more dangerous anti-monopoly alternative. Anti-monopolists favored it too, as a complement to their campaign against "administered prices."[27] But the most spirited support for spending came from those liberals who considered fiscal policy not a temporary stopgap on the way to more lasting solutions, but a solution in itself.

Most of these fiscal liberals promoted other policies as well; some, indeed, were prominent advocates of anti-monopoly efforts. They did, nevertheless, constitute a distinct community within the larger network of New Deal liberalism, a community in which excitement about innovative economic theories overshadowed other concerns. Marriner Eccles stood at the center of this circle, but he was never its intellectual leader. That role fell, for a time at least, to Lauchlin Currie, a deceptively meek young economist who was simultaneously one of the most anonymous and most influential figures of the late New Deal.[28]

Currie entered government in 1934 as a senior financial analyst in the Treasury Department. He was only thirty-two years old, but he had already established a considerable reputation as an instructor in economics at Harvard and as an iconoclastic authority on monetary policy. He was (as he noted in the preface to his 1934 book, *The Supply and Control of Money in the United States*) "severely critical of our banking system and its administration," and it was that stance that had brought him to the attention of the Roosevelt administration. The American monetary system, Currie complained, displayed "a perverse elasticity," because "on the upswing of the business cycle the supply of money automatically tends to expand, and on the downswing to contract." The nation needed a new, more centralized system that would substitute "certainty and precision of control for the existing uncertainty and lack of precision." The monetary system could become an effective "maladjustment-compensating factor," a tool by which government could moderate fluctuations in the business cycle and prevent disastrous booms and busts.[29]

Morgenthau and his colleagues saw in Currie's ideas little more than an interest in banking reform, which they also favored. But the nature of Currie's critique of the monetary system—his impatience with classical economic rules, his belief in the active manipulation of the money supply to advance larger goals, his conviction that trained experts could manage economic life more effectively than fixed laws—all suggested a level of iconoclasm with which most Treasury officials, had they recognized it, would have felt uncomfortable.

After only a few months at Treasury, Currie followed Marriner Eccles to the Federal Reserve Board as Eccles's special assistant. And there his divergence from the Treasury view quickly became clear. Currie immodestly described himself as "a better monetary theorist than anyone on the staff," but he soon turned his chief attention to another economic strategy in which he had long been interested: the use of fiscal policy as a compensatory device. He became, as a magazine profile later called him, an "apostle of spending," the principal fount within the government for the ideas that Morgenthau was trying so hard to suppress.[30]

For the next three years, Currie spent much of his time developing and promoting the case for the use of countercyclical public spending; and he found in Eccles, who was already sympathetic to such ideas, both an eager student and an effective spokesman. Currie established a direct channel to Eccles, ensuring that his analyses, unlike those of most other members of the Federal Reserve Board staff, would not have to pass through the hands of Emmanuel Goldenweiser, the head of research and (in Currie's view) a conservative "bottleneck" whose views "left much to be desired."[31] He took advantage of this relative independence to send a stream of memoranda to his chief promoting his unorthodox fiscal ideas and (beginning in 1936) hailing the theories of John Maynard Keynes, whose ideas Currie had first encountered while studying at the London School of Economics in the 1920s and whose *General Theory* ("pretty tough reading," he told Eccles) he greatly admired. Currie was occasionally frustrated by what he considered Eccles's intellectual naïveté, his attraction to popular theories (such as those of Foster and Catchings) that "could not stand up to academic criticism." But on the whole, the two men worked together effectively and complemented each other well.[32]

Currie's reputation and his personal connections soon spread beyond the Federal Reserve Board, largely through the intervention of Leon Henderson. Henderson had served as an economic adviser to the Democratic National Committee during the 1936 campaign; and at Eccles's suggestion, he had contacted Currie to help him brief party leaders on monetary policy. Impressed with Currie's politics and intellect, Henderson made a point of introducing his new friend to other members of the "liberal crowd" in Washington, and they provided Currie with a wider audience for his economic analyses. By early 1937, he had a network of allies throughout the bureaucracy. Many of them served together on an interagency fiscal policy committee consisting of men whom Currie described as "personally congenial and who all see eye to eye on the urgency of the problem": Corcoran, Cohen, Henderson, Gardiner Means, Isidor Lubin, and Harry Dexter White (one of the few officials in the Treasury Department sympathetic to Currie's spending arguments). Other New Dealers—among them Harry Hopkins, Henry Wallace, Mordecai Ezekiel, William Douglas, National Youth Administration director Aubrey Williams, and SEC commissioner Jerome Frank—also received Currie's memoranda and expressed interest in his ideas.[33]

Currie was not one of the prescient few who predicted the recession of 1937. Like Eccles, he had opposed the spending cuts in the spring of that year; but he had expressed concern simultaneously about the inflationary potential of the new recovery and had called occasionally for increased taxes to stabilize the boom. He had not protested the Federal Reserve Board's tight-money policies.[34] Once the downturn began, however, he had few doubts about its causes or about the appropriate solution; and he wrote a series of powerful briefs (some under his own name, some for Eccles's use) promoting his ideas. The most important of them (indeed, in Currie's view, perhaps the most important document of his career) was a paper entitled "Causes of the Recession," whose contents he, Henderson, and Lubin presented to the President in a private meeting in November 1937. For the next six months, the memo served as a New Deal *samizdat*, continually revised and passed from agency to agency and official to official. It became the central document in the battle for new federal spending.

"From 1934 to 1936," Currie argued in the report, "the largest single factor in the steady recovery movement was the excess of Federal activity-creating expenditures over activity-decreasing receipts." The reduction of the federal deficit in the spring of 1937 represented "a drastic decline of some of the main elements that had previously contributed toward increasing activity." Other factors had also helped produce the recession, Currie conceded diplomatically. But the "unfortunate timing in the withdrawal of the Government's contribution" was both the most significant and the most easily remediable. The appropriate response to the crisis, therefore, would be "a very substantial increase in the Government's contribution to national buying power"—in other words, a major enlargement of federal spending.[35]

THE "STRUGGLE FOR A PROGRAM" (as Henry Morgenthau later termed it) dragged on inconclusively throughout the long recession winter and into the early spring of 1938, as the President wavered and temporized, hoping the crisis would eventually cure itself. Late in March, with nothing resolved, Roosevelt left Washington for his vacation home in Warm Springs, Georgia. A few days later, Morgenthau traveled to Sea Island, Georgia, for a vacation of his own. Marriner Eccles, in the meantime, was resting in Utah; Leon Henderson and Harry Hopkins (recuperating from his cancer surgery) were in Florida. Yet at this unlikely moment, with many of the principals in the policy debate scattered across the landscape, the administration finally settled on a response to the recession—a response that made use, characteristically, of several contending views without fully embracing any of them.

Several events conspired to force Roosevelt's hand at this moment. A series of public opinion polls conducted in March 1938 showed a steady rise in the number of respondents who blamed the "present decline in business" on the administration, and agreed that it deserved the label the "Roosevelt recession." These and other signs of internal political hemorrhaging (at a time when the President was already thinking about the 1938 congressional elections) coincided with an international challenge. On March 12, German troops entered Austria and completed the long-threatened *Anschluss*; and while the generally peaceful invasion aroused relatively little public comment in the United States, it alarmed those in the administration—the President among them—who considered the spread of fascism a result of the failure of Western democracies to end the Great Depression. Eccles played to this concern in a message he sent the President just before leaving for Utah: "The greatest threat to democracy today lies in the growing conviction that it cannot work. . . . I urge that you provide the democratic leadership that will make our system function. Only in that way can the growing threat of Fascism be overcome." Two weeks later, on March 25, the American stock market—after a halting, incomplete recovery from its 1937 doldrums—collapsed again (in response, some charged, to a harsh presidential speech a few days earlier attacking corporate selfishness). The administration could wait no longer.[36]

Over the next few days, advisers converged on Warm Springs from many directions. Henderson and Hopkins traveled north from Florida. Aubrey Williams, a Hopkins ally, and Beardsley Ruml, an economist working as an adviser to the Federal Reserve Board, came down from Washington. All were there for only one reason: to persuade the President to recommend a major increase in public spending. Williams, Ruml, and Henderson took up residence at an inn not far from the "Little White House." Armed with statistics and studies they had brought with them from Washington (including some of Currie's analyses), they prepared elaborate briefings for Hopkins, who—having "camped on the President's doorstep in Warm Springs" (as Morgenthau later uncharitably put it)—was in a position to funnel the spending arguments to Roosevelt.[37]

Hopkins himself had few inhibitions about spending. He tended, his friend Robert Sherwood later wrote, "to regard money (his own as well as other people's) as something to be spent as quickly as possible." But he was aware of Roosevelt's basic fiscal conservatism and continued uneasiness about the deficit. He was careful, therefore, to emphasize that a spending program of the kind he was advocating had many precedents. Henderson helped him make the case. "The question naturally arises,"

Henderson wrote in a long memorandum to Hopkins, "why was there no federal intervention before March, 1933? The answer is that there was— only it took a form that kept us from recognizing it for what it was. That form was alienation of the national domain"—land grants to railroad companies, the opening of gold fields to private miners, the donation of homesteads to western settlers, and other such disbursals. "From the beginning of the Republic, the federal, state and local governments have been making additions to purchasing power through making the national domain, tangible and intangible, available for spending." A federal spending program now would simply make these implicit government contributions explicit. It would be a continuation of a long tradition.[38]

What finally persuaded Roosevelt to act—the worsening economic situation, the political damage it was causing him, the reassurance he received from Hopkins and Henderson that a spending program could be justified in conservative language, or some combination of these and other factors—is impossible to determine. But whatever the reason, by the time the President returned to Washington in early April, he had agreed to support a substantial new spending program. Once back at the White House, he solicited proposals from Ickes, Hopkins, Wallace, and others and began preparing for a major political offensive to sell what he was beginning to call a "compensatory fiscal" program to Congress and the public.[39]

Morgenthau, in the meantime, remained on Sea Island, cut off from the deliberations he had tried so long to shape, blithely unaware of how rapidly circumstances were turning against him. He spent his days working on "an economic program on a balanced budget basis," telephoning the President occasionally to remind him that "We must get our house in order if we are going to continue our leadership for liberalism." Not until April 4, two days after Roosevelt's return to Washington, did he receive an indication of how futile his efforts had suddenly become: a call from Henry Wallace telling him of the President's interest in new spending initiatives. A day later, he heard from his deputy, Roswell Magill, about a Cabinet meeting (which Magill had attended in Morgenthau's absence) at which Roosevelt solicited advice on how best to spend money. But even then, Morgenthau continued to display the deliberate, plodding style that had so often limited his influence in government. He remained in Georgia for another five days, as the spenders consolidated their position, and returned to Washington—too late—on April 10. Armed with a carefully prepared memorandum making the case for "fiscal responsibility," he hurried to the White House to see the President.[40]

From Morgenthau's perspective, the meeting was a disaster. He walked into the President's office at the tail end of a long discussion between Roosevelt and Hopkins, and the first words he heard were the President's: "Well then, we have agreed on a billion 450." Roosevelt then turned to Morgenthau, who recalled the unhappy conversation in his diary:

> The President said, "We have been travelling fast this last week and we have covered a lot of ground and you will have to hurry to catch up." I said, "Mr. President, maybe I never can catch up." He said, "Oh yes you can—in a couple of hours." He then took half an hour to outline the various schemes that he had in mind for spending money.

Morgenthau could not contain his alarm and responded with uncharacteristic fervor: "Well, Mr. President, listening to what you have outlined here not only frightens me but it will frighten the country because it is all so helter-skelter." He dutifully read his own memorandum, which conceded the need for additional spending but emphasized the importance of financing any new programs in ways that would not add to the deficit. And he pleaded with Roosevelt at least to "sleep on it" before he decided. He seemed to recognize, however, that the battle was lost. "They have just stampeded him during the week I was away," he told his staff shortly after the meeting. "They stampeded him like cattle." The President, he wrote, "has lost all sense of proportion." Two days later, after a series of additional, even stormier encounters with Roosevelt, he told the President that he was "seriously thinking about resigning."[41]

Nothing, however, could derail the spending program now: not Morgenthau's threat to resign in protest (which he quickly withdrew); not the actual resignation of Jacob Viner, the Treasury Department's chief economic adviser; not the arguments of Herman Oliphant and others that monetary, not fiscal, measures were the proper response to the recession. On April 14, the President sent to Congress a set of recommendations "to stimulate further recovery": increased appropriations for the WPA and other relief agencies; an easing of credit through an expansion (or "desterilization") of the gold supply by the Treasury and a reduction of reserve requirements by the Federal Reserve Board; and new funding for roads, flood control, housing, and other public works projects. The requests totaled $2.062 billion in added expenditures and $950 million in federal loans. Since the increased gold supply and lowered reserve requirements would presumably add another $2.1 billion to national income, the entire package was described, somewhat misleadingly, as a "$5 billion spending program." The same evening, as if to emphasize the importance he ascribed to the initiative, he delivered his first Fireside Chat since October 1937, to explain and defend the proposal. The title of the talk (assigned to it later by the editors of Roosevelt's public papers) was "Dictatorships Do Not Grow Out of Strong and Successful Governments, but Out of Weak and Helpless Ones."[42]

LEON HENDERSON'S ROLE in promoting the decision to spend—his presence in Warm Springs in March and his participation in writing the Fireside Chat in April—was evidence of how easily and intimately fiscal proposals coexisted with anti-monopoly ones. To Henderson, as to many other New Dealers, no economic program could succeed that did not confront the problem of "administered prices," a problem that required the elimination of anti-competitive practices. The President's spending program would fail, they believed, unless it was accompanied by a fight against artificially high prices. It was unsurprising, therefore, that Roosevelt was considering the monopoly question at the same time he was agreeing to increase public expenditures.[43]

Planning for an anti-monopoly message to Congress had been in progress since at least the previous October and had gathered force in the first months of 1938. As late as the beginning of April, however, the anti-monopoly initiative, like the spending one, had received no definitive support from the President; and at the meetings in Warm Springs that produced the spending decision there was no discussion of monopoly. But the subject was not dormant for long. Corcoran and Cohen had spent the last days of March in Charleston, drafting an anti-monopoly statement for the President; and when they heard about the spending deliberations in Warm Springs, they decided the time was right to secure a commitment on the monopoly question as well. Cohen traveled to Atlanta, met Robert Jackson, and boarded the President's train as it returned to Washington. In the course of that trip, Cohen later recalled, Roosevelt "went over a preliminary draft and I suppose it might be said that he then at least tentatively decided there should be a monopoly message."[44]

For the next several weeks, major New Deal figures lay the groundwork. Hopkins told a Senate committee on April 8 that any solution to the recession would have to involve both "government contribution to purchasing power" and a strenuous effort to restore competition to the marketplace and protect consumers from the "caprice of a few monopolists." In the meantime, additional drafts of a presidential statement circulated around the administration. On April 28, Jackson, Corcoran, and

Cohen joined the President and two secretaries in his study to hammer out the final draft; and the next morning Roosevelt sent it to Congress. Like the spending proposals of several weeks before, the anti-monopoly message combined broad rhetorical claims with relatively modest proposals—most prominently a call for "a thorough study of the concentration of economic power in American industry and the effect of that concentration upon the decline of competition."[45]

By mid-June, after only moderately acrimonious debate, Congress had passed legislation authorizing both the President's spending program, revised but still recognizable, and a special monopoly inquiry. And for a time, at least, it seemed that the administration had succeeded in regaining both the economic and the political initiative. Economic conditions—as measured by industrial production, employment, stock prices, and other basic indices—improved slowly but markedly over the next several months. In the meantime, the New Deal was winning some significant political victories. Senator Claude Pepper of Florida, widely believed to have endangered his position in his home state through his ardent support of the New Deal, won a hotly contested Democratic primary early in May against a conservative opponent—a demonstration, many believed, of Roosevelt's revived political strength. A few days later, partly in response to Pepper's sweeping victory, Congress moved at last on the long-delayed wages and hours bill. Indeed, so decisively did sentiment shift in favor of the measure that congressmen swarmed the well of the House and within a few hours contributed enough signatures to a petition to discharge the bill from the conservative Rules Committee, which had kept the measure bottled up for months. Several weeks later, the bill became law as the Fair Labor Standards Act, which for the first time established a national minimum wage (forty cents an hour) and a maximum workweek (forty hours) for some categories of workers.[46]

But these early successes were illusory. The recession abated over the summer of 1938, but it did not end. Nor was it ever entirely clear that the administration's policies were responsible for what improvement there was. Many economists, then and later, attributed the partial recovery to the normal fluctuations of the business cycle. In the meantime, the New Deal's modest political triumphs in May were quickly followed by a series of disastrous failures. Late in the summer, voters in several southern Senate primaries—most notably in Georgia, South Carolina and Maryland—rejected a personal appeal from Roosevelt to unseat conservative Democratic incumbents and replace them with men more sympathetic to the New Deal. Indeed, Roosevelt's attempted "purge," as it came to be known, seemed actually to help its targets, angering voters unaccustomed to "outside interference" in state politics. It also deepened the already considerable hostility of conservative Democrats toward the President.

The congressional elections in November dealt what many considered a death blow to hopes for further New Deal achievements. The Democrats lost eighty seats in the House and eight in the Senate. And while the party retained majorities in both chambers, liberals no longer had effective control of Congress.[47]

TO MUCH OF the liberal community, however, the April policy initiatives were significant less for their immediate economic or political effects than for the longer-range possibilities they suggested. When viewed in that light, the new measures were both promising and frustratingly incomplete.

The anti-monopoly campaign, its supporters believed, signaled a resolution of the long and often bitter debate between advocates of a planned, noncompetitive economy and advocates of competition. The President seemed to be saying as much in his message to Congress: "Private enterprise is ceasing to be free enterprise and is becoming a cluster of private collectivisms: masking itself as a system of free enterprise after the American model, it is in fact becoming a concealed cartel system after the European model. . . . [W]e must revive and strengthen competition if we wish to preserve and make workable our traditional system of free enterprise." The New Deal was apparently making a choice. The discredited dream of "economic harmony"—the dream of a "business commonwealth," of a revived NRA, of corporatist "industrial councils"—had been consigned to the dust heap.[48]

But the anti-monopoly initiative, for all its rhetorical importance, was in the end little more than an equivocation. However extravagantly the administration might talk about the war against "administered prices" and "economic concentration," the weapon with which it proposed to fight that war was a feeble one: a general public inquiry unaccompanied by any promise of concrete action. "This request for a study," Raymond Moley (one of the architects of the NRA) noted sourly, "was, certainly, the final expression of Roosevelt's personal indecision about what policy his administration ought to follow in its relations with business." It was, the historian Ellis Hawley has noted, "an escape mechanism, a way to deal with a fundamental policy conflict that could not be resolved."[49] The anti-monopolists, therefore, continued to face an imposing task: to turn the investigation into a mechanism for institutionalizing the fight against monopoly. The inquiry would, they hoped, prompt new legislation to give the government additional tools with which to promote competition. It might also stimulate more aggressive and effective use of existing weapons. It was, in short, a tentative beginning to, not a decisive culmination of, the anti-monopoly battle.

Proponents of the spending initiative, both at the time and for many years after, made even more extravagant claims for the significance of the April decisions. This was, they came to argue, a crucial moment in America's "fiscal revolution." The President himself did much to support that interpretation in his public statements promoting the program. His Fireside Chat on April 14 offered elaborate historical precedents for the decision, echoing Henderson's arguments that government had long been making contributions to national purchasing power; the present proposals, Roosevelt claimed, were "following tradition as well as necessity." But the comfortable references to the past accompanied a genuinely unprecedented rationale for federal expenditures. In the past, the President had generally justified spending programs as ways to deal with particular social problems: helping the unemployed, subsidizing farmers or homeowners or troubled industries, building the national infrastructure. Now he described such programs as vehicles for bringing the economy as a whole back to health. "We suffer primarily from a lack of buying power," he explained (drawing now from a memorandum prepared by Beardsley Ruml). The government had the ability, through public spending, "to put idle money and idle men to work, to increase our public wealth and to build up the health and strength of the people—and to help our system of private enterprise to function." Gone, in short, were the narrow, almost apologetic explanations of federal spending of the past. Public spending, Roosevelt now implied, was no longer a necessary evil, to be employed sparingly as a solution to specific problems. It was a positive good, to be used lavishly at times to stimulate economic growth and social progress.[50]

But while the spending initiative represented an important step in the direction of compensatory fiscal policy, it was a small and tentative step—an augury of the timid, halfhearted way in which Americans would embrace Keynesianism for most of the next forty years. The sums Roosevelt proposed to spend in April 1938 were not insignificant, to be sure; they represented a nearly 25 percent increase in the federal budget. But neither were they capable of promoting the dramatic economic growth that spending advocates envisioned and that the President seemed to promise in his April message. "No significant increase [in economic activity] *under the present program* in Government expenditures can be reasonably expected," Marriner Eccles wrote only two weeks after the President made his proposal. "Every effort should be made to increase the total volume of public and private expenditures in the next six months." The spending program, the *New Republic* complained, "is not large enough to do more than prevent the existing situation from growing worse. . . . In our opinion, the President's strategy was mistaken in allowing the spending program to be represented as gigantic when in reality it is small."[51]

Even more important to Eccles, Currie, and other advocates of aggressive fiscal policies was the continued absence of effective institutional mechanisms by which the government could stimulate the economy quickly and efficiently when needed. If every spending request had to move through the slow and cumbersome congressional appropriations process, if all federal money had still to be budgeted a year in advance, if only a crisis as severe as the 1937 recession could prompt swift executive and legislative action, then the dream of using fiscal tools to stabilize the economy and eliminate disastrous swings in the business cycle would remain unrealized. "It appears evident," Currie wrote in the conclusion to his influential "Causes of the Recession" memorandum,

> that if fiscal policy is to be truly compensatory, a far greater degree of flexibility in expenditures and receipts must be possible than is now the case. It may very well be that much flexibility cannot be achieved within the budget. A large proportion of the taxes are levied on the previous year's income and in accordance with prior enactments. The bulk of expenditures is determined by appropriations made far in advance of the period to which they apply. It may be that the solution lies in securing flexibility in large part outside the regular budget.[52]

The spending decision, like the anti-monopoly initiative, resolved nothing by itself. Instead, it encouraged those who believed in fiscal policy to promote the creation of new state institutions that might permit the realization of their dreams.

The recession of 1937–1938 may not have been the most serious crisis the New Deal faced in its long history. It was, however, the most perplexing. Its incomplete and uncertain resolution in the spring of 1938 helped save the Roosevelt administration from political destruction, but it provided only tentative direction to its future efforts. For the next two years, in the ever-lengthening shadows of an international catastrophe, liberals battled both conservative opponents and their own internal divisions as they tried to establish the ideological and institutional foundations for a strengthened national state.

# Chapter Six

# The Anti-monopoly Moment

THE ANTI-MONOPOLY CRUSADE of the late 1930s was, if not the most important, at least the most prominent of the public initiatives of the late New Deal. It heartened those liberals who continued to believe that curbing the power of great corporations was society's most compelling challenge, and who had fought for anti-monopoly policies in the first years of the Roosevelt administration. It dismayed others who considered competition dangerous to a modern economy and believed the best solution to the nation's problems was cooperation, harmony, and planning. Both the hopes and the fears increased in the first months of 1938, partly in response to Thurman Arnold's attempt to re-energize the Antitrust Division of the Justice Department, and partly in response to the launching of an ambitious government inquiry into the structure of the economy—an inquiry clearly designed to expose the costs of monopoly power.

In fact, neither the newly vigorous Antitrust Division nor the highly publicized investigation of economic concentration did very much to support the hopes of their supporters or the fears of their critics. Both initiatives were, ostensibly, efforts to combat economic concentration. But both became, in the end, chapters in the emergence of a new, consumption-oriented liberalism in which economic concentration would come to seem increasingly irrelevant.

"THE ANTITRUST LAWS," Thurman Arnold wrote in *The Folklore of Capitalism*, "were the answer of a society which unconsciously felt the need of great organizations, and at the same time had to deny them a place in the moral and logical ideology of the social structure." Their real effect, he insisted, was not to reduce economic concentration but "to promote the growth of great industrial organizations by deflecting the attack on them into purely moral and ceremonial channels. . . . In this way the antitrust laws became the greatest protection to uncontrolled business dictatorships."[1]

Arnold was writing in 1937, when he was a professor of law at Yale and an occasional consultant to the Justice Department. A year later, he was named head of the department's Antitrust Division, an event, he somewhat sheepishly admitted, he had not anticipated while writing his book and an appointment that his critics likened to putting the fox in charge of the hen house. And yet the man who had dismissed the antitrust laws as "thick priestly incense which hung over the nation like a pillar of fire by night and a cloud of smoke by day" became the most energetic and aggressive antitrust chief in the history of the division. In the course of his five years in office, he filed almost half as many suits as, and won more judgments than, all his predecessors combined.[2]

Arnold's many admirers tended to dismiss his caustic remarks in *Folklore* as rhetorical excess and to see in his later performance a repudiation of his earlier skepticism. But the way Arnold interpreted and employed the antitrust laws while in office was rarely incompatible with the ideas he had expressed in 1937. Antitrust policy in the Arnold years represented both a reinvigoration of the anti-monopoly ideal and a significant redefinition of it—a redefinition that excluded many traditional antitrust aims and substituted others more compatible with the new impulses coursing through liberal ideology in the late 1930s.[3]

Arnold was the product of two very different cultures: the relatively fluid world of the American West where he grew up, and the more established society of the eastern intellectual elite where he was educated and spent most of his adult life. He was born in Laramie, Wyoming, in 1891, the son of a prosperous lawyer-rancher and grandson of a Presbyterian minister unreflectively committed to the stern dogmas of his faith. Among other legacies of his western childhood, Arnold noted in his autobiography, were "the seeds of skepticism about the old-time religion that have plagued and tormented me ever since." In 1907, at the age of sixteen, he entered Wabash College in Indiana, a place he so detested that he left after a year and excluded all mention of it from his memoirs. The next fall, he enrolled at Princeton—an awkward outsider, wearing the wrong clothes and speaking with the wrong accent, largely ostracized from the hierarchical social structure of the college. "My years at Princeton," he recalled, "were chiefly remarkable for their loneliness." They were notable as well for what he considered their intellectual barrenness. Arnold found the rigid classical curriculum "extraordinarily dull":

The ancient texts were studied as if they existed in a vacuum, wholly apart from the culture of the civilizations that created them. This process made them an intolerable bore. . . . It was an age of absolute certainties. . . . The one thing that had to be avoided at all cost was the discussion of new ideas.

Four years later, he entered Harvard Law School, which he found a considerably more inviting place. ("Enough of my Western manners had rubbed off so that I was no longer lonely," he wrote.) But while he considered the professors at Harvard "intellectual giants" compared to those he had encountered at Princeton, Harvard Law School, too, was unsatisfying to Arnold's skeptical intellect. It was, he decided, "as much a world of eternal verities and absolute certainties as it had been at Princeton. . . . The idea that thinking was a form of human behavior lay far beyond the horizon."[4]

After a brief and unsuccessful effort to establish his own practice in Chicago and an unremarkable period of military service during World War I, Arnold returned to Wyoming and joined his father's law office. He became involved as well in local politics, serving first as mayor of Laramie and then as the only Democrat in the state House of Representatives (where he once rose to nominate himself facetiously for speaker, rose again to second the nomination, and rose a third time to attack the "irresponsible Democrat" who had proposed him and withdraw his name). Arnold was too irreverent for conventional politics and too restless for a small-town law practice. And so in 1927, when he received an offer to become dean of the University of West Virginia Law School (on the strength of a recommendation from Dean Roscoe Pound at Harvard), he loaded his family into a car and drove east, never to return except for occasional visits.[5]

In West Virginia, Arnold helped create a commission of experts (on which he himself served) to oversee a reconstruction of the state's legal procedures. The legislature, he implied, could not be trusted to do the job; only an educated elite, insulated from political pressures, was capable of evaluating the real needs of the system. The work in West Virginia brought him to the attention of Dean Charles Clark of Yale Law School, who had been involved in a similar revision of legal procedures in Connecticut. In the fall of 1930, Arnold eagerly accepted the offer of a professorship at Yale.[6]

Yale was appealing to Arnold for many reasons: greater prestige, a higher salary, an escape from the social isolation he and his family had experienced in West Virginia. But its principal attraction, apparently, was an intellectual one. For Yale Law School (unlike Harvard, from which

Arnold refused an almost simultaneous offer) was at the center of a new critique of traditional concepts of the law—legal realism—which Arnold found highly appealing. Legal realists challenged the prevailing belief, generally known as "conceptualism," that legal concepts were fixed, time-less truths (or, as one critic wrote, "supernatural entities which do not have a verifiable existence except to the eyes of faith"). The realists argued, rather, that fixed legal rules and principles were "empty symbols which take on significance only to the extent that they are informed with the social and professional traditions of a particular time and place." Most lawyers and judges claimed to be acting in response to timeless legal principles when in fact they were operating in response to a political, social, and economic context. Realists called for recognizing that contra-diction. Lawyers, they argued, should, as one scholar has written, "shift the focus from legal rules and concepts to facts." Such a shift could help transform the legal system from an instrument used to preserve things as they were into one used to promote social and political change. But at least equally important—since the kinds of changes the realists envi-sioned were actually relatively modest—the redefinition would make the law a more efficient and predictable mechanism, better able to respond to the real situations it encountered.[7]

Arnold found in legal realism a framework and a language for his own long-developing conviction that unexamined beliefs—outmoded myths and symbols—obstructed the effective workings of government and the law. His experiences in Wyoming and West Virginia had also left him with an interest in the "science" of governmental administration, which legal realism—by rejecting fixed, universal principles—invested with great importance.[8] In *Symbols of Government*, his first book, published in 1935, he decried the invidious distinction society had created between the judiciary ("toward which we take an attitude of respect because we use it to symbolize an ideal of impersonal justice") and the bureaucracy ("which has little symbolic function" and which therefore becomes "a gaunt specter" to which society attributes all deviations from its ideals). In reality, he insisted, judges and bureaucrats operated in much the same way, weighing their decisions less against timeless principles than against immediate circumstance. From that he concluded not that society should lower its esteem for the courts, but that it should raise its respect for bureaucracy. The real need was for a political theory that would allow administrators "to come out of the disreputable cellars in which they have been forced to work" and operate in a climate that gave them a place of respect in society's moral universe.[9]

Two years later, in 1937, Arnold published *The Folklore of Capitalism* to wide attention and acclaim. There he called even more explicitly for a new creed (or "folklore") that would give administrative government the same respect society already accorded the courts and private corporations. American political and economic theory, he argued, was "the most unrealistic in the world." It assumed the autonomy of the individual when every other branch of knowledge was conceding the interconnectedness of society. It embraced the "ideal that a great corporation is endowed with the rights and prerogatives of a free individual," when in fact the modern corporation was a great bureaucracy in most respects little different from the state structures with which it was so often (and so favorably) contrasted.[10]

Unlike some realists, Arnold was not innately hostile to "symbols" and "folklore." Indeed, he could not imagine society functioning without them. His concern was with recognizing the mutability of symbols and creating a folklore that served society's present needs, with recognizing that "principles grow out of and must serve organizations." In the age of the Great Depression and the New Deal, he insisted, those needs included a recognition of the positive value of the state. Americans, he wrote, should develop a "religion of government which permits us to face frankly the psychological factors inherent in the development of organizations with public responsibility."[11]

Such sentiments won Arnold a sympathetic audience among liberals in the Roosevelt administration, a significant number of whom were themselves legal realists and some of whom (most notably William O. Douglas, Arnold's close friend) were also from Yale Law School. In the first years of the New Deal, he performed occasional legal chores for the Agricultural Adjustment Administration and the SEC. In 1937, he went on leave from Yale to do trial work for the Justice Department's tax division. By then, he had become a familiar figure within the Washington "liberal crowd," friendly with Felix Frankfurter, Thomas Corcoran, Benjamin Cohen, Robert Jackson, Jerome Frank, and others, all of whom expressed enthusiasm for *The Folklore of Capitalism* (which they interpreted, at least partially correctly, as a defense of the New Deal). It came as no surprise, therefore, when Arnold was offered an important position in the administration.[12]

That he was named to head the Antitrust Division, however, caused considerable surprise and, in some quarters, consternation. Arnold had done some occasional consulting for Robert Jackson, the outgoing antitrust chief; but he had no particular background in antitrust law. His only significant commentary on the field had been his scathing critique of antitrust practice in *The Folklore of Capitalism*.[13] Even Jackson—who had recommended Arnold as his successor when he left the antitrust division to become solicitor general in 1938—conceded that Arnold "had no large interest or faith in the Antitrust laws." But the antitrust directorship was the first major Justice Department post to come open at a moment when liberals in Washington were trying to find a place for Arnold in their midst.[14]

Arnold experienced brief embarrassment during his confirmation hearings when members of the Senate Judiciary Committee (most notably, Senator William Borah of Idaho, about whom Arnold had made some direct and caustic comments in *Folklore*[15]) read passages from his book and asked him to respond. Arnold insisted that he had been criticizing only the enforcement of the antitrust laws, not the laws themselves. Borah asked him, "Do you believe in breaking up monopolies?" Arnold replied, "Certainly." Borah seemed satisfied, but his original concerns were well grounded. Little in Arnold's subsequent career suggests that he did, in fact, believe that enforcing the antitrust laws had very much to do with what Borah defined as "breaking up monopolies."[16]

But if Arnold's philosophy diverged from that of more traditionally populist anti-monopolists, the differences were not immediately apparent once he assumed his new office, for the frenzied activity he brought to the Antitrust Division tended for a time to obscure ideological subtleties. Unlike Jackson, who had believed that reform of the antitrust laws must precede any major campaign of prosecutions, Arnold was determined to use the power he had and to use it immediately. Imperfect as antitrust law was, he wrote, it "is the only instrument we have."[17] In his first two years in office, he succeeded in increasing his budget more than fivefold and in enlarging his staff from fifty-eight lawyers to over three hundred. Most of all, he radically expanded the number and range of prosecutions. In 1938, the division had initiated 11 new cases; in 1940, it began 92. In 1938, 59 major investigations had begun; in 1940, 215. The Justice Department had filed 923 complaints in 1938, and 3,412 in 1940. Arnold was not only active, but effective. He won almost every case he took to trial (31 of 33 in 1940) and settled most others out of court on terms favorable to the government. One reason he was able to win ever larger appropriations for his division was that he could claim to have brought three times as much money into the Treasury in fines and settlements as he spent on prosecutions.[18]

Arnold's innovative application of the antitrust laws was one of the chief ingredients of his success. Among other things, he made consent decrees a powerful tool for enforcement. The Antitrust Division had employed consent decrees throughout its history, filing civil suits against violators of the Sherman Act and then dropping them in exchange for an agreement by the defendant to stop the offending practice. But Arnold believed past use of the consent decree had too often been a "process by which criminal activity was condoned," and he was determined to use it more creatively and intrusively.[19] No longer could defendants avoid prosecution simply by abandoning "the practices for which they had been indicted." They must agree, Arnold insisted, to much more sweeping reforms in their behavior than even a successful criminal prosecution could have produced.[20]

A second departure from traditional practice, closely allied to the first, was Arnold's use of "industry-wide" prosecutions, what he described as "prosecuting simultaneously all of the restraints which hamper the production and distribution of a product from raw material to consumer." Anti-competitive practices were not necessarily confined to individual firms or organizations; they could permeate an entire industry, from top to bottom. The only effective way to preserve competition was, as the journalists Joseph Alsop and Robert Kintner characterized Arnold's view, to "hit hard, hit everyone and hit them all at once."[21]

The most dramatic result of the industry-wide approach, and the biggest project of Arnold's years in office, was a massive nationwide campaign to restore competition to the housing construction industry— "the first [antitrust prosecution] of industry-wide scope ever undertaken in the history of [the] Antitrust Division," Arnold boasted.[22] "In the building industry," Arnold claimed, "we are confronted with a series of restraints, protective tariffs, and aggressive combinations which has practically stopped progress." The Antitrust Division filed nearly a hundred separate criminal suits and several dozen civil actions against defendants at all levels of the industry and in all regions of the country. It prosecuted producers and distributors of building materials, contractors, and (most controversial of all) the building trades unions, which the Antitrust Division claimed had colluded with contractors to protect restrictive agreements.[23]

At the same time, the Antitrust Division was mobilizing other, similarly "massed" assaults on monopolistic practice in the food, transportation, automobile, aluminum, prescription drug, and insurance industries.[24] There were challenges to the way corporations used the patent laws to "build a domestic or international cartel or to stifle enterprise or production." And there were preliminary plans for major actions in other industries as well. Arnold's confidence, and his ambitions for his division, seemed to grow with every success. "In the entire history of the Sherman Act," he boasted in 1940, "there has never been such support for its enforcement."[25]

. . .

BUT ARNOLD DID more than expand the Antitrust Division's administrative capacities and its public profile. He also embraced a conception of the antitrust laws themselves that was subtly but profoundly different from those of earlier generations of reformers.

The anti-monopoly impulse in America has always been a diverse and contested one. The antitrust laws, the major institutional expression of that impulse, had emerged in the late nineteenth and early twentieth centuries in response to the demands of many different groups. Agrarian dissidents hoped to curb the power of railroads and processors. Workers sought to challenge the new factory system that was robbing them of their autonomy. Small producers wanted protection against large-scale organizations. Local merchants looked for a defense against chain stores. Women, working through a dense network of consumer leagues and other voluntary organizations, demanded an end to what they considered the artificially inflated prices trusts and monopolies imposed on them. Yet there were common themes suffusing most of these different approaches. And one of the most important—a theme that almost all anti-monopolists embraced at least in part and that permitted the antitrust cause to engage popular passions—was the urge to combat concentrated power and restore authority to individuals and communities. Farmers, workers, small producers, local merchants, consumers: all resented monopoly power not only because they blamed it for specific economic problems, but also because they considered it an assault on their ability to govern their own lives and determine their own futures. Most believed that a solution must involve some devolution of power from inaccessible corporate institutions to "the people," that the economy must be made more responsive to a larger notion of the public interest than the corporate world itself was likely ever to produce.[26]

Arnold's approach to the problem of monopoly embraced little of the rhetoric and virtually none of the substance of this tradition. Nowhere was that clearer than in his attitude toward the size of corporate organizations. A principled, even moral opposition to the "curse of bigness" had been a conspicuous characteristic of most American anti-monopoly movements from their beginnings in the mid-nineteenth century to the early years of the Great Depression. As Louis Brandeis, who articulated the case against monopoly for many early-twentieth-century Americans, wrote in 1933: "I am so firmly convinced that the large unit is not as efficient—I mean the very large unit—as the smaller unit, that I believe that if it were possible today to make the corporations act in accordance with what doubtless all of us would agree should be the rules of trade no huge corporation would be created, or if created would be successful." Even many younger liberals, imbued with the pragmatic spirit of the New Deal and uninterested in the kind of large-scale "trust-busting" that Brandeis had once advocated, remained suspicious of large organizations, which they considered anti-democratic. They were at least theoretically committed to reducing their size.[27]

But to Arnold, the size of a corporate venture, and the degree to which it responded to the demands of the "people," was barely relevant. The bigness of an organization was not, by itself, a cause for alarm; only when its size, and its behavior, threatened the competitive machinery— as was often the case—was there reason for state intervention. "As a generalization," he said in 1938, "it is as meaningless to say that small units are better than big units as to say that small buildings are better than big ones."[28] Indeed, he spoke frequently, and vehemently, about the value of bigness, about the great contributions of large organizations to the growth of the industrial economy, and about the impossibility (and undesirability) of restoring an atomized, small-scale economy—a goal he dismissed as nostalgic folly. "There can be no greater nonsense," he wrote in 1942, "than the idea that a mechanized age can get along without big business— its research, its technicians, its production managers. Not only our production during the war, but our way of life after the war, depends on big business."[29] If the antitrust laws were allowed to remain "simply an expression of a religion which condemns largeness as economic sin," they would quickly become "an anachronism."[30]

By rejecting the "moral value of trust-busting," by repudiating the idea that "bigness is a curse in itself,"[31] Arnold was also implicitly endorsing a vision of the state quite different from those of many earlier anti-monopolists. The populist and Brandeisian anti-monopoly ideal rested on a fear of concentrated power in both private and public institutions. Large corporations were not only dangers in themselves. They were also dangerous because controlling them would require the state to become a Leviathan. But while Arnold too spoke occasionally of the dangers of excessive government authority, he was, in fact, promoting a significant expansion of the government's regulatory power—and celebrating the possibility of that expansion.[32]

Arnold's view of the state reflected his image of the economy. Unlike some earlier anti-monopolists, he did not believe the modern economy tended naturally toward a "normal" competitive condition, which monopolistic practices artificially disrupted. He believed, rather, that obstacles to competition were so thoroughly woven through the fabric of the economy—so embedded in pricing and production practices at every level—that there was no "natural" competitive structure to which society could "return." Hence if competition was to play a role in economic life, as Arnold believed it must, it would have to be created and sustained by public action. Government could not hope to "set the competitive machinery right" by restructuring the economy, restoring a truly competitive environment, and then withdrawing from the arena. It would have to become a permanent part of the machinery—a "policeman" or "referee," constantly monitoring and regulating business practices. "The maintenance of a free market," he wrote in 1940, "is as much a matter of constant policing as the flow of free traffic on a busy intersection. It does not stay orderly by trusting to the good intentions of the drivers or by preaching to them. It is a simple problem of policing, but a continuous one." A year earlier, he had used another image: "The competitive struggle without effective antitrust enforcement is like a fight without a referee."[33]

Arnold was saying little that was inconsistent with the actual history of antitrust law enforcement, during the New Deal or before. The antitrust laws had relatively rarely been used actually to dismantle industrial combinations or prevent corporate mergers. Indeed, Arnold was more skeptical of mergers—and more inclined to challenge them when they threatened competition—than his predecessors had been. But most earlier defenders of the antitrust laws had at least claimed to believe in dispersing economic power and avoiding centralized authority. Arnold, however, embraced a view of the state that emphasized the role of experts, agencies, and bureaucratic processes in controlling monopoly power and implicitly repudiated the concept of returning economic authority to "the people."

His divergence from earlier views was clear in, among other things, the way Arnold fused his defense of competition with his effort to enhance the power and status of the administrative process and the people who controlled it. He sought (as he had since at least the publication of *Symbols of Government* in 1935) to legitimize an important—and permanent—role for administrators and experts who would be to a large degree independent of "politics." He was willing to permit (and indeed eager to promote) circumstances by which administrators like himself could interpret and apply regulations in ways unforeseen by their legislative drafters. His most important task, he believed, was not defining economic goals, but securing "adequate weapons"—sufficient administrative capacity—to make his agency's presence felt in the economy. In this, he was aligning himself solidly with James Landis and other New Deal champions of regulatory reform to whom process was at least as important as goals.[34]

Arnold distinguished himself from other anti-monopolists, too, in his rejection of, indeed contempt for, the idea of "fundamental solutions" to economic problems. "We have been passing through a period where the case by case method of reaching economic solutions was psychologically difficult because men were too much interested in broad ideas," he wrote in 1940. "The objection to the enforcement of the Sherman Act as a practical solution to our problems was always that we needed a more fundamental cure." But the New Deal, he claimed, had injected a healthy dose of realism into political thought. "Today the pendulum is swinging against broad general solutions.... We can now get down to the tiresome job of handling smaller and more concrete problems in the light of their particular facts. And in such a situation the method of the Sherman Act comes into its own." The business of government, in other words, was not the inspiring task of reaching for a great, permanent "resolution" of economic questions. It was the grubbier job of establishing administrative mechanisms that would become a constant and permanent presence in the economy and that would grapple perpetually with problems that could never be completely "solved."[35]

Arnold also broke decisively with earlier rationales for antitrust activity in the way he defined the ultimate purposes that activity was to advance. Eclectic as it had been, the anti-monopoly impulse had usually included a belief that the public interest would best be served by ensuring that the institutions of the economy remained accountable and responsive to popular needs and desires. It had rested on essentially democratic aspirations. In part, that had reflected a traditional reverence for the democratic potential of small producers (small businesses and manufacturing concerns, independent shops, family farms) and a commitment to protecting them from being "swallowed up" or destroyed by the great combinations. But it had also reflected the belief among consumers that they could hope to control prices and services only if they could themselves influence the behavior of economic institutions; the consumer interest, too, required a change in the structure of production. Arnold's curt rejection of the idea that there was anything intrinsically wrong with "bigness" and his conviction that the best solution to monopoly power was supervision by government experts left him with little sympathy for such democratic and producer-oriented rationales.[36]

By what standards, then, should government judge the effects of monopoly? To Arnold, there was one, simple, absolute standard: the price to the consumer. Whatever artificially inflated consumer prices (and thus reduced economic activity)—whether it was the anti-competitive practices of a great monopoly, the collusive activities of small producers, or the illegitimate demands of powerful labor organizations—was a proper target of antitrust prosecution. Any organization that did not harm the consumer, regardless of its size, had nothing to fear. Emphasis on this narrow conception of the "consumers' aspect"—uncomplicated by any concern about empowering small producers or even consumers themselves—liberated those who enforced the antitrust laws from the impossible task of evaluating the "moral aspects of the offense" and determining "that will-o'-the-wisp corporate intent."[37] They were now free to concentrate instead on assessing the effects of economic activity by a simple, uniform standard.

In this way enforcement of the antitrust laws would contribute to a larger goal that was moving to the center of late New Deal economic policy: increasing mass consumption by stimulating purchasing power. Arnold agreed with the emerging Keynesians in the administration who argued that federal budget cuts had caused the 1937 recession. He vigorously supported the President's spending initiatives in the spring of 1938. He expressed skepticism at times about some aspects of Keynesian theory (criticizing it for insufficient attention to anti-competitive practices within economic institutions). But he accepted Keynes's repudiation of Say's Law (the belief, central to classical economics, that supply automatically created demand) and applauded his emphasis on stimulating mass consumption. An aggressive anti-monopoly program, Arnold argued, was not only compatible with, but necessary to, the achievement of Keynesian goals. With that, most of the consumption-oriented economists associated with the New Deal (and indeed, Keynes himself) generally agreed.[38]


IN SOME RESPECTS, Arnold's tenure in the Antitrust Division was dramatically successful. In the short run, he launched and won an impressive number of important antitrust prosecutions. For the longer term, he greatly expanded the administrative capacities of his division and developed new techniques for enforcement of the antitrust laws. As a result of Arnold's efforts, the Antitrust Division remained for years what it had never been before: a large, well-staffed, and energetic branch of the Justice Department, far more capable of serious action, and much more inclined to take it, than it had once been.

But by the standards Arnold set for himself, his years in the Justice Department must also be seen as a failure. For he had aspired to much more than a technical refurbishment of the Antitrust Division. He had hoped that his own, "modern" conception of the antitrust laws would become a central and enduring part of the liberal state, both administratively and ideologically. It did not.

Arnold recognized that building popular support for this redefined notion of antitrust activity was crucial to his hopes. Indeed, few figures in the New Deal were so assiduous at promoting their work and their ideas. Arnold spoke on radio forums, appeared at the meetings of business and professional groups, wrote articles for both popular and professional periodicals, and in 1940 published a book—*The Bottlenecks of Business*, aimed at a popular audience—explaining his views of the antitrust laws and recounting some of his experiences in enforcing them. Arnold was always a natural showman, with a wry humor that some considered flippant. His irreverence was all the more striking because it stood in such contrast to his staid, almost stuffy appearance. (With his slicked-back hair, his thin mustache, and his dark, double-breasted suits, he looked like a slightly paunchy Ronald Colman.) However personally satisfying the public prominence may have been, his real aim, he insisted, was to promote public understanding of and support for the new standards of economic behavior the Antitrust Division was attempting to establish.[39]

Yet even before he left office in 1943, it was clear that this effort at legitimation had not succeeded. There were many reasons for that failure. Arnold's own limitations—his sardonic approach to public issues that led many of his contemporaries (and some later scholars) to dismiss him as a showman and even a buffoon—at times made it difficult for him to win serious public attention to his ideas. Mobilization for World War II—and the massive shift of power within the federal government away from liberal administrators and toward corporate interests—undercut Arnold's ability to pursue antitrust cases. But most of all, perhaps, Arnold was unable to make an effective case that aggressive antitrust enforcement was essential for promoting mass purchasing power and protecting consumers. There were always other, less controversial, vehicles for pursuing those goals.

Arnold's political problems stemmed in part from his divisive effort to use the antitrust laws against organized labor—an effort he began during his construction industry campaign (with his assault on the building trades unions) and continued well beyond it. His justification for prosecuting unions was, on the surface at least, simple and plausible: Anti-competitive labor regulations, no less than anti-competitive business practices, artificially inflated prices. He was not, he insisted, challenging labor's right to agitate in any reasonable way to advance its aims. He was arguing, rather, that the rights of labor could not supersede the rights of the consumer. As Arnold later wrote, "When a labor union utilized its collective power to destroy another union, or to prevent the introduction of modern labor-saving devices, or to require the employer to pay for useless and unnecessary labor, I believed that the exemption [from the antitrust laws] had been exceeded and that the union was operating in violation of the Sherman Act."[40]

Arnold was not a labor-baiter. He had supported the Wagner Act and the controversial 1937 sit-down strikes. He denounced company unions. Most of the specific anti-competitive union practices he criticized were, as he claimed, ones that even many labor leaders found indefensible.[41] But Arnold's careful, tempered public statements about labor failed to convey the depth of his antipathy toward what he sometimes privately called the "dictatorial" and "autocratic" power of some union hierarchies. His letters on the subject, and even occasionally his published writings, were suffused with a moralistic contempt for anti-competitive labor practices. In 1943, after leaving the Justice Department, he offered a scathing assessment:

> Some of these labor organizations are beginning to take on the color of the old Anti-Saloon crowd in its palmy days before Repeal. . . . Independent businessmen, consumers and farmers have had to sit back in enraged helplessness while labor used coercion for the following purposes: Price control, eliminating cheap methods of distribution, creating local trade barriers by restricting the use of materials made outside the state, preventing organization of new firms, eliminating small competitors and owner-operators, preventing the efficient use of machines and materials. . . . A certain percentage is graft and corruption, but a larger percentage is the result of the age-old struggle for economic power by men who love power.[42]

Such positions naturally won Arnold few friends in the labor movement. They also lost him many friends in the broader liberal community, to most of whose members unwavering support of unionization had become a basic article of faith—and a political necessity as well. Organized labor had allied itself with the New Deal in 1935, during agitation for the Wagner Act. And it had become an increasingly important constituent element in the Democratic party, and in the New Deal coalition, in the years since. Using the antitrust laws to attack labor "abuses" reminded union supporters of earlier and long-since-repudiated uses of the Sherman Act to destroy unions altogether as "organizations in restraint of trade."[43]

In 1941, the Supreme Court, newly reconstituted with liberal appointees of the Roosevelt administration, ruled in *United States* v. *Hutcheson* that Arnold had exceeded his authority in filing an antitrust suit against the AFL's United Brotherhood of Carpenters. The leaders of the AFL were, of course, delighted that the Court had (as one AFL committee put it) "compelled Mr. Arnold to give up his pretext of discharging the alleged duties of his official position." But to Arnold, the decision was, as he privately admitted, "a tremendous blow." Indeed, within a few months the effects of the *Hutcheson* decision had brought his efforts to reshape the construction industry to a virtual halt and had helped stymie plans for launching other, similarly comprehensive campaigns.[44]

More damaging to Arnold's hopes than his frayed relations with labor and its allies was the mobilization for war in 1940 and 1941, which dramatically changed the political climate for anti-monopoly efforts. Arnold argued strenuously that suspension of antitrust enforcement would have dire consequences, that without vigorous prosecutions the Second World War might produce the same kind of dangerous cartels that the first had helped create.[45] Cartelization, he said, had "slowed down production in basic war materials and given Hitler his flying start." The antitrust laws could be "one of the most effective legal means of speeding national defense." They "must not be laid on the shelf in an industrial war."[46]

Arnold tried to accommodate his work to the political and economic requirements of wartime. He created a special unit within the Antitrust Division to give prior approval to defense production plans that manufacturers feared might violate the Sherman Act. The basis of the antitrust laws, Arnold explained, was the "rule of reason." Any measures the war agencies believed essential to national defense were by definition reasonable. "It is not conceivable to me that any plan safeguarded as I have described can be rejected."[47]

Obviously this newly generous standard of "reasonableness" reduced the Antitrust Division's prosecutorial latitude. But in the beginning, at least, Arnold believed that considerable latitude would remain. "Within the last year," he noted cheerily in May 1941, "the clamor to set aside the antitrust laws has died away and been replaced by an awareness that the Antitrust Division is one of the nation's vital defense agencies."[48] But the optimism was premature. Little by little, the ground Arnold had staked out as suitable terrain for antitrust activities eroded as the military, the war agencies, and their allies increased their control over the mechanisms of government and expanded their involvement in ever wider areas of the economy. Arnold had been confident, for example, that a major suit against the petroleum industry (Standard Oil in particular) would meet the new wartime standard of reasonableness. He was attacking the cartelistic relationship between Standard and I. G. Farben, the great German chemical manufacturer, a relationship that Arnold claimed had resulted in the transfer of important technologies to Germany. Standard had, moreover, worked to delay the development of the synthetic rubber industry in America and had resisted participating in other war-related industrial efforts, all in deference to its financial and patent agreements with Farben. Harry Truman, before whose committee on war contracts the Standard matter was aired in the spring of 1942, commented, "I think this approaches treason."

Despite such arguments, the Standard prosecution soon evoked the ire not only of the oil industry but of the War Department, which insisted that the time and energy the company had to spend defending itself against the antitrust suit were interfering with its ability to meet essential war needs. In April 1942, Arnold succumbed to pressure and grudgingly accepted what he considered an unsatisfactory settlement through a consent decree, which simply required Standard to release a number of patents and pay a $50,000 fine.[49]

The Antitrust Division's problems were mounting in other ways as well. The dominant centers of power in Washington in the spring of 1942 were no longer the New Deal agencies staffed by Arnold's liberal friends, but the war agencies, peopled largely by corporate figures instinctively hostile to antitrust efforts. Arnold had, in effect, been forced to give the military and the war agencies the right to veto antitrust initiatives that they believed would interfere with the war effort. By the end of 1942, the War and Navy departments and the War Production Board were using the veto almost indiscriminately, to stop virtually all antitrust projects that involved companies or industries doing war-related work—which was now almost everyone. Within months of the unhappy settlement of the Standard case, such opposition forced Arnold to abandon investigations and prosecutions involving the chemical, electrical, steel, shipbuilding, aircraft, transportation, and other industries—even though some of the cases had been in progress for three years or more and involved activities that had preceded the war.[50]

In February 1943, shortly after the attorney general directed him to abandon a case against the railroads for price fixing, Arnold finally resigned from the Justice Department to accept an appointment as a judge on the First Circuit Court of Appeals. "I guess I'm like the Marx brothers," he said ruefully at the time. "They can be awfully funny for a long while, but finally people get tired of them." In a farewell address a few weeks later, he gave voice to larger concerns. "We are on the verge of a new industrial age," he predicted, "which may bring a higher standard of living than the world has ever known before. . . . And so the cartel leaders are gathering from all parts of the world to protect their system of high prices and low turnover, restricted production and controlled markets—domestic and foreign—against the new enterprise that is coming after the war."[51]

That Arnold failed to survive in the Antitrust Division was perhaps an inevitable result of the changed political circumstances of war. But if the approach to monopoly he tried to entrench had been hardier, it might have been more likely to revive with the return of peace. His departure from the Justice Department, therefore, did not simply mark the triumph of the military-industrial power structure over the New Deal. It also symbolized the failure of liberals to find a lasting place in American politics for antitrust enforcement and the larger concept of combatting monopoly of which it was a part. Arnold had promoted an anti-monopoly ideal largely stripped of its populist and democratic content. The goal of public policy, including antitrust policy, was not, as Arnold (and others) now saw it, to redistribute power but to enhance mass consumption. But efforts to tame monopoly would always seem secondary in a political world in which issues of economic power were secondary. For it was both easier and more efficient to pursue other strategies to achieve the goal of raising consumption: government spending, tax reductions, redistributive welfare policies, and others. It was tempting to avoid the politically and bureaucratically difficult task of confronting capitalist institutions and pressuring them to change their behavior.[52]

In the end, Arnold left behind him an expanded bureaucratic apparatus, but a depleted reservoir of political support for or interest in the antitrust laws. It would be too much to claim that Arnold himself was responsible for depleting that reservoir; the vitiation of anti-monopoly impulses would almost certainly have occurred without him. But his failed effort to create a new "folklore" that would both embrace the new, consumer-oriented liberalism of the late New Deal and secure for the antitrust laws an important place within it illustrates the enormous difficulties that were facing everyone trying to sustain anti-monopoly ideas in the emerging liberal world of the 1940s and beyond.

In 1964 the historian Richard Hofstadter remarked that "once the United States had an antitrust movement without antitrust prosecutions; in our time there have been antitrust prosecutions without an antitrust movement." The statement captures exactly the paradoxical legacy of Thurman Arnold's tenure in the Justice Department.[53]

THE ENERGY and innovation Arnold brought to the Antitrust Division came as something of a surprise to anti-monopolists in and around the late New Deal and helped refute the almost dismissive attitude of many New Dealers (and of the President himself) toward the antitrust laws.[54] But while Arnold was forging ahead with his ambitious plans, the principal focus of anti-monopoly hopes remained the "great investigation" the

President had proposed and Congress had authorized in response to the 1937 recession: the Temporary National Economic Committee (TNEC), which began public hearings, with tremendous fanfare, in December 1938.[55]

In later years, after the TNEC had completed its protracted hearings with no clearly discernible results, it became common for liberals (and many others) to dismiss the whole enterprise as meaningless window dressing, or even as an effort to derail more serious efforts at reform. That was not how the inquiry appeared at the time. Supporters predicted it would become "one of the most important events of our recent history," an effort that might well determine "whether the New Deal will go down in history as Roosevelt's revolution or merely as a milestone on the rocky road to someone else's," an exercise in "broad economic statesmanship of a sort for which one could find no parallel, perhaps, since Hamilton's 'Essay on Manufactures.'" Even critics of the anti-monopoly campaign viewed the new inquiry as an important, if ominous, event. The investigation, Raymond Moley warned in 1940, was a "time bomb," sputtering along misleadingly but certain to produce unwelcome, radical results.[56]

The framers of the TNEC themselves clearly envisioned no ordinary event. They made that clear in the unusual structure they devised for the committee. Members of the administration and of both houses of Congress were to sit together as theoretical equals, symbolizing the presumably broad support the investigation had within the government. The committee consisted of three senators appointed by Vice President John Nance Garner, three representatives chosen by Speaker Sam Rayburn, and administration officials selected by the President representing the Commerce, Justice, Labor, and Treasury departments, the Federal Trade Commission, and the Securities and Exchange Commission. Senator Joseph C. O'Mahoney of Wyoming was named chairman; Leon Henderson, who had first suggested such an inquiry nearly three years earlier, became executive secretary and ran the committee's day-to-day operations.[57]

As among most groups structured to generate consensus, there were almost as many conflicting views within the TNEC as there were members. O'Mahoney and William Borah were anti-monopolists of the old school, although O'Mahoney was now thoroughly entranced by his proposal for federal incorporation laws and at times seemed to view the inquiry as a vehicle for promoting that and nothing else.[58] Senator William King of Utah, Representative Hatton Sumners of Texas, and Representative Carroll Reece of Tennessee (who, with Borah, was one of two Republicans on the committee) were either hostile to or generally uninterested in anti-monopoly measures (or any other serious reforms) and tried to limit the scope of the inquiry's work and recommendations.

Representative Edward Eicher, an Iowa Democrat, was a staunch New Dealer eager simply to advance the administration's aims, if only he could discern them. Among the administration appointees, only one—Richard Patterson of the Commerce Department—was actually hostile to anti-trust efforts. But the other members—William Douglas of the SEC, Isidor Lubin of the Labor Department, Garland Ferguson of the FTC, Herman Oliphant of the Treasury, even Thurman Arnold representing Justice—all had larger agendas than monopoly alone, as did the numerous adminis-tration "alternates," many of whom played as significant a role as the full members. The results of the investigation would hang more on whether any one faction of its membership could establish dominance than on what information its hearings and research produced.[59]

Although some of the administration representatives, and Henderson in particular, worked hard to maintain good relations with their congres-sional colleagues, the investigation never really became an effective joint enterprise. O'Mahoney took his chairmanship seriously and worked dili-gently to make the inquiry a success (and to generate publicity both for it and for himself), but the other congressional members showed much less interest. Even Borah, who was widely expected to be a leading figure on the TNEC, was by 1938 so preoccupied with his zealous defense of isolationism that he had little energy left for the investigation. In any case, he died in January 1940 and was replaced by the obscure and quiescent Wallace White of Maine.

Perhaps inevitably, then, the administration members—who had conceived the inquiry in the first place, and some of whom viewed Congress with condescension bordering on contempt—dominated the committee from the beginning. They recruited most of the staff. They planned the hearings. They bent the investigation to their own goals. In the process, they demonstrated how contested those goals were even within the New Deal itself and how fundamentally liberal thinking about the "economic question" was in flux.[60]

THE EFFORT by the administration to hammer out a consistent strategy for the inquiry (and, through it, for New Deal economic policy in general) began in earnest in June 1938, at a weekend "retreat" on a farm in Leesburg, Virginia, owned by Thomas Blaisdell. Blaisdell was an econo-mist working for the National Resources Committee, the New Deal's principal planning agency. The ostensible reason for the weekend meet-ing was to convene the NRC's "Industrial Committee," which Blaisdell chaired; but the real purpose was to make plans for the monopoly investigation.[61] Among the other participants at the weekend gathering were Lauchlin Currie, Mordecai Ezekiel, Louis Bean, Gardiner Means, Benjamin Cohen, Jerome Frank, and Henderson. (Thurman Arnold was not present, an early indication of the relatively small role he would play on the TNEC.)

So various were the proposals floated at Leesburg that even the participants later disagreed about what they had discussed. One recalled the meeting as a debate over "whether Government effort should be primarily to restore competition or to set up a regulation of business decisions." Another remembered a discussion on technical reforms of the antitrust laws. Still others reported that the "group's attention was centered upon promoting full employment . . . by counteracting cyclical influences in the opposite direction"—that is, through increased government spending (although differences remained over where the spending should be directed). In fact, the participants discussed all these approaches (and others) without ever making definite choices among them—a result characteristic of hasty meetings among busy people, and one typical of many New Deal efforts to generate consensus through group discussion.[62]

As planning for the TNEC continued through the summer and fall of 1938, the range of strategies under consideration continued to grow. Herman Oliphant, as the Treasury Department representative on the committee, insisted that the "fundamental policy and purpose" of the TNEC was simply to reveal obstacles to competition and suggest the means of removing them.[63] Adolf Berle urged a pragmatic search "to find an organization of business that actually works." It was an "illusion," he insisted, to assume that competition was necessarily the best protection against concentration of power or artificially high prices.[64] From other sources flowed recommendations that the committee concentrate not on business organization at all, but on the question of how to promote mass consumption and full employment—recommendations that found a particularly receptive audience. Leon Henderson himself was a staunch advocate of consumption-oriented economic policies and a believer in government spending. The TNEC, he believed, must explore many policy strategies. But high among its priorities would be providing a hearing for new ideas about fiscal policy.[65]

The TNEC began its work, therefore, immersed in the same policy debate that was plaguing the administration as a whole in 1938. Its highly publicized efforts over the next several years did not resolve those dilemmas, but it did provide a stage on which contending approaches could stake their claim to public attention. And if at the beginning several economic strategies seemed to be competing on relatively equal terms, by the time the TNEC issued its final report in 1941, some of those strategies had become more important than others.

IN THE PUBLICITY surrounding the formation of the TNEC, there was a popular assumption, rarely questioned, that the committee would be principally interested in ways to regulate or break up monopoly. That assumption was, to some degree, correct. Much of the committee's public activity was, in fact, devoted to exploring the "monopoly question." Indeed, the TNEC produced what is arguably the most thorough, and certainly the most voluminous, study of the structure of the American economy, and of its monopolistic elements in particular, ever undertaken by any single organization. It conducted exhaustive hearings into the workings of dozens of major industries: construction, petroleum, iron and steel, automobiles, investment banking, life insurance, and others. It investigated specific economic practices that members considered inherently or potentially monopolistic: abuse of the patent laws, price fixing, mergers and acquisitions, cartelization, interstate trade barriers. The committee examined longstanding complaints about "chain stores" and "the problems of small business." It accumulated masses of statistical data about the concentration of wealth and income in the United States in the 1930s (so much that the economic profile of the decade remains today, despite the dramatically advanced statistical capabilities of later years, one of the most exhaustively documented of the century).[66]

And yet it is difficult to look through the dozens of volumes of testimony, monographs, and reports the TNEC issued—and even more difficult to read the private correspondence among its members and staff—without concluding that there was a vaguely dutiful quality to much of the investigation. Seldom did the hearings themselves crackle with the kind of fervor or anger that gave other great public investigations—the Pujo Committee of 1913, the Nye Committee of 1934–1936— their claim to public attention. Almost never did examination of witnesses depart from a respectful tone of academic information gathering to produce any real argument or debate. Rarely was there a hint of class animosity or populist resentment of corporate power. Instead, members of the committee made a considerable effort to assure industry leaders and others of their good intentions. The committee had "no desire of embarrassing or prosecuting anyone," Leon Henderson assured Edward Stettinius, president of U.S. Steel, late in 1938. At private meetings of the committee members and corporate leaders, there was constant talk of "fairness, tolerance, and good will."[67]

In the end, the inquiry was notable above all for its conceptual poverty on the monopoly issue: for its inability to produce any coherent prescription for dealing with the problem. It issued two final reports— one to the committee from its executive secretary, detailing the impressive results of the staff's research; the other an official "Report and Recommendations" signed by O'Mahoney. Neither contained any serious policy recommendations for controlling monopoly power, other than O'Mahoney's longstanding proposal to institute national charters for corporations and some technical and relatively inconsequential proposals for amending the antitrust laws. The committee's principal accomplishment, it lamely boasted, was the accumulation of "a body of information essential to an understanding of the operation of our economic system and which will prove most useful to . . . [the] search for solutions of our economic ills." It had gathered the data. It would be up to others to decide how to use it.[68]

The tentativeness of the TNEC's approach to the monopoly problem was not lost on its critics, some of whom saw larger (and more ominous) designs in the committee's evasions. The indefatigable anti-monopolist John T. Flynn of the *New Republic* complained constantly that while the committee was keeping up "a chatter about the evils of monopoly," its real purpose "is the resurrection of the NRA," the validation of what he considered the obnoxious idea of economic "planning."[69] Flynn was wrong. The TNEC was not being deliberately deceptive; it was not pursuing corporatist goals while hiding behind an anti-monopoly banner. But where twenty, ten, even five years earlier many liberals had considered solutions to the problem of monopoly both vital and possible, the TNEC inquiry suggested a fading confidence in the ability of government to do anything substantial about the problem—as the political commentator Dwight Macdonald charged as early as 1939. "The program of the New Dealers on the Monopoly Committee," he wrote,

> reflects the slow swing of the forces of the small bourgeoisie behind the drive of big business to power. . . . Monopoly constitutes the death of capitalism and the genesis of authoritarian government. . . . The muffled diplomatic tone of [TNEC's] hearings is the hush that men impose on themselves in a sickroom—or around a deathbed.[70]

Macdonald considerably exaggerated the likely impact of the TNEC's work. But he was right in sensing that the committee's behavior was symbolic of a declining hostility toward corporate power—and hence a declining commitment to combatting monopoly—among leading New Dealers. Little wonder, then, that the final reports of the TNEC, which

had been expected to offer powerful remedies to the "problem of economic concentration," were greeted with considerable ridicule and even
some contempt from the relatively few people who chose to discuss
them, and with an even more devastating silence from the many more
who by the end had come to consider the committee too inconsequential
to notice. At the end, most commentators dismissed the committee's
work as a "colossal dud," "a great anticlimax," or, more charitably, a
"magnificent failure." "With all the ammunition the committee had
stored up," commented *Time* magazine, "a terrific broadside might have
been expected. Instead, the committee rolled a rusty BB gun into place
[and] pinged at the nation's economic problems." The TNEC, I. F. Stone
complained, "spent three years digging up the facts and then reinterred
them with as much dispatch as was decently possible."[71] The interment,
whether or not intended, was dismally effective. Within a year of the
TNEC's disbandment, discussion of its findings and recommendations on
the monopoly issue had all but disappeared from public discourse.


BUT THE TNEC had never seen itself as "merely a 'Monopoly Committee,'" Leon Henderson and Isidor Lubin wrote as they finished their
deliberations, despite the strong popular impression to the contrary. And
it was not as completely barren of ideas as its anemic final report on
economic concentration suggested. For it also served, quite deliberately,
as a forum for promoting aggressive federal fiscal policies as a solution to
the nation's economic torpor.[72] Herbert Stein may have exaggerated
when he described the TNEC many years later as a "showcase for Keynesian economics."[73] But he was correct in suggesting that the course of the
inquiry helps illustrate the emerging shift in emphasis among liberal
economists away from traditional monopoly questions toward newer
fiscal ones. In the end, the committee's most important legacy may have
been its modest but not inconsequential contribution to legitimizing the
new economic thinking.

The importance to the TNEC of ideas about spending and consumption was apparent in the first weeks of testimony. The early witnesses
gave only fleeting attention to the size or structure of economic units but
a great deal of attention to the issues of consumption and government
spending. The hearings opened in December 1938 with Isidor Lubin, the
Commissioner of Labor Statistics, presenting an elaborate statistical argument for the importance of mass purchasing power. Fighting artificially
high prices sustained by monopoly power, Lubin conceded, was part of
the solution to underconsumption. But more important was a direct

effort to raise mass purchasing power through "government spending on relief" and other programs. "To me," Lubin said, "it is a problem of keeping the gears of the economic machine constantly in mesh." And the best way to do that was by stimulating greater consumption, "by so distributing our income that it will put into our homes, through a higher standard of living, the goods, that is, the clothing, food, entertainment, education, and so forth, which our economic machine must turn out."[74]

By May 1939, when the first major series of hearings (on savings and investment) was about to begin, the administration members of the committee had solidified their control of the inquiry and felt free to direct the investigation even more energetically toward a discussion of fiscal policy.[75] They did so carefully and self-consciously. They persuaded the White House to release a presidential letter (written by Berle) to open the hearings and endorse the strategy they had already chosen. Roosevelt's message said virtually nothing about monopoly and referred instead to:

> . . . the dollars which the American people save each year [which] are not finding their way back into productive enterprises in sufficient volume to keep our economic machine turning over at the rate required to bring about full employment.[76]

Henderson and his staff orchestrated the testimony of this group of witnesses—economists and public officials firmly committed to the idea of increasing mass purchasing power through public spending—with a care they lavished upon no other phase of the investigation. They arranged "dress rehearsals" of key witnesses in the actual hearing room, and they left as little room for spontaneity and surprise as possible. The preparations were a reflection of how important they considered the committee's "educational" function (and of how limited was their conception of the hearings as genuine investigation).[77]

The May 1939 hearings marked a particularly gratifying victory for Lauchlin Currie, who ever since the Blaisdell meeting nearly a year before had been working to shift the TNEC's emphasis toward the value of government spending (and who decades later continued to remember his role in the TNEC as one of the highlights of his lifelong effort to promote Keynesian ideas). Currie himself testified at length and made a careful, statistical case for the fiscal measures he had been promoting within the administration for three years. But the central figure in the testimony was a man he had helped recruit for the occasion who was not yet widely known in Washington: Alvin H. Hansen, soon to become one of America's most influential economists.[78]

Hansen was not an immediately impressive public figure. The son of Danish immigrants, born on the South Dakota prairie, educated at the University of Wisconsin, he struck some observers as a simple, direct, "folksy" midwesterner. A distinguished professor of economics at the University of Minnesota and, beginning in 1938, at Harvard, he struck others as an archetypical academic. He spoke in an unemotional monotone, referring frequently and distractingly to papers and charts spread out in front of him. In public hearings, as in many other settings, he wore tinted glasses and a signature green eyeshade, which protected his weak eyes from glaring lights but also reinforced his bookish, almost clerklike image. He reminded the journalist Richard Strout of "an old-time Boston and Maine depot master, or maybe the slot man in the news desk of a morning newspaper."[79]

But Hansen was anything but a retiring academic. In 1939, as throughout his long career, he took an intense and active interest in public policy, an interest his move to Harvard (to which many New Deal economists and lawyers had some connection) enabled him to pursue with much greater effect. For at least the next decade, he was seldom far from the center of official circles. Hansen declined to join the TNEC staff; but by mid-1939 he was deeply, if unofficially, involved in the committee's work and ready to play an important public role in its deliberations.[80]

Hansen's intellectual trajectory, the economist Robert Lekachman has written, "is an example of the power of the Keynesian analysis" to transform economic thinking. Through most of the 1930s, Hansen had written cautious and fairly conservative studies of the business cycle (his principal field of expertise) and had been consistently skeptical of public spending as an antidote to recession. His review of Keynes's *General Theory* in 1936 had been decidedly cool. "The continued workability of the system of private enterprise," he predicted, would come not through the policies advocated by Keynes, "but rather by the work of the inventor and the engineer." Keynes's masterwork, he concluded, was "not a landmark in the sense that it lays a foundation for a 'new economics.' . . . [It] is more a symptom of economic trends than a foundation stone upon which a new science can be built." But by 1938, when he published a collection of his essays under the title *Full Recovery or Stagnation?*, he had become a convert—enthusiastically endorsing an aggressive program for stimulating consumption through public spending. Hansen never explained why his thinking had changed, or even openly acknowledged that it had. But it seems likely that he was responding both to the 1937 recession—which jarred the thinking of many people—and to the steadily growing interest in Keynes within the economics profession in the years following publication of the *General Theory*.[81]

His testimony before the TNEC in May 1939 reflected his conversion. He attacked the Social Security tax as a drain on mass purchasing power and described "our current tax system" in general as "unduly repressive on consumption." And he called for a wide range of public spending activities—government investment in new products and industries, creation of a quasi-public corporation to inject capital into the stagnant railroad industry, and funding public works "on a considerable scale to overcome the chronic unemployment problem."[82]

Ultimately, those promoting public spending were no more successful in giving direction to the TNEC itself than were the ineffectual defenders of traditional anti-monopoly ideas. The executive secretary's report in 1941 gave considerable attention to spending and consumption issues and to what it described as the government's increasingly important fiscal role in sustaining economic growth. But it stopped short of explicit recommendations. The committee's official final report (written largely by O'Mahoney and his staff) said virtually nothing about the new fiscal ideas and, indeed, seemed to some members actually to repudiate them— so much so that several members of the TNEC staff submitted dissents.[83]

But unlike the TNEC's frail gestures toward strengthening the antitrust laws and attacking economic concentration, the Keynesian arguments of Hansen, Currie, Lubin, and others had a real impact. They rippled through the government and became part of broader public discussions of economic policy. In the process, they not only helped redefine the way in which many liberals thought about spending. They also helped redefine thinking about the monopoly question itself. Advocates of public spending did not oppose increased regulation of monopoly. On the contrary, most strongly supported such regulation. What upset them was the idea that regulating monopoly was sufficient to promote economic growth. They were proposing fiscal policies not as an alternative to traditional antitrust or regulatory ideas, but as a necessary companion to them. "The two devices," Mordecai Ezekiel wrote in 1939, "are . . . not competitive but complementary."[84]

In the end, then, the most important of the TNEC's efforts was this attempt to fuse two very different approaches to political economy. And for a time, that effort resonated broadly through liberal discourse—taking the TNEC's ideas well beyond the hearing rooms and offices of the committee itself.

WHAT BOUND TOGETHER these two strategies—increased state regulation of private institutions and increased use of fiscal policy to stimulate aggregate growth—was an emerging assumption about the American economy that was suffusing liberal economic thought in the late 1930s and that was an article of faith to many of the leading figures on the TNEC. Even before the 1937 recession, doubts had been growing within the New Deal and well beyond about the capacity of private enterprise ever again to produce the kind of economic growth it had experienced in the half century before the Great Depression. The setbacks of 1937–1938 greatly reinforced those concerns. Sluggish growth and high unemployment, which had now continued for nearly a decade, were beginning to seem part of the natural order of things. Out of such fears emerged the concept of the "mature economy."

The idea of a mature economy reflected a growing conviction that American economic life had settled on something like a permanent plateau, a conviction Lauchlin Currie expressed in 1939. "The economic problem facing America is not a temporary one," he wrote. "The violence of the depression following 1929 obscured for some time the fact that a profound change of a chronic or secular nature had occurred."[85] The age of economic expansion, he argued, had come to an end. The economy was approaching the limits of its capacity to grow. It had reached "maturity." The challenge facing the nation and its government was to find ways of responding to the new economic world this maturity had created.

The argument grew from a long tradition of such predictions in America. (It also anticipated some of the no-growth ideologies of the 1970s and beyond.) It was particularly reminiscent of the historian Frederick Jackson Turner's 1893 "frontier thesis," for it viewed economic expansion in much the same way Turner had viewed territorial expansion—as something finite and now largely at an end. Senator Lewis Schwellenbach of Washington, an ardent New Dealer (and later secretary of labor under Truman), made that connection explicitly in a 1938 speech in Seattle. "You have heard about the last frontier," he told his audience.

> So long as we had an undeveloped West—new lands—new resources—new opportunities—we had no cause to worry. We could permit concentration of wealth. We could permit speculation of our heritage. We could permit waste and erosion by wind and water, but we caught up with ourselves. We reached our Last Frontier.[86]

But the presumed exhaustion of open land and other natural resources was not the principal concern of the mature-economy theorists in the 1930s. It was slackening population growth and the decline of "capital accumulation" (or investment). In retrospect, it is clear that both were temporary phenomena, products of the Depression itself. At the time, however, it was common to assume that they had become permanent conditions.

The rate of population growth had dropped by more than half in the 1930s, and relatively few analysts expected it to rise again soon. The National Resources Committee's 1938 pamphlet *The Problems of a Changing Population*, for example, predicted very little population growth through the second half of the twentieth century and perhaps no growth at all beyond that. The predictions were, of course, wildly inaccurate (in part because they were based on already obsolete assumptions about the relationship between population growth and open land). Between 1940 and 1990, the American population rose consistently at rates 50 to 100 percent greater than the sluggish rate of the 1930s. Accurate or not, however, the predictions of the late 1930s had tremendous appeal to those trying to explain the prolonged stagnation of the American economy. Declining population growth meant a declining increase in demand. The projected populations of future decades, one economist argued, "would be insufficient to consume our wheat and cotton production, at the present level of consumption," much less to consume the products of an expanding industrial economy.[87]

But inadequate population growth was only one of several reasons for what mature-economy theorists predicted would be a very low rate of future capital investment. At least as important was the apparent "maturity" of the nation's principal industries (steel, automobiles, construction, railroads), all of which seemed to have come near the limits of their capacity to grow; and the absence of new industries of comparable importance ready to replace them. "The great automobile industry has risen to maturity and no comparable new industry has appeared to fill the gap," Alvin Hansen argued. "We are more or less through the heavy task of equipping the continent with giant capital expenditures." Like the population-growth predictions that accompanied them, these forecasts were soon disproved, when the nation embarked in the 1940s on the longest and greatest economic expansion in its history, an expansion in which major new industries emerged and some older ones greatly expanded. A few prescient economists said as much at the time—perhaps most notably, Joseph Schumpeter. He wrote scornfully of the mature-economy idea in 1939, describing the Great Depression as a "temporary reaction" to the evolution of capitalism, "no novel occurrence, no unprecedented catastrophe . . . only a recurrence of what at similar junctures had occurred before." Nonetheless, it is not altogether surprising that after a decade of economic stagnation, and after the failure of what seemed to be daring policy innovations to produce a genuine recovery, many Americans were beginning to conclude that the current economic crisis was not a temporary aberration, but part of a fundamental transformation.[88]

"The economic order of the western world is undergoing in this generation a structural change no less basic and profound in character than . . . 'the Industrial Revolution,' " Hansen wrote. "We are passing, so to speak, over a divide which separates the great era of growth and expansion of the nineteenth century from an era which no man . . . can as yet characterize with clarity or precision. We are moving swiftly out of the order in which those of our generation were brought up, into no one knows what." "The peak of the mechanical age has been passed," another partisan claimed in 1938. "The boom of the 1920's was its final flowering and the Empire State building its most splendid monument. . . . It is the culmination of our growth and the ending of a long chapter in our history."[89]

Taken literally, the mature-economy idea could become a source of considerable gloom. John T. Flynn, for example, wrote caustically (but also credulously) of the theory in 1939: "The suspicion has got around that America—dynamic America— . . . [is] more or less finished."[90] But many of the economists and policymakers promoting the idea were more optimistic. Obviously a change of this magnitude called for major shifts in the management of the American economy, they argued. But with enlightened new policies, even a mature economy could continue to prosper. Hence, the theory became above all a powerful rationale for public policies to which New Dealers were already committed.

To some liberals, the mature-economy idea seemed to support arguments for increasing the regulatory functions of the state. An economic climate in which private industry was incapable of creating dynamic growth would place nearly unbearable pressures on capitalists to avoid risks, to collude in raising (or "administering") prices, and hence to produce further stagnation. Only a strong regulatory state could combat this danger. The new realities would also require more intelligent economic choices. Investment could not be left to the whims of the market. There would have to be some kind of central direction, in which the state itself would play a significant role. "Hereafter," Stuart Chase wrote after describing the problems of a mature economy, "economic systems are going to be run deliberately and directly for those ends which everybody knows they should be run for. . . . The welfare of the community will be paramount."[91]

But the mature-economy idea added strength as well to Keynesian arguments for greater government spending. In the absence of large-scale private investment, only the government had the resources (and the broad "national" view of the economic problem) necessary to produce and sustain economic growth. Private investment was no longer an adequate engine for driving the economy forward. To compensate for this decline in investment, it was necessary now to stimulate consumption. The best way to do so was through federal fiscal policies.[92]

The writings and public statements of Alvin Hansen illustrate particularly clearly how the belief in economic maturity was helping to fuse regulatory and spending ideas. Hansen constructed one of the most sophisticated theoretical explanations of the new concept—which he called "secular stagnation" and which became his principal contribution to Keynesian theory (if one that Keynes himself never entirely accepted).[93] In his testimony before the TNEC, as in many of his writings in the late 1930s and early 1940s, Hansen argued that secular stagnation required an entirely new approach to economic policy—one that would combine old anti-monopoly orthodoxies with new fiscal innovations. Now that private institutions had largely lost the ability to create sustained growth through investment, they were likely actually to retard expansion through anti-competitive practices as they struggled to survive in an increasingly difficult economic world. A necessary part of any public strategy, therefore, was a vigorous antitrust policy to restore fluidity to the marketplace and keep prices low enough to permit mass consumption of industrial goods.[94]

But fluidity alone would not be enough. Government must also assume the responsibility of sustaining, and when necessary increasing, mass purchasing power to keep alive the higher levels of consumption upon which the economy would now have to rely. The solution to the maturity of America's productive capacities was a dramatic expansion of the nation's ability to consume. "Let us now turn to a high-consumption economy and develop that as the great frontier of the future," Hansen argued. Economic maturity need not mean stagnation if America could find ways to raise the standard of living of its now essentially stable population. The end of population growth and capital expansion could, in fact, lead to a better life for all—but only if the nation's leaders developed policies to promote full employment and increase mass purchasing power. Hansen was certain that public spending was the best, even if not the only, means to that end.[95]

TO SAY THAT anti-monopoly and fiscal ideas coexisted among advocates of the mature-economy idea is not to say that they were equally powerful. To most liberals wrestling with economic policy at the close of the 1930s—on the staff of the TNEC, within the New Deal, and in the liberal communities around them—confronting economic concentration was rapidly becoming secondary to stimulating consumption.

That was in part because of their growing doubts about the government's capacity to regulate the economy in the direct, institutional way that a serious commitment to fighting monopoly would require. "This government," Leon Henderson wrote not long before joining the TNEC, "even if it thought it wise to attempt their use, does not have the powers, techniques and organization of forces necessary for controlling the national economy within precise bounds. It is limited to exerting a directional influence by choices of governmental policies such as Federal reserve actions, spending, taxation." Three years later, the political scientist Corwin Edwards reminded Henderson of another danger: the possibility of private interests' "capturing" regulatory mechanisms and using them for their own ends. "There are obvious limits to the possibility of either regulating industry or restoring competition. . . . [I]nformation, personnel, and political support are lacking to set up . . . a control which protects the public interest instead of becoming merely a device by which an interested group obtains what it wants by political means." Antitrust laws and other regulatory mechanisms might be helpful in ending "administered prices" in some sectors of the economy and in making some goods more broadly affordable. But they were not an effective solution to the nation's larger economic problems.[96]

The fading importance of anti-monopoly ideas in the thinking of many liberals was even more a result, however, of the availability of an attractive alternative solution: increasing purchasing power, which would itself help bring prices down by encouraging producers to aim for larger markets. If the Depression was a result of underconsumption, as virtually all liberals believed it was, then directing more income to consumers was the best vehicle for fighting it and for laying the groundwork for the long-term prosperity they hoped might follow.

The uneasy and unequal alliance of the anti-monopoly and spending strategies did not, in any case, survive for very long. Within a few years, concern about monopoly and commitment to expanding the regulatory and administrative functions of the state had largely disappeared from liberal rhetoric. They were becoming, as Richard Hofstadter later wrote, "one of the faded passions of American reform."[97] And the faith in fiscal policy, which had emerged so suddenly and haltingly after 1937, had moved to the center of liberal hopes. The reasons for that change were many, but almost all of them were rooted in the American experience in World War II.

## Chapter Seven

# Liberals Embattled

IN THE SPRING of 1917, as the United States prepared finally to enter World War I, Walter Lippmann published an essay in which he expressed something of the excitement many Americans felt when they thought about what joining the conflict might do for their nation. "I do not wish to underestimate the forces of reaction in our country," he wrote. But, he added,

> We shall know how to deal with them. Forces have been let loose which they can no longer control, and out of this immense horror ideas have arisen to possess men's souls. There are times . . . when new sources of energy are tapped, when the impossible becomes possible, when events outrun our calculations. This may be such a time. . . . We can dare to hope for things we never dared to hope for in the past.[1]

A quarter century later, as the United States prepared to enter another, greater war, Lippmann expressed some of the same sentiments. "Let us hope," he wrote a few days after Pearl Harbor, "that in the fires through which we must pass, we shall be purged of the dross which has so nearly undone us, and that out of suffering the American spirit will come forth clean and bright again." For all the philosophical changes he had experienced since 1917, Lippmann retained his youthful faith in the transforming power of war and his hope that it might produce a new international system, a moral regeneration of the American people, even a reformed economic order.[2]

Many liberals, however much they may have disagreed with Lippmann on other things by 1941, shared this optimistic faith in the aftermath of Pearl Harbor. At a dinner for "two hundred leading liberals" hosted by the *New Republic* in March 1942, the mood was surprisingly bright. The editors later claimed that they had not been certain whether the people they had invited "would meet in a spirit of dejection or of hope." But it quickly became clear

> that the spirit of these men was a militant, fighting one—one which asserted that the offensive on our fronts abroad . . . demanded in turn an offensive attitude on the home front, to resist the attacks of reaction upon the liberal faith of our people, and to give meaning and purpose to the war.[3]

Liberal hopes took as many different forms in wartime as they had in peace. In some ways, in fact, those hopes grew broader and more diverse. The war helped draw growing numbers of white liberals, most of whom had slighted the issue during the 1930s, toward a commitment to fighting racial injustice; and it greatly strengthened the determination of African Americans themselves to demand their rights. It propelled liberals (and many others) into a fervent commitment to internationalism—to a revival and strengthening of the broad outlines of the Wilsonian dream that many (among them Franklin Roosevelt) had never repudiated but that most had dismissed as unrealistic during the previous two decades. It raised hopes among many women that the new roles they played during the fighting might be the beginning of a redefinition of gender roles that would provide them with greater power and opportunity in peacetime.[4]

Still, most liberals during the war, like most liberals in the 1930s, continued to believe that their principal domestic goal was creating stable and enduring prosperity and growth—prosperity and growth that would survive the loss of the artificial economic stimulus of war production and would shape the postwar world. Liberals focused their hopes above all on the prospects of using the powers of the federal government to achieve that goal. However much they recoiled from the horrors they knew the war would unleash, they recognized too that the struggle might create unmatched opportunities for progressive change.[5]

But they also sensed danger: the possibility that a wave of reaction might frustrate their hopes, just as a wave of reaction and repression in 1919 had shattered the hopes of an earlier generation of liberals. "Today," the *New Republic* warned early in 1941,

> powerful forces are at work trying to turn the present defense program into a program to recapture privilege, to break the unions, to profiteer out of war and to trample on the New Deal. Insufficient

forces are at work trying to turn the defense program into a program of the people, to defend the people.[6]

By late 1942, such warnings had become commonplace. "Is the sentiment of the public really moved by the vision of a better world," Attorney General Francis Biddle gloomily asked students at the University of Virginia, "or is it merely disturbed by anxiety about increased taxation . . . ? Do the people of our land fight only to win the war and have it over—or to use the war for great and democratic ends?" I. F. Stone commented in response, "The immediate outlook for progressivism is dark."[7]

In the end, the fears proved more prescient than the hopes. For World War II did not, in the end, do very much to promote the expansive aims of American liberals; indeed, it did much to derail those aims. It was not, as so many anticipated in 1941, to be a "New Deal war." Even before Pearl Harbor, the growing conservative tide in national politics had greatly weakened the Roosevelt administration's ability to deal effectively with Congress. An increasing popular weariness with the New Deal expressed itself in growing Republican and conservative strength in congressional elections, a shift in strength that began in 1938 and continued, largely unabated, through the whole of the war. The enormous reservoir of goodwill toward liberal initiatives that the 1936 election seemed to have demonstrated looked very shallow by 1942.[8]

But the war did more than create external obstacles to liberal goals. It also encouraged liberals themselves to reconsider their positions, to adjust to the sobering political realities of the 1940s and to the new ideological world the conflict created. By the end of the war, the liberal world looked very different from the diverse, even chaotic, battleground of ideas that had characterized the New Deal through most of the 1930s. On issues of political economy, at least, something resembling a consensus had begun to emerge behind a new kind of liberalism: a liberalism less inclined to challenge corporate behavior than some of the reform ideas of the 1930s had done, a liberalism more reconciled to the existing structure of the economy, and a liberalism strongly committed to the use of more "compensatory" tools—a combination of Keynesian fiscal measures and enhanced welfare-state mechanisms—in the struggle to ensure prosperity.

The politics of the 1940s would be very different from those of the 1930s. But it was not just conservative opposition that caused those changes. Liberals caused them too.

.   .   .

THE DETERIORATION of congressional and public support for the New Deal had been apparent even before war began in Europe. In the 1938 elections, Democrats lost 70 seats in the House of Representatives and 7 in the Senate; and while they retained substantial majorities in both chambers (a margin of 44 in the Senate and 97 in the House), many of the Democrats who remained were southern conservatives who often voted with the Republicans. In 1940, a presidential election year in which Franklin Roosevelt decisively defeated Wendell Willkie, the party might normally have expected to make substantial gains. It realized virtually none. Democrats picked up only 7 seats in the House, and lost another 3 in the Senate. And in the next mid-term elections, in 1942, the party experienced something close to disaster. Democrats lost 50 seats in the House (reducing to 10 a majority that six years earlier had stood at 242) and another 8 seats in the Senate (lowering their majority to 21 from the 60 they had enjoyed after the 1936 election). "That the Administration has completely lost control over Congress in the November elections is becoming clearer every day," a British diplomat reported to London early in 1943. "The Republicans will of course have working control of Congress," the journalist Eliot Janeway wrote after the election. "On every issue enough anti-Roosevelt Democrats will be with them to enable Congress to boss the Administration at the point of a gun. . . . The balance of [Roosevelt's] term is going to be an obstacle race."9

Things did not turn out to be quite as dire as Janeway predicted. On most matters directly related to the war, Roosevelt remained in control—either by intimidating Congress or by circumventing the legislative branch entirely and using war powers of sometimes dubious constitutionality. On domestic issues, however, the balance of power was clearly shifting. The extent of the change had been evident as early as 1939, when the administration proposed a $3.06 billion program of loans and expenditures on public works, known as the Works Financing Bill. It was to be, in effect, a continuation and expansion of the 1938 spending program Roosevelt had introduced and Congress had approved as an antidote to that year's recession. The new Congress revolted. A coalition of Republicans and southern Democrats first eviscerated the bill in the Senate and then killed it altogether in the House. The defeat shocked and humiliated liberals in the administration and in Congress. Senator Claude Pepper, stunned by what he considered the viciousness of the opposition, spoke for many when he said, "I am unwilling to let this session of the Congress end without lifting my voice to decry the unrighteous partnership of those who have been willing to scuttle the American government and the American people . . . because they hate Roosevelt and what Roosevelt stands for." The opposition wanted Roosevelt to fail, Pepper charged, so they might "give the government of this Nation back to those who have always been the champions of special privilege." The distinguished newspaper editor William Allen White wrote (prematurely) of the "curious ending" of Roosevelt's presidency and argued that he was no longer "a great leader of the Democratic party but a crippled leader of the liberal faction of the Democratic party."[10]

The assault continued over the next several years. Conservatives in Congress worked to frustrate what remained of the President's domestic agenda and even to dismantle earlier achievements. By the end of 1943, Congress had eliminated the Civilian Conservation Corps, the Works Progress Administration, the National Youth Administration, the Home Owners' Loan Corporation, and other New Deal programs of relief and public assistance. They had abolished the National Resources Planning Board, overturned the President's efforts to limit wartime salaries to $25,000 a year, passed legislation restricting labor's right to strike and contribute to political campaigns, and reduced funding for the Office of Price Administration and the Office of War Information, war agencies they considered centers of liberal sentiment. Indeed, Congress seemed to many liberals to have launched a frenzy of indiscriminate budget-cutting, determined, as one New England Republican put it, to "win the war from the New Deal."[11]

In the meantime, the new House Special Committee to Investigate Un-American Activities, chaired by Democrat Martin Dies of Texas, was launching a series of investigations of liberals and reformers in an effort to discredit the New Deal by tying it to radicals and communists. (In 1945, Congress reconstituted it as the House Un-American Activities Committee, better known as HUAC.) Dies spoke of a "gigantic bureaucracy" populated with "hundreds of left-wingers and radicals who do not believe in our system of private enterprise," and who were intent on seizing control of the nation. In an augury of postwar political battles, he charged that there were "not less than two thousand outright Communists and Party-liners still holding jobs in the government in Washington," among them Frances Perkins, Harold Ickes, and Harry Hopkins. Citing the Smith Act of 1940, which made it a crime to advocate the violent overthrow of the government, Dies and his allies in Congress tried to force the dismissal of dozens of federal employees on the basis of unsupported charges of subversion. Strenuous efforts by Democratic leaders in the House thwarted this drive; but the campaign by conservatives to link liberalism with communism—which became devastatingly effective in the late 1940s and early 1950s—was already becoming a factor in national politics.[12]

The administration and its liberal allies had expected strained relations with Congress, especially after the Democratic losses in 1942. But many were astonished by the intensity and bitterness of the opposition. Vice President Henry Wallace spoke in 1943 of "powerful groups who hope to take advantage of the President's concentration on the war effort to destroy everything he has accomplished on the domestic front over the last ten years." James F. Byrnes, a former senator who had been at best moderately supportive of the New Deal in the 1930s, confided to Felix Frankfurter early in 1943 (by which time Byrnes was working in the White House) that he had been watching the performance of Congress with dismay. As Frankfurter recorded the conversation in his diary, Byrnes "never had such a sense of intellectual bankruptcy. He said there was not one thought or idea or bit of illumination in the whole outfit, and the only thing they talked about was that they were committed to abolishing 'bureaucracy.' " The poet Archibald MacLeish, an official in the Office of War Information, told a gathering of politicians and journalists honoring Freda Kirchwey, editor of the *Nation*, early in 1944, "Liberals meet in Washington these days, if they can endure to meet at all, to discuss the tragic outlook for all liberal proposals, the collapse of all liberal leadership, and the inevitable defeat of all liberal aims. It is no longer feared, it is assumed, that the country is headed back to normalcy, that Harding is just around the corner."[13]

The erosion of congressional support for liberal measures did not, of course, occur in a vacuum. It reflected a broad growing popular impatience with the New Deal—and with the taxes, deficits, and expansion of bureaucracy that many voters associated with it. Even many people who continued to admire and support President Roosevelt expressed weariness with some of the liberal causes for which he had long fought, particularly once the wartime economic boom made some of them seem superfluous. Opinion polls recorded rising opposition to New Deal relief agencies and support for their abolition; deepening hostility to the conduct (although not the fact) of labor unions and their leaders, and increasing sentiment for laws to forbid strikes; growing resentment of government regulation and support for the prerogatives of business. Virtually nowhere on the political landscape were there vigorous grassroots movements of the sort so common in the mid-1930s, movements such as those led by (among many others) Upton Sinclair, Floyd Olson, Milo Reno, Robert La Follette, and Huey Long, movements attacking concentrated wealth and corporate power and demanding increased social protections for ordinary people. The most energetic forces of popular dissidence during the war were, instead, various groups on the right expressing their hostility toward both communists and liberals, and often equating them with one another. In the South, in particular, increasing white anxiety about challenges to segregation—and the growing (if premature) suspicion that the national Democratic party was becoming closely tied to the interests of African Americans—hardened what had been as early as 1938 a significant degree of hostility to many New Deal measures that many white southerners had initially supported. At the same time, popular impatience with the war itself, and with the often clumsy and shambling performance of the government agencies charged with running it, also served to erode support for the administration and its goals. The conservative tide ran considerably stronger in Congress than it did in the population as a whole. But the intransigence of the conservative coalition in Washington rested, nevertheless, on a substantial and increasing popular disaffection with many aspects of the New Deal.

NEW DEALERS RECOGNIZED that the rising power of congressional and popular conservatism was a substantial obstacle to their hopes. But they believed that some prospects for liberal action remained. As a result, they were almost as disturbed about the behavior of the Roosevelt administration in the early 1940s as they were about the behavior of Congress. They watched with dismay as the President made increasing (and, many liberals thought, unnecessary) concessions to conservative forces in the name of the war effort and as he proved consistently unwilling to defend the dwindling band of liberals in important policy positions in the administration. Roosevelt, more than Congress, was responsible for the pervasive sense among liberals that the New Deal was in something close to full retreat.

Roosevelt still talked bravely, even inspirationally, at times about the need to sustain the liberal agenda. "I would ask no one to defend a democracy which in turn would not defend everyone in the nation against want and privation," he told a radio audience in December 1940. "The strength of this nation shall not be diluted by the failure of the government to protect the economic well-being of its citizens." A few weeks later, in his State of the Union address to Congress, he spoke for the first time of the Four Freedoms ("freedom of speech and expression," "freedom of every person to worship God in his own way," "freedom from want," and "freedom from fear"), which should, he insisted, be as much a part of the nation's war aims as a military victory. He gave particular attention to the third of these, "freedom from want," and outlined an ambitious "Economic Bill of Rights" that his liberal admirers considered a ringing endorsement of some of their most ambitious goals.

Two years later, in his 1943 State of the Union address, he renewed his promise to make the war a struggle not just for victory but also for social progress. "I have been told that this is no time to speak of a better America after the war," he said. "I dissent. And if the security of the individual citizen, or the family, should become a subject of national debate, the country knows where I stand." In 1944, again, he made a ringing commitment to "a second Bill of Rights under which a new basis of security and prosperity can be established for all."[15]

In the end, however, these bold proclamations proved to be no more than isolated rhetorical gestures, unmatched by serious wartime efforts by the President to sustain his domestic agenda. As early as 1940, Roosevelt was privately conceding that, as Thomas Corcoran confided to Harold Ickes, "he has probably gone as far as he can on domestic questions . . . that someone else would have to mop up after him." Time and again over the next several years, he deflected ambitious and even modest liberal proposals by insisting that "we must start winning the war . . . before we do much general planning for the future." Observers as intimate as his own wife lamented at times that Roosevelt had "put the running of the war ahead of everything else," that (as a British diplomat observed) "for some time he has regarded and treated domestic politics as a mere nuisance." His celebrated statement to reporters in December 1943 that "Dr. New Deal" had been succeeded by "Dr. Win-the-War" was simply a belated public acknowledgment of an already well-advanced abandonment of the liberal agenda.[16]

Roosevelt's apparent loss of interest in domestic issues was alarming to liberals because he had been so central to their hopes for nearly a decade. But it was alarming, too, because no new liberal leader seemed in sight. Liberals were alternately angry and depressed, charging at times that (as Harold Ickes put it) Roosevelt was "abandoning advanced New Deal ground with a vengeance" and noting plaintively at other moments that "we still do not know for certain whether Mr. Roosevelt is fighting for negative or positive ends." But while some warned that liberals had made a mistake in depending "too much on the Great Leader, counting on him to do everything," most agreed that they had no choice but to rely on him still as the last barrier, however frail, against the tides of reaction they sensed rising around them. Leon Henderson, for one, despite growing strains in his own relationship with the President, continued to look to him for progressive leadership as late as 1945. When Henderson visited Roosevelt a few weeks before the President's death, he was frankly "scared" by the obvious signs of physical decline, not just because of his personal affection for Roosevelt but also out of fear that without him the hopes of liberals might be lost. "I had a horrible vision that he might grow weaker and weaker," he later recalled, "that his enemies would trample him underfoot as they did Woodrow Wilson." America, he feared, was "in for a lot of trouble from FDR's decline in energy."[17]

Nothing suggested Roosevelt's declining commitment to his domestic agenda more clearly than the fate of the leading liberals in his administration. Virtually none of them moved into important positions in the war bureaucracies; many of them lost their positions in the civilian agencies in which they had been serving. By the end of 1943, the liberal diaspora was nearly complete. Almost no real "New Dealers" remained. "The big danger here," I. F. Stone warned early in 1943, "is not so much what Congress may do to the New Deal but what the New Deal is doing to itself." Up and down the ranks of the administration, he claimed,

New Deal agencies are quietly beginning to commit hara kiri as progressive instruments of government . . . bringing in conservatives and getting rid of progressives . . . in order to shelter themselves against Congressional inquiry, denunciation, or budget curtailment. . . . One observes a subtle but unmistakable shift of power within the agencies from progressive subordinates to those that are middle-of-the-road or reactionary.[18]

The list of liberal casualties in the first years of the war was a long one. Corcoran resigned his position in the RFC in 1940 to help lead the campaign for Roosevelt's third term. He hoped for appointment as solicitor general after the election, but instead found himself with no position at all. He entered private law practice and had almost no further contact with the President. Ben Cohen remained in the government through most of the war, but in positions increasingly remote from the liberal agenda he had pursued through the 1930s. When Roosevelt refused to name him general counsel to the State Department in 1944, he too resigned. Thurman Arnold's departure from the Antitrust Division in 1943 largely completed the exodus of liberals from the Justice Department, leaving Attorney General Francis Biddle isolated and without great influence. Harry Hopkins remained one of Roosevelt's principal confidants, but after 1940 he was wholly preoccupied with international issues and paid virtually no attention at all to the liberal causes he had once helped promote. Harold Ickes continued as secretary of the interior and took on various additional responsibilities during the war, but he complained constantly of his increasing isolation. "It looks to me," he moaned, "as if the President were throwing away everything that we have gained during the past seven years." Henry Morgenthau's Treasury Department, a half-hearted bastion of liberalism in the best of times, found itself consistently outflanked by corporate figures in the war agencies. Harold Smith, who had used his position as budget director to push liberal fiscal programs, noted in his diary that most of the liberals he spoke to in the administration now considered themselves "pretty much in the doghouse." After hearing their stories, he confessed, "I could not help feeling like a pup myself." Leon Henderson recorded a darker conversation with Smith in his diary: Smith, he wrote, feared things were "passing into control of conservatives and reactionaries—trend toward fascist state."[19]

HENDERSON HIMSELF was one of the few important New Dealers to head a major war agency: the Office of Price Administration (OPA). As a result, his unceremonious departure from government late in 1942 seemed to many liberals a metaphor for what had happened to them generally.

Henderson was one of the most admired and accomplished liberals of the late 1930s, an intellectual and even social leader of the "New Dealers." Born in 1895 to a middle-class New Jersey family, he attended Swarthmore College, taught briefly at the Wharton School of Business and the Carnegie Institute (despite his lack of any advanced degrees), and worked for a time in Pennsylvania state government before becoming a researcher with the Russell Sage Foundation. He entered the administration in 1934 as an adviser to Hugh Johnson, director of the National Recovery Administration, on consumer affairs. That had been an area of special interest to Henderson in the 1920s and an issue on which he had been sharply critical of the NRA. Through the rest of the 1930s, he was an outspoken advocate of increased government regulation of monopoly (so as to end "administered prices" and to lower consumer costs) and of increased federal spending (so as to create consumer demand and stimulate economic growth). He worked on Roosevelt's 1936 re-election campaign. After serving as executive secretary of the TNEC, he became a commissioner of the Securities and Exchange Commission in 1939. Two years later, in April 1941, Roosevelt named him director of the OPA.[20]

Henderson was already controversial. Always disheveled in appearance (his clothes perpetually flecked with ashes from the six or seven cigars he smoked each day), chronically overweight, he had the air of the slightly distracted university teacher he once had been. He also had a famous temper, and he made few efforts to disguise his contempt for those he considered less intelligent than himself, a group that included (among many others) virtually the entire United States Congress. "His impact on Washington has been not unlike that of last year's hurricane on New England," the *New Republic* commented in 1939, "except that the Henderson hurricane, after descending on Washington, has never passed."[21]

But Henderson's problems were less ones of appearance and personality than of ideology. He believed strongly in the regulatory powers of government. He believed that disinterested public administrators like himself should have the authority to direct economic activity. And he believed that politics (congressional and otherwise) should not be allowed to intrude on his important work. His tenure as OPA director exposed the political costs of those views.

The OPA may have been the most intrusive federal bureaucracy ever created in America. It regulated wages and prices in an effort to prevent inflation, and it rationed an increasing number of goods—gasoline, oil, rubber, meat, sugar, and many other items—as the war progressed. Its decisions affected virtually everyone in the United States, shaping patterns of consumption and everyday life in fundamental ways. Henderson exercised this authority efficiently and effectively, but unapologetically. He refused to allow members of Congress to dictate the appointment of OPA officials in their states or districts; the agency, he insisted, "is going to run on non-partisan lines." He was often contemptuous of the complaints of businessmen and producers, convinced that protecting the interests of the consumer was his chief responsibility.[22]

Criticism of the OPA was probably inevitable, whoever its director. Business leaders resented price controls on principle, particularly at a moment when rising consumer demand was giving them their first opportunities for big profits since the 1920s. Conservatives in Congress and the war agencies feared that OPA policies were an opening wedge for increased state control of economic activity in peacetime. Many consumers were annoyed, even outraged, by what they considered inequities and inefficiencies in the administration of rationing. The OPA became, in short, a target for all the frustrations and disappointments of people unaccustomed to regimentation and control. It was, in effect, a jarring reversal of the New Deal of the 1930s: government acting now not to distribute largesse but to restrict access to goods and services. It reminded much of the public that state power could be used not only to assist but to deny. Henderson, one of the most militant and outspoken of New Deal liberals, was running the agency—and running it with an undiplomatic bluntness that at times seemed designed to antagonize his critics. As a result, the attacks upon it, and him, grew especially ferocious. The historian Bruce Catton, who was working in the war agencies in 1942, later wrote of Henderson that he was "the undying reminder that the New Deal was dangerous and hateful."[23]

By the middle of 1942, the effort to "get Henderson" had become something close to an obsession among conservative critics of the New Deal. He was denounced so frequently on the floor of Congress that an unknowing observer might have assumed he was the principal figure in government. More dangerously, conservatives were trimming the OPA's budget, threatening its ability to perform its enormous tasks. Eventually Henderson—pugnacious and difficult to intimidate as he was—became exhausted by the relentlessness of the attacks, particularly in combination with the pain he was suffering from a bad back and strain on his weak eyes. In December 1942, he resigned. "My physical troubles threatened my ability to override political opposition," he later explained, and "it seemed to me a fresh administrator was needed, particularly to get Congressional approval of an adequate budget for OPA."[24]

The "loss of Leon Henderson," as I. F. Stone described it, resonated through liberal circles, a symbol of their declining fortunes. "If there was one group in Washington that was militant and forceful, it was the OPA," the political writer Michael Straight wrote a few days after Henderson's resignation. "If there was one high-ranking leader in government who was right on policy all the way through it was Leon Henderson. . . . He must be brought back." Henderson's departure, Stone lamented, "is part of the general movement away from liberalism. . . . [His] resignation marks the second phase of the New Deal retreat, as the alliance with big business in May, 1940, marked the first." Henderson himself did nothing in retirement to allay the fears his departure from government had raised. "As a rank and file member of the liberal faith," he told a New York audience in June 1943,

> I share with many others the uneasy feeling that liberalism is in temporary eclipse, that many of its leaders seem to have abdicated, and that too many of us have deferred and postponed the vigor of action which has distinguished our faith in recent years. . . . Our work is suffering from a manpower shortage, while our opponents are falling all over themselves in their efforts to strike a disabled liberalism.[25]

A FEW MONTHS LATER, a controversy erupted that seemed, as one liberal writer noted, "perhaps the last straw in the retreat of the New

Deal." On July 15, 1943, the President intervened in a long-simmering dispute between his vice president, Henry A. Wallace, and his secretary of commerce, Jesse H. Jones, and relieved them both of the responsibilities that had produced the controversy. The ostensibly even-handed decision outraged many of Roosevelt's liberal supporters. Wallace was one of the most luminous liberals remaining in the administration, and Jones (in the view of many New Dealers) one of the most notorious conservatives. That the President failed to side with Wallace appeared to confirm the growing distance between him and his most progressive supporters.[26]

The Wallace-Jones controversy was, at its core, a turf battle. Wallace was chairing the Board of Economic Warfare (BEW), which was charged with purchasing critical materials overseas for the war effort. Jones was the Federal Loan Administrator; he was, in effect, the banker from whom Wallace had to secure the funds for his purchases. Wallace assumed he would have something close to a blank check for what he and his aides considered their vital war work. Jones expected to exercise a banker's close supervision of the activities his agencies were funding. Both were major political figures and proud men, so conflicts may have been inevitable. But the personal and ideological differences between them gave those conflicts an especially nasty edge and helped them spiral out of control until Roosevelt, exasperated, wanted nothing more than to wash his hands of the whole affair.

Of all the major figures in the New Deal, only Harold Ickes rivaled Henry Wallace in the reverence he inspired among liberals.[27] Wallace had been a crusading agrarian reformer in Iowa (and editor of a progressive farmers' newspaper) when Roosevelt named him secretary of agriculture in 1933. For the next eight years, he presided over the transformation of federal agricultural policy, assisted by one of the most talented (and liberal) staffs of any department in Washington. The farm policies Wallace's Agriculture Department administered failed to reverse the trend toward corporate control of agriculture, and indeed, if in part inadvertently, did much to advance that trend. But the gap between his record as agriculture secretary and his own earlier commitments did little to dim his luster among New Deal liberals—or his own self-image as a committed progressive reformer.

By the late 1930s, Wallace's interests were expanding beyond traditional agricultural concerns—to the plight of the rural poor, to the unionization struggles of industrial workers, and to the goal of using fiscal policy to expand mass purchasing power and promote economic growth. He became, too, a firm supporter of the moderate internationalism the

Roosevelt administration was gradually embracing. As conservative forces intensified their assaults on the New Deal, Wallace spoke forcefully in its defense. In 1940, Roosevelt decided that he was the ideal choice to succeed John Nance Garner (with whom the President had long been at odds) as vice president; and he stood up against formidable opposition from Democratic conservatives to push Wallace's nomination through a reluctant party convention.[28]

Wallace was in some ways ill equipped for this sudden transfer from the familiar and relatively insular world of agrarian politics into the center of national affairs. He had never run for public office. And however skilled he may have been in maneuvering through the thickets of farm politics, he seemed at times curiously naïve about the larger arena he had now entered. As vice president, of course, he had no statutory authority. But he apparently believed that his position and his relationship with the President entitled him to considerable influence within the bureaucracy. He believed as well that he could (and should) use that influence to promote the same liberal causes he had championed in the 1930s.

His appointment as director of the BEW seemed to confirm his own assumption (and that of many others) that he would be a figure of considerable influence within the administration. Although he delegated much of the work of the agency to his energetic deputy, Milo Perkins, Wallace stood squarely behind the BEW's policies and thrust himself fervently into the center of its public disputes. Early in 1942, Martin Dies, the reactionary chairman of the Special House Committee to Investigate Un-American Activities, launched a typically grotesque attack on the BEW for what he claimed were its ties to the Communist party (and for a 1931 article by one BEW employee, Maurice Parmelee, celebrating nudism). Wallace responded by likening Dies to Goebbels and declared that "the effect on our morale would be less damaging if Mr. Dies were on the Hitler payroll."[29]

Wallace and Perkins together envisioned the BEW as more than simply a purchasing agent for critical materials. It was, they claimed, one of the principal mechanisms for reshaping the postwar world. It operated on the assumption that "plans for the war and plans for the peace are inseparable . . . that the shape of the postwar world will be determined by our present actions." More specifically, they wanted to use the leverage their funds gave them to promote progressive reforms in the nations with which they were doing business—for example, to promote liberal labor policies or combat cartels in Latin American nations. The BEW at times made reforms a condition of their contracts, and at other moments used the threat of termination to pressure a commercial partner into making changes. "The economic highways we have pioneered in war will still be there [in peace]," the Office of Facts and Figures boasted on behalf of the BEW early in 1942. "If we have pioneered well, the blows struck in economic warfare will be blows struck for our future freedom and prosperity, and the freedom and prosperity of all friendly nations, large and small, everywhere." The BEW's effectiveness in forcing social and economic reforms in less developed countries was hard to measure, but probably limited. Its commitment to trying, however, was highly public and even more highly controversial.[30]

In all this, Wallace found himself in the uncomfortable position of having to work intimately with Jesse Jones, a man with whom he could hardly have had less in common. Jones was a Texas banker whose long and unabashed promotion of federal investment in the Southwest had helped win him a position on the Reconstruction Finance Corporation at its founding in 1932. A year later, Roosevelt named him its director, a post he held until 1939, when he assumed the new and more powerful position of Federal Loan Administrator, from which he directed not only the RFC but several federal housing agencies and the Export-Import Bank; a year later, he became secretary of commerce as well.[31] He had direct control over more federal money than did anyone else in government; and he guarded his prerogatives fiercely and jealously, securing his power with a cautious, conservative approach to lending that greatly pleased Republicans and conservative Democrats in Congress. He was also an assiduous flatterer of the President, showering him with expensive gifts and lavish praise (even while quietly deploring and even obstructing much of what Roosevelt tried to do). Like Wallace, he had spent most of his public career as an administrator, not a politician. But unlike Wallace, he had honed his political skills carefully and effectively.[32]

Wallace and Perkins considered Jones a reactionary obstacle to their work, and hence to the successful prosecution of the war. He was, they charged, slow to release funds and slow to make the purchases they asked him to make. "We are helpless," Wallace once complained, "when Jesse Jones, as our banker, refuses to sign checks in accordance with our directives." Over time, they became convinced that Jones was deliberately obstructing their mission because of ideological distaste for their objectives or petty bureaucratic jealousy.[33] Perkins, in particular, came to detest Jones and his combative deputy, Will Clayton. His intemperate comments about them before congressional committees and in the press greatly inflamed the dispute.[34]

Jones and Clayton would likely have resented the BEW whatever it did. They considered it an invasion of their own bureaucratic territory, an agency charged with doing things their own agencies were already doing much more effectively. Jones never failed to point out evidence of inefficiency and incompetence in the work of the BEW. He spoke scornfully of its liberal agenda and charged that the efforts to use the agency to effect social changes abroad was reckless and fiscally irresponsible. "During its brief but bustling life," Jones wrote in his memoirs,

> the [BEW] puffed its personnel to nearly three thousand men and women, scores of whom traveled all over the world at the government's expense having the time of their lives, trying to duplicate work already being efficiently done by RFC's wartime subsidiaries.... For a full year before Mr. Wallace came on the preparedness scene, the RFC and its subsidiaries had been doing the work that the BEW was set up to duplicate.[35]

When Wallace or Perkins criticized the RFC's actions, Jones and Clayton responded in kind. By early 1943, the dispute had become so public and so rancorous that even the President could not subdue it, much as he tried to do so.[36]

Early in July 1943, as part of an increasingly desperate effort to win budgetary autonomy for the BEW, Wallace and Perkins sent several angry statements to the Senate Appropriations Committee attacking Jones for "harmful misrepresentation" of the record of the BEW and for "stalling" and "obstructionist tactics." Jones promptly and publicly labeled these charges "full of malice and misstatements." Attacks and counterattacks escalated further over the next week as Wallace and Jones exchanged acrimonious public letters. James Byrnes, now the President's principal domestic aide, tried to mediate. He even arranged a "peace conference" between the two men in the White House, to no avail. Jones refused to shake hands with Wallace; Wallace leveled new attacks at Jones. Byrnes, fearing that Jones might physically attack the vice president, cut the meeting short. Finally, on July 15, the President sent identical letters to both men informing them that the dispute had made it necessary "to transfer these matters to other hands." He abolished the BEW and replaced it with a new agency, the Office of Economic Warfare (OEW), under Leo T. Crowley. Jones was relieved as Federal Loan Administrator.[37]

The controversy greatly damaged the position of both men. Jones believed at first that the appointment of Crowley, a friend and former associate, to head OEW would permit him to continue controlling overseas purchases. But Crowley proved just as determined as Wallace to win autonomy for his agency, and considerably more successful. He soon won presidential backing for the measure Wallace and Perkins had so strenuously and futilely promoted: complete financial independence for the BEW. Over the next few months, Jones found himself stripped of more and more of his authority. Early in 1945, he unhappily left government altogether.[38]

For Wallace, the cost was probably much higher. He remained vice president, of course, so the loss of his BEW directorship was in itself a relatively small one. But the ugliness of the public dispute, and the anger it produced among conservative Democrats loyal to Jones, almost certainly contributed to the already strong opposition to Wallace's renomination in 1944. The vice president continued to speak vigorously in support of liberal causes. "The New Deal is not dead," he assured liberals in a Jackson Day speech early in 1944. "The New Deal has yet to attain its full strength. . . . The doorway to [freedom from want] is blocked by the deliberate misrepresentation of the paid hirelings of the special interests." Roosevelt remained nominally loyal to Wallace to the end and publicly endorsed him as the Democratic convention began. But while in 1940 the President had been willing to fight off conservative opposition and force the delegates to support his choice, in 1944 he had neither the political strength nor the personal energy to do so. Wallace lost the vice presidency to Harry Truman, and with it his chance to become president. It was gratifying to him and some of his supporters that a few months later Roosevelt agreed to dismiss Jesse Jones as secretary of commerce and appoint Wallace to the post in his place; but that was a small victory next to a towering defeat.[39]

To the larger liberal community, the denouement of the controversy was profoundly depressing—a last, seemingly irrefutable confirmation of their reduced standing with the President and the administration. "The President's action in the case of the Jones-Wallace dispute is the most severe shock to his liberal followers since he has been in office," the *New Republic* lamented. "Until last week, there were only two government agencies left in Washington in which New Deal ways of thinking prevailed, or New Dealers had any important part—the BEW and the Federal Communications Commission. Now there is only one." The struggle between Jones and Wallace, the *Nation* claimed, was part of the struggle "between the most conservative group in the government and the group which is trying to use the federal machinery to hasten the winning of the war even at the expense of the guaranties and safeguards which big business has generally tried to exact as the price of cooperation." By jettisoning Wallace, Roosevelt had bowed to the reactionaries.[40] Those liberals who remained in the administration, already embattled, considered Wallace's removal a personal threat. Some of those outside government who had long assumed (if with ebbing faith) that Roosevelt remained committed to their cause now talked openly of supporting another candidate (perhaps even Wendell Willkie or another liberal Republican) in 1944. The White House mail room was deluged with letters protesting his treatment of one of the few remaining liberal heroes, calling it "a hard blow for liberals," an "appeasement of reactionaries," a "stab in the back." But it was a sign of the changing political climate that the President received almost as many letters—equally impassioned—supporting Jones.[41]

THE POLITICAL ATMOSPHERE of the war years discouraged American liberals. It also forced them to reassess their positions. If the public, the Congress, even the President, were less reliably committed to New Deal measures than had once seemed to be the case, it would be necessary to find new approaches to the nation's problems that had some possibility of success. Pragmatic liberals began searching, therefore, for new and more politically palatable ideas.

But adjustments in liberal thinking were not simply grudging responses to domestic political reality. They were also responses to the greatest and most destructive war in human history and to the social and political horrors the war revealed. Quite apart from what was happening in the United States, the conflict in Europe and the Pacific shaped the way liberals envisioned the future of their nation. In particular, it shaped their sense of the possible uses of the state.

No one giving serious thought to the nature and role of government could remain unaffected by the character of the regimes the United States and its allies were fighting in World War II. As early as the mid-1930s, a revulsion from and fear of the totalitarian states of Europe—Hitler's Germany, Mussolini's Italy, Stalin's Soviet Union—had begun to penetrate the thinking of many liberals and intellectuals just as it had penetrated the thinking of most others. The war itself greatly increased that revulsion and fear. Perhaps inevitably, it prompted some liberals to reconsider their own commitment to an activist managerial state. Statism, they began to believe, could produce tyranny and oppression. However serious the structural problems of the capitalist economy, a statist cure might be worse than the disease.

The idea of dictatorship had never been popular in American society, least of all among those who considered themselves liberals. But opposition to dictatorship had not always been as widespread or intense as it had become by the beginning of World War II. In the 1920s and the first years of the 1930s, there was at times cautious admiration in America for some of the autocratic regimes in Europe that seemed to be handling their economic problems so successfully. There was particular interest in, even praise for, the presumed successes of Mussolini in reviving the Italian economy and restoring order and efficiency to society. Although there were resolutely anti-fascist voices in America (among them the *Nation* magazine) that sharply denounced the European dictators consistently and from the start, there were also respected voices, including some liberal voices, that expressed a certain qualified approval for a time. The social scientist Horace Kallen, for example, wrote in 1927 that "the fascist revolution . . . should have the freest opportunity once it has made a start of demonstrating whether it be an exploitation of men by special interests or a fruitful endeavor after the good life." The prominent progressive editor Herbert Croly wrote the same year that "whatever the dangers of fascism, it has at any rate substituted movement for stagnation, purposive behavior for drifting, and visions of great future for collective pettiness and discouragement."[42]

The rise of Hitler in 1932 helped launch a broad reassessment of fascism and dictatorship among those who had cautiously admired it in the 1920s; and the increasing brutality and racism of the Nazi regime over the next several years hastened that process. So did the Italian invasion of Ethiopia in 1935, the Spanish Civil War, which began in 1936, and the rising visibility of eminent Jewish émigrés from Germany throughout the decade. By the time war began in 1939, the once vaguely tolerant view of dictatorship had given way to a broad hostility. The war itself greatly increased the intensity of that hostility. By the early 1940s, Americans were not only denouncing autocracy as the greatest threat to democracy and peace. They were defining their own nation increasingly as the antithesis of dictatorship (and linking dictatorship to the new and more ominous concept of "totalitarianism"). They were defending their own government to themselves and to others as a nation admirable above all for *not* being a totalitarian state.

As a result, the fear of dictatorship and totalitarianism began to affect popular thinking about government in virtually every area of American life. Conservative opponents of the New Deal strengthened their case by placing the example of Europe at the center of their critique. Corporate foes of economic planning almost invariably invoked the example of Nazi Germany in their attacks on liberal policies. Even progressive business leaders generally sympathetic to the New Deal became outspoken in their warnings. David Sarnoff, the president of RCA, said in a 1943 speech:

If we have learned anything from the history of the past ten years,
we have learned how empty were the claims of those demagogues
who wheedled away the freedoms of their people with the mirage
of an all-powerful state that would provide security at the expense
of liberty.[43]

The publication of two books, one early and one late in the war, helped
galvanize the concerns that were beginning to emerge among intellectuals
(and many others) about the implications of totalitarianism.

One was James Burnham's *The Managerial Revolution*, which appeared in 1941. Burnham had been an active socialist in the 1930s, a
follower of Leon Trotsky, and a sometime supporter of the New Deal.
His 1941 book came at a time in which he, like many leftists, was reas-
sessing his political stance. In Burnham's case, the reassessment marked
the beginning of a journey that would eventually lead him into the
thick of right-wing politics. *The Managerial Revolution*, however, received wide (and largely favorable) critical attention, even from many
liberals.[44]

The thrust of the book, Burnham claimed, was purely descriptive. He
wished to show the ways in which societies dominated by large-scale
organizations experienced a radical transformation of power relationships; he did not propose to pass judgment on that transformation. But
there was a powerful implicit message in his argument, which became
particularly clear in his discussion of the general problem of preserving
individual liberties in "managerial" societies.

The greatest threat to liberty, he argued, lay in the concentration of
excessive power in any one organization; and the greatest threat of such
concentration came from the state. The large institutions of private capitalism presented certain perils to be sure, but their power remained
limited by the dispersion of economic strength among many different
industries and firms, by the inability of the corporate world to unite, and
by the existence of "relatively autonomous social forces" that constantly
challenged (and checked) corporate hegemony. Only the state had the
capacity to concentrate total authority within a single organization. Burnham himself did not explicitly reject the idea of a powerful federal
government; indeed, in some passages he seemed to argue for its virtual
inevitability, even its desirability. Nevertheless, the picture he drew of
the possible effects of the "managerial state" were remarkably (and probably intentionally) chilling.

"Those nations—Russia, Germany, and Italy—which have advanced
furthest toward the managerial social structure," he wrote,

are all of them, at present, *totalitarian* dictatorships. Though there have been many dictatorships in the past, none of them, in a complex culture at any rate, has been so extreme in form as totalitarianism. . . . It should be noted that a totalitarian type of dictatorship would not have been possible in any age previous to our own.

Totalitarianism was not only possible, he suggested, but difficult to avoid in a nation that chose to embark on the dangerous course of state management of the economy. "In managerial society," he insisted, "politics and economics are directly interfused; the state does not recognize its capitalist limits; the economic arena is also the arena of the state."[45]

Although it might be possible for some form of democracy to survive in a managerial society, it would not, Burnham insisted, be a form that most Americans would recognize. There would be no room for a real parliamentary system, no room for the checks and balances produced by opposing economic groups. "The economic structure of managerial society seems to raise obstacles to democracy," he warned:

All major parts of the economy will be planned and controlled by the single integrated set of institutions which will be the managerial state. There would seem, then, to be no independent economic foundation for genuine opposition political groups.[46]

Burnham (who said of himself in 1941 that, since his break with Trotsky, "I have had no politics") claimed not to find anything inherently bad in the transformations he chronicled and predicted. "I do not see with what meaning the human situation as a whole can be called tragic, or comic," he concluded. "There is no background against which to judge the human situation as a whole. It is merely what happens to be." Yet for all his supposed objectivity, for all the reservations and qualifications that suffused the book, Burnham's message was a stark one: The rise of the managerial state was fraught with peril. "This much is clear," he wrote. "The democracy of capitalist society is on the way out, is, in fact, just about gone, and will not come back."[47]

Friedrich A. Hayek's *The Road to Serfdom*, published in 1944, was far more controversial—and influential. Even more than Burnham, Hayek forced into public discourse the question of the compatibility of democracy and statism. And unlike Burnham, he made no pretense of neutrality about the phenomena he described.

Hayek was a distinguished Austrian economist who had emigrated to England in 1931. (He later moved to the United States and settled at the

University of Chicago.) With the memory of totalitarian oppression in central Europe always in mind, he devoted himself to refurbishing the tattered reputation of the anti-statist, classical liberalism of the nineteenth century. He became (along with such others as the American economist Milton Friedman and the English philosopher Michael Oakeshott) an important voice on behalf of some form of libertarianism in modern society. He was a consistent critic from 1930 on of the ideas of Keynes; and he expressed constant doubts about the ability of humans to understand their world well enough to be able to direct or plan its economic life.[48] As early as the mid-1930s, increasingly horrified by the growing popularity of "collectivism" in Britain and America, he began contemplating an "essay" attacking the liberalism of his own time in the name of the truer liberalism he believed he represented. "I wish I could make my 'progressive' friends . . . understand that democracy is possible only under capitalism and that collectivist experiments lead inevitably to fascism of one sort or another," he wrote his friend Walter Lippmann in 1937. "There are now many economists who begin to see the value of the old liberalism."[49]

The essay Hayek was considering in 1937 became *The Road to Serfdom*. He wrote it in London during the Nazi blitz, and it is perhaps not surprising, therefore, that it had a superheated polemical tone. As Hayek readily conceded, it was not a work of scholarship. It was a "political book," a call to arms—a warning, directed at a general readership, of the dangers confronting the West. Somewhat implausibly, it became a major best seller, a *Reader's Digest* condensed book, and a Book-of-the-Month Club selection.[50]

In it, Hayek portrayed the rise of the economic power of the state as an unambiguous disaster, a dangerous threat to human freedom. The development of totalitarianism in Germany and Russia (the reduction of the citizenry of both nations to "serfdom") was proof, he maintained, of the incompatibility of the modern managerial state with personal liberty. But it was not only in central Europe that statism had created great dangers. Britain and America, too, had begun to abandon their fundamental commitment to human freedom in search of an elusive rationalization of their economies. They too had embarked on the road to serfdom. "It is necessary now," he wrote in his impassioned introduction, "to state the unpalatable truth that it is Germany whose fate we are in some danger of repeating."[51]

In Germany, he reminded his readers, the rise of statism had been accompanied by complacent assurances that government could increase its economic power without increasing its infringements on personal liberty. The Nazi and Soviet experiences, Hayek claimed, illustrated the impossibility of maintaining that balance. "Economic control," he wrote, "is not merely control of a sector of human life which can be separated from the rest; it is the control of the means of all our ends." And given that connection, the most dangerous form of economic control was statism. "We have seen before how the separation of economic and political aims is an essential guaranty of individual freedom," he wrote, "and how it is consequently attacked by all collectivists." The greatest threat to human liberty, therefore, was the abandonment of that separation, an abandonment that many American liberals glibly supported.

> What is called economic power, while it can be an instrument of coercion, is, in the hands of private individuals, never exclusive or complete power, never power over the whole life of a person. But centralized as an instrument of political power it creates a degree of dependence scarcely distinguishable from slavery.[52]

Hayek's hostility to the New Deal was longstanding and well known, so the sentiments he expressed in *The Road to Serfdom* came as no surprise to readers familiar with his earlier work. He was, moreover, attacking what was to some degree a straw man, ideas about "planning" and "socialism" that few New Dealers had ever endorsed. "Hayek identifies planning with a basic national policy favoring central governmental control of productive output and distribution," one critic charged, complaining of "loose use of the term planning."[53] Many liberals tried to dismiss the book as a hysterical polemic. Alvin Hansen, for example, wrote of *The Road to Serfdom*: "This kind of writing is not scholarship. It is seeing hobgoblins under every bed." The *New Republic* attacked the "curious and archaic fallacy" that "every effort at the control of corporate power is a step on 'the road to serfdom.' "[54]

But given the book's extraordinary reception, and the totalitarian horrors it so powerfully evoked, few could dismiss it altogether. In fact, running through liberal criticism of the book was a strongly defensive tone, an effort to assure a suspicious world that New Dealers, too, were concerned about the dangers of statism. "These apprehensions, expressed within reason, will be helpful in preserving democracy," the liberal theologian Reinhold Niebuhr wrote in an otherwise critical assessment; "for a too powerful state is dangerous to our liberties, even when its avowed purpose is the achievement of more equal justice." Stuart Chase, in a spirited defense of planning, nevertheless conceded that Hayek had offered a "useful warning . . . which every planner should paste under the glass top of his desk." The essence of the warning, he added, "is this: If citizens surrender all responsibility for economic action to a centralized government, as in Germany and Russia, citizens will lose their civil liberties, their freedom to choose jobs and goods. For Americans this would indeed be a kind of serfdom." Other critics were similarly tentative, describing the book as "an arresting call to all well-intentioned planners and socialists, to all those who are sincere democrats and liberals at heart, to stop, look and listen"; or as "a banner for those who believe that the state needs constant watching if it is not to be a tyrant." Even Hansen, in his scathing review, felt obliged to concede something to Hayek's attacks. "We need now as always to be on guard. We face serious dangers ahead. . . . And as a goad to fresh self-examination it may well be that Hayek's 'Road to Serfdom' is . . . 'good medicine but a bad diet.' "[55]

Burnham and, especially, Hayek were influential not because they had stated any new or original ideas. They affected liberal thought because they had articulated concerns that were already familiar, and deeply rooted in American history. For all the efforts of New Dealers in the 1930s to celebrate and legitimize the new functions they were creating for the state, a broad suspicion of centralized bureaucratic power—rooted in traditions of republicanism and populism stretching back to the earliest years of the American polity—remained a staple of popular discourse and a constant impediment to many liberal aims. The most powerful challenges to the New Deal in the 1930s had come not from capitalists decrying their lost prerogatives, but from middle-class (and even, at times, working-class) men and women in communities throughout the United States fearful that the growing federal bureaucracy would limit their freedom and autonomy. The most controversial government agency during the war was the Office of Price Administration, which infringed on personal liberty more directly than any other. The most evocative rationale for wartime sacrifice was that Americans were fighting for personal and economic freedom, that they were opposing not just enemies of the nation but threats to liberty. In responding to Burnham and Hayek, and to the broader discussion of totalitarianism that was permeating virtually all political discourse in the 1940s, liberals were in fact responding to a powerful strain of Jeffersonian anti-statism in American political culture that a decade of the New Deal had done relatively little to eliminate.[56]

The result was a subtle but important shift in liberal thinking. Although they might accuse conservatives of overreaction and misrepresentation, liberals, too, saw a warning in the examples of Germany, Italy, and the Soviet Union. The fear of autocracy that conservatives and libertarians had long expressed was now penetrating liberal political consciousness as well and eroding (or at least helping to alter) their commitment to an active managerial state. "The rise of totalitarianism," Reinhold Niebuhr noted somberly,

> has prompted the democratic world to view all collectivist answers to our social problems with increased apprehension. Since there are no forms of the socialization of property which do not contain some peril of compounding economic and political power, a wise community will walk warily and test the effect of each new adventure before further adventures.[57]

"Walking warily" was, in fact, already the norm for most liberals by 1945. Some tried to argue that the German and Soviet examples were not the only examples of centralized state power, that Britain, Sweden, Holland, and other "benignly collectivist" societies offered alternative models; that even the United States, with its emerging "mixed economy," was proof that individual liberty and state involvement in the economy could coexist.[58] Still, few liberals could remain unaffected by an environment in which the specter of totalitarianism was a staple of public discourse and private thought. One example was a hortatory tract, *The City of Man*, published in 1940 by a group of liberal intellectuals and academics who called themselves the "Committee on Europe" and who claimed to be championing the "American dream" as an alternative to the totalitarian ideologies of Germany and Italy. In the midst of a bombastic appeal for liberal internationalism, they also expressed (in a tortured language characteristic of most of the document) fears of excessive state power at home. "It is universality that we oppose to totalitarianism," they proclaimed, "republican unity to autarchic despotism, service in brotherhood to regimentation in serfdom." In that light, the early record of the New Deal, which most of them had supported and which many of them still largely admired, took on certain new and ominous implications. "The pluralistic system of the American Commonwealth," the best alternative to the tyrannies of Europe, had, they argued, not only been "prevented so far from reaching a complete expression"; it had even been "visibly weakened in this last decade by the extension of federal power."[59]

Some liberals began to present even their most ambitious proposals as antidotes to totalitarianism. Jerry Voorhis, a liberal congressman from California, introduced a resolution to Congress in 1941 calling for the establishment of a national unemployment commission. His justification rested less on the economic or humanitarian purposes such a commission might serve than on the part it would play in "the contest between the

democratic and autocratic systems of government, both seeking fundamentally to win the allegiance of the peoples of the world." Forceful
action to combat unemployment would refute "the only possible justification which proponents of an autocratic system can advance ... a charge
that democracy cannot successfully cope with the economic problems of
the power age."[60]

Such linkages were, on one level, simply political tactics; but they
were tactics that had subtle effects on what liberals were willing to
support. Justifying reform measures as a way to avoid autocracy created
pressures to avoid proposals that seemed too overtly statist. Vying with
one another in their denunciations of the tyrannies of Europe made
liberals newly sensitive to charges of statist tyranny at home. "How much
freedom," Freda Kirchwey asked in the Nation, "can survive the degree
of collective control necessary to keep the industrial machine going?"
Marriner Eccles wrote the President: "We must devise means for directing voluntary efforts into the necessary channels and limiting the intrusion
of the state, through controls and participation, to the minimum necessary." Max Lerner cited the link between state planning and German
militarism: "Germany's war preparation began crucially with Hitler's first
step in reorganizing the German economy on the basis of planning. The
really dangerous German propaganda is Hitler's propaganda by deed, his
demonstration that planning can raise the national income by inhuman
methods and for inhuman ends." And Lewis Corey, a writer for the
Nation, stated bluntly what many advocates of centralized economic
planning were beginning to fear:

> Denunciations of Stalinism are not enough. Nor is it enough to say
> that a socialist economy must operate under democratic conditions.
> We cannot thus easily dispose of the disturbing conclusion that
> collective ownership is compatible with totalitarianism.[61]

Several years after the end of the war, Adolf Berle—once one of
Roosevelt's most influential advisers and long an advocate of increased
government controls on corporate power—suggested something of how
profound and lasting the impact of totalitarianism had been on the liberal
view of the state. He said in a lecture at the University of Pennsylvania:

> ... if fear of the giant corporation exists, apprehension of the
> leviathan state is surely no less. A generation which has watched the
> extreme of police-state organization in Soviet Russia and its equally
> frightening off-shoot ... , the Nazi and Fascist organizations in

Germany and Italy, is not likely to underestimate the possibility that an overmastering state likewise can become a tyrant.[62]

The challenge, then, was to define a role for the state in the management of the economy that would prevent the dislocations of unregulated capitalism without creating the tyranny of fascism or communism. In dealing with that challenge, those liberals who continued to support planning, regulation, associationalism, and other methods spoke in increasingly defensive terms. Charles Merriam, an important champion of national planning, decried the arguments of "those who contend . . . that no substantial advance can be made toward the readjustment of our internal social problems unless all is planned in totalitarian style." The planning he and other liberals advocated, he claimed, "is not autocracy, totalitarianism, or violence, but is intelligent cooperation." Marion Hedges, in a 1943 defense of planning as "the one chance left for humanity in a robot world," insisted repeatedly that his notion of planning had nothing to do with the Nazi version. "The state," he said, "must constantly strive to divest itself of its own power." John Chamberlain wrote in the *New Republic* of the difference between "democratic" planning and that of Germany and the Soviet Union:

> Western planners . . . have developed a technique . . . of limited, or partial, planning. This technique does not require totalitarian control of the means of production, for it begins by research and ends in the consulting chamber, with all claims—the claims of management, the claims of labor, the claims of ownership—represented in a final compromise. The planners are not the bosses nor are they rubber-stamps for the bosses; they merely act as advisers.

Waldo Frank, a disillusioned socialist, concluded more darkly that "regimentation is upon us. . . . Only the principle of human freedom, positing a strongly knit community of mature persons, can modulate collectivism away from its natural result—some form of fascism."[63]

If the "natural result" of collectivism was "some form of fascism," as many liberals (and even some socialists) now began to fear, what was the alternative to the unregulated capitalism of the past, which had visited such disasters upon the nation? To an increasing number of liberals, the need to answer that question strengthened what was already their growing inclination: to turn away from the dangerous effort to control production and focus instead on sustaining and increasing consumption. As Leon Henderson explained:

National contribution to purchasing power may take two forms, a contribution to production or a contribution to consumption. National intervention to stimulate production is the method of the totalitarian state, Russian, Italian and German. . . . National intervention to stimulate consumption is the democratic method, since purchasing power freely in the hands of consumers must be won by competition.[64]

Similar comments could be found in many defenses of proposals for of consumption-oriented policies to promote full employment after the war. Henry Wallace spoke in 1943 of "the need to demonstrate that the consuming power of the people can be made to equal their productive power" and warned that if America failed in that effort "Prussian or Marxian doctrine will take us over." James Patton of the National Farmers Union and James Loeb, director of the newly formed Union for Democratic Action, wrote in defense of full-employment programs in 1945, insisting that "we must banish the banshee of 'inevitable' boom-and-bust, feast or famine." But they were careful to differentiate their proposals from producer-centered regulatory measures. "This could be done in various ways," they claimed, "some of which are obviously statism in its worst form and would ultimately mean fascism. Others [including their own plan for stimulating consumption] are compatible with and will promote the essentials of genuine democracy and opportunity."[65]

In the shadow of a war that virtually everyone considered a struggle between freedom and tyranny, the feature of American society to which liberals now found themselves most attracted was individual liberty. Few, of course, had ever opposed liberty; but many in the 1930s had balanced it against other values that they had considered equally important: economic justice, equality, efficiency. Now, with concern for personal freedom taking on new urgency, other, competing goals began to seem less crucial, and the statist economic reforms many liberals had once supported began to seem more threatening. The result was not a sudden or decisive ideological shift, but a slow adjustment of beliefs—a gradual movement away from the celebration of the state that had marked liberal thinking in the late 1930s, an ebbing of commitment to the "religion of government" that Thurman Arnold had once invoked. The specter of totalitarianism helped direct American liberals toward a revised vision of the postwar state.

THIS STRENGTHENED concern for personal freedom in the face of the totalitarian menace led, in turn, to another major change in the character of American liberalism, although one that did not become fully visible until after the war. The intensified commitment to democratic rights, and the effort to define America as the antithesis of its autocratic foes, helped lay the groundwork for one of the central preoccupations of postwar liberals: the struggle for racial justice.

In the 1930s, the New Deal had responded intermittently and usually timidly to the demands of African Americans for equality. There were a few mid-level black officials within the Roosevelt administration, among them Robert C. Weaver, Alfred Edgar Smith, William H. Hastie, and Mary McLeod Bethune. They formed an informal network known as the "Black Cabinet," and through it they worked—with occasional success— on behalf of policies they believed would benefit others of their race. They received substantial public support at times from more prominent figures, most notably Harold Ickes and Eleanor Roosevelt. And they achieved some significant symbolic triumphs. But the New Deal as a whole never made race an important part of its agenda. And the larger liberal community rarely devoted more than passing attention to racial problems in the 1930s.[66]

The reasons for this apparent indifference lay in some of the core assumptions of the "reform" liberalism that had shaped the New Deal from the beginning. Progressives of the early twentieth century had devoted considerable attention to racial and ethnic issues and stressed the importance of somehow overcoming cultural divisions through "assimilation" and "Americanization." But beginning shortly after World War I—particularly after the frenzy of racial hatred the nation experienced in 1919—many liberals began to recoil from a direct engagement with race. As the philosopher John Dewey somewhat complacently observed in 1918, "Not only have we separated the church from the state, but we have separated language, cultural traditions, all that is called race, from the state—that is from problems of political organization and power."

The ugly cultural politics of the 1920s (as symbolized by the rise of the second Ku Klux Klan and the passage of immigration restriction legislation) and the near self-destruction of the Democratic party in 1924 (largely because of battles over racial and cultural issues) only reinforced the inclination to seek a non-racial basis for liberalism. Roosevelt himself, drawing from his own political experiences in the 1920s, had a strong aversion to the kind of divisive regional and cultural issues he believed had crippled the Democratic party in those years. Linking the party to controversial racial demands, he feared, would cripple it again in the 1930s, and destroy his own coalition in the process.

Instead of defining social problems in terms of race, ethnicity, and culture, therefore, liberals increasingly chose to present public issues almost entirely in terms of economics and class. Most liberals detested racial prejudice, to be sure; but pursuing the politics of race, they believed, risked unleashing the kind of mass irrationality they believed they had seen in 1919 and the mid-1920s. The best hope for aiding oppressed minorities was economic reform. By attacking problems on a class basis, by defining people in economic rather than cultural terms, liberalism might hope to alleviate the material problems of African Americans without having to confront prejudice openly.

Hence, even the relatively few New Dealers actively concerned with the condition of African Americans approached racial problems in predominantly economic terms. The obstacles facing blacks were, they argued, simply an exaggerated version of the obstacles facing many whites—and subject to the same solutions. The irrationality of racial prejudice, they believed, would ultimately wither away if blacks and other minorities achieved real economic gains. The most important New Deal contribution to black Americans, therefore, was its creation of relief and welfare programs. Few such programs made special provisions for blacks, and some permitted substantial discrimination against them. But the New Deal did give significant economic assistance to many African Americans, and Roosevelt received overwhelming support from black voters in return.[67]

Immediate political realities also strengthened that tendency within the New Deal. Not without reason, the President believed that any direct assault on discrimination and segregation would alienate powerful Southerners in Congress and loyal Democratic voters in the South. That was why, for example, he was never willing to support legislation before Congress to make lynching a federal crime, despite his private sympathy for the measure. The anti-lynching bill was an important cause for the NAACP and other black leaders; but it was anathema to many white Southerners, who (whatever their feelings about lynching itself) considered the proposed law a challenge to states' rights and a first step toward a federal assault on white supremacy. "I did not choose the tools with which I must work," the President told Walter White, secretary of the NAACP, in 1934, in response to White's request that he intercede more forcefully on behalf of anti-lynching legislation.

> Had I been permitted to choose them I would have selected quite
> different ones. But I've got to get legislation passed by Congress to
> save America. Southerners, by reason of the seniority rule in Congress, are chairmen or occupy strategic places on most of the Senate
> and House committees. If I come out for the anti-lynching bill now,

they will block every bill I ask Congress to pass to keep America from collapsing. I just can't take that risk.[68]

On the surface, at least, relatively little in the behavior of white liberals (or of the Roosevelt administration) changed during the war. The President established a Fair Employment Practices Commission in 1940 to enhance black employment opportunities in war industries. But he did so largely to prevent the march on Washington that A. Philip Randolph, president of the Brotherhood of Sleeping Car Porters, was threatening to stage, not out of any broader commitment to confronting the racial problem. Officially sanctioned discrimination continued throughout the war in the military and in many areas of the federal government. There were few significant efforts to raise racial issues to a prominent place on the liberal agenda.[69]

And yet the war was a critical moment, nevertheless, in the movement of liberals toward a commitment to racial justice. The most important reason for that change in the 1940s, as in subsequent decades, was the increasing assertiveness of African Americans themselves, their growing power within the Democratic party, and their effort to associate their struggle with the basic issues in the world conflict. "To win a cheap military victory over the Axis," the black journalist Horace Cayton wrote in 1943,

> and then continue the exploitation of subject peoples within the British Empire and the subordination of Negroes in the United States is to set the stage for the next world war—probably a war of color. . . . Somehow, through some mechanism, there must be achieved in America and in the world a moral order which will include the American Negro and all other oppressed peoples. The present war must be considered as one phase of a larger struggle to achieve this new moral order.[70]

But another important reason was the new centrality of the notion of liberty and "rights" among white liberals as they sought to identify what best differentiated their society and its political ideas from the totalitarian regimes the United States was fighting. Liberals were slow at first to apply this enhanced conception of rights to the American racial dilemma, although the pages of liberal journals and the private correspondence of liberal activists in the first years of the war reveal a small but significant increase in attention to the subject. But a series of race riots in the summer of 1943, the largest in Detroit, helped inspire some significant liberal soul-searching. "It is time," the *Nation* wrote, "for us to clear our minds and hearts of the contradictions that are rotting our moral position and undermining our purpose. We cannot fight fascism at home while turning a blind eye to fascism at home. We cannot inscribe on our banners: For democracy and a caste system."[71]

By late 1943, race was becoming ever more visible in discussions of the liberal mission after the war. It was racial hatred, many Americans now argued, that had caused "the greatest storm in all history" in the first place. "Unless civilized man awakens from the baleful delusion that there are by nature master races, and slave races," Alvin Johnson, a former editor of the *New Republic*, warned, there would be "greater storms" in the future. "At the very moment when America is proving one of the leaders of the world in the crusade for democracy," Otelia Cromwell wrote in *The American Scholar*, "thirteen million American citizens are deprived of the democracy for which the sons of America—including many of that thirteen million—have gove forth to war. . . . What the Negro desires seems to him the spirit actuating the effort of the Allied Nations."[72]

Out of this growing awareness of the nation's racial burdens emerged, haltingly and incompletely, a revised liberal definition of society. Perhaps the problems of the modern world were not purely economic, many liberals began to consider. Perhaps class was not the only, or even the best, concept with which to analyze social problems. Perhaps race, ethnicity, religion, and culture—the divisive, "irrational" issues from which liberals had taken pains to distance themselves in the past—were, in fact, essential to understanding America after all. "One of the greatest problems of democratic civilization," Reinhold Niebuhr wrote in 1944, "is how to integrate the life of its various subordinate ethnic, religious and economic groups in the community in such a way that the richness and harmony of the whole community will be enhanced and not destroyed by them." Deriding the smug liberal confidence of an earlier time that had anticipated a "frictionless harmony of ethnic groups" and the capacity of economic progress alone to achieve "their eventual assimilation in one racial unity," Niebuhr called on "democratic society" to use "every stratagem of education and every resource of religion" to fight the influence of racial bigotry—a bigotry that would not wither away simply as a result of material prosperity.[73]

And then, early in 1944, an explosive event helped galvanize this growing but still inchoate political and intellectual debate: the publication of Gunnar Myrdal's *An American Dilemma*. The book was a major factor in drawing white liberal attention to problems of race—precisely because Myrdal himself discussed racial injustice as a rebuke to the nation's increasingly vocal claim to be the defender of democracy and personal freedom in a world menaced by totalitarianism.

Myrdal was an eminent Swedish sociologist whom the Carnegie Foundation commissioned in the late 1930s to supervise a major examination of the problem of race in the United States. After collaborating with dozens of scholars and writers and accumulating a massive body of research, he wrote the book itself during the war. His acute awareness of the dangers of fascism (and his particular concern about its impact on his native Sweden, which maintained a precarious neutrality throughout the war) helped shape his approach to his subject. The "American dilemma," Myrdal argued, was not simply an economic problem. It was a moral one—a problem of the tension between the reality of racial oppression in the South and the deep American faith in human rights and personal liberty (what he called the "American creed"). It was a problem in the hearts and minds of white Americans, a problem born of the impossible attempt to reconcile a commitment to freedom and democracy with the effort to deny one group of citizens a set of basic rights guaranteed to everyone else. In the shadow of Nazi tyranny, such a contradiction seemed to Myrdal—and to many readers of his book—especially glaring, as he made clear in his powerful concluding chapter:

> The three great wars of this country have been fought for the ideals of liberty and equality to which the nation was pledged. . . . Now America is again in a life-and-death struggle for liberty and equality, and the American Negro is again watching for signs of what war and victory will mean in terms of opportunity and rights for him in his native land. To the white American, too, the Negro problem has taken on a significance greater than it has ever had since the Civil War. . . . The world conflict and America's exposed position as the defender of the democratic faith is thus accelerating an ideological process which was well under way.

That process, of course, was an assault on the "caste system" that preserved racial inequality and injustice.[74]

Reaction to *An American Dilemma* was stunning, and its reputation (and the reputation of its author) grew steadily over the next several years. That Myrdal was a European and an eminent scholar; that his findings were couched in the presumably "objective" language of social science; that a respected, non-partisan foundation had sponsored the project and that a large number of prominent academics had collaborated on it; that the book was nearly fifteen hundred pages long, with over five hundred pages of footnotes lending it an unmistakable aura of scholarly authority: all helped make it seem almost unassailable, a "study to end all studies," something close to a definitive analysis of the problem.

Robert Lynd called it "the most penetrating and important book on our contemporary American civilization that has been written." The African-American novelist J. Saunders Redding, reviewing the book in the *New Republic*, declared that Myrdal's book would end the "stalemate" in race relations and force Americans to acknowledge the moral character of the problem. The war—"this time of momentous redefinition and change"—had, he argued, raised the stakes. "Either the American creed must prevail and the world sustain its hope in democracy, or the American deed must prevail and the faith in human goodness be destroyed." There were dissenters, to be sure, not all of them defenders of white supremacy: white liberals, who feared the consequences of the direct assaults on the caste system Myrdal proposed; Marxists, who continued to see racial problems as secondary to the class struggle; and others. But the praise for the book all but drowned out the dissenters.[75]

The Myrdal study was not the only thing, perhaps not even the most important thing, moving awareness of racial injustice into the center of liberal orthodoxy. Its remarkable impact did, however, both reveal and accelerate that movement.

The war, in short, was a significant moment in the shift of American liberalism from a preoccupation with "reform" (with a set of essentially class-based issues centered around confronting the problem of monopoly and economic disorder) and toward a preoccupation with "rights" (a commitment to the liberties and entitlements of individuals and thus to the liberation of oppressed people and groups). "Rights-based" liberalism was in some respects part of a retreat from a broad range of economic issues that had been important to progressives and New Dealers for decades: issues involving the structure of the industrial economy and the distribution of wealth and power within it. But it also opened the way to an enormous host of new commitments that would emerge after the war and that relatively few progressives or New Dealers had ever seriously contemplated before. Above all, it led to the postwar identification of liberalism with the effort to secure civil rights for African Americans and, later, many other groups—and to the many triumphs and travails that identification would ultimately produce.

THE SPECTER of totalitarianism was encouraging liberals to reassess their earlier faith in a managerial state.[76] The intensifying defense of democracy was encouraging them to think less about issues of class and economic power and more about issues of racial and cultural injustice. But such shifts in focus would have been unlikely had liberals not begun to sense an imminent resolution of the economic crisis that had dominated American public life for the previous decade. In the end, the most important effect of the war on liberal thought may have been the way it suggested just such a resolution.

In the last years of the Great Depression, many liberals had reached the pessimistic conclusion that stagnation had become the normal condition of modern industrial economies; that America, having reached "economic maturity," would need to be managed since it could no longer be expected to grow. But World War II, quickly and decisively, destroyed the economic-maturity thesis and, with it, much of the rationale for a highly planned and regulated economy. Between 1940 and 1944, the United States experienced the greatest expansion of industrial production in its history and an increase of more than 50 percent in gross national product. The massive unemployment of the 1930s gave way to virtually full employment and increasing mass consumption. After a decade of depression, a decade of declining confidence in capitalism and despair about the prospects for future growth, the American economy restored itself and, perhaps more important for the future of national politics, redeemed itself in a single stroke.[77]

The wartime economic experience—the booming expansion, the virtual end of unemployment, the creation of new industries, new "frontiers"—served as a rebuke to the "mature economy" idea and restored the concept of growth to the center of liberal hopes. The capitalist economy, liberals suddenly discovered, was not irretrievably stagnant. Economic expansion could achieve, in fact had achieved, dimensions beyond the wildest dreams of the 1930s.

Assaults on the concept of the "mature economy" and "secular stagnation" were emerging as early as 1940, and gathered force throughout the war. Alvin Hansen, who had long been one of the principal theorists of secular stagnation, himself repudiated the idea in 1941 ("All of us had our sights too low," he admitted). The *New Republic* and the *Nation*, both of which had embraced the idea in 1938 and 1939, openly rejected it in the 1940s—not only rejected it but celebrated its demise. The country had achieved a "break," exulted the *Nation*, "from the defeatist thinking that held us in economic thralldom through the thirties, when it was assumed that we could not afford full employment or full production in this country. The war has shown the absurdity of this contention."[78]

In addition to the renewed faith in capitalism that liberals developed in these years, they also acquired a greater willingness to trust capitalists themselves: a growing, if usually tentative, belief in the competence and integrity of the corporate world and its leaders. Suspicion of the business community had been an important (if never universal) part of New Deal liberalism during much of the 1930s and during decades of progressivism earlier—a hostility deepened by the 1937 recession and the widespread belief that it had been the result of a "capital strike." Such sentiments diminished (although they never entirely disappeared) during the war. In their place arose a belief that many leaders of private enterprise could, in fact, at once protect their own economic interests and serve the nation responsibly and effectively, with only limited government interference.

This new respect for the business community remained grudging and incomplete. New Dealers and other liberals observing wartime mobilization efforts complained frequently about the predominance of representatives of big business in the most important positions and worried that this penetration of the administration by the corporate world would mean an abandonment of hopes for domestic reform.[79] But increasingly as the war dragged on, liberals made distinctions: between reactionary businessmen determined to undermine liberal progress, on the one hand, and more enlightened businessmen, receptive to at least some of the New Deal's achievements, on the other. The presence of major industrialists at the center of the federal government, staffing the most important war agencies, filling crucial positions in the War, Navy, and State departments, often acting with what appeared to be unselfish commitment, helped dispel much of the reflexive suspicion with which liberals had in the past regarded them. The remarkable feats of wartime production, which provided the underpinnings of the Allied military victory (and the domestic economic recovery), further enhanced the reputation of the corporate world.[80]

The war, moreover, brought some New Deal liberals into close and constant contact with business leaders over a prolonged period of time, a wholly new and highly revealing experience for many on both sides. There were tensions and conflicts, to be sure; but the process of working together also helped create a sense of shared purpose in the face of a great national emergency and often led to a recognition of common values and assumptions. "As I leave Washington, I leave behind me in you a man whom I have learned to work with, to like and to respect," one business executive wrote to a New Deal official after the two had worked closely together for several years:

When I first came on the horizon, you quite naturally had grave doubts as to the length of my horns and on the other hand, I had many to warn me of pitfalls. We soon learned that we could deal together across the table. I soon learned that you were willing to work on the up and up with anyone who was working for the war effort. . . . You have worked with and cooperated with both of us in as fine a manner as any man in the world could do.[81]

Many New Dealers in turn came to revise their own views of the corporate world, to admit that businessmen too did not always have "horns," and to recognize that there were important potential allies for the new liberal agenda in some areas of the private sector. In particular, the war helped strengthen the bond between New Dealers and the group of financial and industrial leaders whom historians would later describe (usually pejoratively) as "corporate liberals." Some such businessmen had forged ties to the New Deal as early as 1933, through the Business Advisory Council of the Commerce Department. And there survived throughout the 1930s a significant core of financiers and industrialists committed to forging a workable relationship with the New Deal.[82]

The experience of the war—and the new set of liberal assumptions emerging from that experience—greatly strengthened that support. The accommodation with government that had been modestly attractive to some industrialists in the 1930s became far more appealing in the 1940s, as the focus of liberal economic policy turned away from overt regulation and reform and toward Keynesian and welfare state measures. The campaign for social security became more palatable once that campaign became linked to the maintenance of purchasing power. Even liberal labor policies became tolerable when higher wages could be seen as a contribution to the larger health of the economy. The Committee for Economic Development (CED), a businessmen's "planning" organization created in 1942 and closely tied to the Business Advisory Council, accepted and attempted to reinforce some of the central premises of the new liberalism of the 1940s. In particular, members of the CED were committed to the idea that the health of the postwar American (and world) economy as a whole was of more importance than the immediate market environments of particular sectors; and like the Keynesian liberals within the administration, they commissioned studies on full employment fiscal policies, on social insurance, and on new forms of labor-management accommodation. The CED became, in fact, one of the most important sources of the new economic thought, both during and after the war, and the bureaucratic home of such influential Keynesians as Beardsley Ruml and (later) Herbert Stein.[83]

Liberals within the government and those within the corporate world found, in short, substantial common ground: an interest in maintaining economic growth and a belief that liberal social policies could contribute to that task. They also discovered an increasing mutual respect, based on an adjustment of positions on both sides, that narrowed the gap between liberal aspirations and corporate interests. Henry Wallace, for example, spoke in 1944 of a breed of business leader "oftentimes more interested in increasing production, and thereby serving humanity, than in making money for money's sake. . . . Such men are in some ways the hope of America and the world." Charles Wilson, the president of General Electric and, in 1944, a major figure in the war production bureaucracy, won a broad reputation among liberals as an "industrial statesman" when he supported the liberal call for postwar full employment. "If only more business leaders would take this viewpoint," Chester Bowles wrote the President in 1944, "there would be very little question of our ability to come through the next few difficult years with a vigorous economy and a unified people." Roosevelt himself, although he complained often about the anti–New Deal businessmen who found their way into government, always insisted that "there are at least thirty-times-three men [from the business world] of equal ability who have believed in us in the past, who have said so, who are not ashamed of it, and who would give . . . just as good service!"[84]

"I begin to feel a new spirit rising in this country," Thurman Arnold wrote late in 1943:

> I believe that men like Henry Kaiser, whom I got to know very well in my efforts to prosecute the steel companies for preventing him from getting into production on the Pacific Coast, are going to get strong enough through this war so that they cannot be stopped. If they do, liberalism in this country is going to change.[85]

Liberalism was indeed changing in the war years, even if not in precisely the directions Arnold envisioned. Out of the inconclusive battles of the late 1930s was emerging a new liberalism—less statist than its earlier counterparts, less concerned with issues of class, less hostile to existing patterns of economic power, committed above all to a newer vision of a consumer-driven economy. Older, more producer-oriented reform ideas were still alive, and at times highly visible. But their purchase on liberal loyalties was rapidly declining—as became clear both in the way the state mobilized the economy for war and in the way the American labor movement adjusted to the new challenges and opportunities the conflict created for workers.

## Chapter Eight

# Mobilizing for War

THE HOPES AND FEARS liberals experienced as they girded for American entry into World War II were nowhere clearer than in their attitude toward economic mobilization. How the government orchestrated the great feats of production and distribution necessary for the war would, they assumed, have a decisive impact on the structure of the economy in peacetime. And for those who believed that structure should include a much greater role for the state, it seemed possible, at least for a time, to hope that wartime mobilization might advance their aims. "We have learned," Clifford Durr, chairman of the Federal Communications Commission, wrote in 1943, "that we cannot obtain the production we need for waging the war as an undirected by-product of what we commonly refer to as 'sound business principles.' Neither can we expect such by-product to furnish us after the war with the standard of living which we shall be warranted in expecting. . . . There must be some over-all source of direction more concerned with [these] objectives than with the profits or losses of individual business concerns."[1] Or as Herbert Emmerich, another New Deal official, wrote in 1941, "With a farewell to normalcy and an appreciation of the greater opportunities that the war crisis presents, public administrators today have an opportunity to enhance and permanently to establish the prestige of their calling in the United States."[2] But just as at other critical moments in the shaping of New Deal public policy—1933, 1935, 1938—these hopes for an enhanced state role in managing the economy took many different forms.

Anti-monopolists and advocates of increased state regulation and planning of the economy hoped the war would help legitimize an expansion of government's power to regulate corporate behavior.[3] But they also knew that war had the potential to be disastrous to their hopes—that control of the economy might move, as some believed it had during World War I, into the hands of self-interested businessmen, that all the reforms they had been struggling to introduce for the previous eight years might fall victim to the clamor for increased production.[4] And so, as plans for war mobilization began to take shape, some liberals prepared again to do battle with the forces of monopoly and reaction, to defend the autonomy of the state in regulating private enterprise.

To another group of New Dealers—those who believed in forging a partnership among business, labor, and government—there seemed more reason for optimism. The economic mobilization during World War I, after all, had helped legitimize a generation of efforts to create an "ordered economic world." It had inspired associational experiments throughout the 1920s and had served as a model to those who constructed the National Recovery Administration in 1933. It did not seem too much to hope that the new World War would do the same.

Ultimately, however, the economic mobilization of World War II proved satisfying to none of the liberal factions within the New Deal. That was not because government coordination of the economy failed. On the contrary, the wartime economy was a spectacular success. It produced virtually everything the Allied military forces needed while simultaneously meeting the basic requirements of American consumers. It created full employment for the first time in over a decade, and it launched a period of dramatic economic growth that would continue—with only brief and occasional interruptions—for nearly thirty years. It did what the New Deal, after eight years of trying, had never been able to do. It ended the Great Depression. And whatever role government agencies may or may not have played in producing these successes, they had at least as much right to claim credit for them as had the equivalent agencies of World War I.

Even so, in 1945 the war agencies emerged from four years of effort and achievement with nothing even remotely comparable to the standing and authority the war boards of World War I had enjoyed at the end of 1918. If they served as models at all, they were models of the perils of state management of the economy, not of its promise. Far from legitimizing an increased government role in the managing of investment and production, as some had hoped, the wartime mobilization added strength to the already growing inclination among many liberals to find a role for government that would allow it to manage the economy without managing the institutions of the economy.

To many anti-monopolists and regulators, this result was disappointing but not entirely surprising. But to the corporatists within the New Deal, the wartime experience was especially discouraging. For them, the story of how the government mobilized the American economy for war became, in the end, the story of how the dream of an "ordered economic world"—a dream that had occupied an important, if contested, place in liberal hopes for nearly three decades—all but expired. Corporatist economic arrangements survived World War II and in some areas of the economy even flourished. But formal corporatist institutions and ideas found no important place in the postwar state.

THE GOVERNMENT AGENCIES that managed the wartime economy in the 1940s were not notably different in most respects from those that had managed the economy during World War I—with a significant and ultimately decisive exception. Unlike the earlier war boards, the World War II organizations were never able to mask the bitter conflicts and rampant inefficiencies that accompanied their considerable achievements. To some liberals, the war agencies were repugnant because they were inequitable, because they ceded too much power to corporate interests or to the military, or because they favored big business over small. But even those who believed in some form of corporate self-government were dismayed by the image of chaos that constantly surrounded the agencies. The mobilization, they concluded, not only failed to achieve equity; it failed to achieve the efficiency and order that formed the basis of their hopes for it.

The bureaucratic chaos that surrounded the mobilization was in part a product of the confused, stumbling process by which the administration responded to the economic demands of the war from the start. In trying to formulate a plan for war production, Roosevelt faced a dilemma of his own making. On the one hand, he was determined not to cede control of the economy to private or quasi-private authorities, not to create an independent "super-manager" who would usurp what he considered his own legitimate powers. On the other hand, there existed no administrative mechanisms within the government capable of handling the enormous new tasks the war had imposed on it. The federal bureaucracy had expanded considerably in the 1930s, but very little of that growth had enhanced the state's capacity to administer industrial production. The civil service and the professional political community had little experience in supervising the behavior of corporations; even the NRA experiment, ambitious as it was, had relied largely on business leaders to manage their own relationships with one another. The one major effort to "modernize" the federal bureaucracy and equip it to perform more advanced managerial tasks—Roosevelt's executive reorganization plan of 1938—had ultimately produced only modest reforms. As a result, the President careened from one form of organization to another in a futile search for a mechanism that would fulfill his contradictory demands.

The search began in the summer of 1939, before the outbreak of war in Europe, when Assistant Secretary of War Louis Johnson persuaded Roosevelt to create a committee—known eventually as the War Resources Board (WRB)—to draft plans for full-scale economic mobilization. To Johnson, launching the WRB was an important skirmish in his bitter battle with his superior, Secretary of War Harry Woodring, a feckless isolationist whom Johnson despised and aspired to replace. To Roosevelt, however, it seemed a reasonably uncontroversial way of exploring scenarios that most of the public was as yet unwilling to contemplate. The beginning of war in Europe only a few weeks later added urgency to the task. By late September, the WRB had prepared its final report. The President read it, rejected it, and finally disbanded the board.[5]

The failure of the War Resources Board illustrated many of the problems that would bedevil mobilization efforts for the next six years. No sooner had Roosevelt approved the creation of the committee than battles began raging within the administration over who would control it. The President laid down few requirements for the WRB, but one of them was that Bernard Baruch, the director of the War Industries Board during World War I, should not be a member. As always, Roosevelt was guarding against the emergence of an alternative center of authority within the government; he feared that Baruch's stature—the product of years of efforts by Baruch and others to mythologize his achievements in 1918—would make the WRB's recommendations difficult to reject.[6]

But Louis Johnson, as maladroit as he was ambitious, proceeded to appoint several close allies of Baruch anyway—antagonizing Roosevelt and heightening the suspicions of many administration liberals, who already considered the WRB a gathering of "economic royalists" intent on undoing the New Deal. (Liberals were alarmed, too, that Edward Stettinius, the thirty-nine-year-old chairman of U.S. Steel, was named—at the President's request—to preside over the board.) There were complaints that the WRB excluded representatives of labor and agriculture, and that the economists it was consulting were too conservative.[7] There were also objections—from Adolf Berle and others hostile to the aims of the New Dealers—that the "Tommy boys" (Corcoran and his allies) were actively undermining the WRB. They were, Berle complained, "men ... as ruthless in their desire to get hold of and use power for personal ends as any group of spoilsmen or Tammany pols."[8]

But the WRB's fate was, in the end, less the result of this internecine feuding than of other factors. Among them was its name. The WRB submitted its report only days after the German invasion of Poland in September 1939 that marked the beginning of World War II. In those anxious early months of the conflict, an agency with "war" in its title was bound to become the target of angry attacks from isolationists both within Congress and outside it, and the WRB was on the defensive against such assaults throughout its brief existence. More damaging still was the substance of its own final report. The Board's mandate, Stettinius and Johnson believed, was to revise the now eight-year-old Industrial Mobilization Plan—a document originally prepared by the War Department in 1931 as a guide to "the effective and equitable utilization of the industrial resources of the United States in time of war." Roosevelt made clear from the start his distaste for the plan, which he believed ceded too much authority to the military and infringed on the President's prerogatives; but Johnson, characteristically, proceeded on his own course and made no effort to consult the White House along the way. As a result, the plan the WRB produced was no more acceptable to the President than the one he had already rejected. It made modest reductions in the amount of control the armed services would have over industrial mobilization, but it called for the creation of a powerful War Resources Administration, whose director would become (in the President's view, at least) an "economic czar" and whose members, the report proposed, "should be obtained from the patriotic business leaders of the Nation." As he looked over these proposals, Roosevelt complained angrily, "What do they think they are doing, setting up a second Government?" Still determined to keep control of mobilization in the White House, he thanked the members of the War Resources Board for their efforts, classified their report, and never mentioned it again. It did not become public until after the war was over.[9]

To much of the press (and to many New Dealers), the demise of the WRB represented a significant victory for the "liberals" in the administration and a serious setback for advocates of a rapprochement between government and business. The *Wall Street Journal*, for example, ran rueful headlines declaring: "Left Wingers on Top; Preparedness Will Be Handled on New Deal Lines."[10] But such conclusions were premature. For one thing, the collapse of the WRB coincided with Roosevelt's dramatic shakeup of the War and Navy departments. The discredited Woodring was fired as secretary of war, to be succeeded not by the striving Johnson (who also lost his post) but by Henry Stimson, a lifelong Republican, a corporate lawyer, and one of the great figures of the American establishment. The lightly regarded Charles Edison was eased out of the Navy Department, to be succeeded by Frank Knox, the powerful publisher of the Chicago *Daily News* and 1936 Republican vice-presidential candidate. By appointing men of such stature, Roosevelt strengthened the role of the War and Navy departments—the departments liberals most mistrusted—in planning for war mobilization. Naming two Republicans to the Cabinet also made clear Roosevelt's preference for a centrist, bipartisan approach to preparing for war—an approach that would, of necessity, limit the role of liberals.

For months after the WRB fiasco, the President did almost nothing about economic mobilization. Already faced with the difficult prospect of seeking an unprecedented third term, he was unwilling to compound his problems by seeming to move too quickly toward war in an election year. Events, however, soon forced his hand. In May 1940, Nazi Germany launched its devastating invasion of France and the Low Countries—the "blitzkrieg"—and quickly occupied most of western Europe. Britain, now standing virtually alone, removed Neville Chamberlain as prime minister and replaced him with Winston Churchill, who immediately stepped up demands for American munitions. They were, Churchill insisted, essential to Great Britain's survival. In an atmosphere of escalating crisis, pressures grew once again for some level of state management of industrial production, particularly since public support for aid to Britain was rapidly and dramatically increasing. In response, Roosevelt created two new agencies: the Office of Emergency Management (OEM), lodged in the White House, "to maintain coordination between the President and whatever defense agencies would be established"; and the National Defense Advisory Commission (NDAC), a committee of business leaders and government officials with vaguely defined powers to supervise production. It was to report directly to Roosevelt, and it would have no chairman. When William Knudsen, president of General Motors and a prominent member of the commission, asked who would be "the boss," Roosevelt replied, "I am."[11]

To anti-monopolists and regulators within the New Deal, the NDAC was as ominous as the WRB. The President, they came to believe, was ceding power to the corporate world and freezing out those within the government who had been struggling to expand the role of the state in managing the economy. Harold Ickes, writing in his diary of a lunch meeting in June of members of the "liberal crowd" (William O. Douglas, Thomas Corcoran, Benjamin Cohen, Archibald MacLeish, among others), noted that "All of us were very much worried. . . . I was of the opinion that whatever the purpose [of delegating so much authority to business leaders], the President would soon find himself in so deep that he would not be able to extricate himself. All of us realize that the whole New Deal accomplishment to date has been placed in grave jeopardy."[12]

In the end, however, the NDAC also failed—not because it displeased liberals, but because it was unable to satisfy the very people it had been designed to placate: business leaders and those who believed in creating a workable partnership between capital and the state. The commission stumbled along for several months, never able to resolve the problems of its own undefined authority and divided leadership (limitations imposed on it by the President), never able to create any effective order in the chaotic process of converting industry to war production. In January 1941, a little more than six months after creating the NDAC (and two months after winning reelection), Roosevelt abolished it.[13]

Authority now shifted to the new Office of Production Management (OPM), which had somewhat greater authority and a somewhat more centralized structure of command than the NDAC, but which still lacked what Baruch and others were demanding: a "single, responsible head." The OPM had two chairmen of ostensibly equal authority: Knudsen and Sidney Hillman, head of the CIO's Amalgamated Clothing Workers of America. And while the OPM's responsibilities and powers grew considerably during its year-long existence, it too very quickly disillusioned almost everyone. Liberals complained that it was Knudsen and other corporate leaders (many of them simply shifted over from the NDAC) who really controlled the organization, despite Hillman's theoretical authority, and that the agency was, in any case, incapable of standing up to the Army and Navy. Corporatists lamented the OPM's failure to reduce the continuing inefficiency and disorder of the industrial economy and kept up the call for a single leader.[14]

In August 1941, bowing to pressure from liberal critics, Roosevelt created a new agency, to operate in tandem with the OPM: the Supply Priorities and Allocations Board (SPAB). Donald Nelson, a Sears, Roebuck executive who had been director of purchasing in OPM, was named chairman of the new organization and later described its duties as "dividing the available supply of materials among material needs, defense aid needs, and the total civilian needs." Nelson had a reputation as a "New Deal businessman," and his elevation pleased many liberals who had been complaining for months about the dominance (and incompetence) of Knudsen and his "cronies." "It would seem," *Business Week* reported in September, "that, at last, the New Dealers had routed the business men from the management of the defense program." But so blurry were the lines dividing SPAB's authority from that of the OPM, and so intense were the bureaucratic rivalries that the overlapping agencies spawned, that even liberals soon found the new arrangement no more appealing than the old one.[15]

To Baruch, Berle, and others enamored of the World War I model of mobilization, the war agencies of 1939 through 1941—from the War Resources Board to the NDAC to OPM and SPAB—had one great, glaring deficiency: the absence of a strong central leader capable of bringing order out of the chaos of conversion. But creating a new Baruch (or restoring Baruch himself to his former preeminence) was precisely what Roosevelt was trying to avoid. To most liberals, who were no more enamored than Roosevelt of the prospect of creating a "second government" or an "economic czar," the problem was somewhat different. What the war economy most needed, they believed, was expanded plant capacity. But private industry was, on the whole, profoundly reluctant to invest in new plants; most businessmen had spent a decade saddled with the cost of excess capacity, and they feared any expansion now would become redundant as soon as the war was over. The only solution was forceful intervention by the government. The creation of SPAB, many liberals hoped (and some businessmen feared), was a step in the direction of more effective state planning of industrial investment and production; it placed advocates of plant expansion firmly in the saddle and shunted aside those (including Knudsen) whom liberals had come to consider obstacles to effective conversion. But it soon became apparent to everyone that, whatever the inclinations of its leaders, SPAB lacked the authority to solve the problem of inadequate war production.[16]

And so by late 1941, even before Pearl Harbor, the clamor for yet another reorganization of the mobilization effort was rising once again. When the Japanese attack came that December 7, the shock waves it sent through the leaders of government sped the creation of a new and presumably more powerful agency to eliminate the problems and inefficiencies created by the stumbling efforts of the previous two years.

ON JANUARY 13, 1942, little more than a month after the United States formally entered the war, Donald Nelson was presiding over a dreary meeting of the Supply Priorities and Allocations Board when he received a note instructing him to report to the White House. An hour later, as Nelson later described it in his sunny, generally unrevealing memoirs, he was sitting in the Oval Office listening with some puzzlement as Roosevelt described to him the changes he wanted to make in the machinery of war production. Foremost among them was the creation of a new agency to replace OPM and SPAB and the appointment of "one man" to direct the entire enterprise. Nelson recalled "sitting mute for more than an hour" as the President rambled on. "I felt a little embarrassed and thought I ought to do or say something. So I asked the President what he proposed to call the new agency. 'The War Production Administration?' I offered." No, the President replied. An agency with the initials WPA would be confused with (and perhaps carry the political baggage of) the

Works Progress Administration. He suggested "War Production Board" instead. Nelson agreed.

"I'm glad you approve," he remembered the President saying, "because you are the Chairman of the War Production Board." A news release announcing the appointment was going out over the wires before Nelson left the White House. (William Knudsen, co-chairman of the OPM, discovered that his agency, and his job, had been abolished when the news came over the teletype in his office. He reportedly went home and wept.) The next morning the "WPB," the most important, but not the last, production agency of the war, began its troubled life.[17]

At first, the creation of the new board generated almost universal enthusiasm. Critics of the OPM, which by January 1942 included almost everyone with an opinion on the subject, differed on many things; but virtually all of them agreed that what the war production bureaucracy needed above all else was a single, strong leader capable of taming the contending interests and vast bureaucracies that were hampering war production. Creating the WPB and appointing Nelson to head it seemed to do exactly that. "His powers over procurement and production are absolute," a *New York Times Magazine* article observed. "Every Federal department, establishment and agency must take orders from him." He had "authority greater than any U.S. citizen except the President himself has ever had," *Time* exclaimed, "greater even than that wielded by sage old Bernard Mannes Baruch" during World War I. "It is," said *Life*, "the biggest single job in the world today."[18]

The enthusiasm was a result in large part of the broad popularity of Nelson himself, who had now spent two years in the war-production bureaucracy and had managed, implausibly, to impress New Dealers and business leaders alike. Liberals considered him almost one of their own, willing to stand up to the "economic royalists" and assert the power of the state over the fractious private economy. Corporate executives judged him competent and trustworthy, a reliable buffer against the "radical" demands of New Deal reformers. The *New Republic* called him a "really able man." *Business Week* lauded his "knack for getting along with those around him and for getting teamwork out of them." Others praised his "almost inhuman control over his emotions," his "patience about almost anything except delay," his willingness to work "fifteen or sixteen hours a day, seven days a week," his "keen, driving intensity of purpose," even the "persistent twinkle in his eye." World War II, it seemed, had found its Baruch; and no one was more aware of that than Baruch himself, who many believed still coveted the job and had expected to receive it. Baruch had not suggested Nelson for the post when Roosevelt asked him for recommendations; but, always alert to where power lay, he began immediately to forge a close relationship with the new "economic czar."[19]

Donald Nelson seemed an unlikely candidate for such adulation. He was born in 1888 to a family of modest means in Hannibal, Missouri, and grew up there in the home of his grandmother. (His mother died when he was a young boy, and his father, a railroad engineer, was frequently away.) His grandmother's emotional reticence and stern Victorian values had a lasting effect on the boy. Even years later, he seemed to some who knew him "more like a nineteenth-century man than a twentieth-century man," carefully guarding his emotions behind a calm, unruffled exterior. He attended the University of Missouri, studied chemistry, and in 1912 took a job with Sears, Roebuck, planning to work there for a year or two before returning to academia. He remained at Sears for three decades.[20]

Sears sent him first to work as a textile chemist with Utica Mills in New York, one of its subcontractors; and when Nelson discovered that he was being paid simultaneously by both firms, he began returning his Sears paychecks to the company headquarters. This small act of integrity brought him to the notice of Julius Rosenwald, the president of Sears, who ordered Nelson back to Chicago, put him to work in merchandising, and soon named him manager of the boys' clothing department. In 1927, he became general merchandising manager (a position from which he helped launch Sears's first retail stores). Twelve years later, he became executive vice president, in charge of purchasing.

His rapid rise was not a result of intellectual brilliance or personal magnetism. Nelson was likable, and undoubtedly intelligent, but he was also rather dull. He disliked reading, hated writing, and had few interests outside his work. His unremarkable owlish face, his austere steel-rimmed glasses, his plain wardrobe, his flat voice: all worked to produce an image of ordinariness. His greatest assets were his honesty, his diligence, and his calm, somewhat self-effacing personal style, which allowed him to get along with almost everyone in the company—no small feat in a large, competitive corporate bureaucracy.[21]

Nelson's first brush with government service came in 1934, when he moved briefly to Washington to serve on the Industrial Advisory Board of the National Recovery Administration. After the demise of the NRA, he retained a connection with Washington through his membership in the Commerce Department's Business Advisory Council. In 1940, Robert E. Wood, who had succeeded Rosenwald as president of Sears (and had become a leading figure in the isolationist America First organization), sent Nelson to help Secretary of the Treasury Henry Morgenthau with purchasing problems in the struggling NDAC. Morgenthau named him "coordinator of purchases," and Wood somewhat grudgingly agreed to grant Nelson a leave from Sears. He would never return.[22]

Over the next two years, as Nelson moved steadily up the ladder of the ever-changing war production bureaucracy, he displayed the same characteristics that had made him so successful at Sears. He worked hard; he showed a remarkable ability to manage paperwork efficiently; and, in the words of the War Production Board's official historians,

> . . . he occupied the middle ground and commanded the confidence of both extremes. His long and successful business career made him acceptable to the industrially minded, while his record with the National Recovery Administration indicated a capacity to see the economy as a whole and recognize the importance of winning the cooperation of all groups of the population in the defense program. However much they might disagree with him, each group . . . preferred Nelson to the other group, and so he became in fact the unifying force.

Even Nelson's few critics inadvertently assisted him. Leon Henderson was delighted to hear in 1940 that Edward Stettinius had denounced Nelson as a "traitor to his class." Such stories burnished Nelson's image with the New Dealers and sped his ascent.[23]

Roosevelt never confided to anyone his reasons for choosing Nelson for the daunting task of running the WPB and passing over more eminent candidates: Baruch, Wendell Willkie, Henry Wallace, William O. Douglas (all of whom the President briefly considered, and most of whom were apparently eager for the job). One reason, certainly, was Nelson's strong identification with those within the war bureaucracy who favored a thorough and speedy conversion of industry to war production (a position that at the time was far from popular among many of the corporate figures working in Washington). But Roosevelt was also probably swayed by his belief that such an ingratiating and palpably unambitious man would not likely challenge the President's own political and administrative pre-eminence. In later years, some of those analyzing Roosevelt's often devious use of power argued that he selected Nelson because he expected him to fail; there is no evidence that was true. But it does seem likely that one of Nelson's attractions was that he was unlikely to succeed too brilliantly. "I don't think there are any supermen," Nelson said at his first press conference after his appointment. "I know I'm not one." The President evidently agreed.[24]

But Nelson's efforts to dampen expectations had little effect among the public, the press, and the troubled bureaucracies he was now called upon to tame. Critics of the mobilization effort had pushed for the appointment of a "single, responsible head" so hard and for so long that few paused to notice that the new War Production Board was in most other respects quite similar to its failed predecessors.[25] Nelson's authority within the WPB was, in theory at least, solidly established; but his ability to control competing bureaucracies—and the powerful, insatiable military procurement offices in particular—was less clear. An aggressive, assertive leader might have been able to take advantage of the frenzied atmosphere of the first weeks of 1942 to enlist the President behind him, vanquish his competitors, and establish supremacy. But Nelson's affable, conciliatory leadership style, along with his distant, deferential relationship with Roosevelt, was not well adapted to bureaucratic warfare. Problems mounted and disillusionment set in quickly, especially among those liberals who had hoped Nelson would transform the WPB into an effective instrument not only of economic mobilization, but also of reform. Their criticisms of the WPB clustered in three related areas: the failure to wrest control of procurement from the military; the domination of the mobilization machinery by representatives of the business world; and the neglect of small business in awarding government contracts.

NELSON'S BIGGEST PROBLEM—a source of almost all his many troubles—was the relationship between the WPB and the military. On paper, Nelson had the authority to seize control of the vast purchasing program the expansion of the armed forces required. But actually to do so would have been extraordinarily difficult.[26] For by the beginning of 1942, the American military high command was no longer the provincial, myopic elite it had been in the 1930s—the elite that had resisted expansion as late as early 1940. Under the leadership of Stimson, Knox, and a large cadre of young, tough, energetic administrators drawn largely from the law firms and brokerage houses of Wall Street, the War and Navy departments were fighting with unprecedented ferocity and skill to win control over industrial production and bend virtually the entire American economy to their needs.[27]

Among those leading the charge was Robert Patterson, a former federal judge whom Stimson recruited in 1940 to oversee army procurement as assistant secretary of war. His task, as he saw it, was to reduce civilian influence over the economy (including the influence of the WPB) as radically as possible. Patterson was a ferocious bureaucratic warrior, humorless and self-righteous; one of his antagonists described him as "a man who believes he has a monopoly on patriotism . . . that anyone who disagrees with him not only is wrong, but is wrong from bad motives—probably treasonable." Patterson's personal crusade was eliminating what he considered unnecessary civilian production. He once tried to pressure Nelson to ban comic strips from newspapers—they were a waste of paper and introduced what he considered inappropriate levity into the grim business of war. He was renowned in the WPB for what became known as the "Seven-Up defense." Whenever anyone requested scarce materials for civilian production, Patterson would produce a devastating (if usually irrelevant) anecdote, the most famous of which involved seeing a Seven-Up delivery truck driving around Washington. "So long as gas and tires and equipment are being wasted on that kind of damn foolishness," he said, "the civilian economy doesn't deserve *anything*."[28]

An even more daunting obstacle to hopes that the WPB would seize effective control of production was General Brehon Burke Somervell, the officer in charge of the army's procurement and supply division. Somervell was smoother and less contentious than Patterson, but at least equally determined that the military, not the WPB, would control production.[29] By the beginning of 1942, Somervell had established a substantial procurement bureaucracy of his own, complete with committees for each major industry. He had made the Army Navy Munitions Board (ANMB), originally established as a coordinating body to prevent the services from competing with one another for scarce materials, into a powerful procurement agency, headed by Ferdinand Eberstadt, a tough, talented New York investment banker. Manufacturers had grown accustomed, *Time* noted in 1942, "to thinking of the Army as the source of orders" and of OPM and WPB as "a source of questionnaires." Somervell had, in effect, created a bureaucracy within the War Department that almost precisely paralleled what Nelson and most New Dealers expected the WPB to become. And he defended its prerogatives with single-minded intensity.[30]

Nelson thus faced an unenviable choice as he began shaping the WPB early in 1942. He could try to seize control of procurement from the military. But that would have meant doing battle with Patterson, Somervell, and the powerful bureaucracies they had already created—a daunting prospect, particularly since Nelson had no assurance that the President would support him in the struggle. And it would have required setting up new industry committees within the WPB—an enormous administrative task that would have taken months at a moment when achievements were being measured in days.[31]

Instead, Nelson chose to try to work through the existing military agencies and sent his own men to serve on and represent the WPB's interests before the various boards the army and navy had created. Many such officials quickly developed stronger loyalties to the military than to the WPB, particularly those whom the shrewd Somervell commissioned as officers. Nelson himself, moreover, showed little inclination to stand up to the more assertive figures he encountered in uniform (the men liberals describe contemptuously as the "brass hats"). Although he resisted some of Somervell's most extravagant proposals (including one to give the military complete power over allocation of raw materials), he seemed powerless to stop the War and Navy departments from tightening their grip over relations with defense contractors. As one of his associates later described it, "One of these War Department Generals will stick a knife into Nelson and all Nelson does is pull the knife out and hand it back and say, 'General, I believe you dropped something.' And the general will say, 'Why Don, thanks, I believe I did'—and right away he sticks it back in again."[32]

Nelson's inability to prevent the military from taking over procurement placed the WPB in an almost untenable position. Rather than the agency that controlled basic economic decisions, it was becoming, in effect, the arbitrator of conflicts between the military and civilian sectors of the economy. And since the civilian sector had no effective organization representing its interests, certainly none as powerful as the War and Navy departments, the WPB itself became, in effect, the sole guardian of civilian needs. In the end, then, Nelson was not even really a mediator; he had inadvertently turned himself into the defender of the civilian economy—of the comic strips and the Seven-Up trucks—in a struggle in which almost all political strength lay with his opponents.

Within weeks of its creation, the WPB began hearing the drumbeat of criticism that would plague it throughout its existence. It was weak, disorganized, confused. It had abdicated its most important authority to others. It had not "taken charge." "The WPB itself is a classic fifth wheel," the New Republic complained, "and this is because Nelson lacked both the ability and the drive to make it anything else," because the Board had failed "to rip the procurement powers out of the military's hands, which it was supposed to do."[33]

By the end of the summer, Nelson was virtually under siege—both from liberals who wanted him to be tougher in standing up to the military, and from the military itself. (Somervell was orchestrating a concerted attack on the WPB through carefully planted leaks and off-the-record criticism.) Nelson left Washington for a brief vacation, apparently on the verge of resigning. But a week later he returned, a "changed man," reporters said, determined to do battle with Patterson and Somervell and restore the credibility of his agency. In a rare press conference he displayed an even rarer burst of emotion. "I am going to get tough enough to get this job done," he told reporters, pounding his desk for emphasis. "From now on, anybody who crosses my path is going to have his head taken off."[34] Above all, he insisted, he was going to seize control of allocating critical materials—a power that was the key to controlling production generally and one he had long since ceded to the military. But the great battle he envisioned soon turned into a characteristic process of compromise. Control of critical materials would, indeed, revert to the WPB; but the man exercising the authority would be Eberstadt, who had been handling similar decisions for the ANMB and who now moved to the WPB. Eberstadt, it soon became clear, would remain loyal to Somervell and the army despite his new bureaucratic address.[35]

NELSON'S CRITICS were not mollified. As I. F. Stone noted, even if Nelson's forces were able to prevail over the military, which was far from certain, "they still have a long way to go." For they faced as well another battle—a battle that, to most liberals at least, was at least as important as, and closely related to, the conflict with the armed forces. Nelson and his allies would have to stand up against the conservative corporate figures who were flooding into the war agencies and threatening, many liberals feared, to turn them into agents of monopoly.[36]

In 1939 and early 1940, when preparation for war was still largely theoretical, most liberals within the administration (and many outside it) lobbied for a mobilization plan that would make use of the established institutions of the federal government. The Commerce Department, for example, might manage industrial mobilization; the Labor Department would handle labor problems. Each department would bring in advisers and subordinates from the business world, but the regular officers of government would largely dominate the process. That would ensure a war effort managed by people committed to New Deal principles. It would also guarantee that the state itself, not an improvised hybrid, would control the war economy. In the process, many liberals hoped, the state would legitimize and expand its role as an effective instrument for planning and regulation. Roosevelt, in short, should not organize the economy according to the World War I model; he should not, Harold Ickes warned in 1939, "allow the fat cats of Wall Street to run the war activities."[37]

In the end, of course, the mobilization did follow the World War I model. That was partly a result of bureaucratic necessity—of the lack of capacity and experience within the existing departments for the vast responsibilities mobilization would have imposed on them. But it was also a deliberate political choice. Roosevelt feared that entrusting the war economy to existing agencies would create damaging partisan divisions; and he believed that businessmen would respond more readily to direction from other businessmen than to orders from what they considered a hostile federal government. The result was a collection of war bureaucracies most of which were state agencies only in name. Indeed, some liberals looked on them not as agencies of government at all, but as the malign arms of monopoly capital, staffed by people less loyal to the needs of the nation than to the needs of their own industries. From the first days of the war mobilization to the last, the most pervasive liberal criticism of the process rested on the power of "monopolists" within it.[38]

Business executives assumed positions within the WPB and other war agencies in several different ways. Some (Nelson among them) resigned from their firms and took salaried government positions, which almost always meant a substantial reduction in income. Others took temporary (often paid) leaves from their companies and worked in Washington as, in effect, volunteers, without any official appointment or salary; they were known as "WOCs," people working "without compensation." But the most prominent, if not the most numerous, business figures in Washington—and the ones who came to symbolize the larger problem of "monopolists" in government—were the "dollar-a-year men," executives who had official appointments in the war bureaucracy but who continued to receive their corporate salaries. The government paid them a token "dollar a year."[39]

"Dollar-a-year men" had been the focus of criticism from progressives during World War I, and liberals started warning against a new dollar-a-year regime as early as 1939, before any real mobilization began. By mid-1942—by which time over ten thousand business executives (most of them Republicans) had moved into offices, cubicles, and even converted bathrooms in the hopelessly overcrowded headquarters of the war agencies—the complaints were reaching a crescendo.[40] The *Nation* called them "business men who are more worried about their competitive position after the war than about winning the war." The *New Republic* described them as men whose "concern for the war is secondary to self-interest and the jealous protection of their competitive positions," and as "self-seeking industrialists." "What we have in the WPB," I. F. Stone complained, "is 'self-regulation' of business with all its inevitable evils, the same subordination of our country's safety to private interests that helped ruin France."[41]

Through much of 1942, complaints about the presumed conflicts of interest the dollar-a-year men had created centered around the case of Robert Guthrie, a former department store executive and stockbroker who had come to Washington in 1940. He eventually acquired the arcane title of "assistant chief of Bureau of Industry Branches" in the WPB and was placed in charge of supervising conversion of several crucial civilian industries to war production. Guthrie was a tough, humorless administrator who pushed relentlessly, often over the objections of his colleagues, for full and immediate conversion. In the spring of 1942, he either resigned or was dismissed from his post, depending on who was telling the story, and complained publicly that dollar-a-year men in the WPB were holding up production of war material while continuing to channel scarce commodities to their own, civilian industries. He did not name names, but other WPB critics quickly singled out Guthrie's immediate superior: Philip Reed, chairman of General Electric and a dollar-a-year man par excellence, whom Guthrie had apparently enraged by pressing for a rapid halt in the production of radios for civilian consumption.

The charges, true or not, hit a nerve among people in and out of government who were already critical of the slow pace of conversion and the industry representatives they considered responsible for it. Senator Harry Truman's Special Committee to Investigate the National Defense Program (known as the "Truman Committee") began an inquiry into the Guthrie affair and issued a report mildly critical of the dollar-a-year men generally and of Reed in particular. When Nelson tried—unsuccessfully—to suppress the report, suspicions of the WPB's motives intensified. For a brief moment, the "Guthrie affair" became a potent symbol to liberals of everything they considered wrong with the war agencies. "The arsenal of democracy, as the Guthrie case and the reactions to the [Truman Committee] report show," I. F. Stone wrote contemptuously, "is still being operated with one eye on the war and the other on the convenience of big business." Guthrie's departure, Michael Straight complained, "exposes a state of rottenness at the heart of the production effort." Even *Business Week* concluded in the wake of the Guthrie report that it was "undesirable to rely upon [the large industrialists] exclusively for the direction of the war production program."[42]

Complaints about conflicts of interest within the WPB continued until the end of the war. The liberal magazines, the Truman Committee, and perhaps most of all the few remaining liberals within the Roosevelt administration found many opportunities to point out the duplicity and disloyalty of dollar-a-year Republicans. Leon Henderson, for example, warned the President that William Jeffers (a railroad executive placed in charge of wartime rubber production) "has been playing politics with his job and making alliances with people who hate you and your supporters. He debauches public service." But even among those making the complaints, hopes that anything would change were steadily and visibly flagging.[43]

TO SOME NEW DEALERS, this shift of power away from liberals (and away from the permanent state structures they largely controlled) and toward private interests was the most troubling problem of the war agencies. But to another group of liberals, the problem of the War Production Board was very different. Those of more traditionally anti-monopolist and populist inclinations, including many members of Congress, considered the most alarming feature of the WPB not its resistance to liberal influence but its "discrimination" against small business.[44]

It was hard to deny that small business was having difficulty getting war contracts. The military procurement agencies and the WPB itself almost instinctively offered contracts to larger firms. That was partly because the men working in the war agencies were, on the whole, products of those companies; and it was partly because it was harder for bureaucrats to identify and sustain relationships with many small firms than it was to work with a few big ones. It was also because there was a general, and generally unquestioned, belief within the war agencies that "the largest and best organized business concerns ... would be best suited to take care of the defense program." Whatever the reason, small businesses found themselves largely shut out of war production. And since raw materials for civilian production were becoming increasingly scarce, many could not even continue their normal civilian operations. From the beginning of the war to the end, they clamored for relief.[45]

In the process, they enlisted some powerful allies in Congress. In the House, Wright Patman of Texas kept up a steady cry throughout the war demanding a wider dispersion of war contracts. Senator James E. Murray of Montana used the Senate Small Business Committee to reveal the extent to which the war agencies were favoring large corporations. Early in 1942, for example, the committee disclosed that 75 percent of all contracts had gone to 56 large corporations. A year later, Joseph O'Mahoney of Wyoming, fresh from his work on the TNEC, found no significant improvement. Seventy percent of all war-contract money, he charged, had gone to 100 "super-colossal corporations."[46]

Together, Murray and Patman shepherded legislation through Congress in the spring of 1942 establishing the Smaller War Plants Corporation

(SWPC) within the WPB.[47] The new sub-agency was capitalized at a modest $150 million. It was directed to help smaller plants convert to war production and to divert war contracts from big firms to small ones. Nelson, who had bristled at other criticisms of the dollar-a-year men, accepted this new mandate willingly, even eagerly. He seemed genuinely to believe in the importance of drawing small business into the war effort, and he moved quickly to put the SWPC into operation.[48]

But the SWPC failed to satisfy the hopes of its founders and did little to still the criticisms of the WPB from defenders of small business. Its first director was Lou Holland, owner of a small sprinkler company in Kansas City and, perhaps more significant, a friend of Harry Truman. Truman's Senate committee was boring in on the WPB's failure to protect small businesses, and the chairman himself at one point referred to the agency (in a letter to small-business constituents) as "the Gestapo." The appointment of Holland was, in part at least, an effort by the WPB to placate Truman.[49] Holland worked hard, and he spoke often and loudly about the importance of his task. But his conception of the SWPC role was limited largely to exhorting small businesses to compete more aggressively for war contracts; and his administrative skills (not to mention his budget) were entirely inadequate to the massive bureaucratic tasks he encountered. He started his job in July 1942. By early 1943, he was back at his sprinkler company in Kansas City, complaining bitterly that he had been undermined by "fanatics" and that his achievements had not been sufficiently appreciated.[50]

Faced with the necessity of finding a replacement for Holland, Roosevelt privately confessed that he was "baffled" by the small-business problem. "We have not met it," he admitted, "and I am not sure it can be met." He tried to recruit Joseph Kennedy to take over the post, but Kennedy refused, expressing doubts "that anyone could accomplish anything of value to small business."[51] The White House settled instead on Robert Wood Johnson, president of the Johnson and Johnson surgical supply company in New Jersey. Johnson, a longtime member of the Business Advisory Council of the Commerce Department, was more comfortable in Washington than the dyspeptic Holland, and he quickly developed good relations with the army (which made him a brigadier general) and the WPB. He made modest progress in diverting war contracts to smaller firms, and he used part of the SWPC's capital to help "small industry in distress." In the end, however, he was no more able than Holland to force a significant change in the way contracts were allotted. After a little less than a year on the job, he resigned late in 1943 (citing health reasons) and returned to New Jersey.[52]

Maury Maverick, the last director of the SWPC, perceived his task in different terms. A former mayor of San Antonio and two-term member of Congress, he had a well-earned reputation as a firebrand; and he was known above all for his defense of the interests of small producers against what he considered the predatory character of modern industrial capitalism. His appointment to the SWPC seemed to promise a new, confrontational approach to the small-business problem. But by early 1944, when Maverick took over (evidently as a result of the President's election-year conversion to concern for the problems of small business), securing major new military orders for smaller firms was probably already a lost cause. The most important war contracts had long since been negotiated. Maverick managed to raise the percentage of new orders going to small business from about 13 percent in 1943 to 27 percent in 1945; but he was, essentially, ensuring a fairer distribution of a rapidly shrinking pie. As a result, he focused instead on reconversion to civilian production. Having been largely excluded from the bounty of war contracts, Maverick argued, small firms deserved some measure of preference in the conversion back to peacetime production.[53]

When the success of the Normandy invasion in June 1944 suggested that the end of the war might be in sight, Maverick stepped up his efforts—and, perhaps most significant, drew Nelson into the battle with him. Together they began to lobby for allowing some small businesses to resume civilian production before the formal end of the war (and thus ahead of their large competitors, who were still engaged in military production). Such a policy, they argued, would not only help small business; it would ease the transition to a postwar economy for everyone.[54]

But the efforts to speed reconversion were, if anything, less successful than the efforts to redistribute war contracts. They aroused the ire of the major industrialists, who naturally opposed giving their competitors a head start in the civilian market. More important, they encountered implacable opposition from both the civilian and uniformed leaders of the armed forces, who insisted that any movement toward peacetime production would endanger military procurement and undermine civilian morale. This second concern, in particular, captured the ear of the White House, which dismissed Nelson's and Maverick's proposals with a breezy endorsement of the position of the Joint Chiefs of Staff. It also created considerable dissension within the WPB itself and contributed to the crumbling of Nelson's power, a process that was by then already far advanced.[55]

·   ·   ·

THAT NELSON was unlikely ever to become the "Baruch of World War II," as some observers had hopefully predicted early in 1942, had been obvious from the start to those who knew him. But even his early critics failed to predict how quickly his authority within the WPB would erode. His bitter battle with the military over procurement in the summer of 1942 was only the first of many unpleasant struggles that would cloud (and finally end) his three-year tenure as WPB chief and, in the process, besmirch the reputation of the agency itself.

The growing dissatisfaction with Nelson's leadership came to a head in the first months of 1943, in part as a result of his efforts to dispel it. Nelson had brought Ferdinand Eberstadt into the WPB late the previous summer in an attempt both to enhance the agency's authority and to settle his feud with the military. Eberstadt created what became known as the Controlled Materials Plan, which redirected the agency's efforts away from actual purchasing; the military, Lend-Lease, and the various agencies controlling civilian production would retain principal responsibility for that. Instead, the WPB would be in charge of allocating among the various claimants available supplies of critical raw materials. The Controlled Materials Plan quickly established itself as the most efficient and successful of the WPB's many undertakings. "Everybody who knows and thinks about it feels that the Controlled Materials Plan is what brought order out of chaos in the War Production Board," Baruch later wrote Eberstadt. That the plan worked well was partly because its task was simpler than most others the WPB had attempted and partly because Eberstadt was a talented administrator. Its successes increased an already strong inclination within the military and elsewhere—an inclination actively cultivated by Eberstadt himself—to restrict the WPB's role to materials allocation alone.[56]

Nelson felt differently, at least in part because defining the WPB's mission in such a narrow way would greatly enhance Eberstadt's position and diminish his own. By early 1943, he had managed to persuade Roosevelt to appoint yet another senior administrator to the WPB: Charles E. Wilson, formerly the president of General Electric, whom Nelson now made director of production. Wilson's mission, Nelson explained, was to involve the WPB more deeply in the production and purchasing decisions that the military had until then largely controlled. Wilson's real job, some believed, was to help Nelson win authority back from Eberstadt. Inevitably, and virtually immediately, Wilson and Eberstadt found themselves at odds. Wilson soon discovered that managing production was impossible without some control of materials; he began to demand a share of that control. Late in 1942, Nelson obliged him by wresting five of the industry committees from Eberstadt and transferring them to Wilson. Eberstadt quietly began making plans to resign.[57]

The dispute between Eberstadt and Wilson dominated both the internal politics of the WPB and the public discussion of its activities through the last months of 1942 and the first weeks of 1943. It was more than simply a struggle over bureaucratic turf. Eberstadt's position, supported by the military, Baruch, and some business leaders, seemed to liberals to reflect the essentially conservative belief that war production must be promoted carefully, to avoid disrupting the fragile equilibrium of American industry. Pushing industry to expand and produce too quickly might lead to instability and, eventually, to the same problems of overproduction that Eberstadt and his allies believed had caused the Great Depression in the first place. Neither the armed forces nor consumers could be permitted to demand more than the economy was capable of producing. The strict control of raw materials that Eberstadt had introduced was, in other words, a vehicle for stabilizing, and thus limiting, levels of production. It was also, some critics charged, a vehicle for maintaining the "Old Wall Street–Army combination."[58]

Wilson, although no liberal himself, had the support of many New Dealers because he believed above all in expanded production. Liberals portrayed him, perhaps inaccurately, as the spokesman for a more expansive and dynamic view of economic life. The WPB, they argued, should not strive simply to stabilize the existing timid, anti-competitive industrial world; it should move aggressively to promote greatly expanded production—both to meet the nation's war needs and to ensure greater production (and hence greater employment) after the war. "Wilson is now carrying the ball for civilian control," Mordecai Ezekiel wrote Henry Wallace late in 1942. "He is a symbol of American democracy. . . . If we let him go down, there will be nothing left to stop the Army-Eberstadt-Baruch clique from obtaining complete power and control over the organization of industry for the war, and probably for the peace as well."[59]

Nelson clearly sided with Wilson in the dispute, but he soon became the target of criticism from dismayed partisans of both camps for the acrimony and confusion the battle created. Eberstadt supporters began lobbying vigorously for replacing Nelson with their ally Baruch. Liberals, many of whom liked Baruch even less than Eberstadt, began to promote Wilson himself as the most promising champion of full production. Nelson meant well, New Dealers argued, but his weakness and ineptitude crippled his best intentions. "Nelson is the failure that many were afraid that he would be but hoped that he wouldn't be," Harold Ickes wrote in late summer 1942, even before the Eberstadt-Wilson conflict.

"He likes to please everybody which means that he has to make compromises. He frequently reverses himself. . . . He can't fire people."[60] In January 1943, the beleaguered Nelson asked the pollster Elmo Roper to do an informal survey on his standing in Washington. "The major criticism," Roper gingerly reported, was that "you have turned out to be a poor administrator. . . . You are also criticized for publicly announcing you were going to 'get tough.' . . . You aren't the kind of fellow who can get results by trying to get tough."[61]

By early February, it was no longer possible for the President to view the problems of the WPB as normal bureaucratic confusion of the sort he himself often liked to create. The problems had become serious enough to threaten the public image of his administration and, according to many critics, the nation's ability to conduct the war. Weary with what was now a four-year struggle to find a workable system, disillusioned with the various business leaders who had tried to bring order out of the chaos, he grudgingly acceded to pressure from the military and some of his own, more conservative advisers (most notably James F. Byrnes, now head of the new Office of Economic Stabilization, and soon himself to become another "czar" of war production). Roosevelt decided at last to offer Nelson's job to Baruch.[62]

What followed was an almost comic episode of political and bureaucratic intrigue in which Nelson, to the surprise of almost everyone, temporarily outflanked his rivals. On February 6, Byrnes personally delivered a letter to Baruch, written by himself but signed by the President, asking the financier to assume the directorship of the WPB. Baruch promised an answer the next morning; but he left for New York that night and did not contact the White House for ten days. He claimed he had become ill on the train and had returned to Washington as soon as he had recovered. But the more likely explanation, according to one biographer, is that he was genuinely reluctant to take the onerous job and needed time to consider it. (He was seventy-two years old and increasingly deaf. "When evening comes," he complained at the time, "I am tired.") In the end, however, Baruch decided to accept and returned to Washington February 17 for an afternoon meeting with the President.[63]

But early that morning, Nelson finally heard about his own impending ouster. He had previously signaled a willingness to leave the WPB (and accept a face-saving mission to Australia) if Wilson became his successor. But the idea of stepping aside for Baruch, whose appointment Nelson believed would be seen as a repudiation of his own leadership, was much less appealing. Within hours, he fired Eberstadt and named Wilson his chief deputy.[64]

The President, taken by surprise, now faced a situation in which replacing Nelson with Baruch would appear to be an endorsement of Eberstadt and a repudiation of Wilson. He decided, as was his custom in such cases, to do nothing. Baruch arrived at the White House that morning to "report for duty." The President greeted him with an amiable but irrelevant monologue about political problems in the Middle East and then excused himself to attend a meeting. He did not mention the WPB job, then or ever. It remained for embarrassed aides to explain to Baruch what had happened.[65]

The sound and fury that accompanied these bureaucratic maneuvers saved Nelson's job, but it signified almost nothing else. Nelson's decisive actions to keep himself in office challenged his public image of weakness and incompetence only briefly. Within weeks, the drumbeat of dismissive criticism resumed. Wilson, once freed from turf battles, soon proved almost as unwilling as Eberstadt had been to challenge the military's control of purchasing or its opposition to reconversion. By the fall of 1943, he was already at odds with Nelson; and for the next year, the two men battled for supremacy within the agency.[66] Late in 1944, both were replaced by Julius Krug, a stolid administrator with vaguely New Deal sympathies who supervised the WPB's waning months without fundamentally altering its role.[67]

In the meantime, Roosevelt had created yet another agency: the Office of War Mobilization (OWM), based in the White House and directed by Byrnes. Its ostensible job was to mediate among the contending economic mobilization agencies. In fact, Byrnes quickly became the principal civilian figure in the war production bureaucracy, and he gravitated almost instinctively to the relatively conservative approach advocated by Baruch, Eberstadt, and the military. He favored stabilizing, rather than expanding, the economy; he left largely unchallenged the military's control over purchasing; he showed no particular interest in the problems of small business; he opposed most early reconversion plans.[68] More than two years of political and bureaucratic battles had left the basic structure of the economic mobilization for war essentially unchanged.

WHAT, IN THE END, was the political and ideological legacy of the troubled War Production Board experiment? What was its contribution to the structure of the postwar state and to the character of liberal thinking about the role of government? There are at least two broad areas in which the WPB seems to have had lasting, and contradictory, impacts.

On the one hand, the widespread unpopularity of the WPB among liberals in and out of government ensured that after the war virtually no one would cite it as a model to which the peacetime state should aspire. Almost no one called, as many reformers had after World War I, for continuing the government's wartime role in regulating production and coordinating the private economy. No one claimed that the WPB had charted a path to an "ordered economic world." Bernard Baruch had emerged from World War I a national hero; and for the rest of his life he remained an influential and widely respected sage, revered as the wizard of one of the most successful economic experiments of modern times. After World War II, Donald Nelson sank quickly into obscurity. He spent his last days serving as a public relations executive for a minor Hollywood trade association and pursuing other, generally unsuccessful business ventures. When he published his plodding memoirs in 1946, many reviewers took the occasion to compare him unfavorably to Baruch.[69]

The WPB experience, in short, served not as a model to liberals, but as a warning. For those who had long championed the corporatist arrangements to which the agency at times aspired, its failure was so disillusioning that many of them ceased to promote those earlier dreams. For those who had always viewed "public-private partnerships" with distrust, the WPB became the NRA writ large—a compelling illustration of how state efforts to coordinate production and investment led to a "capture" of government agencies by powerful corporate interests. Frustration with the WPB weakened liberal's faith in the regulatory and planning potential of the state and strengthened their already growing inclination to look to fiscal and compensatory strategies for managing the economy instead.

But if the WPB's ideological legacy was greatly to weaken corporatist and planning visions, its institutional legacy was very different—a result, in part, of Nelson's failure to wrest control of purchasing from the military. In the course of the war there emerged the foundations of what would later become known as the "military-industrial complex," a vast, cartelistic partnership between the armed forces and private industry, largely invulnerable to political attacks; a national security state, which forged intimate partnerships with the corporate world, constantly blurring the distinctions between public and private. The bureaucratic empire that Brehon Somervell and Ferdinand Eberstadt created was, they had argued (and had perhaps believed) at the time, a temporary expedient for winning the war. Peace, however, led not to a general demobilization but to the Cold War and decades of massive military spending and defense production. Liberals agreed in the late 1940s and beyond that the Cold War required continued and even expanded military preparedness. But the model of political economy to which they had by then gravitated left them with no tools for regulating the economic consequences of that preparedness. Perhaps the

WPB's most important institutional legacy, therefore, was its failure to exert (and legitimize) effective civilian control over the Army Navy Munitions Board. For in the postwar era, the WPB disappeared, while the ANMB and its successors—largely unencumbered by civilian oversight—went on and on.[70]

## Chapter Nine

# The New Unionism
# and the New Liberalism

ORGANIZED LABOR had more reason than most other groups to feel ambivalent about the prospect of mobilizing for war. American workers had much to gain from the massive economic expansion the conflict would inevitably produce. But memories of World War I suggested that they had much to lose as well. As the government moved slowly in the months before Pearl Harbor to increase production and shift it to military purposes, labor leaders jockeyed to find a significant role for themselves and their unions in the process—a role that would avoid the setbacks of the last war and exploit the opportunities of the new conflict. Out of that jockeying emerged several bold plans for restructuring the relationship between management and labor. The story of what happened to those plans, and what emerged to replace them, is an important part of the larger story of how the war was reshaping liberal approaches to political economy.

THE RISE OF the American labor movement had been one of the most striking social developments of the 1930s. As the Depression began, the great majority of American workers remained wholly unrepresented in the process of determining their own economic fates. Most unskilled workers had no organizations at all; many skilled workers belonged to unions which employers refused to recognize or with which they refused to bargain. By the end of the 1930s, workers had created powerful new unions committed to representing the unskilled through the Congress of Industrial Organizations (CIO). And employers were recognizing both new and old unions and engaging—many for the first time—in collective bargaining with their workers. As a result, union membership grew from under 3 million in 1933 to 8.5 million in 1940 and 10.5 million in 1941.[1]

Crucial to this change was the rising militancy of workers themselves, who fought strenuously throughout the decade for some control over their economic lives. Equally crucial were new policies of the federal government, embodied most notably in the 1935 National Labor Relations (or Wagner) Act and the National Labor Relations Board (NLRB) it created. For the first time, the power of the state stood firmly behind the right of workers to organize and bargain collectively.

But the passage of the Wagner Act and the triumphant organizing battles that followed it did not resolve the "labor question"; nor did they fully satisfy either union leaders or the rank and file. The American Federation of Labor (AFL), although it supported the Wagner Act in 1935, quickly grew disenchanted. This was partly because of the AFL's historic reluctance to rely on government assistance (a reluctance born of the conviction that once labor became dependent on the state it could be—and would be—oppressed by the state). It was also partly because of the belief among many AFL leaders that the NLRB mediating process tended to favor the CIO in the bitter jurisdictional battles between the rival organizations.[2]

The CIO, which had benefited more than any other group from New Deal labor legislation, also had reasons for disenchantment. By the end of the 1930s, some CIO leaders (and, if the demands voiced in some labor actions were any indication, much of the CIO rank and file) had become convinced that the NLRB and the courts were using the Wagner Act not only to advance, but also to limit, labor's goals. The law, labor critics complained, had been used to enshrine a process that protected collective bargaining over wages, benefits, and work rules, but implicitly (and at times explicitly) denied labor's right to challenge employers in any other way or on any other issues. A new bureaucratic species—the labor mediator, seen by many in the CIO as a gray-suited *apparatchik* committed to industrial stability and uninterested in, if not openly hostile to, the movement's larger aims—had emerged to occupy a crucial place in the middle of the battle. To those who hoped the CIO would become a vehicle for creating a new labor party or for transferring a significant share of control of the workplace from capital to labor or for other, even more radical forms of social change, the presence of the state in the center of the conflict had become a significant obstacle.[3]

The dangers facing the labor movement were, therefore, clear. During World War I, the state had allowed control of economic mobilization to flow into the hands of corporate figures and had offered workers only transitory benefits—almost all of them stripped away, sometimes violently, in the immediate aftermath of the conflict. World War II had the potential to do the same: to reinvigorate capital and derail the labor movement's most ambitious and controversial aims. The war bureaucracy could accelerate the process the NLRB had already begun, the process of defining labor-management relations narrowly and entrenching labor mediators at the center of those relations. That was the principal reason for John L. Lewis's outspoken opposition to Roosevelt's interventionist policy in 1940 and 1941 (and part of the reason for his ill-fated decision to support the Republican candidate, Wendell Willkie, in the 1940 presidential election); he feared war would destroy whatever chances remained for progressive change (which in his view meant enhanced labor power) at home.[4]

But the opportunities were also clear. The war would require unprecedented industrial production under emergency conditions. A stable and productive workforce would be as crucial to victory as a well-trained military. Labor could, therefore, expect an end to the problems of unemployment and underemployment that had plagued American workers for a decade. It could also hope to exercise some influence over the organization of the economy for war. In the process, it might establish precedents that would lead to lasting gains for workers in peacetime as well. In the months before and just after Pearl Harbor, several ideas emerged from within organized labor that seemed for a time to have a real chance of success. They were ideas that promised not just a solution to the immediate problems of war mobilization, but a significant change in the way the industrial economy as a whole would operate.

THE MOST IMPORTANT of these ideas emerged from within the CIO, from its new president, Philip Murray, and—in a more elaborate and politically palatable form—from Walter Reuther of the United Auto Workers (UAW). Although the plans differed in detail, they were similar in concept. Both centered on the vaguely corporatist idea of "industrial councils," tripartite groups in which labor, capital, and government would collaborate in the supervision of industries.

The industrial-council idea had roots in a number of earlier, failed efforts to advance labor-management cooperation, and in several broad intellectual and social traditions: in abortive efforts to create similar bodies during World War I, in the concept (if seldom the reality) of some company unions in the 1920s, in the code authorities of the National Recovery Administration in the early New Deal, and in at least some versions of the "industrial democracy" vision that had been an important part of labor thinking for at least twenty years. Catholic labor leaders

(Murray among them) drew as well from Catholic social reform ideas, ideas drawn from the papal encyclicals of Leo XIII and Pius XI and from notions of community, derived from St. Thomas Aquinas, on which the encyclicals were to a large degree based.[5]

But the CIO version of the plan emerged most directly from the writings of Mordecai Ezekiel, the New Deal agricultural economist and unabashed champion of economic expansion. In his 1936 book, *$2500 a Year*, Ezekiel had called for aggressive efforts to increase production and consumption (as opposed to cautious efforts to stabilize economic institutions). He called his plan "Industrial Adjustment." It would rely, he claimed, on government policies that would spur (or even compel) businesses to produce more. It would also enable consumers to buy more. That meant industries would need to empower their workers—primarily by paying them enough (a $2500 a year minimum family income) so they could enjoy "abundant living," but also, he suggested, by giving them a greater voice in the running of their industries.[6]

By the end of the decade, Ezekiel had become even more convinced of the importance of introducing "effective democracy into many economic areas where no democracy exists today." And so he outlined a plan for what he called "industry authorities" on which representatives of capital, labor, consumers, and the state would sit and collaborate on making basic decisions about their industries. Ezekiel envisioned something more than the collective bargaining recognized by the NLRB, something more than adversarial negotiations over wages and benefits. He proposed a real sharing of power. Citing the historian Charles Beard, he wrote (in his 1939 book, *Jobs for All*):

> [Frederick Winslow] Taylor, the founder of modern efficiency engineering, was wrong and inhuman in regarding the worker simply as an unthinking set of arms. . . . Modern efficiency engineers find it is more effective to give the worker some responsibility, to leave him some intellectual part in planning and running his job.

By choosing representatives to participate in setting "the economic policies of his industry," the worker would experience "real participation." The plan would "help him see his place as part of the whole" and "develop the intellectual side of [his] job."[7]

Murray was familiar with and intrigued by Ezekiel's proposals, which intersected with some of the labor and Catholic traditions in which he himself had long been immersed. He began talking about industrial councils as a solution to the problems of war mobilization as early as the fall of 1940 and started pushing them in earnest in the spring of 1941, as his disillusionment with the Office of Production Management (and with Sidney Hillman, labor's representative on it) grew. The CIO should not allow itself to become dependent on agencies of the state, as Hillman seemed to propose. ("What the government gives," Murray once said, in an echo of the traditional AFL position, "the government can take away.") Labor must strive instead for an independent power base. The industrial councils could provide one.[8]

The councils, as he described them, would perform many of the functions currently housed within the Office of Production Management (OPM) and other war agencies. They would "ascertain the domestic and armament requirements of each respective industry, coordinate the production facilities of each industry to meet these requirements speedily and accurately, and expand production facilities where they are inadequate to fulfill these requirements." They would be responsible for the "granting and re-allocating of armament contracts"; they would "fill the labor requirements of the industry"; and they would ensure "industrial peace through the perfection and extension of sound collective bargaining relations between management and organized labor." Perhaps most important of all, the industry council was to be "an administrative agency, not an advisory council." It was, in other words, to be very different from the weak, dependent labor advisory bodies Hillman had proposed and that Murray and others had emphatically rejected.[9]

Murray's hopes for his plan rested on two assumptions. One was that the administration needed labor's cooperation desperately enough that it would be willing to consider unconventional, perhaps even radical, reforms to win it. The other was that the stumbling, confused performance of the war agencies would support his argument that control of economic mobilization should be moved out of Washington and into the industries themselves. But to Roosevelt, and to most others involved in planning for war, the critical issue in 1941 was finding a way to increase production. Murray's proposal offered breezy assurances that the industrial council plan would, in fact, contribute to higher production; but it did not emphasize that claim and offered no concrete evidence to support it. As a result, it received relatively little attention outside labor circles beyond the alarmed and hostile response of several business organizations.[10]

But while the Murray Plan languished, interest grew rapidly in a similar proposal drafted by Walter Reuther, a young, energetic, and rapidly rising United Auto Workers official who headed an important union local in Detroit. (He would become president of the national union in 1946 and five years later president of the CIO.) Born in West Virginia in 1907 into a socialist union family, he trained as a tool and die maker. By his early twenties he was a well-paid skilled worker in Ford's River Rouge plant and, along with his brothers Victor and Roy, an active figure in socialist and union politics. When Henry Ford supplied a Soviet automobile factory with equipment from his own plants in the early 1930s, Walter and Victor volunteered to spend a year in Gorky teaching Russian workers how to use the new tools. They were excited by the experience and, like many American socialists of those years, enamored of the Soviet experiment in state economic planning. Their rapturous letters home about the "Workers' Fatherland" ("We are actually helping to build a society that will forever end the exploitation of man by man," they wrote in 1934) later became fodder for FBI efforts to discredit them.

Back in Detroit in 1935, Walter Reuther threw himself into the organizing battles of the UAW and rose steadily through the union hierarchy. He gradually lost interest in socialist politics, but he continued to advocate economic reforms that would, he believed, distribute power and wealth more broadly and democratically. The approach of war encouraged him to think such plans might at last win an audience outside the labor movement itself; but unlike Murray, he also understood that to win support for such reforms, he would have to justify them not just in terms of the needs of workers, but also in terms of the needs of the war effort as a whole. The Reuther Plan, as it came to be known, was cagily (although not hypocritically) packaged to emphasize its contributions to production first and its restructuring of economic relations second.[11]

In presenting his plan in late 1940, Reuther echoed what was already a widely shared frustration within the Roosevelt administration over the slow pace of conversion to war production. One of Roosevelt's highest priorities was a dramatic increase in the production of airplanes; he had called for the building of "50,000 planes a year." But progress toward that goal had been hobbled by the underdeveloped state of the aviation industry. Almost everyone assumed that production could increase only after new aircraft factories were built. Reuther, however, proposed what seemed to many a dazzling alternative. Automobile factories were the largest manufacturing plants in the country. Many of them were sitting idle. They could, he insisted, be converted to airplane production in much less time than it would take to build new factories; and they would come equipped with a trained labor force. Production would increase rapidly enough to meet and even to exceed the President's goals. Auto workers, Reuther predicted, could eventually turn out "5,000 planes a day."[12]

Folded into this bold proposal—and, Reuther believed, essential to it—were two more controversial plans. One was to require auto manufacturers to pool their efforts. The military would allocate contracts for different parts of planes to different companies, depending on whose plants were most suitable for particular tasks. One company might construct an airplane engine; another might make body parts; a third might actually assemble the plane. The plan also called for the creation of industrial councils in the automobile industry—to be structured like those Murray had outlined in his own plan—which would allow workers to participate in basic production decisions. Reuther did not say so, but it seems clear that to him and to many other union leaders this was the most important provision of the proposal—and one designed to establish precedents that would shape labor-management relations beyond the war itself.[13]

In the confused economic and political climate of 1941, the Reuther Plan appeared to many frustrated liberals (and even to some conservatives) a daring solution to what had come to seem an intractable problem. It would break the impasse in production. It would ensure harmony between workers and managers at a critical moment—and perhaps well beyond the war. It would join labor and capital in a common, cooperative quest for full production and full employment. "It represents the whole direction of trade-union striving," Max Lerner wrote excitedly in the *New Republic* early in 1941. "For labor is no longer to be seen as just a pressure group. Its stake in democracy is a stake in raising the whole national income. It is a stake in productive and social efficiency for the large." Labor was asking for a "simple thing," the renowned sociologist Robert S. Lynd argued: ". . . the right to participate in terms that have meaning to the participant." Bruce Catton, who worked in the war agencies and later wrote a bitter memoir of his experiences, remembered the Reuther Plan as one of the few bright spots of those years. "This wasn't going to be like the last war," he wrote, in describing Reuther's hopes, "with the trade associations running industry and Gompers exhorting the boys not to strike in return for management agreement to a temporary cessation of union-busting. Labor was coming up to the quarter-deck just as if it had a right to be there. . . . It was a revolutionary proposal, . . . something breath-takingly new."[14]

For a time, the plan received favorable attention from major figures in the administration as well. Under Secretary of War Robert Patterson, a zealot on the issue of increasing military production, was growing increasingly irritated at the reluctance of the automobile industry to give up any of its lucrative civilian business. He seemed receptive to the Reuther idea for a time. Donald Nelson (then chairman of the Supply Priorities and Allocation Board) was cautiously interested as well. And most of the liberal New Dealers still serving in the administration rallied to it enthusiastically, as a last, frail vessel for their dreams of a progressive, democratically structured war economy. Jerome Frank, for example, hosted a breakfast at the Cosmos Club in Washington so that Reuther could explain his plan to such sympathetic New Dealers as Lauchlin Currie, Thomas Corcoran, former Indiana governor Paul McNutt, and Leon Henderson, all of whom expressed enthusiasm. The President himself showed at least momentary interest.[15]

But the plan also aroused substantial, and ultimately fatal, opposition. Auto manufacturers were, not surprisingly, aghast. Many of them were still resisting conversion to war production of any kind in the months before Pearl Harbor, particularly since civilian auto sales were rebounding so impressively from the lean Depression years. They insisted that their factories were unsuitable for airplane production, that even with retooling they could never manufacture the delicate parts required for aviation. (In this, they had the fervent support of the aviation industry, which wanted to preserve the lucrative airplane contracts for itself, however unequipped it was to fulfill them.) But those auto executives who recognized the inevitability of conversion were even more alarmed. They strongly opposed the Reuther Plan's provisions for pooling efforts across company lines. In an industry in which each auto company had a carefully nurtured, insular culture, such alliances seemed unthinkable; to the "Big Three"—General Motors, Ford, and Chrysler—it also seemed a threat to their competitive supremacy over smaller rivals. Most of all, of course, managers recoiled at the notion of sharing power with their workers. The industrial councils struck them as an opening wedge in an assault on the entire hierarchical structure of industry. According to Charles E. Wilson, president of General Motors (no relation to Charles E. Wilson of the War Production Board), "To divide the responsibility of management would be to destroy the very foundations upon which America's unparalleled record of accomplishment is built." If Reuther wanted a role in running the automobile industry, Wilson said, GM would hire him as a manager.[16]

Perhaps the biggest obstacle to the plan, however, was the new war bureaucracy in Washington. However stumbling and inefficient the OPM might have been in other ways, it still managed effectively to defend the interests of the dominant group within it, the corporate "dollar-a-year men." That OPM's chairman, William Knudsen, was a former president of General Motors ensured a particularly obdurate hostility to Reuther's proposal. Early in 1941, when the plan was receiving widespread favorable publicity for its "patriotic" commitment to war production, Knudsen worked quietly to destroy it—ignoring it in public, stalling or disparaging it in private. After the first wave of enthusiasm subsided, he became more outspoken.[17]

Pearl Harbor robbed the Reuther Plan of one of its most important assets: its promise to force the auto industry to convert. Once the United States formally entered the war, conversion was no longer a question. Government agencies quickly forbade further production of civilian automobiles; the auto companies turned entirely to war production, manufacturing jeeps, tanks, and (despite their earlier claims that they could not do so) airplane parts. Reuther's proposal was no longer appealing because it promised rapid conversion; the conversion was taking place without it. It was now primarily a device for restructuring labor-management relations. Many liberals continued to support it for that very reason; but most others—especially those in the military and the war agencies who had once been favorably disposed—quickly lost interest. By late 1942, it had vanished almost without a trace. There were feeble and intermittent efforts to revive it over the next three years; but by then the course of labor relations had begun to move onto a very different path.[18]

THE REAL PATTERN of wartime labor policy emerged finally in the immediate aftermath of Pearl Harbor and rested largely on three important accords between union leaders and the wartime government. Together, those agreements produced an accommodation between capital and the state and formed the outline of what would eventually become the dominant form of postwar labor politics.

The first agreement emerged in late 1941 and early 1942, a response to the frenzied patriotism and exaggerated fears that Pearl Harbor helped create. In quick succession, the AFL, the CIO, and most of the major unions in both organizations promised to abstain from disruptive labor actions for the duration of the war. The agreement became known as the "no-strike pledge." The no-strike pledge reflected the eagerness of labor leaders to demonstrate their support for the war effort. But it also reflected their fear that, if they did not take action themselves to curb strikes, others would take it for them, in a much more draconian way.[19]

Over two million workers had gone on strike in 1941, more than in any years but 1937 and 1919. Communist labor leaders, hostile to preparedness efforts in the period of the Nazi-Soviet pact, had helped inspire some of the strikes, a fact cited and greatly exaggerated by labor's critics. But the real source of labor militancy was the perceived opportunity to win some real economic gains in the booming, defense-driven economy, after more than a decade of depression.[20]

Whatever the reasons, the strikes enraged many conservatives (and some liberals). Even before Pearl Harbor, they began to accuse labor of obstructing the nation's preparations for war. The National Defense Mediation Board (NDMB), the federal agency Roosevelt established in March 1941 to arbitrate labor disputes and prevent work stoppages, lacked enforcement authority and proved largely ineffective. After the Board failed to resolve a major coal strike in September 1941, its CIO members resigned, the President implicitly repudiated it, and the agency in effect collapsed. By late 1941, Congress was beginning to consider legislation to make strikes illegal and even to conscript industrial workers in the same way the government was drafting soldiers. The no-strike pledge was, among other things, an effort to stop this antistrike drive. In return, the unions asked the administration to replace the decrepit NDMB; Roosevelt responded by creating the War Labor Board (WLB) in January 1942 (at the same time he was establishing the new War Production Board), headed by William H. Davis, a patent attorney and experienced labor mediator. It was authorized to spur enforcement of its rulings against obdurate unions or employers by asking the President to seize plants and operate them on behalf of the government.[21]

The WLB did not, however, have much latitude in awarding wage increases. That was because it was bound by a second agreement wrested from union leaders by the administration in 1941, designed to prevent labor's understandable demand for a share of the profits of the wartime economic boom from producing inflation. Price-control administrators in the war agencies had called for an absolute freeze on wages for the duration of the war; but labor and its defenders insisted that such a freeze would lock workers into the unfavorable position they occupied at the end of the Depression. The result, a compromise, was the so-called Little Steel formula, a device designed to limit without absolutely forbidding wage increases for industrial workers.[22]

The formula was based on one of the WLB's first important decisions: a ruling in July 1942 to award workers in four steel companies (all of them smaller than the giant of the industry, U.S. Steel, and hence known collectively as "Little Steel") a wage increase based strictly on rises in the inflation rate between January 1, 1941, and May 1, 1942. The cost of living had risen 15 percent in those sixteen months, the WLB claimed, and steelworkers were thus entitled to a 15 percent wage increase (approximately ten cents an hour) over their January 1941 base. The new wage rate would continue for the duration of the war. More important, the same formula would govern future WLB decisions for workers in other industries, which in some cases meant no wage increases at all. Miners, for example, had won a 16 percent wage increase in 1941; under the Little Steel formula, they could expect no more.[23]

The Little Steel formula was hard for many union leaders to swallow. It limited wage increases at just the moment when great economic gains for workers at last seemed possible. It also transformed the WLB from an agency for mediating labor-management disputes into one for fighting inflation. "The WLB violates the government agreement with labor each day that it operates," John L. Lewis bitterly charged. "Under its arbitrary and miserably stupid formula, it chains labor to the wheels of industry without compensation for increased costs, while other agencies of government reward and fatten industry by charging its increased costs to the public purse." Philip Murray complained of the WLB's "callous abdication of its responsibility" in refusing to adjudicate "certain types of disputes."[24]

To make the new arrangements more palatable, the administration offered labor a third new agreement. In exchange for honoring the no-strike pledge and accepting the Little Steel formula, the government would guarantee the institutional stability of industrial unions through the "maintenance-of-membership" plan.

The maintenance-of-membership plan, which the major unions quickly accepted, was an effort to resolve one of the most hotly contested labor issues of the late 1930s and early 1940s: the question of whether workers in unionized plants could be required to become and remain members of the union. The WLB rejected the union demand for a closed shop (a shop in which only union members can be hired). It proposed instead a modified version of the union shop (a shop in which all workers must join the union after being hired). All workers in unionized plants would automatically become union members and remain so for the duration of the union contract unless they resigned from the union during their first fifteen days on the job (or during the first fifteen days of a new contract). This "escape clause" was a crucial concession to employers and conservatives, who detested the idea of a closed or union shop. It had, however, little practical effect; few workers exercised the option. The result of the agreement was a tremendous increase in the dues-paying membership of most unions; the ranks of organized labor grew from 10.5 million in 1941 to 14.75 million in 1945. But along with this important contribution to the size and prosperity of unions came a much greater dependence on federal agencies. Maintenance of membership, the WLB insisted, was a "privilege," something the government could give or take away according to the way workers behaved. Unions that failed to abide by other parts of the wartime accords—the no-strike pledge or the Little

Steel formula—could find themselves stripped of maintenance-of-membership protections.[25]

WHEN  COMPARED  TO the bold visions of shared decision-making in the Murray and Reuther plans, the wartime "contract" that emerged from these three agreements seems to represent a notable retreat by organized labor. Instead of an active participant in the councils of industry, the labor movement had become, in effect, a ward of the state. Without the option of striking and with wage increases sharply limited by government fiat, unions had to depend on the goodwill of the war agencies for whatever gains or protections they hoped to secure.[26]

Workers themselves were not oblivious to these dangers. Although the war brought them the stable, secure employment for which they had been waiting for over a decade, it brought as well a marked retreat from some of the more expansive visions that had emerged from the labor movement during the Depression. In the mid- and late 1930s, much of the industrial rank-and-file had engaged in a prolonged and at times militant battle on behalf of an agenda shaped not by the state but by workers themselves. They had demanded more than recognition of their unions, better wages and hours, and improved working conditions, enormously important as these things were to them; many had worked, as well, to make the labor movement an at least quasi-independent force in the industrial economy and in American politics generally. The discovery of their own power was a heady experience for many workers, and it enabled them to envision significant new relationships between labor and management and between labor and the state—a vision of an "industrial democracy" that they believed could transform not just the lives of workers but the character of American society.

There was no single vision of industrial democracy. It mean different things to different groups of workers, and the concept thus embraced a wide range of goals, some moderate or even conservative, others strikingly radical. In some industries, workers demanded almost complete control of the shop floor, including hiring and firing. In others, to the horror of their employers, they demanded the right to inspect the company's books as part of periodic negotiations over wages. Almost all industrial workers supported the New Deal as it created the foundations of the modern welfare state, but most envisioned a much more expansive and generous system of social insurance than the government actually created. Some workers called for aggressive policies to redistribute wealth, others for some form of state control of private industry. The important role social-

ists and, above all, communists played in the early phases of the organizing battles of the 1930s ensured that many activities embraced even more
radical visions. Some workers expected labor to become the dominant
force in the Democratic party; others anticipated the formation of a new,
independent labor party championing industrial democracy.[27]

Workers had welcomed the federal government's intervention in
labor-management relations through the New Deal's labor laws. The 1935
National Industrial Relations Act, the 1938 Fair Labor Standards Act, and
allied measures owed their passage in part to the growing political clout
of unions and their activist rank and file. Government support and enforcement of workers' right to organize had been critical to the success
of the CIO, in particular, in the late 1930s. But many workers saw such
laws as only the beginning, not the end, of their quest for power, a first
step toward a greatly expanded voice for workers in the running of their
shops, their industries, and perhaps even the national economy as a
whole.[28]

The gap between the hopes they embraced in the 1930s and the
reality they encountered during the war was one of the reasons for the
widespread discontent and, at times, defiance among labor's rank and file
in the 1940s. Although the no-strike pledge seemed generally effective in
1942, worker displeasure with the Little Steel formula, in particular, was
evident. The Office of War Information, for example, circulated an
"intelligence report" in August 1942 warning that "if labor dissatisfaction
is not reduced, workers will turn to more radical methods and more
radical leaders. They may resort to unauthorized strikes." By mid-1943, the
no-strike pledge seemed in danger of collapsing altogether. The WLB
complained to the President that, while wages were being restrained by
the Little Steel formula, prices were continuing to rise—a violation of
"the policy promised to the wage-earners of the nation." Without decisive action to roll back prices, they warned, "workers' spontaneous revolt
against the rising cost of living is imminent." Union leaders were more
direct. "It is feared that within 60 days there will be a complete breakdown which may by itself threaten the entire existence of the machinery
of war," a CIO committee predicted. "These are hard days for Labor men
who are trying to keep the wheels rolling," Daniel Tobin of the Team-
sters Union wrote privately to the President.[29]

A "complete breakdown" never occurred. But "wildcat" strikes
(strikes unauthorized by union leadership) were widespread in 1943: a
walkout by shipyard workers in San Francisco in March; a strike by
rubber workers in Akron in April; another by Chrysler employees in
May; strikes by workers in aviation, leather, and many other industries;

a threatened railroad strike that the government prevented only by seizing the lines and granting workers the wage increase they demanded; and
above all a series of coal strikes that accounted for nearly two-thirds of
the hours lost to walkouts in 1943. Over three million workers engaged
in strikes in that year, more than three times the number in 1942. And
while the damage to war production was, in fact, relatively slight, some
wildcatters made clear that they were willing to strike regardless of the
degree of damage.

Not all wildcat strikes were a response to economic or even political
frustrations. Some were a result of racial tensions—of white workers
protesting the hiring or promotion of African Americans; some were the
actions of workers new to the factories (and to the unions), whose
grievances and demands were often vague. But many wildcats were,
indeed, expressions of frustration at what some workers considered a
betrayal by their leadership. "The most important thing in this war is to
preserve the system of government that we have, and among other things,
the procedure for adjudicating union troubles," a striking New York
aviation worker told an interviewer who accused him of endangering
American troops by interfering with war production.

> There is no sense in winning the war if we are going to lose all these
> privileges. . . . If I had brothers at the front who needed 10 or 12 planes
> that were sacrificed, I'd let them die, if necessary, to preserve our
> way of life or rights or whatever you call it. . . . What's more, if I were
> in their place, I'd expect them to do the same thing. I'd expect them
> to let me die.[30]

And yet despite the increasingly widespread discontent among the
rank and file, despite the growing number of wildcat strikes, despite their
own unhappiness with the Little Steel formula and the price-control
efforts of the war agencies, the leaders of most major unions continued
to support the no-strike pledge and to work earnestly, if not always
effectively, to enforce it. Walter Reuther, for example, appeared before
striking Chrysler workers and was greeted with boos and catcalls when
he asked them to return to work. Philip Murray of the CIO and William
Green of the AFL insisted (correctly but ineffectively) that the wildcat
strikes were relatively limited, that the vast majority of workers were
abiding by the no-strike pledge; and they lamely suggested at times that
workers who were violating the pledge were the victims of radicals or
malcontents in union locals.[31]

Union leaders continued to support the wartime agreements in part because they sensed they had no real alternative. The wildcat strikes, however limited their impact on war production, enraged much of the public and sharply eroded labor's standing in Congress and with the administration. Much anti-labor agitation came from predictable places: the National Chamber of Commerce and other employer organizations, business publications, conservative politicians, and newspapers that had always been hostile to unions.[32] But such animosity was spreading well beyond these traditional sources. The Gallup Poll, for example, conducted a number of surveys in 1942 and 1943 that found overwhelming popular opposition to unions and their demands: 81 percent of respondents supported "a law forbidding strikes in war industries." Seventy-eight percent favored requiring war workers to work a forty-eight-hour week before receiving overtime (instead of the forty-hour week established by law in 1938). The most frequent response to the question "What . . . is the chief cause of strikes" was "unjust demands of workers"; the second most frequent response was "labor leaders who seek personal power."[33]

Even some of labor's friends were beginning to express alarm at how unions were forfeiting their public support. Max Lerner, writing in the *New Republic*, worried about the anti-labor sentiments of "young people . . . who are starting out on jobs or careers or the perilous voyage of the mind." Liberals had "for some time been building up for them a fighting faith in labor as a creative social force." Now that faith was rapidly eroding. The *Nation* noted that "the public at large is convinced that union workers are coining big money out of the war in callous disregard for the national need." Labor's "pivotal" task, it claimed, was "the winning of public opinion. . . . Labor's position will remain precarious until the trade-union movement achieves acceptance and recognition by the public as a permanent and basic institution of American life."[34] Union leaders themselves railed against the unfair charges and false reports they believed were responsible for their declining popularity. Victor Reuther, for example, complained of the "deliberate amplification of minor misdeeds by labor unions."[35]

Nothing revealed the precariousness of labor's position more than the controversial coal strikes of 1943, the largest labor actions of the war. By early 1943, unhappiness among miners with the Little Steel formula was such that John L. Lewis might have felt compelled to act even if he had not opposed the formula (and the War Labor Board) from the start. Coal miners were among the lowest paid of all unionized workers, and the Little Steel formula guaranteed that they would receive no significant wage increases as long as the war continued. Price controls, erratically effective in the best of circumstances, were particularly unreliable in the small towns in which most miners worked; having started at a low point on the economic ladder, many miners were actually moving downward as inflation eroded their earnings—even as the industry's profits were soaring. Lewis publicly condemned a series of wildcat strikes early in 1943 called by locals demanding a two-dollar-a-day wage increase; but he shared the wildcatters' contempt for government labor policies, and he recognized that their grievances could not be contained within the existing mediation machinery. He finally persuaded the strikers to return to work only by agreeing to support their demand for a pay raise. "The coal miners of America are hungry," Lewis said in March, as he began negotiations with the mine operators on a new contract. "They are ill-fed and undernourished below the standard of their neighbors and other citizens."[36]

When negotiations with the operators broke down, Lewis defied the WLB (which had moved in to mediate the dispute, and which Lewis assumed would support the owners) and ordered several brief strikes in May and June to demonstrate the union's resolve. The popular and political response was savage. Although a clear majority of respondents in public opinion polls said they believed the miners deserved a wage increase, 87 percent expressed hostility to Lewis. Members of Congress began calling on the administration to charge him with treason. The President, who already disliked Lewis, ordered the Justice Department to consider indicting him. "John L. Lewis is just about the most irritating man on the public scene today," the New Republic charged in the midst of one of the coal strikes, even as it conceded the justice of the miners' demands. "His criminal recklessness in ignoring the effect of a strike on the outcome of the war is outrageous to the last degree."[37]

The coal dispute dragged on for more than six months, until finally Harold Ickes (more sympathetic to Lewis and the UMW than most other administration officials) negotiated a settlement that gave miners an effective $1.50 a day wage increase on terms that artfully avoided a direct violation of the Little Steel formula.[38] But the political fallout from the conflict revealed the relative weakness of labor and its inability to defend its own interests against a hostile public and an increasingly hostile government. Conservatives in Congress, who had failed to pass antistrike and labor conscription legislation in 1941, now revived it in the form of the War Labor Disputes (or Smith-Connally) Act, which easily passed both houses and even survived a halfhearted presidential veto. The new law required workers in nonwar plants to observe a thirty-day "cooling off" period before striking; gave the President authority to seize struck war plants; established criminal penalties for anyone encouraging war workers to strike; and made union contributions to political campaigns illegal. The law, in fact, gave the government relatively few new powers (seizing struck plants was the most notable exception) and had little direct impact on the ability of unions to act. But it demonstrated the degree to which the labor movement was losing political leverage.[39]

BUT IT WAS not simply because of external pressures that the labor movement acquiesced in the wartime system of labor-management relations. Despite the restiveness of much of the rank and file, despite the rebelliousness of some labor leaders and the quiet discontent of others, there was an important and growing faction within the movement that found in labor's new alliance with the state a promising, if still imperfect, model for the future. Lewis and other militants continued to advocate an autonomous labor movement, capable of fighting independently for its own agenda of social and economic change. But other, more conciliatory leaders were working to construct a different role for labor. And while important battles within the movement continued until at least the late 1940s, the war produced the outlines of the accommodation between labor and the state that would ultimately prevail.

If the symbol of labor's wartime defiance was John L. Lewis, the symbol of its effort to ally itself with the Roosevelt administration and the state was Sidney Hillman. As president of the Amalgamated Clothing Workers of America (ACWA), Hillman had played an important role in the formation of the CIO. But in the course of the 1930s and 1940s, he also assumed the role of "labor statesman," the movement's representative within the councils of government.

Hillman was born in Lithuania in 1887 to a pious Jewish merchant family that included several generations of rabbis. As a boy, he showed promise as a Talmudic scholar; his parents hoped—and expected—that he too would become a rabbi. But Hillman found himself drawn instead to another intellectual force gaining strength in the Pale: a secular interest in socialist and trade-union politics that had produced the General League of Jewish Workers of Lithuania, Poland, and Russia—the "Bund." An active participant in socialist study groups, he joined the Bund officially in 1903. He quickly became an ardent socialist revolutionary, leading strikes and demonstrations and twice before he was twenty spending several months in jail. In 1906, as official repression of socialists grew harsher, he escaped a third arrest warrant by fleeing Lithuania. He lived briefly in England, then migrated to the United States in 1907 and settled in Chicago. After two years of menial jobs, he became an apprentice garment cutter at Hart, Schaffner, and Marx.

Hillman was not a particularly skilled cutter, but he quickly demonstrated considerable gifts as an activist and organizer. When Chicago garment workers staged a major strike in 1910, Hillman became one of the leading insurgents. Four years later, he moved to New York and became president of the new ACWA, founded as an alternative to the conservative, anti-Semitic, and often thuggish United Garment Workers Union of the AFL, which had failed to support the 1910 strike. By then, Hillman was already closely connected with and greatly admired among middle-class supporters of the labor movement—and already convinced of the importance of his alliance with them. He had also developed what would be a lifelong hostility to the AFL.

During and after World War I, as Hillman struggled to establish and sustain his fledgling union, he forged relationships with a group of progressive intellectuals and businessmen (among them Felix Frankfurter, the Taylorite reformer Morris Cooke, the Boston businessman Edward Filene, and labor economist William Leiserson) who, together, were trying to envision a new pattern of labor-management relations, a "new unionism." The new unionism would, Hillman argued, produce a more cooperative relationship between workers and employers, born of a shared commitment to efficiency and increased production. Workers would acquiesce in the efforts of Taylorites and other advocates of scientific management to make factory work more rational and productive. But they would also, through their unions, be fully represented in decisions on setting production standards and other policies within their industries. Their goal would not be to overturn capitalism. It would be to make it more rational and democratic. And it would be to make the state, as it had been briefly during World War I, an active champion of industrial democracy.[40]

Hillman promoted the new unionism throughout the 1920s. He also began to argue that the interests of labor depended above all on economic growth, an idea that would become increasingly important to him (and to other labor leaders) in the 1930s and beyond. "The question of a high living standard," he claimed, "is a matter of vital importance for the whole nation." As he explained on another occasion, "It is essential to our system of mass production to create a consumer's demand for almost unlimited output. . . . [The labor movement's] insistence upon a sane and responsible democracy in industry and the progressive improvement in standards of living are essential for the maintenance and progress of our industrial system." Labor's future, in other words, lay not in making itself a powerful adversary of capital and the middle class, but by demonstrating that working-class interests were in many ways the same as those of other groups.[41]

The Great Depression, which devastated the clothing industry as it did the rest of the American economy, produced in Hillman something close to despair. But it also reinforced his already growing conviction that the future of the economy (and of labor within it) rested on the revival of mass consumption, which the economic crisis had disastrously reduced. And because he believed the revival and stimulation of demand required "planning on a national scale," he became increasingly convinced that the success of the labor movement would depend on its ability to form a close alliance with the state. An enthusiastic supporter of Roosevelt from the start, Hillman eagerly accepted appointment to the Labor Advisory Board of the National Recovery Administration in 1933 and, in the following year, to the National Industrial Recovery Review Board, which briefly replaced the faltering leadership of the NRA's original director, Hugh Johnson. In those roles he displayed a pattern of behavior that would find an echo a decade later, when he became an important figure in the war bureaucracy. As the NRA experiment unraveled, as the initial enthusiasm for it among labor organizations faded, Hillman dug in his heels and fought to preserve it (and, not incidentally, to justify his own role within it). "The NRA will go as far as the labor movement pushes it forward," he insisted. "There's no need talking about Leninism, Trotskyism, and other theories and theoreticians. . . . We must get out of our little circle and into national life."[42]

When the Supreme Court struck down the NRA in 1935, Hillman spoke bravely of how labor would "go ahead on our own." But even as he moved into the thick of the controversies within the labor movement and became a major actor in the events that led to the creation of the CIO, he continued to make national politics the principal focus of his attention. In April 1936, he joined John L. Lewis, David Dubinsky, George L. Berry, and others to form Labor's Non-Partisan League, whose goal was mobilizing labor support for Roosevelt's re-election. Hillman became its treasurer and raised over $1 million. By contributing to the President's victory, Hillman hoped, labor might strengthen its crucial ties to the state and its ability to promote the policies necessary for recovery. "The NRA was not repassed because labor was supine," he told his union. "But I think now that if we could get another situation like the NRA . . . that with this group of people in the CIO, we could really get somewhere."[43]

The 1936 election greatly strengthened Hillman's reputation as the most important link between the Roosevelt administration and the labor movement. His strenuous and apparently effective efforts on behalf of the Fair Labor Standards Act of 1938 further burnished his credentials, as did his furious denunciations of John L. Lewis's endorsement of Wendell Willkie in 1940. In the meantime, he was articulating more clearly than before his emerging vision of a new political economy and labor's place within it. "Labor cannot act independently, in isolation from other progressive groups," he wrote in 1939. "Organized Labor represents the hard core around which all progressive political action must be built. But it has no program and no objectives which are not shared by the great majority of forward-looking Americans."[44]

Hillman's emphasis on alliances with the government (and collaboration with the Roosevelt administration), his belief in the transforming value of economic growth, his apparent lack of interest in structural economic change, and his own apparent political ambitions (illustrated by an abortive attempt in 1938 to run as a Democrat for the U.S. Senate): all combined to drive a wedge between him and many of the more militant factions within the CIO, who continued to believe in the importance of an autonomous labor movement and even an independent labor party. Hillman's efforts to undermine and discredit John L. Lewis in 1940 also angered many of his CIO colleagues, including many who disagreed with Lewis but found Hillman's attacks on him distasteful. Outside union circles, Hillman was being praised as a "labor statesman." Within the movement, there was growing criticism of him as a sycophant, currying favor with the President to enhance his own power.[45]

Both reputations grew as a result of Hillman's intimate involvement with the federal government's war agencies. From the start, he was the principal labor representative in the defense bureaucracy—a member of the National Defense Advisory Commission and, beginning in early 1941, co-chairman (with William Knudsen) of the OPM. Although Knudsen and Hillman had a cordial personal relationship, it was clear almost from the beginning that Hillman was, in effect, the junior partner in an agency of uncertain authority. His principal mission, it seemed, was to find a way to prevent strikes—a responsibility he accepted with what some of his labor and liberal colleagues considered unseemly fervor. "Every time there was a threat of a strike or a strike took place," Isidor Lubin said of Hillman, "the heavens were going to fall." His principal accomplishment was to organize the labor-management conference of January 1942 that produced the no-strike pledge.[46]

It may be that nothing Hillman could have done would have made the war agencies more effective protectors of labor's interests. But to many of his critics, Hillman simply did not try very hard. He expressed cautious interest at first in the Murray and Reuther plans (plans that embodied ideas about labor-management cooperation he had himself promoted before the war). But when it became clear that the plans had little support within the OPM (and had attracted the adamant hostility of Knudsen and many others), he backed away from them. "Labor's plea in the defense program is being made from day to day," he told members of the Steelworkers' Organizing Committee (later the United Steelworkers of America) in explaining his failure to support the Reuther plan. There was no need for industrial councils to do what Hillman himself was already doing. To the President, he spoke even more dismissively about the CIO proposals. "No one not wholly responsible to the government can be expected to have the necessary information and detachment," he said. "In short, 130,000,000 people cannot delegate to any combination of private interests final decisions in matters of basic policy."[47]

Not even Hillman's humiliating departure from the war bureaucracy in 1942 seriously shook his faith in the beneficence of the Roosevelt administration. When the President replaced the faltering OPM with the new War Production Board, Hillman advocated creating what became the War Labor Board to represent worker interests. Roosevelt took his advice. But instead of naming Hillman to head the WLB (as Hillman himself had hoped), he chose William H. Davis. Later, the President created the War Manpower Commission (WMC), an agency charged with allocating scarce labor resources to various areas of the economy. Hillman, who had helped draft the plan for the new agency, was passed over again. The chairmanship went to Paul McNutt, the former governor of Indiana. Both agencies, in the end, proved relatively ineffective as defenders of labor's interests.[48]

Hillman continued to defend the Roosevelt administration despite these slights, even though agreements he had worked to produce and sustain—the no-strike pledge, the Little Steel formula—were becoming increasingly unpopular, and even though he had failed to win any significant role for labor in war mobilization. The result was an erosion in Hillman's standing, not just within the labor movement, but among some of his erstwhile liberal admirers outside it. "Hillman is turning out to be a weak man in that combination," his friend Harold Ickes wrote of the collaboration with Knudsen. "His activities should have been confined to labor." Felix Frankfurter concluded that Hillman's "leadership . . . has not been so bold as the times required," and worried about the "inferiority complexes" that have "produced in him an unfortunately [*sic*] timidity and ineptitude." Others were even less kind, suggesting that Hillman had abandoned his principles in a sycophantic effort to cement his relationship with Roosevelt. Benjamin Stolberg, a longtime labor reporter who had written admiringly of Hillman in the 1920s, published a profile in the *Saturday Evening Post* in 1940 in which he complained bitterly about how much Hillman had changed. Stolberg discovered a photograph of Hillman as a young man, and he was struck by the contrast between what he saw in it and what he saw in the mature Hillman of his own time. The physical contrast, he nastily suggested, was a symbol of an intellectual and moral change as well:

> A photograph of Hillman at the age of twenty-one shows a sensitive and wistful youth. The bone structure of the face is delicate, almost feminine, and the high cheekbones give it a curiously romantic lift. The upward glance is dreamy, shy, idealistic. Today, one wonders what happened to this proletarian Shelley in the course of thirty years. The delicate bone structure, even the high cheekbones, have completely disappeared in a squarish, somewhat jowly face. The sensitiveness has given way to an assured complacency, relieved only by a touch of slyness. There is, startlingly, no psychic continuity in these two faces—in fact no physical resemblance.[49]

But while Hillman's personal relationship with the President was certainly of great importance to him, sycophancy was not the only cause of his evolving view of labor relations in the 1940s. He was also attempting, quite deliberately, to find a new position for the labor movement within the changing liberal world of his time. And in doing so, he was proving a much more accurate barometer of the future course of the movement than his many critics were offering. Hillman believed that labor's hopes could no longer realistically rest on the dream of a socialist revolution, or a labor party, or most of the other large social changes workers had envisioned in the long history of their struggle. Labor could best advance by becoming part of the liberal political order—allying itself with the New Deal and the Democratic party and working to achieve its aims by establishing real power within conventional politics.

In the aftermath of the 1942 congressional elections, in which Republicans and conservatives gained considerable strength, Hillman created the CIO's Political Action Committee (PAC), which would, he hoped, enable labor to campaign effectively for the President and other sympathetic Democrats in 1944. It would prove that labor could be more politically valuable to the Democratic party than the conservative urban machines, most of which were hostile to union aims. Ultimately, he believed, PAC would make the CIO a forceful lobby as well, capable of influencing not just elections, but legislation. In the 1944 elections, PAC proved itself an effective fundraiser and seemed to demonstrate real political clout. In a number of close congressional races, PAC support appeared to provide the margin of victory for candidates it endorsed. (It took credit for, among other things, the defeat in the Texas Democratic primary of Representative Martin Dies, the red-baiting, labor-baiting chairman of the Special House Committee on Un-American Activities.) Perhaps that was why Republicans and conservatives complained so bitterly about the "capture" of the Democratic party by Hillman and organized labor; and why Roosevelt's alleged order that his aides "clear it with Sidney" before he chose Harry Truman as his running mate became a major issue in the 1944 campaign.[50]

But the creation of PAC signaled more than an attempt to increase labor's political clout. It was part of an effort by Hillman and others within the movement to shed what they considered the self-defeating independence and radicalism of working-class politics and make labor a permanent ally of the Democratic party and the emerging, consumer-oriented liberal order they hoped it would represent. Hillman, who had once supported the idea of a labor party, now all but scoffed at suggestions that labor should chart its own political course. "It is definitely not the policy of the CIO to organize a third party, but rather to abstain from and discourage any move in that direction," he insisted. Any such move would "serve to divide labor and the progressive forces." American workers "can no longer work out even their most immediate day to day problems through negotiations with their employers and the terms of their collective agreements. Their wages, hours, and working conditions have become increasingly dependent upon policies adopted by Congress and the National Administration."[51]

Nor would PAC spend much time worrying about the structure of the economy, the power of "monopolists," or even the shape of the workplace. It would align itself squarely with the larger liberal agenda of countercyclical public spending and generous programs of social protection. "As a result of this war and the victory that will be achieved at the conclusion of it," Hillman said in 1944, "we must move forward to a broad program of social and economic security for the men and women of this nation." Labor's future lay in the ability of workers to wrest from their employers and their government enough purchasing power and economic security to become effective consumers. Workers' interests were, in the end, synonymous with the interests of the economy, and the society, as a whole.[52]

Other labor leaders might have resented Hillman's prominence and his ambition, but they, too, were gravitating increasingly to the positions he and PAC were promoting. Victor Reuther, for example, wrote in 1943 that "labor must not only speak but also act in a fashion that will prove beyond any doubt that the unions are genuinely exerting themselves to make democracy work to the benefit of all." His brother Walter continued to press proposals for power sharing within industry; but by the end of the war, he was also promoting the idea of workers as consumers and emphasizing programs to ensure a high-consumption economy, an idea that within a few years would become his principal concern. He proposed, among other things, a guaranteed annual wage for auto workers, which, he argued, would be

> the greatest "back to work" movement in the history of labor relations. . . . It offers the expectation of a continually growing market by placing pay checks regularly in the hands of the millions of American workers who are the great consumers of the products of this country's assembly lines.

AFL President William Green, despite his organization's traditional suspicion of government, was beginning to identify labor's hopes with federal policies "for the maintenance of a high national income . . . [and] equilibrium between producing and consuming power." R. J. Thomas, Reuther's rival in the United Auto Workers, spoke bluntly about his own lack of interest in wide-ranging economic reform. "I don't know much about the class struggle," he said in 1945. "I'm interested in wages, hours and working conditions."[53]

SOME ACCOUNTS of the wartime experiences of American labor depict a historic lost opportunity. By forging an alliance with the Democratic party and the liberal state, and by abandoning such larger goals as the industrial-council plan or the idea of a labor party, organized workers gave up the chance of becoming an independent political movement. More than that, they forsook the struggle to win a significant redistribution of wealth and power within the industrial economy—the chance to create a genuine industrial democracy. For in its new partnership with Democrats, liberals, and the state, trade unions were destined to be a subordinate force, incapable of shaping the liberal agenda in more than marginal ways. Before the war, the labor movement had included a substantial faction of militant, crusading workers promoting advanced, often radical, approaches to economic reform. By 1945, the movement was on its way to assuming its modern form as a highly bureaucratized (and occasionally corrupt) interest group, with relatively narrow (and at times illiberal) aims, committed mainly to its own institutional survival.[54]

Workers did achieve a great deal—both during and after the war—

from the new arrangements their leaders and the state crafted for them. Their incomes, and thus their standard of living, rose dramatically (one reason why the 1940s became the only decade in the twentieth century to witness a downward redistribution of wealth). They achieved substantial new benefits (limitations on working hours, increased pay for overtime, paid vacations, among others) that a decade earlier would have seemed almost inconceivable. Unions may not have won real control over the workplace, but in most organized industries they established at least a modicum of power to limit abuses of management authority. Some working-class aspirations were thwarted in the 1940s, but labor emerged from the war and its aftermath with substantial gains as well.[55]

Could they have achieved more? Many workers, and some union leaders, believed they could have; and some continued struggling to broaden the agenda of the labor movement into at least the late 1940s.[56] But while the possibility of transforming the industrial world did not disappear altogether during the war, the prospects for such a transformation—never great in the best of times—declined substantially. The prospects declined because labor failed in wartime to overcome the internal divisions that had often limited it in peace—divisions along ideological, regional, ethnic, racial, and gender lines that would only grow sharper after 1945. They declined because of the savage popular and political opposition the labor movement attracted during the war, despite its generally tame and conciliatory posture—opposition that would also only intensify during the Cold War. And the prospects declined because many of labor's most important liberal allies, and many of labor's own leaders, were already gravitating in the early 1940s toward a new vision of political economy in which the idea of "industrial democracy" played no important role.

It was, of course, theoretically possible for union leaders or rank-and-file workers to repudiate the accommodations with capital and the state that labor accepted during the war (as some tried to do) and transform the trade union movement into the more independent, militant, and confrontational force that some of its members wanted it to become. The postwar political landscape might have looked very different if leaders more like Lewis than Hillman had managed to shape trade union decisions in those years. Ultimately—in the grimmer times that began in the late 1960s—such a movement might have been better suited to dealing with the deteriorating status of workers than the more conciliatory structure that actually emerged. But in the conservative climate of the 1940s and 1950s, it is difficult to imagine labor achieving much more (and quite possible to imagine it achieving less—at least in material terms) with a more radical leadership. The "lost alternative" of the 1940s was probably not labor's emergence as an equal partner within the industrial economy. It was, rather, the survival of an independent social and political force capable of raising challenges to existing ideas and institutions from a position of relative weakness.

In any case, the trade union movement during World War II, like American liberalism as a whole, was beginning to shed its commitment to structural economic reforms and to a redistribution of wealth and power. Instead, it was, slowly embracing the emerging liberal belief that the key to a successful society was economic growth through high levels of consumption. The working-class agenda, at least as expressed by the principal labor organizations, was beginning to resemble the liberal agenda of what remained of the New Deal: a belief in the capacity of American abundance to smooth over questions of class and power by creating a nation of consumers.

## Chapter Ten

# Planning for Full Employment

ARCHIBALD MACLEISH considered himself a poet and playwright above all else. But through much of the 1940s, he was at least as well known for his official posts (Librarian of Congress, deputy director of the Office of War Information, assistant secretary of state) and for the political essays he often wrote for liberal journals. There were moments, however, when MacLeish the poet and MacLeish the liberal political activist seemed to converge, when he tried to fuse his own poetic language and imagination to the discussion of public issues. One such moment was the spring of 1943, when MacLeish was invited to deliver the Charter Day address at the University of California at Berkeley, an address he titled "The Unimagined America."

MacLeish had spent the first years of the war working in the Office of Facts and Figures and its successor, the Office of War Information, the government's principal wartime information and propaganda agencies. During World War I, the equivalent agency, the Committee on Public Information, had devoted much of its energy to creating lurid images of the enemy, discrediting dissenters, and exhorting Americans to be on the alert for signs of disloyalty.[1] The Office of War Information (or at least the area of it in which MacLeish principally worked, its propaganda division) conceived its task differently—in self-consciously liberal terms. MacLeish sought to keep the public's gaze fastened on the future beyond the war. He hoped to persuade Americans that out of the struggle would come a new and better world in which the liberal promise of the New Deal could be realized and expanded both in America and in other societies.[2]

In his speech at Berkeley, he spoke in poetic (if perhaps somewhat mawkish) terms about the importance of "imagining" that future, of seizing it and harnessing it to some great purpose:

The great majority of the American people understand very well that this war is not a war only, but an end and a beginning—an end to things known and a beginning of things unknown. We have smelled the wind in the streets that changes weather. We know that whatever the world will be when the war ends, the world will be different. . . . There is a deep, unreasoning conviction in the minds of people here, as in the minds of people elsewhere, that this war, whatever was true of wars before, *must* have consequences—that anything that costs in life and suffering what this war is costing *must* purchase, not merely an end to itself, but something else, something admirable, something of human worth and human significance.[3]

As MacLeish's words suggest, the debate over how the United States, and its economy, would return to peace began long before the war came to an end, even before some of the great Soviet and Anglo-American victories that made an Allied victory seem imminent. Almost everyone involved in this debate over reconversion shared certain concerns. Most remembered the chaotic aftermath of World War I, which had ended before anyone had made plans for the peace and had led to nearly three years of economic instability.[4] Everyone remembered the Great Depression and feared that the end of the fighting would bring a return to the dismal conditions of the 1930s.[5] And most hoped, as MacLeish did, that America would emerge from the struggle a stronger and better nation than it had been before the fighting began. Beyond these general areas of agreement, however, there were intense, at times bitter, disputes about how reconversion should proceed and what the peace should be like.

To liberals, in particular, the coming of peace seemed a great moment of opportunity. Having failed to shape the wartime government as they had hoped, they quickly turned their gaze to the process by which the nation would return to peace, and to the kind of world (and the kind of state) peace might bring.[6] There was considerable disagreement among liberals about how to proceed with reconversion, just as there had been disagreement among them in the 1930s and during the early days of wartime mobilization about what the New Deal should do. But their disagreements occupied a considerably narrower ideological spectrum than they had a decade earlier. In planning for peace, liberals revealed, even if unwittingly, how decisively their goals were shifting in response to the experiences of the years since the heyday of the New Deal.

Increasingly, liberal discussion of the postwar world centered on a single, highly resonant phrase: "full employment," a term that came to mean much more than simply an end to joblessness. In defining full employment—what I. F. Stone called "that new, glamorous, and socially explosive slogan"[7]—liberals were defining their vision of the postwar state.

THE FOCUS ON "full employment" in the wartime discussions of political economy reflected the cumulative impact of several years of ideological change among American liberals. There was nothing new about wanting to end widespread unemployment, of course; that had been a goal of New Dealers (and many others) from the beginning of the Great Depression. But through most of the 1930s, and through much of the earlier history of American public policy, the idea of *full* employment had seemed, even to most liberals, both unrealistic and peripheral to the more urgent economic need to stabilize prices and production. Many employers actively feared full employment, convinced that it would drive up wages and reduce the "incentive to work." And even some liberals shared their concern that a labor shortage would depress economic activity. Most New Dealers envisioned a decline in joblessness as a welcome by-product of a healthy economy, but not as the principal measurement of the economy's health.

The rise of the concept of full employment as the central economic goal of New Deal liberals marked the triumph of those who had been arguing throughout the 1930s that the proper focus of public policy was not stabilization but growth and who had insisted that the route to growth lay less through production than consumption. Full employment was necessary, they argued, not just to spare individuals the pain of joblessness, but also—and more important—to provide the nation with the largest possible body of consumers. And full employment was possible, they believed, because consumption-oriented fiscal policies, which had been gaining favor in liberal circles since at least 1937, provided a vehicle with which government could stimulate permanent economic growth without engaging in the politically difficult process of forcing structural change on economic institutions.

"Our objective," the liberal journalist George Soule wrote in a 1942 essay on postwar planning, "is simply full employment. Not merely full employment in some particular year or on rare occasions, but continuous full employment, year after year." Milo Perkins, staff director of the Bureau of Economic Warfare, spoke to the Swarthmore College commencement the same year about the importance of "full-blast production" after the war for a "gradually rising standard of living" and proclaimed that "the job of the future will be to build up a mass consumption great enough to use this mass production." The great break-through in liberal thought was the belief that such objectives were attainable.[8]

Central to the concept of full employment was a renewed emphasis on "planning." Planning had always had a special appeal to the statist liberals of the New Deal. (It had also been the special target of those who had attacked the Roosevelt administration as intrusive and tyrannical.) But there was a particular urgency to the calls for planning in the early years of World War II, as if the war itself were a reproach to society for not having heeded such calls earlier. The magazines and journals of the nation's many planning organizations were filled with almost frenzied calls for a national embrace of the planning ideal before it was too late; even more mainstream liberal publications published many such appeals. To some, the belief in planning took on an almost religious quality; the planning faithful, like the religious faithful, tended to assume that those who did not share their views were simply unenlightened. "The future is now aborning," the director of a local planning council in California wrote exuberantly in 1945. "An expanded community is in the making. The opportunity to create something new and better is at hand." Planning, he wrote, may not be "the answer to all of life's problems." But nothing else had its potential for contributing to human happiness. Some prominent planners went so far as to develop the implausible argument that the framers of the Republic had been committed to their cause. "Jefferson was not only a philosopher of democracy," the prominent planning advocates Charles Merriam and Frank Bourgin wrote in 1943; "he was also, in the modern sense of the term, a planner of national resources, both physical and human."[9]

Through most of the 1930s, indeed through most of the history of the idea of planning in modern America, planners had thought primarily in terms of reshaping the nation's social and economic structure. Rexford Tugwell, one of the principal champions of planning in the first years of the New Deal, had advocated (and continued in the 1940s to advocate) an increased state presence in supervising, and stabilizing, production and pricing. Other planners, emerging from urban and regional planning backgrounds, similarly envisioned a new political order in which the state played some role in shaping the development of communities and the distribution of resources.[10]

The full-employment planners of the 1940s, however, had a different vision, even if they continued to use traditional planning language in describing it. America needed a planned economy, they maintained; but the plan would not, indeed should not, involve direct government intervention in decisions about production or investment. Instead, as the economist Gardiner Means argued, planning should focus on demand, on the "expansion of civilian consumption." It should strive to ensure an avid consumer market for the products of the American economy, to guarantee sufficient economic activity to create genuine "abundance" after the war.[11]

Mordecai Ezekiel, the Agriculture Department economist who had written extensively in the 1930s about ways to produce industrial growth, became during the war an energetic advocate of planning for full employment. In the 1930s, his blueprints for planning had included elaborate proposals for coordinating the investment and production decisions of the private sector. But in the 1940s, he talked increasingly about planning for greater consumer demand. Indeed, in a memorandum he wrote in 1943 for a White House study of the postwar economy, he seemed to repudiate many of the ideas he had expressed only a few years before. His 1939 book, *Jobs for All Through Industrial Expansion*, had laid out an ambitious plan for pressuring the industrial economy to reform its ways so as to create a high-demand, high-production economy. He had repeated such proposals as recently as 1942.[12] But in his 1943 analysis, he wrote:

> It is not essential that business develop a wider distribution of income after the war, or provide employment for the great mass of those now in the services or working at war industries. We know now that what business fails to do government can do, through heavy progressive taxation and/or large deficit expenditures.[13]

Ezekiel was overstating his own case. Few advocates of full employment really thought, as Ezekiel seemed to be saying, that government no longer need be concerned about what business did; most liberals continued to support vigorous use of the state's antitrust and regulatory mechanisms. Using "government fiscal policies as a stimulus" to economic growth will "go for naught," the *New Republic* argued in 1943, "if private enterprise continues its pre-war tendency to restrict output in the interest of scarcity profits."[14] But those commitments, tempered by wartime experiences and earlier failures, were no longer at the center of their hopes. The prospects for postwar abundance, they claimed, would rise or fall more on the basis of how government dealt with "aggregate demand" than on the basis of how successfully it controlled corporate behavior.[15]

It was, in fact, that shift of emphasis from planning production to planning consumption that made the idea of full employment so appealing. No longer was it necessary to deal with popular fears of "a huge permanent staff of office holders [who] will come to regiment us day and night, and gradually destroy our liberties," the liberal journalist Stuart Chase wrote in 1943. Instead, he argued, it was possible to plan for a "compensatory economy which will *reduce* the bureaucracy, regimentation, and restraints on liberties from which we are already suffering in the war—a post-war economy with controls at the minimum."[16]

Advocates of full employment offered a range of strategies for achieving that goal, but virtually all such strategies rested on a faith in the potential of government fiscal policies. Government spending "is the crux of the matter," the economist Seymour Harris wrote in 1945, for "private consumption and investment may not be adequate" to produce full employment.[17] The growing primacy of that conviction rested in part on the rapidly increasing influence of John Maynard Keynes on American economic thought—in academia and beyond.

Keynes was personally responsible for at least some of his growing presence in American political debate. Convinced that the postwar health of the Western democracies depended above all on a thriving American economy, Keynes devoted considerable attention to the United States throughout the war. He corresponded with sympathetic American policymakers and economists. He made periodic visits to Washington, visits that became occasions for dinner-party gatherings of liberals, eager for the presence of the man who was becoming so central to their thinking. In the process, Keynes reinforced his allies and won new converts. But in the end, he exercised only limited control over the uses Americans would make of his ideas.[18]

That was in part because his own ideas were so protean: ranging from a conservative, minimalist conception of a state that managed economic growth purely through monetary policy to a much more expansive, even radical vision—born of his occasional despair over the obtuseness of capitalists—of socialized investment to ensure full employment. Those wishing to use Keynes as a source of public policy had to choose among his own, diverse prescriptions.[19] Given the recent history of New Deal experiments in fiscal and monetary policy, it was not surprising that American policymakers chose among the more moderate versions of Keynesianism, which emphasized the active use of fiscal policy and de-emphasized Keynes's own, occasional interest in more direct state intervention in the economy. These were the people Bruce Bliven of the *New Republic* called "practical Keynesians" (and whom some more recent scholars have called "commercial Keynesians"): those who were already chiefly concerned "with income distribution and purchasing power" and saw in Keynes's ideas a way of "getting money into the pockets of the mass of the people."[20]

Foremost among them was Alvin Hansen, the Harvard economist who had played such an important role on the TNEC and who remained throughout the war (and beyond) the single most influential economist in Washington. By the mid-1940s Hansen had become a tireless proselytizer for the energetic use of government's fiscal powers to promote economic growth and full employment. "Dr. Hansen does not give a whoop about the New Deal, one way or another," the columnist Richard Strout observed early in the war. And while Strout undoubtedly exaggerated on that point, he was certainly correct in saying that "what he cares about is his revolutionary vision of a brave new America after the war. An America in which factories work overtime on peace goods and there are jobs for all."[21]

Like most of the other advocates of full-employment policies, Hansen was promoting a "high-consumption" economy, in which the "propensity to consume" would drive economic growth. That meant more than simply encouraging individuals to spend more money on themselves. It also meant finding government policies that would put more money in consumers' pockets. In 1944, he prepared a memorandum outlining a "Postwar Employment Program," which he submitted to the administration's economic policymakers. He took pains to point out that he was not calling for state ownership or control of productive activities (except in "limited fields such as public power and . . . public housing"). On the contrary, the role of the federal government was a "marginal" one, designed to "promote the growth and expansion of private enterprise." But that the role was marginal did not mean it was unambitious. Hansen called on the government to "ensure and underwrite an adequate volume of purchasing power and effective demand" by greatly increasing its commitment to public investment and social welfare. The state could ensure full employment "by maintaining a national minimum of social services, by undertaking an improvement and development program of public works, regional resource development, urban redevelopment and public housing, and by underwriting and making loans to private business and foreign countries." All these undertakings would have beneficial social results in specific areas; but the larger justification for them would be their contribution to the health of the economy as a whole.[22]

Crucial to the successful completion of this project was a new approach to the question of deficit spending, and it was on this issue that Hansen found himself most indebted to Keynes. The entire concept of "full employment" rested on the belief that government must step in and stimulate economic growth at times when the private economy fell short; that meant, almost by definition, that the state's spending obligations would be highest when its revenues were lowest. The Roosevelt administration, which had run budget deficits in every year of its existence, had nevertheless been slow to challenge the balanced-budget orthodoxy it had inherited; even the President's important 1938 commitment to large-scale federal spending as a way to fight recession had not included any overt challenges to the supporters of balanced budgets.

To Hansen, and to virtually everyone else gravitating to the idea of "full employment," it was now necessary to mount such a challenge. "We cannot in this country change the propensity to consume rapidly enough to achieve full employment without a considerable volume of loan expenditures by the government," he wrote in 1945. But that should be no reason for concern. The public debt, he argued, "is not at all like personal debt." Government spending could serve to increase economic activity and hence increase national wealth. It was "more like investment" than ordinary debt. It represented not fiscal irresponsibility, but the nation's commitment "to do something . . . which the citizens could not accomplish individually and the cost of which is not possible or desirable to distribute at once among them." Hence, an internal public debt "need never be paid," he argued; indeed, it "need never even be reduced, except . . . when it has become so large that taxation to service it disrupts the functioning of the economy." That was an unlikely event, Hansen argued, since "a compensatory program and a large-scale development program would not in any probability absorb so large a figure as 5 per cent of national income. . . . No impossible breakdown need occur over the moderate use of public credit for long-range development projects."[23] Stuart Chase, who had also become an inveterate publicist of the full-employment idea by the early 1940s, made the same point more bluntly. The fear of public debt, so paralyzing to public action, was "largely groundless," he wrote. "Great nations do not go bankrupt in the way a person or a business does, for the debt they owe is largely to themselves."[24]

The idea of full employment was, in the end, an expression of both faith and fear: faith in the ability of the state to manage the economy effectively through its fiscal powers, fear that in the absence of state intervention the end of the war would bring a return to, even a worsening of, the depression conditions of the 1930s. It was a concept that provided a reasonably coherent framework for many of the discrete and halting adjustments liberals had been making in their goals for the state since at least the late 1930s. It represented an effort to define a role for government less threatening to capitalists (and hence less politically and bureaucratically difficult) than the regulatory and managerial strategies of the early New Deal and before; but one that nevertheless gave the state an active and powerful part in ensuring that the capitalist economy would work on behalf of all the nation's people.[25]

Advocates of full employment were not naive. They boasted of broad public support for their goals, but they knew there would be substantial opposition. Achieving full employment would not be easy. Yet they were also optimists, even at times visionaries—men and women convinced that they had, at last, found the answer to the problems of the modern industrial economy, an answer that lay within the nation's grasp. "In these war years we have rediscovered our economic power," Hansen wrote ebulliently in 1943. In the 1930s, no one had believed the American economy could grow as rapidly and substantially as it had in the 1940s. "These things were just not believed possible. But here they are.... Thus our sights all along the line have been raised." A "compensatory fiscal policy" could make wartime growth continue in the postwar world, without "direct controls on business," with "individual enterprise quite free to operate within the framework of a free market." The reformers' battles over the structure of corporate power had not been won, certainly, but perhaps now it was not necessary to win them. "The old standards are obsolete," Hansen insisted.[26]

"We stand at the gates of the age of plenty, key in hand, fumbling at the lock," the liberal planner Charles Merriam said at the beginning of the war. "But make no mistake, we face a new era. We are not going back, but forward, to build in the New World a new and finer form of American democratic state, a loftier realm to which human personality may wing its way and find its home."[27] A bold new world beckoned. What remained was to find the vehicles, and the political support, to allow the United States to grasp it.

THE STRUGGLE TO DEFINE a full-employment policy proceeded on many fronts, and it revealed the degree to which older notions of economic reform—anti-monopoly impulses, the belief in regulating production, and others—continued to mingle with the emerging consumption-oriented ideas that were at the heart of the new liberalism. That mingling of impulses was particularly clear in one of the first skirmishes of the full-employment battle. It occurred within the War Production Board—the government agency whose troubled stewardship of the wartime economy had done much both to legitimize the idea of full employment and to delegitimize the idea of state management of production. Within the WPB, as elsewhere, the question of how and when to begin the reconversion process became the subject of heated debate. It also became part of the endgame by which Donald Nelson terminated his unhappy tenure as chairman.

By late 1943, Nelson and the WPB had essentially lost the battle to control the war economy in any genuinely independent way. Most purchasing decisions were firmly in the hands of the military. Materials allocation, still under the nominal control of the WPB, was responsive above all to the War and Navy departments and the Army-Navy Munitions Board. Efforts to funnel war contracts to small businesses had largely failed. WPB personnel, whom the military had skillfully cultivated, were often more loyal to the armed services than to their own agency. Clearly, it was now too late in the war to hope for any basic change in the system of war production and procurement.

Nelson and his dwindling band of allies within the WPB gradually turned their attention, therefore, to the question that was beginning to preoccupy many liberals: how to convert the war economy to civilian purposes. And they moved quickly to associate themselves with the growing commitment to full employment. In April 1943, Nelson commissioned the first of several WPB studies of reconversion policies. Its recommendations, as he had undoubtedly intended, included giving the WPB substantial authority over the reconversion process. More important, it endorsed the full-employment agenda many liberals were by now vigorously promoting in other places. "The modern industrial economy has always been characterized by the low degree of utilization of its existing plant," WPB reconversion planners claimed. Even in wartime, substantial resources (perhaps most notably the plants and facilities of the thousands of small businesses shut out of war production) remained untapped. The WPB should take the lead, through a vigorous program of early reconversion, in getting the economy ready not just for stability, but for robust growth after the war. It should prepare for "resumption of civilian production with full employment as quickly as possible."[28]

As early as 1943, there were already areas of the economy in which military orders were slowing and unemployment was on the rise. By the spring of 1944, the number of such areas was rapidly growing. And after the success of the Normandy invasion in June 1944, confidence grew rapidly that the European war might end relatively quickly. To Nelson and his allies, that made moving toward reconversion an urgent priority; and they began struggling to authorize a limited return to civilian production. Nelson was careful, as always, to do nothing overtly confrontational.

He outlined a series of plans that would, he insisted, promote reconversion only when there was no possibility of interfering with military needs. Industries shifting to civilian production, moreover, would not be permitted to hire workers who might be needed for war production.[29] But despite the caution, Nelson was emphatic about one thing: Reconversion policies should assist in creating a high-growth, full-employment economy after the war, with as little productive slack as possible. And they should target the areas most likely to contribute to a resumption of and increase in civilian consumption in peacetime.[30]

The WPB reconversion plan had to compete, of course, with similar prescriptions from many other areas of government—even from some civilian agencies that shared Nelson's goals but hoped themselves to control reconversion.[31] But Nelson's most serious opposition came from those unsympathetic to reconversion of any kind. One source was predictable: the War Department and the uniformed services, which had consistently fought all but the most minimal civilian production during the war and which strongly opposed all but the most minimal plans for reconversion while fighting was still in progress.[32] Another was something of a surprise: Charles E. Wilson.

When Nelson fired Ferdinand Eberstadt in February 1943 and made Wilson his principal deputy, he was not just acting to secure his own job. He was tying himself to a man who seemed to be his ally in his struggles against the War Department, the military, and corporate figures who took a conservative, restrictionist view of economic policy. In the battle with Eberstadt, Wilson had been a champion of expanding, not just stabilizing, production. Nelson expected him also to support policies shifting the economy toward civilian production before the war was over, so as to guard against a recession and massive layoffs when peace finally came. But while Wilson was a champion of increasing war production, he showed minimal interest in defending civilian production and even less in promoting early reconversion. Once freed from his turf battle with Eberstadt, moreover, he quickly allied himself almost as closely with the military as Eberstadt had done. Although he gave lip service to the need for reconversion planning (and complained bitterly when accused of opposing it), he resisted Nelson's ambitious reconversion schemes and at times fought strenuously to derail them.[33]

By mid-1944, therefore, Nelson was almost entirely isolated within the WPB itself and was casting about for allies from outside the agency. He found them among liberal enthusiasts for full employment—in the Bureau of the Budget in the administration, on the Truman Committee in Congress, and among some of the liberal journals of opinion that had generally treated him with disdain but now began once again to lionize him. ("It is strange, but true, that the most progressive voice in this fight is that of Donald M. Nelson," the *New Republic* noted in July 1944.[34]) In his last months in government, as his power within the bureaucracy waned, he moved deeper and deeper into the liberals' embrace, becoming at last the committed New Dealer that his early supporters had wrongly assumed he was in 1942.

Nelson also allied himself with one of the few remaining divisions in the WPB whose staff remained loyal to him: the Smaller War Plants Corporation (whose last director, Maury Maverick, once called Nelson "the outstanding industrial statesman of all times"). And in doing so, he brought to his enthusiasm for full employment a commitment many other liberals had by now largely abandoned: a concern about the power of monopoly and a commitment to protecting smaller economic units. Nelson backed Maverick's proposal that small businesses, having shared relatively little in the lucrative war contracts, should have a head start in converting to civilian production. That would serve both the cause of justice (by compensating small businesses for their wartime losses) and the cause of efficiency (because small business plants were, Maverick claimed, easier and speedier to convert than larger factories, and because they were more likely to produce the consumer goods that would be the keys to postwar prosperity).[35] Nelson echoed such arguments in his 1944 reconversion plan. "If the small user is bound by the same rules of civilian production as the big plant," he wrote, "the cumulative effect may be to close down small businesses." The WPB should not so much "give small business a break" as "try to equalize the breaks between smaller and larger businesses."[36]

Such plans met predictable opposition. The military resisted virtually any moves toward reconversion, whatever the size of the plants. "Household goods won't win the war," Assistant Secretary of War Robert Patterson said in a characteristically stern and caustic radio address late in 1944. "Our fighting men could not maintain their brilliant gains with vacuum cleaners, refrigerators, and lawn mowers."[37] And corporate figures within the WPB, most of whom represented larger corporations, feared that the proposals Maverick and Nelson were promoting would work to the disadvantage of their own companies. "One consideration should guide all reconversion planning as the dollar-a-year men saw it," Bruce Catton later wrote, somewhat polemically. "The old competitive patterns of industry must be preserved intact."[38]

Nelson responded to the opposition with what was, for him, unusual bitterness. His complaints about the military he kept largely to himself—

at least until publication of his memoirs in 1946, when he charged that "the Army was, quite openly, out to protect war production by the simple means of creating pools of unemployment."[39] But he responded publicly and bluntly to the criticism from his fellow businessmen. "As to the fear that the competitive position of certain companies may be injured by permitting their competitors to get into production first," he wrote in a 1944 memorandum,

> we cannot allow that fear to prevent action needed to protect the overall economy. The powers of the War Production Board should not be used to preserve the competitive pattern of industry which existed before the war.... The welfare of the overall economy takes precedence over the interest of any individual or groups.[40]

But neither Nelson's uncharacteristically forceful rhetoric nor his support from full-employment liberals was of much help to him in the end within the increasingly savage war production bureaucracy. Part of the problem was clashing personalities. By mid-1944, Nelson's feud with Wilson had grown to almost epic proportions. Virtually the entire WPB had taken sides in the dispute, with the most powerful members of the staff aligning themselves with Wilson—who was by now virtually ignoring Nelson and behaving as if he were himself the chairman. Nelson could not even get a respectful hearing at WPB staff meetings; he was greeted by his ostensible subordinates with such contempt and even derision that he all but stopped attending.[41]

But part of the problem was Nelson's increasingly fervent commitment to the cause of small business. That cause had scant sympathy in any part of the WPB other than the beleaguered Smaller War Plants Corporation (SWPC). Even Nelson's liberal defenders had difficulty supporting it with any genuine enthusiasm. A reconversion policy designed to ensure postwar growth would have been difficult for Wilson and Nelson's other critics to oppose; indeed, Wilson insisted repeatedly, if somewhat disingenuously, that he not only supported such plans but had set them in motion. But a reconversion policy designed to strengthen small businesses aroused much more fervent opposition. And, except among members of the Truman Committee and among a few scattered anti-monopolists in other parts of the government, it generated little real enthusiasm.[42]

In August 1944, the President finally intervened. Reluctant to antagonize either Nelson's or Wilson's constituency, he crafted what he believed to be a face-saving compromise. Nelson would step aside "temporarily" as WPB chairman to accept a special mission to China (the purpose of which was conspicuously vague). Wilson would become acting chairman in Nelson's absence. But the compromise fooled, and placated, no one. Nelson accepted the China assignment (to the dismay of his many supporters among small businessmen)[43]; but, convinced that Wilson would destroy any chance of an early reconversion, he and his allies sought commitments from the White House that there would be no change in policy once he departed. Wilson, enraged once again that he was being "slandered" by Nelson's supporters, submitted another in what had become a long string of overheated letters of resignation. The President and Office of War Mobilization director James F. Byrnes had refused them in the past; this time, finally weary of the battle (and reluctant to antagonize liberals by seeming to side with Wilson), they accepted.[44]

Julius Krug, a longtime Nelson subordinate with no clear ideological profile, became acting chairman. A few months later, Nelson formally resigned and Krug took formal possession of the job. He was more sympathetic to reconversion than Wilson, but not committed enough (and not powerful enough) to win any significant victories. The last months of the war passed with only token efforts by the WPB to plan for conversion to peace—and virtually no efforts to give small business any special protection in the process.[45]

"A powerful battle of the most immediate importance to every American is raging inside the War Production Board over who will control the American economy in the transition to peace," the New Republic columnist T.R.B. (a vocal full-employment enthusiast) had written in July 1944. "Whether men are to have jobs will depend on the decisions of the WPB. The type of economic development we are to have in the next generation will be determined by who wins out in the tremendous struggle that is now being waged." Two months later, it was clear that liberals had lost the struggle for the soul of the WPB—at least in part because of the attempt to link the quest for full employment with a defense of small business. Full employment enthusiasts would have to seek support for their dreams in other ways and in other places.[46]

A SECOND, THWARTED effort to attach the search for full employment to an older idea of state economic management emerged in discussions of an obscure but very important wartime bureaucracy: the Defense Plants Corporation. The DPC was the brainchild of New Deal officials who, more than a year before Pearl Harbor, became convinced that private capital would not (and probably could not) invest enough in expanded plant capacity to meet the nation's likely production requirements in wartime.

The new corporation, which a talented group of New Deal administrators created over the fall and summer of 1940, was housed fully within the Reconstruction Finance Corporation and was dependent on the RFC (and its director, Jesse Jones) for everything from money to office space to paper clips. But within the RFC it created a reasonably autonomous bureaucracy of its own, and it survived a series of challenges from other areas of government. Conservatives in Congress and in various war agencies worried that the existence of government-owned plants would make the state too powerful a force in the industrial economy after the war and tried to restrict the DPC to building facilities with no conceivable peacetime uses. General Somervell and the Army Navy Munitions Board tried to seize the function for themselves. But the DPC had powerful allies too, including Robert Patterson and other important figures in the War Department, who considered it the best vehicle for rapid plant expansion and who were content to worry about the postwar implications of the experiment later.[47]

The Defense Plants Corporation was the most important source of capital investment in the nation during the war. Private investment in plant and equipment between 1940 and 1945 was over $11 billion, more than private sources had invested in all of the 1930s. But by as early as 1943, the government had invested almost $15 billion, nearly two-thirds of it through the DPC, to build some of the newest and most efficient manufacturing facilities in the United States. DPC plants controlled virtually all the nation's synthetic rubber and magnesium production, nearly three-quarters of the aircraft manufacturing, more than half the aluminum production, a substantial proportion of the raw materials industries, and important segments of steel, pipelines, barge production, and other industries.[48]

The government did not itself operate the plants; the DPC leased them to private manufacturers. And there were numerous complaints from liberals—mirroring many of their objections to the War Production Board—that the process by which private companies gained access to these plants (which cost them nothing to build and from which they derived profits far out of proportion to the modest leasing fees they paid the government) favored already powerful corporations. If the government was going to offer what were, in effect, subsidies to private industry, critics argued, it should not favor "monopolists" when it did so. I. F. Stone charged that Jesse Jones, "a Shylock in dealing with ordinary business men, negotiated a contract with the Aluminum Company of America that gave it everything but a second mortgage on the White House." The government's "vast plant-building activity," Dwight Macdonald complained, "simply reproduces on a larger scale the present balance of forces in the economy." To those liberals whose vision of the state included a commitment to altering that "balance of forces," this was a strong indictment indeed.[49]

Liberals won some successes in influencing the distribution of DPC plants. The agency, under pressure from the Justice Department, leased some new aluminum factories to competitors of Alcoa, which liberals considered a notorious monopoly. And while most of the DPC funds went to such already industrialized areas as New York, Chicago, Cleveland, and Detroit (the site of the mammoth Willow Run aviation plant, leased to Ford), a considerable portion of the agency's investment went to relatively undeveloped areas—Texas, California, the Pacific Northwest, and elsewhere—helping break the concentration of industry and credit in the East. That pleased, among others, Harold Ickes.[50]

But such victories were few, and most liberals gave up early trying to influence the distribution of DPC funds during the war. As they began to consider the shape of the peace in 1943 and 1944, however, many of them turned their attention to the defense plants again. The government may not have operated the plants during the war, but it did own them. And that ownership, some liberals insisted, could give the state an important lever with which to influence the postwar economy. "The type of financing now being carried on by the Defense Plants Corporation," Clifford Durr (one of its founders) wrote in 1943,

> . . . may serve to encourage ventures into new fields where the possibilities are great but the risks are too heavy to be assumed by private business. . . . With the government holding title to the plants, the prospect of useful productive capacity being destroyed in an endeavor to increase prices by limiting production will be greatly reduced.[51]

At the least, the *Nation* argued early in 1945, the government must not allow the plants "to fall into the hands of giant monopolies which seek to maintain prices and profits by creating artificial scarcities." The CIO-PAC proposed that the sale of any DPC plant be contingent on "a guaranty that the purchaser will fully utilize its productive capacity." Maury Maverick urged that the facilities be subdivided and sold in pieces to give small business a chance to bid on them. Harold Ickes offered a plan for selling the plants to veterans, thus "giving ten million young persons shares of stock in the America for which they risked their lives."[52]

Some liberals went further, insisting that the best solution lay in continued government ownership of many of the DPC facilities. Plant ownership would allow the state, as the New Deal economist H. S. Person wrote in the *New Republic*, "to prevent monopolies and cartels and otherwise regulate industry." They could, in particular, counter efforts by monopolists to inflate prices artificially. State-owned factories could serve the same "yardstick" function the TVA had served earlier in driving down prices for electric power and combatting the restrictionist policies of utilities. If the nation genuinely aspired to full employment, public ownership of strategically placed factories would permit the state to play an important role in creating a high-production, high-consumption economy.[53]

Ultimately, however, hopes for a "liberal" approach to the disposal of the DPC plants proved as futile as hopes for a "New Deal" approach to reconversion by the WPB. Within the administration, the few liberals who remained in positions of power tried to influence the President to take an interest in the issue, but to no avail. Control of decisions remained in the hands of Byrnes, Jones, and others with scant sympathy for the liberal position. Late in 1943, in response to warnings that reconversion planning was in chaos, Byrnes recruited the redoubtable Bernard Baruch to prepare a set of recommendations for reconversion policies, among them suggestions for dealing with government-owned war plants. Baruch recruited his longtime collaborator John Hancock to help him, and together they released a report in February 1944 that confirmed many of the worst fears of liberals about the direction of reconversion planning.

The Baruch-Hancock report was not an entirely reactionary document. It supported, in a general way, the concept of full employment (although perhaps insincerely, since Baruch himself was really more concerned with preserving stability than ensuring economic expansion). It called for measures to guard against a resurgence of monopoly power, although it offered few guidelines as to what those measures should be. But on most specific issues, the report took reliably conservative positions. Baruch spoke privately of his fear that reconversion policies would fall into the reckless hands of New Dealers ("the long-haired boys") once the businessmen in the WPB and elsewhere left Washington; to prevent that, he crafted plans to leave as little of the war production apparatus behind as possible. That included, above all, the war plants of the DPC. "People will not invest money in new plants," he wrote privately to Byrnes, "if Government-owned plants are hanging over the market. . . . Business confidence cannot exist in the period of uncertainty as to such an important aspect of the whole economy. Unless business confidence does exist, reasonably full employment cannot exist."[54]

The report called for the appointment of a surplus property administrator within the Office of War Mobilization (Byrnes's agency), with specific instructions to sell off government plants to private industry as quickly as possible. The administrators should try to avoid promoting monopoly power. They might, on occasion, contemplate leasing plants to private operators. But Baruch and Hancock were emphatic in stating that under no circumstances should the government actually control plants, even if it continued to own some of them. Nor should the government have any leverage over the production and pricing decisions of any firm. *"Leasing,"* they wrote, italicizing the passage for emphasis, *"must not become a hidden device for the Government to compete with private plants.* . . . Once plants leave the Government's hands, they must stand on their own feet competitively."[55]

Some liberals found the rhetoric of the Baruch-Hancock report so appealing (and surprising) that they overlooked its conservative substance. Eleanor Roosevelt, for example, told Harry Hopkins (who had criticized the document), "I read the Baruch report and it does not seem to me it ignores all the human side of demobilization." The *New Republic* ran an editorial praising the general tone (although not all the specific suggestions) of the report.[56] But most liberals responded with dismay. I. F. Stone lamented the lost opportunity to use DPC property "to break monopolistic restrictions on the market, a task two generations of trust-busting has been unable to accomplish." He described the report as a "triple-plated guaranty that no such use will be made of government plants." By November 1944, the *New Republic* editorialists who had viewed the Baruch-Hancock report favorably the previous March, had begun vigorously to attack it. They now saw the report as advocating that "established plants . . . have first access to raw materials; that cartels . . . continue their control over international trade"; the DPC factories would become the "spoils of monopoly," and the economy overall would "return to the past . . . squelching all predictions of new consumer products after the war." Most of all, the critics argued, the plan had missed the principal lesson of the war: that (as J. Donald Kingsley, an official in the War Manpower Commission, wrote in 1944) "large-scale global intervention can produce full employment and can carry levels of production to previously unimagined heights." The Baruch-Hancock plan, by contrast, was "Victorian both in its economics and its optimism."[57]

Four days after receiving the report, the White House moved to enact Baruch and Hancock's principal recommendations (in what I. F. Stone called "a kind of right-wing economic coup"). The President created the office of Surplus Property Administrator within the OWM and, at Baruch's urging, named Will Clayton (Jesse Jones's close associate, whom the *New Republic* described as "a fanatical believer in unrestricted free enterprise") to the post. There was never any doubt about Clayton's intentions. He would dispose of government plants as quickly and efficiently as possible. And his motive for doing so would not be (as liberals had hoped) to advance the prospects of full employment, but simply to get the government out of the private economy and allow "free enterprise" to blossom. "It is beginning to look as if the words 'free enterprise' are going to take the place of 'rugged individualism' . . . as a cloak for corporate exploitation," Thurman Arnold complained shortly after hearing of the appointment. Clayton, he said, "dreads and hates the very idea of full production of anything." Sale of the plants (at what critics, with considerable justification, considered outrageously low prices) began even before the fighting ended In most cases the purchasers were the corporations that had run the plants during the war. By the end of 1945, virtually all the most desirable plants were in private hands. By 1949, the government had sold the last of them.[58]

The jettisoning of the government-owned plants was clearly a defeat for liberals, and more evidence of their dwindling political influence within the Roosevelt administration. But it was also evidence of their own shifting priorities. Most liberals would have preferred to see the government dispose of the DPC facilities differently, or not at all; most believed that the Baruch-Clayton approach destroyed a valuable opportunity to strengthen the chances for full employment. But relatively few liberals considered the issue central to their hopes. They were focusing, instead, on different prospects for government action.


AS THE IDEA of planning for full employment grew more attractive in the early 1940s, many supporters of the concept began to look to a relatively obscure government agency: the National Resources Planning Board. All but unnoticed during most of its ten-year life, the NRPB managed for a brief moment in the midst of the war to articulate a coherent liberal vision of the future, a vision that inspired broad, even rapturous enthusiasm among full-employment enthusiasts and many others.

In the short term, at least, the NRPB and its supporters were not much more successful than the War Production Board liberals or the Defense Plant Corporation planners in achieving their goals. Indeed, the NRPB—an agency designed to play a permanent role in government— actually expired well before either the WPB or the DPC, which were both explicitly temporary. But important parts of the NRPB vision survived as a centerpiece of liberal hopes long after the agency itself ceased to exist.

The NRPB began its life in the shadows of one of the first great New Deal bureaucracies. When Congress created the Public Works Administration (under the National Industrial Recovery Act) in 1933, Harold Ickes, the director of the new agency, established an office to help coordinate its work: the National Planning Board.[59] He did so at the behest of Charles W. Eliot II, the young scion of a distinguished Massachusetts family (and the grandson of a celebrated Harvard president). Eliot came out of a well-established tradition of city and regional planners; his uncle, and namesake, was one of the leading urban planners of the early twentieth century and the architect of a plan that helped shape the modern city of Boston. The younger Eliot was himself a landscape architect by training, and he had worked previously as a city planner in Massachusetts and with the National Capital Park and Planning Commission.

The planning board Ickes created in response to Eliot's suggestion had the clear stamp of that background. Its chairman, Frederic A. Delano (the President's uncle), had helped write the New York City regional plan in the 1920s and later directed the National Capital Park and Planning Commission on which Eliot had served; Eliot became the new board's staff director. In its statement of purpose, the board set for itself the goal of preparing "comprehensive and coordinated plans for regional areas," to help the PWA decide which public works projects to finance. It considered its mission an enlarged version of the same kind of resources and development planning that Eliot, Delano, and many others had grown accustomed to considering for cities and regions. *The American City*, an urban planning journal, excitedly described the members of the board in 1933 in explicit city-planning terms, as "architects building a habitation for a new social order" engaged in "the most worthwhile and inspiring job in the United States today."[60]

But the new board embodied another, broader planning impulse as well. It embraced an ambitious program of research into "the distribution and trends of population, land uses, industry, housing, and natural resources" and the "social and economic habits, trends, and values involved in development projects and plans." Out of that research would come planning on a genuinely national scale, planning for the structure and performance of the economy and the society as a whole. Charles E. Merriam, who was (along with Delano and the economist Wesley Mitchell) one of the three original "citizen members" of the board, described this second purpose as the creation of "a plan for national planning."

Merriam, in fact, was the most influential figure in the new agency almost from the beginning. An eminent political scientist at the University of Chicago and an academic enterpreneur par excellence, he had a social scientist's faith in the value of surveys and research. He had been one of the founders of President Hoover's Social Science Research Council, which had prepared a series of reports in the early 1930s on broad social trends. He was accustomed to thinking of planning in national terms. Indeed, he spent his life trying to fit his deep faith in planning into the structure of democratic politics. The new board, he came to believe, could become a mechanism by which planners would have a permanent voice in government, through which they could persuade the public and the political system to make rational choices about the future.[61]

In its early years, the board devoted most of its energies to "resource planning": crafting proposals for the regulation and development of land, water, forests, and other natural resources. But the broader planning agenda was never far from the surface. "There is need for government economic planning," Merriam wrote in 1935, in a discussion of the agency's early work, "not to replace business planning, but to render services to the general public, and to business itself, which business cannot render . . . . Business cannot protect itself effectively against the business cycle hazard."[62]

In the course of the 1930s, the planning board moved through several incarnations. Each of them helped push it closer to Merriam's vision of an agency committed to broad concepts of research and planning with influence at the highest levels of government. And each of them increased the strains between Merriam and Eliot, whose interest in planning was always more project-oriented. In 1934, the President folded the National Planning Board into a new National Resources Board, an independent agency indirectly responsible to the President; no longer was it just an adjunct of a public works program. A year later he renamed it the National Resources Committee, in a largely technical effort to detach it from the National Industrial Recovery Act (under whose auspices it had been created) after the Supreme Court struck the legislation down. And in 1939, as part of the larger reorganization of the executive branch that Merriam and the NRC had helped initiate, it became the National Resources Planning Board—a formal part of the executive office of the President, reporting directly to Roosevelt.[63]

The NRPB was in many respects simply a continuation under a different name of the three planning boards that had preceded it. Delano was still the chair; Merriam, now vice-chair, continued to dominate the substantive work of the agency; Eliot remained the staff director. (George Yantis, an economist from Washington state with a background in natural resource issues, replaced Wesley Mitchell as the third citizen member; his impact on the board was never great.) But there were important differences. Unlike its predecessors, the NRPB needed direct congressional appropriations to survive; as a result it no longer had the relative protection from partisan politics it had enjoyed in its earlier lives. At the same time, the board was accelerating its already significant movement away from choosing sites for dams and public buildings and toward broader questions of industrial production, consumer expenditures, and employment levels—the kinds of questions Merriam had been pressing the board to consider from the beginning.[64]

One indication of this changing focus was the increasing involvement of Alvin Hansen in the board's deliberations. Eliot and others wrote him frequently asking advice on economic questions. Hansen used his relationship with the board to promote his own ideas on full employment and fiscal policy. He was the author or co-author of many of its most important reports.[65]

Another indication was the close relationship between the NRPB and the Fiscal and Monetary Advisory Board, which had been created in 1938 (at the urging of Delano and Merriam) to advise the President on "Government spending, taxation and monetary activities in such a way as to smooth out so far as possible the upswings and downswings of the business cycle." Its principal members were Delano, Henry Morgenthau, Marriner Eccles, and Harold Smith, director of the Bureau of the Budget; its "basic purpose," according to the original proposal, "is to develop studies and plans for high living standards." (It, too, frequently consulted with Hansen.)[66]

But the Fiscal and Monetary Advisory Board was an unsatisfactory answer to Merriam's call for a planning body concerned with the structure and performance of the economy. It was an informal group, and it met only occasionally. Its work suffered, moreover, from a lack of sympathy for its central task by its highest-ranking member, Secretary of the Treasury Morgenthau. The committee issued a few reports promoting increased government spending to spur full employment, and it had a few meetings with the President (who talked with the members mostly about the political obstacles in the way of their proposals). It soon lapsed into obscurity. As the inadequacy of the Fiscal and Monetary Advisory Board became clear, some members of the planning board grew increasingly interested in taking over its functions.[67]

Discussions of how to achieve full employment were well under way within the National Resources Committee as early as 1938. At a meeting on industrial policy that year, members and staff agreed that "Government policy should include both direct efforts to place more funds in the hands of consumers and direct efforts to influence the nature of production and price policies." Most participants agreed that both efforts were important. But the question remained (as Thomas Blaisdell put it in 1938) "whether the orientation of intervention should be toward the producer or toward the consumer." Over the next several years, the most influential members of the committee came to favor the latter.[68]

In June 1940, the newly reorganized NRPB issued one of its first major publications, *The Structure of the American Economy: Part II*. Part I, published in 1939 by the National Resources Committee, had described "basic characteristics" of the economy; Part II outlined an ambitious agenda for making "full use of resources" and raising the "general standard of living." It referred in passing to other work of the board (reflected in such publications of 1940 as *Deficiencies in Hydrologic Research, Land Classification in the United States*, or *Housing: The Continuing Problem*) as useful complements to "this broad purpose"—a reference that no doubt annoyed Eliot and others, who still considered such projects the NRPB's primary mission. But the document had little time for the details of public works and regional planning; it attempted, rather, to explain the importance of a firm commitment to the idea of full employment through increased consumption:

> The development and adoption of techniques for bringing about and maintaining reasonably full employment of men and machines is not only a major problem, but is today the Nation's most pressing economic problem, relegating all other economic problems to a secondary position so long as it remains unsolved.[69]

The five economists who contributed essays to the "symposium" (as the NRPB called it) were not in full agreement. But all of them emphasized the degree to which the ostensible subject of their publication—the "structure" of the economy—was, in fact, less important than what one called its "operating characteristics." There was nothing wrong, they conceded, in considering structural changes—in challenging excessive economic concentration, for example. But such efforts would always be inadequate to the task of achieving full employment, which had more to do with changing the way consumers and producers alike behaved in their daily lives than in changing the structure of institutions. More important than reforming or regulating production, then, would be policies designed to encourage consumers to spend more and producers to produce and invest more, as well as policies to discourage everyone from excessive, unproductive saving. Over the next two years, the NRPB would elaborate on those ideas and make them the basis of several extraordinary documents.[70]

AMERICAN INVOLVEMENT in World War II changed the NRPB's mission substantially. No longer was the board part of the effort to produce economic recovery; war production had ended the Depression quickly and decisively. No longer was it making plans for New Deal public works programs; most such programs quickly ceased operations as the government shifted resources and energies to war production. Instead, the NRPB began to plan for the world after the war. How could the United States ensure that the Depression would not return once the fighting ended? What policies would guarantee the continuation of full production and full employment in peacetime? The board addressed these questions in most of the dozens of pamphlets and reports it issued in 1942 and 1943.[71]

The NPRB continued during the war to propose public works projects and to insist on their importance; but even more than in 1940, it now portrayed such projects less as vehicles for remaking the environment than as tools for countercyclical government spending. Its mission was to create a "shelf" of potential public undertakings from which the government could, "at a moment's notice," draw projects "as insurance against industrial collapse and unemployment"; the intrinsic value of the projects themselves in terms of older notions of urban or regional planning had become decidedly secondary.[72]

The NRPB's principal mission now was to devise policies that would create a high-production, full-employment economy. Its wartime reports called explicitly and repeatedly for government programs to maintain a "dynamic expanding economy on the order of 100 to 125 billions national income," a figure that only a few years before would have seemed preposterously high, but one which suddenly seemed sustainable in light of the wartime boom; the 1942 "national income" was $137 billion. "We must plan for full employment," members of the board wrote in a 1942 article explaining their proposals. "We shall plan to balance our national production-consumption budget at a high level with full employment, not at a low level with mass unemployment."[73]

Of the many things the NRPB published in its ten-year life, nothing had as great an impact as *Security, Work, and Relief Policies*, a prosaically titled report released in March 1943 (after Roosevelt, skittish about its political impact, had held it for over a year). The report attempted to lay out a coherent plan for a postwar social order. To many liberals, the document became something close to a programmatic bible; to conservatives, it was evidence of the dangerously statist designs of the NRPB and the New Deal as a whole. It simultaneously ensured the NRPB's centrality to liberal thinking and guaranteed its demise.[74]

*Security, Work, and Relief Policies* outlined a program of "social security" of such breadth and ambition that it was widely dubbed the "American Beveridge Plan," a counterpart to the contemporaneous report in Great Britain (the product of a planning commission chaired by Sir William Beveridge of the London School of Economics), which outlined the framework of what became the postwar British welfare state. There was, in fact, some modest communication between the two planning efforts (and considerable mutual admiration and congratulation when their reports appeared). Beveridge himself made a well-publicized visit to the United States in May 1943, during which he met with most of the members of the NRPB and many other American full-employment enthusiasts.[75] But the NRPB report was distinctively a product of the emerging American liberalism of the war years—particularly in its ebullience. The Beveridge plan tempered its proposals with a sense of economic and fiscal limits; not until 1945, in a second report, did Beveridge become a real convert to the full-employment idea. The NRPB's proposals were wholly rooted in the concept of full-employment planning from the start, and they reflected the degree to which American liberals had repudiated the "mature economy" idea and had come to believe in the potentially limitless resources of the American economy.[76]

For most of its more than six hundred pages, *Security, Work, and Relief Policies* laid out a broad and ambitious plan to make "adequate provision for those who have no means of livelihood or only inadequate means"—a plan that accepted, but greatly expanded upon, the outlines of the social insurance and social provision systems the New Deal had created in the 1930s. Even sixty years later, its proposals are striking for their sweep—and for the generosity of spirit (so seldom evident in discussions of public assistance in America) that surrounded them. The report spoke of the

> millions of cases where deep anxiety, haunting fear of want, acute suffering and distress blight and sear the lives of men and women, and children, too. Most of the drifting souls are those on whom the door of hope has been closed either by nature's equipment or by the unfortunate circumstances of unkind social experience.

And it rejected outright the idea that a "complete system of social security" would destroy incentives and encourage people to avoid work:

> We must and do assume that the bulk of mankind who are able to work are willing to work, and that they will strive for something more than a doghouse subsistence on a dole.[77]

The report called for extensive federal work programs, administered through a new Federal Work Agency (modeled vaguely on the New Deal's Works Progress Administration), to provide jobs for "all who are able and willing to work." It outlined a greatly expanded program of social insurance for the unemployed, the disabled, and the elderly, based on the Social Security system the New Deal had created in 1935. It called for significant increases in "general public assistance" for those whom the work programs and the social insurance did not cover—again an extension of programs the Roosevelt administration had launched in the 1930s. And it endorsed generous new programs of public services in health and education, even if it provided few details about how such programs would work. Together, its proposals embraced much of what became the liberal social agenda for decades after World War II.[78]

But the NRPB plan reflected more than social generosity. It was a product, too, of a firm commitment to the goal of a "high-income, full-employment" economy and of a belief that programs of public aid would help create it. "Full economic activity and full employment are our first need," the authors of the report claimed. A full-employment economy would create the resources necessary to support the ambitious NRPB agenda. ("Financial problems need be no hindrance," they confidently declared.) But an extensive program of public aid would also help create and maintain full employment. "All the various elements in the public-aid programs have a common quality in that they put money into the hands of individuals in the low-income brackets," the authors explained. The experience of the 1930s made clear that such programs "substantially contributed to the consumers' expenditures of these years," and it was equally clear that such programs, if "coordinated with the broader economic and monetary policies of government," would contribute to maintaining high levels of employment and consumption. For example, "if an expansionist [fiscal] program is desired, the unemployment compensation systems, suitably amended, offer a speedy and almost automatically operating mechanism for distributing funds to those who will spend them."[79]

The report did not wholly ignore other, more traditional approaches to economic and social reform. Improved labor relations, it said, could play an important role in creating the new economic order. So could effective use of antitrust laws. But what was striking about the discussion of these issues was, first, the exceptionally small role they played in the fabric of the report as a whole; and second, the modest, even tentative character of the NRPB's embrace of them. The report talked of the need for "statesmanlike union leaders and managers" to refashion labor relations to serve the demands of the new full-employment, high-consumption economy; building such an economy, it suggested, would do more than any reform of the workplace in improving the lives of workers and capitalists alike. It conceded the possible value of using the antitrust laws in situations where "monopolistic power restricts employment opportunity and the expansion of national income." But it said nothing of the value of the laws in increasing opportunities for producers, and it noted the ways in which anti-monopoly efforts could actually harm the prospects for full employment, could "become destructive of labor standards and produce poverty and wage slavery instead of full employment and high incomes." Structural reform of the economy was clearly secondary. "Full economic activity and full employment are our first need," the authors stated bluntly. The systems of public aid the NRPB was proposing were important vehicles for achieving those goals.[80]

*Security, Work, and Relief Policies* was a product of the Committee on Long-Range Work and Relief Policies, which the NRPB had created late in 1939. William Haber, a liberal economist at the University of Michigan, chaired the committee; Eveline Burns, an economist from Columbia University who had once studied at the London School of Economics (where Beveridge taught), was the director of research. They did their work in relative isolation from the other parts of the NRPB. And in transmitting their report to the President, Delano was careful to indicate that its proposals—welcome as they may have been—did not embrace all the board's aims. It had a "strategic place" in the NRPB's plans for the economy, but it was not the whole of those plans. As if to make that clear, the board published (almost simultaneously with the security report) Alvin Hansen's *After the War—Full Employment*, a bold summary of his already well-known views on the importance of using fiscal policy and, if necessary, deficit spending to raise consumption, stimulate economic growth, and achieve full employment. "It is the responsibility of Government to do its part to insure a sustained demand," he wrote. "We know from past experience that private enterprise has done this for limited periods only." Programs of social insurance and public aid would be useful complements to this goal, but they were clearly secondary to it.[81]

THE SIMULTANEOUS RELEASE in early 1943 of *Security, Work, and Relief Policies* and *After the War—Full Employment* made the NRPB, for the first time in its history, the focus of considerable public attention. The breadth of the reports, and, perhaps equally important, the boldness of their language, excited many full-employment liberals and alarmed many of their more conservative critics. In the short term, at least, the critics prevailed.

But that was not for lack of effort among those who admired the reports and embraced their recommendations. The AFL, the CIO, the National Farmers Union, and others gave immediate, fulsome endorsements. Liberals in Congress called them, as one put it, "nothing short of magnificent." The *Security* report, a *Nation* editorial proclaimed, "has given the American people a dramatic reply to the question: 'What are we fighting for?' . . . It epitomizes, as no other statement has done, the contrast between the way of life of free men and the way of life in the dictatorships. It is a natural supplement to the Atlantic Charter, but it is . . . far more inspiring to the average man." A special issue of the *New Republic* called the NRPB plans "a revolutionary answer to the needs of a revolutionary age," and a potentially powerful weapon in "demoralizing the enemy," "heartening our friends," and "winning the war." Although there were complaints about the vagueness of the reports and about their neglect of some issues (most notably the failure to endorse a comprehensive national health care system), there was widespread enthusiasm for the NRPB's larger aims.[82]

But if the reaction to the reports suggested the outlines of a new liberal agenda for the postwar era, it also revealed the strength of the obstacles to that agenda. Within days of their release, a storm of conservative attacks—in the press, in Congress, and among New Deal critics everywhere—engulfed the reports. The NRPB proposals were "nonsense," Ohio Senator Robert A. Taft claimed; if the United States were to embrace such fiscally irresponsible plans, he said, "we will be ruined long before the war is over." A Republican congressman from Ohio called the reports a plan for "nothing less than the absorption by the state of all economic functions and the complete demolition of free enterprise." A Georgia Democrat concluded that the NRPB program "looks like a $50,000,000,000-a-year proposition. I don't see where we could get that kind of money." Others dismissed the reports as nothing more than the President's "opening gun for a fourth term." The *New York Times* compared them, preposterously, to "Bismarck's state insurance systems, which laid the foundation for the German welfare state that ended in naziism." The head of the U.S. Chamber of Commerce denounced them as a "totalitarian scheme." Such extravagant rhetoric was not uncommon among the NRPB's foes.[83]

Within weeks, critics were consigning the NRPB reports to the dustheap. It was the "flop of the year," *Time* magazine crowed. "Seldom has so important a report disappeared from public debate so quickly," *Newsweek* claimed.[84] The NRPB itself was already a target of conservatives in Congress even before the release of the reports. In the first half of 1943 the abuse escalated dramatically, and hostile members began working to destroy the agency altogether. Members of the board flailed about, arguing first for the importance of their work, then considering a mass resignation—in hopes of saving the agency itself, even if not their own jobs. The President enlisted Donald Nelson and others to make the case for the NRPB's importance to the war effort, and he wrote privately to several crucial senators and congressmen urging the survival of the board; but as on other issues not directly related to the war, he made no strenuous efforts. In the end, Congress authorized no funds for the board in the budget it approved in June. Ten years after its creation in the first heady days of the New Deal, and little more than ten weeks after the release of its two most important reports, the National Resources Planning Board was dead.[85]

In part, the NRPB fell victim to the frenzied efforts by conservatives in Congress—Democrats and Republicans both—to use the war to dismantle as much of the New Deal as possible and to rehabilitate what they considered the tattered principle of fiscal responsibility. Taft and others were neglecting no opportunity in 1943 to denounce high taxes and "wasteful" spending and to demand a balanced budget as soon as the war was over. In part, too, it was a casualty of its own political failings: the passivity of the aging Frederic Delano; the ineffectiveness and unpopularity of Charles W. Eliot, the staff director; the fuzzy, abstract character of many of the NRPB's proposals; the insistence of Charles Merriam that the board should (as a critical observer at the time wrote) "merely offer the elder statesmen a kind of counsel and shun the tough battles that would be necessary to perform the essential functions of planning."[86] But the most important reasons for the board's demise were two larger fears.

One was a concern, primarily within Congress, about the growing power of the executive branch at the expense of the legislature. Merriam's association with the Executive Reorganization bills of 1938 and 1939, which had crystallized that concern, made the NRPB particularly vulnerable to such criticisms. But so did its reports, which did indeed propose a series of measures that would have centralized considerable new authority in the White House. The NRPB's call in some earlier documents for the creation of new regional planning authorities, what some called "Seven Little TVAs," was particularly alarming to members of Congress who saw it, correctly, as an effort to circumvent local political leaders and reduce opportunities for patronage. But even more disturbing was the very existence of the board itself, which served as a symbol to many members of Congress of their increasing irrelevance to basic policy-making. Legislators had been aware for years of the contempt with which many New Deal liberals viewed Congress, and of the liberal thirst for vehicles of governance independent of legislative authority. That had been one of the reasons for the intense hostility to the President's executive reorganization plan in 1937 and 1938. Now the war was producing a plethora of new agencies, many exercising unprecedented power, over which Congress had scant control. The NRPB, many members feared, gave the executive branch tools with which it could erode the authority of Congress further in peacetime.[87]

The other, greater fear extended well beyond Congress. This was the broad popular fear of bureaucracy and state power—a powerful element of American political culture throughout the nation's history. Even at the height of its popularity, the New Deal had aroused considerable misgivings on this score. Many Americans had liked the benefits the Roosevelt administration was providing them and, indeed, quickly came to think of them as basic rights (or "entitlements"). But even as they called for enhancing the services the state provided them, many of those same people remained uneasy about expanding the power of the state. Farmers, for example, were indefatigable in fighting for federal controls and subsidies to stabilize their economic situation; and yet the leading farm organization (the American Farm Bureau Federation) and many, perhaps most, of the farmers it represented were continually critical of the New Deal for extending the reach of bureaucracy and eroding individual freedom. During the war, the unprecedented government intrusiveness into everyday life greatly inflamed such concerns. And the NRPB, with its expansive vision of planning and social provision and its blithe indifference to the political climate in which it was operating, became a natural target of those in Congress attempting to exploit and inflame those popular resentments.[88]

Whatever the reasons, the demise of the NRPB struck many liberals as a heavy blow to their hopes for full employment after the war. For the government to play its proper role in creating and sustaining economic growth in peacetime, it would need (in the New Republic editor Bruce Bliven's words) a new "postwar layer" of administrative capacity. The

NRPB did not have to be that layer; but the hostility to bureaucracy the battle against it revealed made clear how difficult it would be to create it elsewhere. "It is one of the besetting evils of an irresponsible press and a partisan-minded Congress," Bliven complained, "that all advances in the administrative arts must be made under the hail of the most virulent abuse." Even more important, others argued, was the danger the NRPB's institutional collapse posed to the proposals it had made in its last reports—its efforts to tie the concept of full employment to a broad expansion of social insurance and social welfare. Congress was, it seemed, killing more than the messenger. It was killing the message itself. "And so without fanfare or lament," the editors of *Commonweal* concluded at the close of the battle, "dies the present hope of an intelligent, self-disciplined America based on an economy of abundance."[89]

The National Resources Planning Board reports captured more fully than any other documents of their time the contours of what would soon become the heart of postwar American liberalism. They outlined an active role for the federal government in stabilizing the economy and promoting economic growth—a role related to, but also significantly different from, earlier progressive and New Deal notions of economic policy. The reports did not advocate substantial state intrusions into the affairs of capitalist institutions. They called instead for the federal government to make aggressive use of its fiscal powers—spending and taxation—to prevent future depressions and ensure full employment. They outlined, too, an expansive role for the state in protecting American citizens from the vicissitudes of the industrial economy: a substantial expansion of the social insurance and social welfare mechanisms the New Deal had created in the 1930s.

Both those ideas survived to shape the liberal agenda for at least a generation after World War II. But another part of the NRPB vision did not survive nearly so successfully: the idea that the two ideas were connected. The 1943 reports—indeed virtually the entire wartime record of the planning board—represented an effort to link the commitment to full employment with the commitment to a generous welfare state. The two efforts would complement one another: Economic growth would make a generous welfare state possible; a generous welfare state would help stimulate economic growth. But even before the end of the war, it became clear that the linkage between the two ideas was a frail one. By early 1946, the two commitments had begun to move along quite separate paths—with important consequences for both. Two pieces of legislation—the Servicemen's Readjustment Act of 1944 (better known as the "G.I. Bill") and the Employment Act of 1946—

revealed both the extent of and the substantial obstacles to the new liberal agenda.

ALTHOUGH CONGRESS passed the G.I. Bill well after the NRPB had ceased to exist, the planning board was centrally involved in shaping it. In July 1942, the NRPB convened a Conference on Post-War Readjustment of Civilian and Military Personnel in response to a vague directive from the President—who was already feeling pressures from some corners of his administration to begin planning for demobilization.[90] A year later, it presented Roosevelt with a report outlining a series of measures to ensure that returning veterans had access to jobs, education, and—when necessary—financial assistance. Similar recommendations were coming simultaneously from a War Department committee the President had established late in 1943 to study the same questions, and from the American Legion, the nation's most powerful veterans' organization.[91]

Roosevelt endorsed the idea of special benefits for veterans in a fireside chat in July 1943, following the advice of several members of the administration that making provisions for returning soldiers "is not only the right thing to advocate, but it also has enormous appeal." "Among many other things," the President told his radio audience,

> we are, today, laying plans for the return to civilian life of our gallant men and women in the armed services. They must not be demobilized into an environment of inflation and unemployment, to a place on the bread line or on a corner selling apples. We must, this time, have plans ready—instead of waiting to do a hasty, inefficient, and ill-considered job at the last moment.

In October, he sent a formal message to Congress (although no specific legislation) proposing a broad range of veterans' benefits.[92]

Early in 1944, the American Legion presented Congress with a single, comprehensive veterans' bill that became, after modest amendments, the Servicemen's Readjustment Act of 1944. (It was the Legion that coined the title "G.I. Bill of Rights.") Roosevelt allowed the Legion's bill to supersede his own, less-well-developed proposals. One of the most expansive social programs in American history, it passed through Congress with remarkable ease. The Senate approved it unanimously, after a perfunctory forty-minute debate. In the House, deliberations took longer—in part because the Mississippi segregationist John Rankin insisted on amendments diluting some of the education and unemployment benefits, which, he claimed, would encourage "50,000 Negroes" from his state to "remain unemployed for at least a year." In the end, however, the House unanimously passed a bill only slightly less generous than the Senate's version. The President signed it in June.[93]

The G.I. Bill provided veterans with many of the benefits the NRPB, and other liberals, had hoped to provide all Americans after the war. It gave them enhanced unemployment and pension benefits, significant help in finding new jobs, generous economic assistance for all levels of education, and low-interest loans for buying homes, farms, and businesses. Later legislation added a comprehensive national health care system centered in an expanded network of Veterans Administration hospitals. The program won the support of liberals in part because they hoped it would strengthen the case for a broader network of social programs aimed at the entire population. But it won the support of conservatives precisely because it was limited to veterans and because many elements of it would, presumably, wither away as the veterans re-established themselves in society, aged, and ceased to need public assistance.[94]

Like the elaborate pension system established for Civil War veterans in the 1860s, the G.I. Bill could generate broad support because it aimed its benefits at a specific population who most Americans (and thus most politicians) believed had a special claim on public generosity. And like the Civil War pensions, which some late-nineteenth century reformers had hoped in vain might become a first step toward more universal social assistance programs, the G.I. Bill failed to become a basis for a broader program of social assistance. It placed administration of its programs within the Veterans Administration, which reduced the chances of their expanding to serve a larger constituency. It reinforced invidious distinctions between "deserving" and "undeserving" citizens and sustained the popular belief that public generosity should be reserved for those with a special claim to public attention. (Men in uniform, the President argued, had "been compelled to make greater economic sacrifice and every other kind of sacrifice than the rest of us.") And the framers and promoters of the G.I. Bill did nothing to link this vast program of public spending to the larger vision of a full-employment economy sustained by an elaborate welfare and social insurance system.[95]

AT ALMOST THE same time that Congress was embracing the G.I. Bill, it was agonizing over another legacy of the National Resources Planning Board: legislation that would have committed the federal government to ensuring full employment in the postwar era. The Full Employment Bill, as it was widely known, emerged from many sources. The President's 1944 State of the Union Address, apparently influenced by the NRPB reports, seemed to endorse a full-employment strategy with its call for an "economic bill of rights"—among them "the right to a useful and remunerative job" and "the right to earn enough to provide adequate food and clothing and recreation." Political rights alone, Roosevelt said, were "inadequate to assure us equality in the pursuit of happiness." Individual freedom could not exist "without economic security and independence." The speech emboldened liberals in Washington and elsewhere to press for legislative action.[96]

Progressives in the labor movement (most notably the CIO's new Political Action Committee) lobbied vigorously and effectively for full-employment policies as part of any reconversion legislation.[97] Agrarian progressives, mobilized through the National Farmers Union, were at the center of the battle as well. Keynesian economists, who saw the transition to peace as their best opportunity to entrench their ideas in public policy, promoted guarantees of full employment as the best vehicle for ensuring postwar prosperity. Alvin Hansen, in particular, produced a flurry of articles in popular magazines in support of legislation.[98] The Union for Democratic Action (later reconstituted as Americans for Democratic Action) was a liberal organization founded in 1941 to unite anti-fascist groups in support of the war. By 1944, it was fighting for a progressive postwar agenda, and it too made the battle for full-employment legislation its principal commitment. Liberal members of Congress, convinced that the public expected protection from the prospect of a peacetime economic slump, considered full employment a politically attractive cause.[99]

By the time James E. Murray of Montana introduced the Full Employment Bill to the Senate on January 22, 1945, many of its provisions had already been bouncing around the legislative process for months. Much of the early initiative came from the National Farmers Union, which represented mostly small farmers and which embraced a much more progressive economic agenda than its more powerful counterpart, the American Farm Bureau Federation (which was linked to commercial farmers). In 1944, the NFU's energetic president, James Patton, had helped persuade the sponsors of a bill expanding postwar unemployment benefits (the Kilgore Reconversion Bill) to attach an amendment mandating the federal government to guarantee full employment after the war through aggressive fiscal policies. Both the amendment and the bill had died in the Senate. But the concept of government-guaranteed full employment generated considerable popular support, both in opinion polls and—indirectly, at least—in the 1944 presidential election. Despite the forced removal from the Democratic ticket of Henry Wallace, one of the leading proponents of full employment, most liberals interpreted Roosevelt's substantial fourth-term victory as an endorsement of the economic bill of rights he had presented earlier in the year.[100]

The bill Murray introduced early in 1945 included a defensive endorsement of "free competitive enterprise," one of a number of largely cosmetic changes to the NFU proposal designed to make the law politically palatable to moderates. But the heart of the bill was the statement that "all Americans able to work and seeking work have the right to a useful and remunerative job. . . . [I]t is essential that continuing full employment be maintained in the United States." The legislation called for the President to prepare each year a National Production and Employment Budget. It would estimate the "number of jobs needed during the ensuing fiscal year or years to assure continuing full employment," and it would calculate "the estimated dollar value of the gross national product . . . required to provide such a number of jobs." If it seemed likely that private-sector spending and investment would not create the necessary jobs, the government would be expected to step in with a program of loans, expenditures, and public investments to bring the economy up to full-employment levels.[101]

The Full Employment Bill did not specify what kind of spending the government should use to create the necessary jobs. Nor did it contain any explicit call for expanded programs of social insurance and public assistance, as the NRPB reports had done. But the full-employment liberals who had embraced the NRPB ideas in 1943 considered the bill a vehicle capable of sustaining their highest hopes. It was the "most imaginative [proposal] yet made for postwar America," and "a beginning of a far-reaching program for progressives"; it would "create the conditions for greater enjoyment of traditional as well as new liberties"; it would "provide a framework for an economy at once sufficiently planned to maintain full employment and sufficiently flexible to give ample scope to . . . free enterprise"; it would be "a firm assurance that unemployment never again will be permitted to become a national problem"; it was "probably our only alternative to an otherwise irresistible drift toward real socialism."[102]

Perhaps most important, the bill made possible (even if it did not require) the linkage that had been so important to the NRPB: the connection between a generous program of social insurance and an aggressive program of government spending to ensure economic growth. It called for the kind of sustained economic planning that the NRPB had hoped to provide, and it gave the government tools with which to convert its plans into policy. The bill did nothing, its supporters conceded, to attack the "problems of monopoly." But it would solve through other means the problems monopoly helped cause without creating a "creeping bureaucracy all of us want to avoid." And after April 12, 1945, when Franklin D. Roosevelt died suddenly of a massive stroke, many supporters of the bill began calling it a fitting memorial to the fallen president.[103]

Supporters of the Full Employment Bill—among them the new president, Harry S. Truman, struggling to claim Roosevelt's mantle—considered it an effective "middle way" between a heavily statist solution to the problems of the economy and a return to the kind of unmediated private enterprise that had produced the Great Depression. But opponents in Congress and elsewhere had no such faith. While virtually no one openly challenged the goal of reducing unemployment, there was considerable debate about the desirability (and the meaning) of the idea of *full* employment. Even the most fervent champions of full employment had never proposed a literal "right to a job" for every individual; they envisioned, rather, an economy that would theoretically produce enough jobs to employ everyone, conceding that there would, nevertheless, always be some people—whether because of geography, training, or preference—who would still be unable or unwilling to find work. But opponents in Congress and elsewhere seized on the phrase and warned demagogically of a vast state bureaucracy that would compel everyone to work and determine what jobs they could have. Ultimately, the bill's sponsors agreed to a new phrase—"maximum employment"—which they hoped would seem less threatening.[104]

Some of the conservative opposition, however, was based on a more rational calculation of the likely economic effects of the bill. Employers (mobilized through the Chambers of Commerce and the National Association of Manufacturers) and commercial farmers (mobilized through the American Farm Bureau Federation) feared that a high-employment economy would raise their labor costs and make it difficult to find workers for menial jobs such as seasonal farm work. Fiscal conservatives recoiled at the idea of using deficit spending as a normal tool of economic planning and sought to remove from the bill any suggestion that government spending would be the preferred route to economic growth. Skeptical economists pointed to the difficulty of preparing accurate economic forecasts, as the Murray bill required; that the debate on the bill occurred at the same time that widespread predictions of a postwar depression were proving inaccurate only increased the skepticism. Most of all, perhaps, conservative members of Congress of both parties, who had spent a decade chafing against what they considered a dangerous concentration of power in the executive branch (and who had killed the NRPB in 1943 to express their unhappiness with that trend), saw the Full Employment Bill as another vehicle for inflating the President's power at the expense of their own.[105]

In the end, the strength of conservatives in Congress was too much for the uneasy coalition of liberals who were supporting the Full Employment Bill. Having lost 50 seats in the House in 1942 (reducing their majority to 10), Democrats gained only 22 in the 1944 elections. Their Senate majority actually declined by one. The wartime coalition of Republicans and conservative Democrats continued to dominate Congress; and that coalition, although not powerful enough to kill the bill altogether, voted a series of amendments that substantially, some believed fundamentally, changed its character. By the time both houses of Congress finally approved a bill in early 1946—after considering it intermittently for more than a year—it was no longer the *Full* Employment Bill; it was the Employment Act of 1946. Gone was the ringing mandate for the President and Congress to ensure "full employment" (a phrase that appeared nowhere in the final version of the law). In its place was a statement of purpose so filled with qualifications and ambiguities that it was almost meaningless:

> The Congress hereby declares that it is the continuing policy and responsibility of the Federal Government to use all practicable means consistent with its needs and obligations and other essential considerations of national policy with the assistance and cooperation of industry, agriculture, labor, and State and local governments, to coordinate and utilize all its plans, functions, and resources for the purpose of creating and maintaining, in a manner calculated to foster and promote free competitive enterprise and the general welfare, conditions under which there will be afforded useful employment, for those able, willing, and seeking to work, and to promote maximum employment, production, and purchasing power.

The law created a Council of Economic Advisers, to be located in the White House and appointed by the President, "to formulate and recommend national economic policy to promote employment, production, and purchasing power under free competitive enterprise." Nothing in the law required either the President or the Congress to respond to the council's recommendations in any particular way.[106]

Reaction to the Employment Act among its original supporters was mixed. Some were relieved to have salvaged anything from the brutal legislative process, and they comforted themselves with the thought that, as Marriner Eccles put it, "Congress has gone a long way . . . in recognizing that the Government has definite economic responsibilities and in stating as a mandate the objectives toward which public policy and action should be directed. This is a tremendous step." The Council of Economic Advisers, Eccles and others believed, could, if staffed with progressives and supported by the President, become a potent force within the federal bureaucracy for a full-employment agenda.[107] But others saw in the "badly watered down" bill of 1946 a symbol of liberal impotence. Having adjusted their goals to an increasingly conservative, anti-statist climate, having avoided politically explosive efforts to regulate corporate power and attack monopoly, liberals had been unable to salvage more than a few rhetorical gestures even from their revised and, they believed, modest agenda.[108] Both evaluations contained elements of truth.

The fight for the Full Employment Bill, and its ambiguous conclusion, were in one sense an ending. It was the last great legislative battle of the Roosevelt presidency (even though most of it occurred after Roosevelt's death). And as such, it was, in effect, the last great battle for the New Deal. But it was also a beginning. The bill itself revealed much of what by early 1946 had already become the postwar agenda of most American liberals. And the evisceration of the bill at the hands of determined opponents revealed many of the obstacles that agenda would encounter over the next quarter century. Its supporters did not say so, and perhaps were not even aware of it, but both in struggling to win passage of the bill, and in compromising on a pale version of their real hopes, they were suggesting the outlines of the postwar liberal world.

*Epilogue*

# The Reconstruction
# of New Deal Liberalism

SYSTEMS OF BELIEF are never uniform and never static. The ideas of American liberals in 1945 displayed, as they had in the past, considerable diversity. They continued to change, and continued to produce internecine debates, in the years that followed. Still, broad transformations in the contours of liberal thought were clearly visible by the end of World War II.

That the new framework was significantly different from the old was most evident in the way many postwar liberals came to define the legacy of the 1930s. Most continued to consider themselves "New Dealers." But few liberals any longer expressed much interest or faith in many of the reform ideas that had once been central to the New Deal. In particular, they abandoned or greatly de-emphasized the abortive experiments in statist planning, the failed efforts to create cooperative associational arrangements, the vigorous if short-lived anti-monopoly crusades, the overt celebration of government, and the open skepticism toward capitalism and its captains.

A few lamented this retreat from reform, but saw no real prospects of reversing it. Chester Bowles, the last director of the OPA and a major liberal spokesman in the first years after the war, conceded that "the original fight against monopoly has been lost. Theodore Roosevelt, Wilson and Bob La Follette were right in the supreme effort they made twenty or thirty years ago. But that effort failed and, in all likelihood, the U.S. Steel Corporation, International Harvester, and the rest are here to stay." William Leuchtenburg, a young historian and political activist later to become one of the leading chroniclers of the New Deal, wrote resignedly in 1948 of the legacy of the Roosevelt years: "Democratic orators filled the air with denunciation of monopoly for most of the decade, but corporations are more powerful today then they were in 1933."[1]

For most liberals, however, the end of reform was not something to regret. It was evidence of maturity and success. Liberals were becoming content to offer "partial remedies" to problems for which they had once proposed "fundamental cures," Stuart Chase wrote in 1945. And there was no need to apologize for the change: "Americans should be grown-up enough by this time to stop looking for cure-alls." Adolf Berle, who in the 1930s had called for new forms of public control over corporate power, decided not long after the war that such controls were unnecessary. American corporations, he claimed, had become socially responsible— through a combination of dispersal of control (a result of progressive taxation) and acculturation of corporate managers. He seemed at times almost embarrassed by the alarmist views he had expressed during the Depression.[2] And Arthur M. Schlesinger, Jr. (who, like Leuchtenburg, would soon become one of the great historians of the Roosevelt era), conceded in a 1948 essay that the New Deal "made no fundamental attempt to grapple with the problem of the economies of concentration." But that was not the point:

> The New Deal took a broken and despairing land and gave it new confidence in itself. . . . Roosevelt had a vision of a democratic America and the strength to realize a good part of that vision. All his solutions were incomplete. But then all great problems are insoluble.

Instead of lamenting the New Deal's failure to achieve the reforms they once had considered essential, most postwar liberals lauded what they now considered its successes. They praised the New Deal for having solved the problems of capitalism without altering the structure of capitalism; for having used the state to save the economy without intruding the state too far into the economy. They cited the New Deal's contributions to the creation of a welfare state, and they credited the New Deal with legitimizing government fiscal policies as the best way to deal with fluctuations in the business cycle and to promote full employment.

This reconstruction of New Deal liberalism was a result of many things: of the failures and unintended consequences of some of the reform efforts of the early 1930s; of the impact of the recession of 1937–38, the frustrations that unexpected crisis had created, and the reassessments it had inspired; of the emergence of a new set of economic ideas—ultimately identified chiefly with John Maynard Keynes—that provided an alternative to older, more institutional approaches; of the dramatic economic growth of the 1940s, the experiences of wartime economic mobilization, the resurgence of popular conservatism, and the growing fear of totalitarianism. The new liberal outlook had emerged so slowly, so halt-ingly, in response to so many different influences that some of those who embraced it did not always recognize how much it had changed—or why.

But for those who cared to look, signs of the change abounded. It was visible, for example, in the character of the postwar liberal community. Most of the "planners," "regulators," and "anti-monopolists" who had dominated liberal circles eight years earlier were no longer central figures in the discussion of public policy. Rexford Tugwell was a political science professor at the University of Chicago. Donald Richberg was teaching law at the University of Virginia. Thurman Arnold, Robert Jackson, and William O. Douglas were sitting on federal courts. Thomas Corcoran was practicing law in Washington. Benjamin Cohen was accepting occasional assignments as a delegate to international conferences. Leon Henderson, one of the last of the true "New Dealers" to hold a major administrative post during the war, had resigned as head of the Office of Price Adminis-tration in December 1942 and had become an embittered (and increas-ingly obscure) critic of the government's failures, convinced that without more assertive state planning and regulation the nation faced an economic disaster after the war.[3]

No comparably powerful network could be said to have emerged by 1945 to take their place. By then, many liberals were preoccupied with international questions and with the emerging schism within their ranks over the Soviet Union, and were paying less attention to domestic issues than they once had. But those who did attempt to define a domestic agenda were largely people fired with enthusiasm for the vision of a full-employment economy, people who considered the New Deal's prin-cipal legacy the idea of effective use of fiscal policy and the expansion of social welfare and insurance programs. In the place of the reform liberals who had helped define public discourse in the 1930s were "compensa-tory" liberals such as Alvin Hansen, architect of the NRPB reports and the Full Employment Bill; Chester Bowles, whose widely regarded 1946 book *Tomorrow Without Fear* called not for an expansion, or even a continua-tion, of the regulatory experiments with which he had been involved during the war, but for the pursuit of full employment through an increased use of fiscal policy; and Eleanor Roosevelt, who for more than fifteen years after her husband's death served as a revered symbol of the New Deal and a powerful voice of liberal hopes—hopes that, for her, had always centered more around visions of a generous system of welfare and social insurance than around efforts to reshape the capitalist world.[4]

The Democratic party platform in 1944 was another sign of the changing political landscape. Four years earlier, the party platform had called for measures against the "unbridled concentration of economic power and the exploitation of the consumer and the investor." It had boasted of the New Deal's regulatory innovations, its aggressive antitrust policies, its war on "the extortionate methods of monopoly." The 1944 platform also praised the administration's anti-monopoly and regulatory efforts—in a perfunctory sentence near the end. But most of its limited discussion of domestic issues centered on how the New Deal had "found the road to prosperity" through aggressive compensatory measures: fiscal policies and social welfare innovations.[5]

At the heart of these shifts in the character of liberal thought was a basic change in the way many Americans had come to look at modern economic life. The liberal vision of political economy in the 1940s rested squarely on a conviction that would have seemed heretical to most economists and intellectuals a generation before (although not to much of the public). It rested on the belief that protecting consumers and encouraging mass consumption, more than protecting producers and promoting savings, were the principal responsibilities of the liberal state. In its pursuit of full employment, the government would not seek to regulate corporate institutions so much as it would try to influence the business cycle. It would not try to redistribute economic power and limit inequality so much as it would create a compensatory welfare system (what later generations would call a "safety net") for those whom capitalism had failed. It would not reshape capitalist institutions. It would reshape the economic and social environment in which those institutions worked.

THE IMPORTANCE of the New Deal lies in large part, of course, in its actual legislative and institutional achievements: the Social Security System, the Wagner Act, the TVA, the farm subsidy programs, the regulation of wages and hours, the construction of vast systems of public works, the new regulatory mechanisms for important areas of the economy, and others—achievements that together transformed the federal government and its relationship to the economy and to the American people. But the New Deal's significance lies as well in its impact on subsequent generations of liberals and, through them, on two decades of postwar government activism. And in that light, the New Deal appears not just as a bright moment in which reform energies briefly prevailed but as part of a long process of ideological adaptation.

For more than half a century, Americans concerned about the impact of industrialization on their society—about economic instability and social injustice—had harbored deep and continuing doubts about the institutional structure of modern corporate capitalism. Relatively few had wanted to destroy that structure, but many had wanted to reshape it; that desire had been at the center of "progressive" and "reform" hopes from the late nineteenth century through the early 1930s. Much of the history of the New Deal, by contrast, and in particular its history from the troubled years after 1937 through the conclusion of the war, is the story of a slow, unstated, but nevertheless decisive repudiation of such hopes and the elevation of other aspirations to replace them.

By 1945, American liberals, as the result of countless small adaptations to a broad range of experiences, had reached an accommodation with modern capitalism that served, in effect, to settle many of the most divisive conflicts of the first decades of the century. They had done so by convincing themselves that the achievements of the New Deal had already eliminated the most dangerous features of the corporate capitalist system; by committing themselves to the belief that economic growth was the surest route to social progress and that consumption, more than production, was the surest route to economic growth; and by defining a role for the state that would, they believed, permit it to compensate for capitalism's inevitable flaws and omissions without interfering very much with its internal workings. They had, in effect, detached liberalism from its earlier emphasis on reform—its preoccupation with issues of class, its tendency to equate freedom and democracy with economic autonomy, its hostility to concentrated economic power. They had redefined citizenship to de-emphasize the role of men and women as producers and to elevate their roles as consumers.

As the reform liberalism of the New Deal years gave way to the consumer-oriented liberalism of the postwar era, new issues—some of them already becoming visible by the end of World War II—became a part of liberal discourse and the liberal agenda, joining the Keynesian–welfare state approach to political economy around which liberals had coalesced during the war. The first, and for a time most important, was a fervent commitment to internationalism, and to the global struggle against communism, a commitment that at times seemed to overshadow all else. But liberals embraced other new goals as well, most notably a growing interest in the expansion of rights for individuals and groups.

For over a generation, the new liberalism did much to justify the hopes of those who had shaped it. The United States enjoyed the most dramatic period of economic growth in its history in the first thirty years after World War II, and liberal economic policies were at times instrumental in sustaining and accelerating that growth. The American welfare state steadily expanded from the basis the New Deal had established in 1935, and in the 1960s, a great flurry of social legislation extended the welfare state into new realms altogether. The United States confronted many of its oldest and most difficult social problems, the oppression of African Americans most prominent among them; the New Deal (and some previous generations of progressives and reformers) had determinedly avoided such problems, but postwar liberals eagerly embraced them. Taken together, the liberal achievements of the postwar era have few, if any, parallels in American history. In some respects, they exceeded those of the New Deal itself.

Ultimately, however, the new liberalism proved inadequate to the tasks it set for itself. The effort to create economic growth and full employment through consumer-oriented fiscal policies floundered after 1973 in the face of global competition, environmental degradation, and deindustrialization. The welfare state failed to solve the problems of deteriorating inner city communities and rising violence; ultimately it could not even withstand assaults from those who believed it had helped create those problems. The white liberal commitment to the struggle for racial justice wavered as the relatively straightforward legal and moral issues of the early 1960s gave way to more complicated and controversial economic ones. The effort to expand the notion of individual and group rights—and the related efforts to move race, ethnicity, gender, and sexuality to the center of political life—ultimately produced a series of divisive cultural battles that most liberals had not anticipated and few welcomed. In the face of these and other frustrations, postwar liberalism ultimately seemed to exhaust itself—to become paralyzed by its inability to find satisfactory answers to the problems it had so eagerly embraced.

It can be argued, of course, that all these shortcomings were less a result of the weaknesses of liberalism itself than of the strength of external opposition; that liberalism did not succeed because it never had a genuine chance to try. Real Keynesian management of the postwar economy occurred, at best, in fits and starts. Never did the American state organize itself to use its fiscal policies in the way the liberals of the 1940s had hoped. The modern welfare state, despite its considerable growth, has fallen far short of the expansive visions of wartime liberals. It has never become anything like the generous system of universal social insurance and broad social protections the NRPB and others envisioned and thus has never had the opportunity to demonstrate what many liberals still believe is its potential to solve what have come to seem intractable problems. The many crusades for rights, which have produced such frustration and controversy in recent years, have suffered more from conservative opposition and the persistence of longstanding prejudices than from liberal misconceptions or irresolution. But while liberalism was not the only cause of its own failures, neither was it blameless. Its redefinition in the last years of the New Deal made possible many of its later achievements. But that redefinition also stripped postwar liberalism of its ability to deal with some enduring and inescapable problems.

In the late 1930s and early 1940s, American liberals began a broad retreat from many of the commitments that had once defined their politics: concerns about the problems of production and about the limitations of the market. They did so with confidence, certain that their new consumer-oriented approach to political economy had freed them at last from the need to reform capitalist institutions and from the pressure to redistribute wealth and economic power. The industrial economy, most liberals now believed, could take care of itself. Intelligent fiscal policies and a generous welfare state would be sufficient to sustain economic growth and ensure at least minimal levels of social justice. For nearly three decades, an unprecedented, largely uninterrupted prosperity seemed to justify those assumptions.

But once the great postwar expansion came to a close—replaced by an erratic and often stagnant economy, increasing inequality, and growing social instability—confidence in the capacity of compensatory liberalism to solve the nation's problems became more difficult to sustain. The result has been confusion and at times paralysis among liberals themselves, and the growth of a powerful conservative opposition casting doubt on the ability of government to play any useful role in resolving America's dilemmas.

In the end, it was not as easy as many liberals once expected to create a just and prosperous society without worrying about the problems of production and the structure of the economy. And it does not seem too much to imagine, therefore, that the New Deal's retreat from reform in its waning years is among the sources of American liberalism's present travails.

# Archival Sources

**Adams MSS:** James Truslow Adams Papers, Columbia University Library, New York, New York

**Arnold MSS:** Thurman W. Arnold Papers, University of Wyoming Library, Laramie, Wyoming

**Baruch MSS:** Bernard M. Baruch Papers, Seeley G. Mudd Manuscripts Library, Princeton University, Princeton, New Jersey

**Bean MSS:** Louis H. Bean Papers, Franklin D. Roosevelt Library, Hyde Park, New York

**Berge MSS:** Wendell Berge Papers, Manuscripts Division, Library of Congress, Washington, D.C.

**Berle MSS:** Adolf A. Berle Papers, Roosevelt Library

**Beveridge MSS:** William H. Beveridge Papers, British Library of Political and Economic Science, London School of Economics, London

**Black MSS:** Hugo Black Papers, Manuscripts Division, Library of Congress

**Borah MSS:** William E. Borah Papers, Manuscripts Division, Library of Congress

**Bowles MSS:** Chester B. Bowles Papers, Manuscripts and Archives, Sterling Library, Yale University, New Haven, Connecticut

**Brant MSS:** Irving Brant Papers, Manuscripts Division, Library of Congress

**Budget, RG 51, NA:** Bureau of the Budget Archives, Record Group 51, National Archives, Washington, D.C.

**Clapper MSS:** Raymond Clapper Papers, Manuscripts Division, Library of Congress

**Cohen MSS:** Benjamin V. Cohen Papers, Manuscripts Division, Library of Congress

**Corcoran MSS:** Thomas G. Corcoran Papers, Manuscripts Division, Library of Congress

**Coy MSS:** A. Wayne Coy Papers, Roosevelt Library

**Davis MSS:** Elmer Davis Papers, Manuscripts Division, Library of Congress

**Delano MSS:** Frederic A. Delano Papers, Roosevelt Library

**DNC MSS:** Democratic National Committee Papers, Roosevelt Library

**Douglas MSS:** William O. Douglas Papers, Manuscripts Division, Library of Congress

**Eberstadt MSS:** Ferdinand Eberstadt Papers, Seeley G. Mudd Manuscripts Library, Princeton University

**Eccles MSS:** Marriner S. Eccles Papers, Marriott Library, University of Utah, Salt Lake City, Utah

**Ezekiel MSS:** Mordecai Ezekiel Papers, Roosevelt Library

**Farley MSS:** James A. Farley Papers, Manuscripts Division, Library of Congress

**FO.371, PRO:** Foreign Office Records, General Correspondence, Political, Public Records Office, Kew, London

**Frank MSS:** Jerome Frank Papers, Yale University Library

**Frankfurter MSS:** Felix Frankfurter Papers, Manuscripts Division, Library of Congress

**Frey MSS:** John P. Frey Papers, Manuscripts Division, Library of Congress

**Hansen MSS:** Alvin Henry Hansen Papers, Harvard University Archives, Pusey Library, Harvard University, Cambridge, Massachusetts

**Henderson MSS:** Leon Henderson Papers, Roosevelt Library

**Hillman MSS:** Sidney Hillman Papers, Industrial and Labor Relations Library, Cornell University, Ithaca, New York

**Hopkins Letters:** Hopkins Personal Letters, Roosevelt Library

**Hopkins MSS:** Harry L. Hopkins Papers, Roosevelt Library

**Ickes MSS:** Harold Ickes Papers, Manuscripts Division, Library of Congress

**Interior, RG48, NA:** Interior Department Records, Record Group 48, National Archives, Washington, D.C.

**Jackson MSS:** Robert H. Jackson Papers, Manuscripts Division, Library of Congress

**Jones MSS:** Jesse H. Jones Papers, Manuscripts Division, Library of Congress

**Krug MSS:** Julius Krug Papers, Manuscripts Division, Library of Congress

**La Follette MSS:** Robert M. La Follette, Jr. Papers, La Follette Family Papers, Manuscripts Division, Library of Congress

**Lerner MSS:** Max Lerner Papers, Yale University Library

**Lippmann MSS:** Walter Lippmann Papers, Yale University Library

**Lubin MSS:** Isidor Lubin Papers, Roosevelt Library

**MacLeish MSS:** Archibald MacLeish Papers, Manuscripts Division, Library of Congress

**Means MSS:** Gardiner Means Papers, Roosevelt Library

**Morgenthau Diaries:** Henry Morgenthau, Jr., Presidential Diaries, Roosevelt Library

**Morgenthau MSS:** Henry Morgenthau, Jr., Papers, Roosevelt Library

**Nelson MSS:** Donald Marr Nelson Papers, Huntington Library, San Marino, California

**Niebuhr MSS:** Reinhold Niebuhr Papers, Manuscripts Division, Library of Congress

**NRPB, RG187, NA:** National Resource Planning Board Records, Record Group 187, National Archives

**O'Mahoney MSS:** Joseph O'Mahoney Papers, University of Wyoming Library

**PIN.8, PRO:** Pensions and Insurance Records, Public Records Office

**Richberg MSS:** Donald Richberg Papers, Manuscripts Division, Library of Congress

**Rogers MSS:** James Harvey Rogers Papers, Yale University

**OF, FDRL:** Franklin D. Roosevelt Presidential Papers, Official File, Roosevelt Library

**PPF, FDRL:** Franklin D. Roosevelt Presidential Papers, President's Personal File, Roosevelt Library

**PSF, FDRL:** Franklin D. Roosevelt Presidential Papers, President's Secretary's File, Roosevelt Library

**Schwellenbach MSS:** Lewis Schwellenbach Papers, Manuscripts Division, Library of Congress

**Smith MSS:** Harold Smith Papers, Roosevelt Library

**Stettinius MSS:** Walter J. Stettinius, Jr., Papers, Alderman Library Manuscripts Department, University of Virginia, Charlottesville, Virginia

**Taft MSS:** Robert A. Taft Papers, Manuscripts Division, Library of Congress

**TNEC, RG144, NA:** Temporary National Economic Committee Records, Record Group 144, National Archives

**Truman Family MSS:** Harry S Truman Family Correspondence, Harry S Truman Library, Independence, Missouri

**Truman Pre-Presidential MSS, HSTL:** Harry S Truman Pre-Presidential Papers, Senatorial File, Truman Library

**OF, HSTL:** Harry S Truman Presidential Papers, Official File, Truman Library

**PPF, HSTL:** Harry S Truman Presidential Papers, President's Personal File, Truman Library

**PSF, HSTL:** Harry S Truman Presidential Papers, President's Secretary's File, Truman Library

**Tumulty MSS:** Joseph Tumulty Papers, Manuscripts Division, Library of Congress

**CAB.87, PRO:** War Cabinet Records, CAB.87, Public Records Office

**White MSS:** William Allen White Papers, Manuscripts Division, Library of Congress

**WPB, RG 179, NA:** War Production Board Records, Record Group 179, National Archives

# Notes

## Introduction

1. There is a large and diverse literature on the political and intellectual origins of New Deal thought. Otis Graham, *Encore for Reform: Old Progressives and the New Deal* (New York: Oxford University Press, 1967), and Ronald L. Feinman, *Twilight of Progressivism: The Western Republican Senators and the New Deal* (Baltimore: Johns Hopkins University Press, 1981), examine some of the progressive influences on the New Deal. William Leuchtenburg, "The New Deal and the Analogue of War," in John Braeman et al., eds., *Change and Continuity in Twentieth-Century America* (Columbus: Ohio State University Press, 1964), pp. 81–143, examines some of the legacies of World War I—both concrete and metaphorical—for the New Deal. Arthur S. Link, "What Happened to the Progressive Movement in the 1920s?," *American Historical Review* 64 (1959), 833–51; Robert F. Himmelberg, "The Origins of the National Recovery Administration: Business, Government, and the Trade Association Issue, 1921–1933" (New York: Fordham University Press, 1976); and Ellis Hawley, *The Great War and the Search for a Modern Order: A History of the American People and Their Institutions, 1917–1933* (New York: St. Martin's Press, 1979), are among the works suggesting the links between the New Deal and various reform impulses of the 1920s. Richard Hofstadter, *The Age of Reform: From Bryan to FDR* (New York: Alfred A. Knopf, 1955), is a classic interpretation of, among other things, the roots of New Deal reform. See also (among many others) Alan Dawley, *Struggles for Justice: Social Responsibility and the Liberal State* (Cambridge: Harvard University Press, 1991), and Alan Brinkley, "The New Deal: Prelude," *Wilson Quarterly* 6 (1982), 50–61.

2. Alvin H. Hansen, "Toward Full Employment," speech at the University of Cincinnati, March 15, 1940, Hansen MSS 3.10; Hofstadter, *The Age of Reform*, p. 307. William Leuchtenburg challenges the idea of the New Deal's "ideological innocence" in *Franklin D. Roosevelt and the New Deal* (New York: Harper & Row, 1963), p. 34.

3. Ellis Hawley, *The New Deal and the Problem of Monopoly* (Princeton: Princeton University Press, 1966), remains the fullest and most perceptive study of New Deal political economy from 1933 to 1938. See also, among many other works, Thomas K. McCraw, "The New Deal and the Mixed Economy," in Harvard Sitkoff, ed., *Fifty Years Later: The New Deal Evaluated* (New York: Alfred A. Knopf, 1985), pp. 37–66; McCraw, *Prophets of Regulation* (Cambridge: Harvard University Press, 1984), pp. 210–12.

4. See, e.g., Carl Dreher, "The American Way: A Voice from the Left," in David Cushman Coyle, ed., *The American Way* (New York: Harper, 1938), pp. 75–88.

5. See Thomas K. McCraw, *Morgan vs. Lilienthal: The Feud Within the TVA* (Chicago: Loyola University Press, 1970), and *TVA and the Power Fight, 1933–1939* (Philadelphia: Lippincott, 1971); Roy Talbert, Jr., *FDR's Utopian: Arthur Morgan of the TVA* (Jackson: University Press of Mississippi, 1987); David E. Lilienthal, *The Journals of David E. Lilienthal*, vol. 1, *The TVA Years, 1939–1945* (New York: Harper & Row, 1964).

6. See Jordan Schwarz, *The New Dealers: Power Politics in the Age of Roosevelt* (New York: Alfred A. Knopf, 1993).

7. Elements and variations of this argument can be found in, among others, Richard P. Adelstein, " 'The Nation as an Economic Unit': Keynes, Roosevelt, and the Managerial Ideal," *Journal of American History* 78 (1991), 160–87; Alan Brinkley, "The New Deal and the Idea of the State," in Steve Fraser and Gary Gerstle, eds., *The Rise and Fall of the New Deal Order: 1933–1980* (Princeton: Princeton University Press, 1989), pp. 85–121; John W. Jeffries, "The 'New' New Deal: FDR and American Liberalism, 1937–1945," *Political Science Quarterly* 105 (1990), 397–418; Theodore Rosenof, *Patterns of Political Economy in America: The Failure to Develop a Democratic Left Synthesis, 1933–1950* (New York: Garland, 1983); Robert Skidelsky, "Keynes and the Reconstruction of Liberalism," *Encounter* 52 (1979), 29–39; Herbert Stein, *The Fiscal Revolution in America* (Chicago: University of Chicago Press, 1969), chaps. 6–9; Dean L. May, *From New Deal to New Economics: The American Liberal Response to the Recession of 1937* (New York: Garland, 1981); William E. Stoneman, *A History of Economic Analysis of the Great Depression in America* (New York: Garland, 1979). Richard N. Chapman, *Contours of Public Policy, 1939–1945* (New York: Garland, 1981), is a capable narrative of policy developments in the last years of the New Deal.

8. One of the classic statements of this assumption is Louis Hartz, *The Liberal Tradition in America* (New York: Harper, 1955). At least equally influential was Richard Hofstadter, *The American Political Tradition and Those Who Made It* (New York: Alfred A. Knopf, 1948).

9. See Joyce Appleby, *Liberalism and Republicanism in the Historical Imagination* (Cambridge: Harvard University Press, 1992), Introduction. She refers to liberalism as a "loose association of unexamined assumptions" (p. 1).

10. See, e.g., Richard Hofstadter, *Social Darwinism in American Thought* (Philadelphia: University of Pennsylvania Press, 1944); Hartz, *The Liberal Tradition in America*; Sidney Fine, *Laissez-Faire and the General Welfare State* (Ann Arbor: University of Michigan Press, 1964); Edward C. Kirkland, *Dream and Thought in the Business Community* (Ithaca: Cornell University Press, 1956); R. Jeffrey Lustig, *Corporate Liberalism: The Origins of Modern*

*American Political Theory, 1890–1920* (Berkeley: University of California Press, 1982), chap. 1; Theodore J. Lowi, *The End of Liberalism: Ideology, Policy, and the Crisis of Public Authority* (New York: W. W. Norton, 1969), chap. 1.

11. Merle Fainsod et al., *Government and the American Economy*, 3rd ed. (New York: W. W. Norton, 1959), illustrates some of the contradictions between the idea of laissez-faire liberalism and the reality of state intervention on behalf of capitalists. See Paul Avrich, *The Haymarket Tragedy* (Princeton: Princeton University Press, 1984), for an example of the reliance of capital on the state in suppressing labor unrest.

12. See, e.g., Peter G. Filene, "An Obituary for the Progressive Movement," *American Quarterly* 22 (1970), 20–34; and Daniel T. Rodgers, "In Search of Progressivism," *Reviews in American History* 10 (1982), 113–32; Charles Forcey, *The Crossroads of Liberalism: Croly, Weyl, Lippmann and the Progressive Era, 1900–1925* (New York: Oxford University Press, 1961); Dawley, *Struggles for Justice*, chaps. 2–4.

13. For a discussion of how New Dealers appropriated the term "liberal," see Ronald D. Rotunda, "The 'Liberal' Label: Roosevelt's Capture of a Symbol," *Public Policy* 17 (1968), 377–408.

14. Gary Gerstle, "The Protean Character of American Liberalism," *American Historical Review* 99 (1944), 15–23. For a discussion of the centrality of "corruption" and political reform to progressivism, see Richard L. McCormick, *The Party Period and Public Policy: American Politics from the Age of Jackson to the Progressive Era* (New York: Oxford University Press, 1986), and especially his important essay in that volume, "The Discovery That Business Corrupts Politics: A Reappraisal of the Origins of Progressivism," pp. 311–56. The Roosevelt quotation is from Fred Siegel, "Liberalism," in Eric Foner and John A. Garraty, eds., *The Reader's Companion to American History*, p. 654.

15. Rights-based liberalism is not, of course, new to the postwar era. The defense of rights and freedoms has been a vital part, many would argue the central part, of the liberal tradition throughout American history. But the particular form rights-based liberalism has recently assumed, and its centrality within liberal politics, is largely new to the period since the New Deal. Among its most important theoretical texts are John Rawls, *A Theory of Justice* (Cambridge: Harvard University Press, 1971), and his elaboration on the theory in *Political Liberalism* (New York: Columbia University Press, 1993). For more skeptical views of modern liberalism, see Theodore J. Lowi, *The End of Liberalism: Ideology, Policy, and the Crisis of Public Authority* (New York: W. W. Norton, 1969), and Michael J. Sandel, *Liberalism and the Limits of Justice* (New York: Cambridge University Press, 1982).

16. See, e.g., David B. Truman, *The Governmental Process* (New York: Alfred A. Knopf, 1951); Harold Wilensky and Charles N. Lebeaux, *Industrial Society and Social Welfare* (New York: Russell Sage, 1958); Gabriel Almond and James S. Coleman, eds., *The Politics of Developing Areas* (Princeton: Princeton University Press, 1960); Michael Shalev, "The Social Democratic Model and Beyond: Two Generations of Comparative Research on the Welfare State," *Comparative Social Research* 6 (1983), 315–51; Frances Fox Piven and Richard Cloward, *Regulating the Poor: The Functions of Public Welfare* (New York: Pantheon, 1971).

17. Eric A. Nordlinger, *On the Autonomy of the Democratic State* (Cambridge: Harvard University Press, 1981), p. 1. More complex discussions of a state-centered approach to politics and public policy can be found in Peter B. Evans, Dietrich Rueschemeyer, and Theda Skocpol, *Bringing the State Back In* (New York: Cambridge University Press, 1985); see especially Skocpol, "Bringing the State Back In: Strategies of Analysis in Current Research," pp. 3–37. Theda Skocpol has recently described her approach as "polity-centered," to suggest her belief that politically active institutions and groups outside the formal structure of the state must be part of any explanation of state behavior. See *Protecting Soldiers and Mothers: The Political Origins of Social Policy in the United States* (Cambridge: Harvard University Press, 1992), esp. pp. 41–62.

18. Arthur M. Schlesinger, Jr., *The Age of Roosevelt*, 3 vols. (Boston: Houghton Mifflin, 1957–60), is the classic statement of this view. Leuchtenburg, *Franklin D. Roosevelt and the New Deal*, is the most influential general history of the New Deal and offers a more muted and qualified version of this approach.

19. See Ronald Radosh, "The Myth of the New Deal," in Radosh and Murray Rothbard, eds. *A New History of the Leviathan: Essays on the Rise of the American Corporate State* (New York: Dutton, 1972), pp. 146–87; Barton J. Bernstein, "The New Deal: The Conservative Achievements of Liberal Reform," in Bernstein, ed., *Towards a New Past: Dissenting Essays in American History* (New York: Alfred A. Knopf, 1968), pp. 263–88.

20. Among studies of the New Deal that emphasize its subordination to corporate power instrumentally (through the direct influence of capitalist leaders)—as opposed to functionally (through the efforts of public officials to serve the interests of capitalism)—are Thomas Ferguson, "From Normalcy to New Deal: Industrial Structure, Party Competition, and American Public Policy in the Great Depression," *International Organization* 38 (1984), 41–94, and Ferguson, "Industrial Conflict and the Coming of the New Deal: The Triumph of Multinational Liberalism in America," in Fraser and Gerstle, eds., *The Rise and Fall of the New Deal Order*, pp. 3–31. The fullest discussion so far of the role of capitalists in shaping New Deal policies is in Colin Gordon, *New Deals: Business, Labor, and Politics in America, 1920–1935* (New York: Cambridge University Press, 1994).

21. See, for example, Lizabeth Cohen, *Making a New Deal: Industrial Workers in Chicago, 1919–1939* (New York: Cambridge University Press, 1990), esp. chaps. 6–7; Grant McConnell, *The Decline of Agrarian Democracy* (Berkeley: University of California Press, 1953), esp. chaps. 7–8; Alan Brinkley, *Voices of Protest: Huey Long, Father Coughlin, and the Great Depression* (New York: Alfred A. Knopf, 1982), esp. chaps. 3, 11; Linda Gordon, "Social Insurance and Public Assistance: The Influence of Gender in Welfare Thought in the United States, 1890–1935," *American Historical Review* 97 (1992), 19–54, Gordon, "Black and White Visions of Welfare: Women's Welfare Activism, 1890–1945," *Journal of American History* 78 (1991), 559–90, and Gordon, ed., *Women, the State, and Welfare* (Madison: University of Wisconsin Press, 1990), esp. pp. 9–35.

22. There is, of course, significant scholarship on this period, even if less

plentiful and less renowned than the work on the earlier years of the New Deal. In addition to an extensive journal literature, there are a number of important books on the politics and policy of the late 1930s and 1940s, among them: Richard N. Chapman, *Contours of Public Policy;* Rosenof, *Patterns of Political Economy;* May, *From New Deal to New Economics;* Stein, *The Fiscal Revolution in America;* James T. Patterson, *Congressional Conservatism and the New Deal: The Growth of the Conservative Coalition in Congress, 1933–1939* (Lexington: University of Kentucky Press, 1967); Barry Karl, *Executive Reorganization and Reform in the New Deal* (Chicago: University of Chicago Press, 1963); Richard Polenberg, *Reorganizing Roosevelt's Government, 1936–1939: The Controversy over Executive Reorganization* (Cambridge: Harvard University Press, 1966); Sidney M. Milkis, *The President and the Parties: The Transformation of the American Party System Since the New Deal* (New York: Oxford University Press, 1993); John Morton Blum, *V Was for Victory: Politics and American Culture During World War II* (New York: Harcourt Brace Jovanovich, 1976); Richard Polenberg, *War and Society: The United States, 1919–1945* (Philadelphia: J. B. Lippincott, 1972); Roland Young, *Congressional Politics in the Second World War* (New York: Columbia University Press, 1956); Steve Fraser, *Labor Will Rule: Sidney Hillman and the Rise of American Labor* (New York: The Free Press, 1991); Nelson Lichtenstein, *Labor's War at Home: The CIO and World War II* (New York: Cambridge University Press, 1982).

## Chapter One

1. "Masterpiece," *Time*, November 9, 1936, p. 23; *New York Times*, November 4, 1936.

2. "Triumph," *Time*, November 16, 1936, p. 23; "Election," *Newsweek*, November 7, 1936, pp. 7–8.

3. "The Shape of Things," *Nation*, November 7, 1936, p. 533; "The Week," *New Republic*, November 11, 1936, pp. 29–30; "Mr. Roosevelt's Blank Check," ibid., p. 31; Maury Maverick, "The Next Four Years. I: In Congress," *New Republic*, November 25, 1936, pp. 99–102; Max Lerner, "The Task for Roosevelt," *Nation*, November 14, 1936, pp. 569–70; Heywood Broun, "The President Needs a Gadfly," ibid., p. 577; Sidney M. Milkis, "Franklin D. Roosevelt and the Transcendence of Party Politics," *Political Science Quarterly* 100 (1985), 479–505.

4. Second Inaugural Address, January 20, 1937, in Samuel Rosenman, ed., *The Public Papers and Addresses of Franklin D. Roosevelt*, 4 vols. (New York: Macmillan, 1941), 1937 volume, pp. 1–5. The *Public Papers and Addresses*, which are cited frequently below, were published in several sets by several different publishers. The first set of five volumes, published in 1938 by Random House, contains material from 1928 up to Roosevelt's second inaugural in 1937. A second set of four volumes, published by Macmillan, contains material from the 1937 inaugural through 1940. A final set of four volumes, published by Harper, contains material from 1941 through Roosevelt's death in 1945. The first five volumes are identified by volume number (1–5); the

next eight volumes are identified by the years their contents represent (e.g., "1937 volume").

5. The phrase is from Paul Mallon, writing in the Chicago *Daily News*, January 5, 1937, quoted in Mark Leff, *The Limits of Symbolic Reform: The New Deal and Taxation, 1933–1939* (New York: Cambridge University Press, 1984), p. 205.

6. The classic account of the rise of congressional opposition to Roosevelt is James T. Patterson, *Congressional Conservatism and the New Deal: The Growth of the Conservative Coalition in Congress, 1933–1939* (Lexington: University of Kentucky Press, 1967), pp. 211–49 and passim. See also Sidney M. Milkis, *The President and the Parties: The Transformation of the American Party System since the New Deal* (New York: Oxford University Press, 1993), pp. 79–97; and Milkis, "Presidents and Party Purges: With Special Emphasis on the Lessons of 1938," in Robert Harmel, ed., *Presidents and Their Parties: Leadership or Neglect?* (New York: Praeger, 1984), pp. 151–75.

7. Press conference, May 31, 1935, in Rosenman, ed., *The Public Papers and Addresses of Franklin D. Roosevelt*, 4 vols. (New York: Random House, 1938), 4: 205, 212, 221; William E. Leuchtenburg, "The Origins of Franklin D. Roosevelt's 'Court-Packing' Plan," *Supreme Court Review*, 1966, p. 357; Arthur M. Schlesinger, Jr., *The Politics of Upheaval* (Boston: Houghton Mifflin, 1960), pp. 284–87.

8. Leuchtenburg, "Origins of Franklin D. Roosevelt's 'Court-Packing' Plan," pp. 359–80. Other accounts of the genesis of the judicial reorganization plan can be found in Joseph Alsop and Turner Catledge, *The 168 Days* (Garden City: Doubleday, Doran, 1938), pp. 17–60; Leonard Baker, *Back to Back: The Duel Between FDR and the Supreme Court* (New York: Macmillan, 1967), pp. 109–36; and Milkis, *The President and the Parties*, pp. 111–13.

9. Inaugural Address, in Rosenman, ed., *Public Papers and Addresses*, 1937 volume, p. 2.

10. Message to Congress, February 5, 1937, and "Fireside Chat," March 9, 1937, both in ibid., pp. 51–52, 127. Only in public statements did the administration claim to be concerned about judicial delays. Privately, liberal New Dealers spoke frankly about their real motives. Benjamin Cohen, for example, wrote to Justice Brandeis in July 1937 that the plan was a way "to resolve conflicts which recurrently arise between the Court and the Congress during periods of social and economic change." Cohen to Brandeis, July 30, 1937, Corcoran MSS 190.

11. Morton J. Horowitz, *The Transformation of American Law, 1870–1960: The Crisis of Legal Orthodoxy* (New York: Oxford University Press, 1992), pp. 258–68; Leuchtenburg, "Franklin D. Roosevelt's Supreme Court 'Packing' Plan," in Harold M. Hollingsworth and William F. Holmes, eds., *Essays on the New Deal* (Austin: University of Texas Press, 1969), p. 115; Leuchtenburg, "The Constitutional Revolution of 1937," in Victor Hoar, ed., *The Great Depression: Essays and Memoirs from Canada and the United States* (Vancouver: Copp Clark, 1969), pp. 31–83.

12. James Truslow Adams, "An Historian Looks at the Supreme Court," radio address, March 8, 1937, Adams MSS; *New Republic*, May 12, 1937, p. 15; Robert Jackson, draft autobiography, p. 121, Jackson MSS 188.

13. Leuchtenburg, "Roosevelt's Supreme Court 'Packing' Plan," pp. 83–91, 109–15.

14. Barry D. Karl, *Executive Reorganization and Reform in the New Deal: The Genesis of Administrative Management, 1900–1939* (Cambridge: Harvard University Press, 1963), pp. 205–10; Peri E. Arnold, *Making the Managerial Presidency: Comprehensive Reorganization Planning, 1905–1980* (Princeton: Princeton University Press, 1986), pp. 81–95.

15. Karl, *Executive Reorganization*, pp. 80, 217–18; Arnold, *Making the Managerial Presidency*, pp. 99–117. The Brownlow Report's characterization of the American state prior to the New Deal anticipated Stephen Skowronek's later description of American government at the turn-of-the-century as a "state of courts and parties." See Skowronek, *Building a New Administrative State: The Expansion of National Administrative Capacities, 1877–1920* (New York: Cambridge University Press, 1982).

16. Barry Karl, "Executive Reorganization and Presidential Power," *Supreme Court Review*, 1977, pp. 26–27; Sidney Milkis, "The New Deal, Administrative Reform, and the Transcendence of Partisan Politics," *Administration and Society* 18 (1987), 433–72; Milkis, *The President and Parties*, pp. 104–11, 113–34.

17. James Farley diary, April 7, 1938, Farley MSS 43; FDR to heads of departments, August 7, 1939, Jesse Jones MSS 30; Lewis Schwellenbach radio address, March 10, 1938, Schwellenbach MSS 3; John Carter to Thomas Corcoran, July 8, 1937, Corcoran MSS 192.

18. Some historians have made a similar argument by describing the initiatives of 1937 and 1938 as part of a "Third New Deal," by which the administration sought to effect a major shift of power into the executive branch. See, e.g., Barry Karl, *The Uneasy State* (Chicago: University of Chicago Press, 1983), pp. 155–81; Karl, "Constitution and Central Planning: The Third New Deal Revisited," *Supreme Court Review*, 1989, pp. 163–201; Otis Graham, "Franklin Roosevelt and the Intended New Deal," in Thomas E. Cronin and Michael R. Beschloss, eds., *Essays in Honor of James MacGregor Burns* (Englewood Cliffs: Prentice Hall, 1989), pp. 85–86; John W. Jeffries, "The 'New' New Deal: FDR and American Liberalism, 1937–1945," *Political Science Quarterly* 105 (1990), 397–418; Milkis, *The President and the Parties*, pp. 98–104.

19. "Whose Recovery?" *New Republic*, April 20, 1938, p. 319; "Reorganization Jitters," *New Republic*, April 6, 1938, p. 263; Harold L. Ickes, *The Secret Diary of Harold L. Ickes*, 3 vols. (New York: Simon and Schuster, 1953–1954), II: 325–26; Richard Polenberg, *Reorganizing Roosevelt's Government: The Controversy Over Executive Reorganization, 1936–1939* (Cambridge: Harvard University Press, 1966), pp. 127, 148–49, 153–54; Patterson, *Congressional Conservatism*, pp. 213–27. The Senate, after an acrimonious battle, had passed the reorganization bill 49-42; but the debate helped awaken popular opposition that contributed to the bill's demise in the House.

20. *New Republic*, April 27, 1938, pp. 358–59.

21. George Soule, "This Recovery: What Brought It? And Will it Last?" *Harper's*, March 1937, p. 337; Leon Henderson, "Boom and Bust," March 29, 1937, and Mariner Eccles, "How to Prevent Another 1929 in 1940," April 5,

1937, both in PSF 155, FDRL; Lauchlin Currie, "An Appraisal of Current Prospects and a Tentative Program," May 18, 1937, and Will Clayton to Eccles, April 18, 1937, both in Eccles MSS 72-14.

22. Eccles, "How to Prevent Another 1929 in 1940"; Currie, "An Appraisal of Current Prospects," and "Current Business Situation," September 20, 1937, Eccles MSS 73-3; Henderson to Hopkins, August 31, 1937, Hopkins MSS 54. Henderson accompanied his prediction with warnings of rising prices and declining purchasing power. See also Henderson to Hopkins, September [n.d.], 1937, ibid.

23. National income, for example, had been $87 billion in 1929. Simon Kuznets, *National Income and Its Composition, 1919–1938*, 2 vols. (New York: National Bureau of Economic Research, 1941), pp. 137–38; Rudolph L. Weissman, ed., *Economic Balance and a Balanced Budget: Public Papers of Marriner S. Eccles* (New York: Harper & Brothers, 1940), p. 293; Kenneth D. Roose, *Economics of Recession and Revival: An Interpretation of 1937–38* (New Haven: Yale University Press, 1954), pp. 23–58; Melvin D. Brockie, "The Rally, Crisis, and Depression, 1935–38" (Ph.D. Dissertation, UCLA, 1948), pp. 8–15, 71–80.

24. "Big July 4 a Good Business Omen," *Business Week*, July 10, 1937, p. 13; "Fall Business: Fair and Warmer," *Business Week*, September 4, 1937, p. 13; "Recovery," *Newsweek*, July 31, 1937, p. 28; Raymond Moley, "The Case for Optimism," *Newsweek*, July 3, 1937, p. 36.

25. The federal budget deficits for the first four years of the Roosevelt administration were $3.6 billion in FY 1934, $2.8 billion in FY 1935, $4.4 billion in FY 1936, and $2.8 billion in FY 1937. The entire federal budget in that same period never exceeded $8.5 billion in any one year; the deficit accounted for 46 percent of all federal expenditures during Roosevelt's first term. Lewis H. Kimmel, *Federal Budget and Fiscal Policy, 1789–1958* (Washington: The Brookings Institution, 1959), pp. 179, 319.

26. Ibid., pp. 176–84; campaign addresses, October 1, 10, 12, 21, 1936, in Rosenman, ed., *Public Papers and Addresses* 5: 401–08, 423–24, 448, 526–29; Chester B. Bowles, *Promises to Keep: My Years in Public Life, 1941–1969* (New York: Harper & Row, 1971), p. 117; Stanley High, "Mr. Roosevelt and the Future," *Harper's*, September 1937, p. 340.

27. The case for the weakness of the 1935–1937 recovery can be found in Michael A. Bernstein, *The Great Depression: Delayed Recovery and Economic Change in America, 1929–1939* (New York: Cambridge University Press, 1987), pp. 33–35, 103–20; in Brockie, "Rally, Crisis, and Depression," pp. 4–17, 75–77; and in Dean L. May, *From New Deal to New Economics: The American Liberal Response to the Recession of 1937* (New York: Garland, 1981), p. 95.

28. Annual Message to Congress, January 3, 1936, in Rosenman, ed., *Public Papers and Addresses* 5: 17; May, *From New Deal to New Economics*, pp. 36–37, 93–95.

29. "The Budget Deficit," *Nation*, April 24, 1937, p. 453; Roosevelt Press Conference, March 19, 1936, and Treasury Statement, December 22, 1936, both in Rosenman, ed., *Public Papers and Addresses*, 1937 volume, pp. 141–42, 171, 617–18; G. Griffith Johnson, Jr., *The Treasury and Monetary Policy, 1933–1938* (Cambridge: Harvard University Press, 1939), pp. 110–14; *Federal Reserve Bulletin* 23 (1937), 95–97; R. C. Leffingwell, "Managing Our Economy," *Yale*

*Review*, Summer 1945, pp. 606–07; Donald M. Marvin and Gertrude M. Williams, *Design for Recovery* (New York: Harper & Brothers, 1939), pp. 78–80; Alvin H. Hansen, *Full Employment or Stagnation?* (New York: Norton, 1938), pp. 271–72; Sidney Hyman, *Marriner Eccles: Private Entrepreneur and Public Servant* (Stanford: Stanford University Graduate School of Business, 1976), pp. 227–34; Broadus Mitchell, *Depression Decade: From New Era through New Deal, 1929–1941* (New York: Rinehart, 1947), p. 22; Herbert Stein, *The Fiscal Revolution in America* (Chicago: University of Chicago Press, 1969), pp. 96–98; William Greider, *Secrets of the Temple: How the Federal Reserve Runs the Country* (New York: Simon and Schuster, 1987), pp. 320–31.

30. Ickes, *Secret Diary*, I: 221–24, 240, 245; Arthur M. Schlesinger, Jr., *The Coming of the New Deal* (Boston: Houghton Mifflin, 1958), pp. 243, 537–38; Rexford G. Tugwell, *The Democratic Roosevelt* (Garden City: Doubleday, 1957), pp. 442–43.

31. Ibid., pp. 243–45; John Morton Blum, *From the Morgenthau Diaries*, 3 vols. (Boston: Houghton Mifflin, 1959–1969), I: 2–77.

32. Alan Sweezy, "The Keynesians and Government Policy, 1933–1939," *American Economic Review* 62 (1972), 119–21; May, *From New Deal to New Economics*, pp. 22–26, 36–37, 91–95.

33. Henry Morgenthau, Jr., "The Morgenthau Diaries: 1. The Fight to Balance the Budget," *Collier's*, September 27, 1944, pp. 12–13, 80–82; Robert Lekachman, *The Age of Keynes* (New York: Random House, 1966), p. 124; Blum, *From the Morgenthau Diaries*, I: 263–85, 274–75, 280–83, 387–89; Leuchtenburg, *Franklin D. Roosevelt*, pp. 244–45; Annual Budget Message, January 7, 1937, in Rosenman, ed., *Public Papers and Addresses*, 5: 642–44.

34. Eccles, "How to Prevent Another 1929 in 1940"; Eccles, *Beckoning Frontiers: Public and Personal Recollections* (New York: Alfred A. Knopf, 1951), pp. 294–300; Blum, *Morgenthau Diaries*, I: 279–80.

35. Ibid., pp. 282–83, 296; Executive Order, April 13, 1937, and Message to Congress, April 20, 1937, both in Rosenman, ed., *Public Papers and Addresses*, 1937 volume, pp. 156, 163–68; May, *From New Deal to New Economics*, pp. 88–89.

36. Stock prices had been declining rapidly before October 19, and the events of the new "Black Tuesday" did not, in the end, lower prices any further. After a wave of panic selling in the morning, the market recovered that afternoon to about the levels of the day before; and prices actually rose through the remainder of the week, before beginning another, more prolonged downward slide. Nevertheless, the events of that day were sufficiently dramatic to create widespread consternation. "Henceforth Tuesday October 19 can lay claim to being the most startling single day in stock market history since famed Oct. 29, 1929," *Time* reported. "When you are in a panic," *Newsweek* reported (quoting a market observer), "you are beyond the limits of logical explanations." "Stocks and Commodities Fall to Year's Low," *Newsweek*, October 18, 1937, pp. 28–29; "Bathysphere," *Time*, November 1, 1937, p. 63; "Market Goes on a Bender," *Newsweek*, November 1, 1937, pp. 7–9; Berle diary, October 19, 1937, Berle MSS 210; Max Lerner, "Notes on 'Black Tuesday,'" *Nation*, October 30, 1937, p. 468.

37. "Recessional," *Time*, November 22, 1937, p. 15; "Business Prospects,"

*Nation*, January 1, 1938; Roose, *Economics of Recession and Revival*, p. 237; Brockie, "Rally, Crisis, and Depression," pp. 83–86; Leonard P. Ayres, "This Business Relapse," *Atlantic Monthly*, February 1938, p. 151.

38. James MacGregor Burns, *Roosevelt: The Lion and the Fox* (New York: Harcourt, Brace, 1956), pp. 319–21; Farley diary, February 10, 1938, Farley MSS 42. The term "depression" had itself been coined by members of the Hoover administration as a supposedly soothing alternative to the more familiar term "panic." Roosevelt evidently considered "recession" an even milder term, although, like "depression," it did nothing to disquise the dire conditions it described.

39. Diary entry, October 19, 1937, Morgenthau Diaries 92: 230; Max Lerner, "Fear Hits the New Deal," *Nation*, November 30, 1937, p. 551; Katie Louchheim, ed., *The Making of the New Deal: The Insiders Speak* (Cambridge: Harvard University Press, 1983), p. 274; Morgenthau to FDR, November 4, 1937, Morgenthau Diaries 94: 48; Monetary and Fiscal Policy Committee memorandum, "Current Business Conditions," October 19, 1937, Eccles MSS 38-1.

40. Ickes, *Secret Diary*, II: 240, 317.

41. Richard B. Henderson, *Maury Maverick: A Political Biography* (Austin: University of Texas Press, 1970), p. 166.

42. Chester Davis to Marriner Eccles, October 30, 1937, Eccles MSS 38-2; Morgenthau to FDR, November 4, 1937, Morgenthau Diaries 94: 48; Monetary and Fiscal Policy Committee, "Current Business Conditions"; Lauchlin Currie, Leon Henderson, Isidor Lubin to FDR, November 8, 1937, Eccles MSS 5-7.

## Chapter Two

1. Henry Morgenthau, Jr., "The Morgenthau Diaries: 2. The Struggle for a Program," *Collier's*, October 4, 1947, p. 21.

2. Among the clearest statements of the "business confidence" argument is Douglas A. Hayes, "Business Confidence and Business Activity: A Case Study of the Recession of 1937," *Michigan Business Studies* 10 (June 1951), 118–26 and passim. See also Jerome Frank to Louis Bean, February 28, 1940, Frank MSS 21.

3. Alvin H. Hansen, *Fiscal Policy and Business Cycles* (New York: W. W. Norton, 1941), pp. 84–88; Simon Kuznets, *National Income and Its Composition, 1919–1938* (New York: National Bureau of Economic Research, 1941), pp. 268–74; Melvin D. Brockie, "The Rally, Crisis, and Depression, 1933–1938" (Ph.D. Dissertation, UCLA, 1948), pp. 13–16, 97–98, 106, and Brockie, "Theories of the 1937–38 Crisis and Depression," *Economics Journal* 60 (1950), 304–10; Kenneth D. Roose, *The Economics of Recession and Revival: An Interpretation of 1937–38* (New Haven: Yale University Press, 1954), pp. 179–82. Brockie and Roose both cite the unwillingness of business to invest as the principal cause of the 1937 recession. Michael Bernstein has demonstrated a pattern of investment that varies widely from one industry to another in the 1930s; he offers no specific explanation of the 1937 downturn, but he concludes that inadequate aggregate private investment was a central cause of

the persistence of the Depression. *The Great Depression* (New York: Cambridge University Press, 1987), pp. 103–20.

4. "Aldrich Blames Market Slump on 'Government Policies,'" *Newsweek*, October 25, 1937, p. 28; Hayes, "Business Confidence and Business Activity," pp. 19–21. C. O. Hardy, "An Appraisal of the Factors ('Natural' and 'Artificial') Which Stopped Short the Recovery Development in the United States," *American Economic Review Supplement* 29, part 2 (March 1939), 170–82, makes a case for New Deal labor policies as a cause of the recession. See also Bernard Baruch to Harry Hopkins, September 28, 1937, Hopkins MSS 85; Adolf Berle diary, July 9, 1939, Berle MSS 210; R. W. Estey to Marriner Eccles, December 27, 1937, Eccles MSS 7-4; "Storm Over Taxes," *New Republic*, May 4, 1938, pp. 381–82; Chester J. La Roche to William O. Douglas, August 23, 1938, Douglas MSS 18; "Roosevelt Over Business," *Business Week*, October 23, 1937, p. 64.

5. Berle diary, May 10, 1939, Berle MSS 210.

6. Speech draft, [n.d.], Morgenthau Diaries 95; transcript of meeting, September 13, 1937, ibid.; transcript of Morgenthau conversation with James A. Farley, October 8, 1937, and Roswell Magill to Morgenthau, October 7, 1937, both in ibid. 91; memorandum, October 12, 1937, ibid. 92; John Morton Blum, *From the Morgenthau Diaries*, 3 vols. (Boston: Houghton Mifflin, 1959–1969), I: 380–86; Dean L. May, *From New Deal to New Economics: The Liberal Response to the Recession* (New York: Garland, 1981), pp. 93–95, 103. A good statement of balanced budget orthodoxy from a disenchanted supporter of the administration is Lewis Douglas, *The Liberal Tradition: A Free People and a Free Economy* (New York: Van Nostrand, 1935), pp. 61–68.

7. Wayne Taylor to Morgenthau, November 1937, and transcripts of meetings, November 4, 5, 1937, Morgenthau Diaries 94; Blum, *From the Morgenthau Diaries*, I: 387–89; May, *From New Deal to New Economics*, pp. 98–103.

8. Transcript of Cabinet meeting, November 4, 1937, Morgenthau Diaries 94.

9. Ibid.; transcript of Treasury meeting, November 4, 1937, Morgenthau Diaries 95; speech, November 10, 1937, ibid. 97; Blum, *From the Morgenthau Diaries* I: 392–97. Roosevelt read and approved Morgenthau's speech in advance, although on November 6 he penciled in a number of revisions, all clearly designed to weaken and qualify Morgenthau's commitment to balancing the budget. The basic thrust of the speech, however, remained as Morgenthau had intended it. See May, *From New Deal to New Economics*, pp. 107–08.

10. See Adolf Berle to Louis Brandeis, February 19, 1932: "Now the concentration has progressed so far that it seems unlikely to break up even in a period of stress. I can see nothing at the moment but to take this trend as it stands endeavoring to mold it so as to be useful." Quoted in Michael E. Parrish, *Felix Frankfurter and His Times: The Reform Years* (New York: The Free Press, 1982), p. 207; Arthur M. Schlesinger, Jr., *The Crisis of the Old Order* (Boston: Houghton Mifflin, 1957), pp. 400–01.

11. Edward Bellamy, *Looking Backward, 2000–1887* (New York: Ticknor, 1887); John L. Thomas, *Alternative America* (Cambridge: Harvard University Press, 1983), pp. 237–87; William E. Akin, *Technocracy and the American*

*Dream* (Berkeley: University of California Press, 1977); Ellis Hawley, *The New Deal and the Problem of Monopoly* (Princeton: Princeton University Press, 1967), p. 44; George Q. Flynn, *American Catholics and the Roosevelt Presidency* (Lexington: University of Kentucky Press, 1968), pp. 22–35; David J. O'Brien, *American Catholics and Social Reform: The New Deal Years* (New York: Oxford University Press, 1968), pp. 17–21, 120–49; Pope Leo XIII, "On the Condition of Workers," in *Two Basic Social Encyclicals* (New York: Benziger Brothers, 1943), pp. 3–81; Pope Pius XI, *Quadragesimo Anno / Forty Years After "On Reconstructing Social Order"* (New York: Benziger Brothers, 1943), pp. 20–24.

12. Robert D. Cuff, *The War Industries Board: Business-Government Relations during World War I* (Baltimore: The Johns Hopkins University Press, 1973), pp. 125–48, 190, 219–20, 268–69; Cuff, "War Mobilization, Social Learning, and State Building in the United States," unpublished paper, 1986, pp. 16–18, 29–32; William E. Leuchtenburg, "The New Deal and the Analogue of War," in John Braeman et al., eds., *Change and Continuity in Twentieth Century America* (Columbus: Ohio State University Press, 1964), pp. 90–93; Richard P. Adelstein, " 'The Nation as an Economic Unit': Keynes, Roosevelt, and the Managerial Ideal," *Journal of American History* 78 (1991), 166–68; David M. Kennedy, *Over Here: The First World War and American Society* (New York: Oxford University Press, 1980), pp. 126–43; David Brody, "The New Deal and World War II," in John Braeman, Robert H. Bremner, David Brody, eds., *The New Deal* (Columbus: Ohio State University Press, 1975) I: 267–70.

13. Bernard M. Baruch, *American Industry in the War* (New York: Prentice Hall, 1941), pp. 105–06.

14. Grosvenor B. Clarkson, *Industrial America in the World War: The Strategy Behind the Line, 1917–1918* (Boston: Houghton Mifflin, 1923), pp. 312, 475–88.

15. Ellis W. Hawley, "Herbert Hoover and Economic Stabilization, 1921–22," in Hawley, ed., *Herbert Hoover as Secretary of Commerce* (Iowa City: University of Iowa Press, 1981), pp. 43–77; Colin Gordon, *New Deals: Business, Labor, and Politics in America, 1920–1935* (New York: Cambridge University Press, 1994), pp. 39–40, 47–49, 85–86, 128–59; Robert F. Himmelberg, *The Origins of the National Recovery Administration: Business, Government, and the Trade Association Issue, 1921–1933* (New York: Fordham University Press, 1976), pp. 43–74; Adelstein, " 'The Nation as an Economic Unit,' " pp. 168–71; Louis Galambos, *Competition and Cooperation: The Emergence of a National Trade Association* (Baltimore: The Johns Hopkins University Press, 1966), pp. 89–138. For a discussion of the roots of New Deal corporatism in the decades preceding the Depression, see (in addition to the works cited above) Donald Brand, *Corporatism and the Rule of Law: A Study of the National Recovery Administration* (Ithaca: Cornell University Press, 1988), part I.

16. Charles R. Stevenson, *The Way Out* (New York: Stevenson, Jordan & Harrison Management Engineers, [1932]), pp. 24–28, 30–36; Edgar L. Heermance, *Can Business Govern Itself? A Study of Industrial Planning* (New York: Harper & Brothers, 1933), pp. 8–30, 61–75, 105–22, 242–59.

17. Gerard Swope, *The Swope Plan*, ed. J. George Frederick (New York: The Business Bourse, 1931), pp. 19–45, 219–21; Gordon, *New Deals*, pp. 167–69.

18. Adolf A. Berle, Jr., and Gardiner C. Means, *The Modern Corporation and Private Property* (New York: Macmillan, 1932), pp. v, 124–25, 352, 356, and passim. In a 1932 letter to Walter Lippmann discussing the message of the book, Berle argued that a fundamental change in the industrial system was inevitable and that the only question remaining was the path along which the change would move: a reversion to "the individualism of the last century," a business-dominated centralization "through the extension of mergers and the like," or (the alternative he clearly preferred) a process by which "the government will step in and in some form or other conscript the various units into a harmonious system." Berle to Lippmann, July 20, 1932, Lippmann MSS III, 56.

19. Raymond Moley, *After Seven Years* (New York: Harper & Brothers, 1939), pp. 14, 23–24, 62, 184, 189–90; Rexford G. Tugwell, *The Industrial Discipline and the Governmental Arts* (New York: Columbia University Press, 1933), pp. 4–6, 189–219; Tugwell, *The Democratic Roosevelt* (Garden City: Doubleday, 1957), pp. 229–30, 284–86, 308–11; Samuel H. Beer, "The Idea of the Nation," *New Republic*, July 19, 26, 1982, pp. 27–28. An early statement of the idea, so appealing to members of the "brains trust," that concentration of industry was on the whole a good thing and that the challenge was to impose some level of planning and public control on the economy was Charles R. Van Hise, *Concentration and Control: A Solution of the Trust Problem in the United States* (New York: Macmillan, 1912), esp. pp. 8–20, 277–78.

20. For a time in the 1920s, Roosevelt had served as president of the American Construction Council, a trade association whose unsuccessful efforts to stabilize the building industry apparently left him with both a general sympathy for associational ideas and a conviction that "voluntary self-regulation did not work," that government must play a larger role if such ventures were to succeed. Although he did not speak often about his broad economic vision before 1932, he did at times express support for the idea of a "natural harmony of interests within the economy" and for the possibilities of voluntary cooperative planning within industries. His celebrated Commonwealth Club address in San Francisco during the 1932 campaign returned to those themes. See Tugwell, *The Democratic Roosevelt*, pp. 142–44; Frank Freidel, *Franklin D. Roosevelt: The Ordeal* (Boston: Little, Brown, 1954), pp. 151–58; Daniel R. Fusfeld, *The Economic Thought of Franklin D. Roosevelt and the Origins of the New Deal* (New York: Columbia University Press, 1954), pp. 102–05, 253–56.

21. Frances Perkins, *The Roosevelt I Knew* (New York: Viking, 1946), p. 240.

22. Ernest B. Fricke, "The New Deal and the Modernization of Small Business: The Mcreary Tire & Rubber Company, 1930–1940," *Business History Review* 56 (1982), 566–76.

23. Perkins, *The Roosevelt I Knew*, p. 206. John A. Garraty, "The New Deal, National Socialism, and the Great Depression," *American Historical Review* 78 (1973), 907–45; Donald R. Brand, "Corporatism, the NRA, and the

Oil Industry," *Political Science Quarterly* 98 (1984), 99–118, and Brand, *Corporatism and the Rule of Law*, part II, all make the case for the corporatist character of the NRA.

24. White House memorandum, "Summary of Critique of NRA Policies and Economic Planning," n.d. [1934], PSF 158, FDRL; V. S. von Szeliski to Mordecai Ezekiel, August 15, 1934, Frank MSS 21.

25. William H. Davis, "Memorandum," PSF 158, FDRL; Henry Stimson to FDR, June 4, 1935, PPF 20, FDRL. For general accounts of the NRA and its demise, see Hawley, *The New Deal and the Problem of Monopoly*, pp. 19–146; Bernard Bellush, *The Failure of the NRA* (New York: Norton, 1975), pp. 30–84, 136–79; William E. Leuchtenburg, *Franklin D. Roosevelt and the New Deal* (New York: Harper & Row, 1963), pp. 64–70, 145–46.

26. L. M. Graves, "The Folly of Industrial Planning: Why the Government Could Not Regulate Production," *Harper's*, February 1938, pp. 270–78; Freda Kirchwey, "Old Liberties for a New World," *Nation*, February 10, 1940, pp. 145–46. Kirchwey described "collective control" as "necessary to keep the industrial machine going"; New Deal reforms, therefore, must be "enormously extended. Collective control over our natural resources, the railroads and other major monopolies must be accepted as obvious first steps in the direction of industrial planning."

27. Roosevelt made these remarks in a message (read in his absence) to a reunion dinner for the NRA general staff in 1941. FDR to Donald Nelson, January 15, 1941, Nelson MSS 2; FDR to Donald Richberg, January 15, 1941, Richberg MSS 2. See also Leuchtenburg, *Franklin D. Roosevelt and the New Deal*, pp. 145–46; Otis L. Graham, Jr., "Frankin Roosevelt and the Intended New Deal," in Thomas E. Cronin and Michael R. Beschloss, eds., *Essays in Honor of James MacGregor Burns* (Englewood Cliffs: Prentice-Hall, 1989), pp. 83–84.

28. Felix Bruner, "Major Berry—Always Available," *American Mercury*, January 1937, pp. 83–90; George Creel, "Handy Man," *Collier's*, August 28, 1937, pp. 36–37. *Newsweek*, [n.d.], quoted in "George L. Berry," *Current Biography*, January 1948, pp. 48–50.

29. "Major Berry Invites," *Business Week*, November 16, 1935, p. 8; "Berry (Not Industry) Conference," ibid., December 14, 1935, pp. 7–8; "Berry Tries Again," ibid., January 4, 1936, p. 11; "All Set for Berry's Show," ibid., December 5, 1936, pp. 20–21; "New Deal's Big Day," *Literary Digest*, December 7, 1935, pp. 5–6; "Troubles at Convention," ibid., December 21, 1935, pp. 3–4; "Better Life," ibid., December 19, 1936, pp. 11–12; George L. Berry to Marvin McIntyre, February 26, 1936, and Robert Wood Johnson to McIntyre, December 3, 1936, both in OF 2452, FDRL; Berry to FDR, March 25, 1937, and Berry, "Proposed Law to Set Up an Instrumentality to Inform the President on the Economic State of the Nation and to Promote Industrial Peace," both in PSF 155, FDRL; Hawley, *The New Deal and the Problem of Monopoly*, pp. 161–62.

30. Gerard Swope to Louis Howe, November 2, 1933; and Swope, "Opening Statement for the Meeting of the Business Advisory and Planning Council," November 1, 1933, both in OF 3-Q, FDRL; Kim McQuaid, *Big Business and Presidential Power: From FDR to Reagan* (New York: William Morrow, 1982), pp. 30–33.

31. See, e.g., Richard Patterson to William O. Douglas, June 14, 1938, Douglas MSS 20; Edward J. Stettinius, "Washington Notes," February–October 1938, Stettinius MSS 64.

32. The hypothesis of a "corporate liberalism"—a liberalism (or progressivism) that serves, rather than challenges, the interests of capital—is a staple of the scholarship on twentieth-century political economy. It has been particularly influential in shaping interpretations of progressive economic reform. See, for example, Gabriel Kolko, *The Triumph of Conservatism: A Reinterpretation of American History, 1900–1916* (New York: The Free Press, 1963); James Weinstein, *The Corporate Ideal in the Liberal State, 1900–1918* (Boston: Beacon Press, 1968); R. Jeffrey Lustig, *Corporate Liberalism: The Origins of Modern American Political Theory, 1890–1920* (Berkeley: University of California Press, 1982); Martin J. Sklar, *The Corporate Reconstruction of American Capitalism: 1890–1916* (New York: Cambridge University Press, 1988). A similar, if for many years less well developed, argument has informed revisionist critiques of the New Deal. See, for example, Barton J. Bernstein, "The New Deal: The Conservative Achievements of Liberal Reform," in Bernstein, ed., *Towards a New Past: Dissenting Essays in American History* (New York: Random House, 1967), pp. 263–88; Ronald Radosh, "The Myth of the New Deal," in Radosh and Murray Rothbard, eds. *A New History of the Leviathan: Essays on the Rise of the American Corporate State* (New York: Dutton, 1972), pp. 146–87. More recent variants on this argument are visible in Thomas Ferguson, "From Normalcy to New Deal: Industrial Structure, Party Competition, and American Public Policy in the Great Depression," *International Organization* 38 (1984), 47–61; Kim McQuaid, "Corporate Liberalism in the American Community," *Business History Review* 52 (1978), 309–20; McQuaid, *Big Business and Presidential Power*, pp. 29–61, 306–10; Theda Skocpol, "Political Response to Capitalist Crisis: Neo-Marxist Theories of the State and the Case of the New Deal," *Politics and Society* 10 (1980), 157–201; and Colin Gordon, *New Deals*, which offers the most thorough and sophisticated version so far. The corporate liberal model takes many forms and explains the impact of corporate interests on New Deal policy in various ways—ranging from arguments for direct, overt interventions in policymaking by capitalists (the "instrumental" approach) to arguments that the state naturally reflects the interests of the corporate community, even when business leaders oppose its actions (the "functional" approach). But whatever its variations, it is, in the end, as Colin Gordon has written, "a broad stream of interpretation that has stressed the primacy of business interests in the formulation of U.S. public policy and the essential conservatism of the New Deal." (p. 4.)

My own view is that the corporate liberal model is in many ways correct, but also incomplete. Business interests have always been more powerful in American politics and policymaking than any other single group, and the New Deal years were no exception. It goes almost without saying that the American political system seldom, if ever, produces policies that are genuinely hostile to capitalism (despite the belief of many capitalists to the contrary); sustaining the health of private enterprise has, in the twentieth century at least, always been the chief commitment of the state. That so many businessmen despised the New Deal is not, in itself, proof that the New Deal was hostile to their interests. Still, the corporate world has never been the only influence on the state, and in the 1930s and since it has competed frequently with other groups (including groups within the state itself) in the shaping of public policy. And if, as many corporate liberal interpretations suggest, the chief project of capitalists in the 1930s was to enlist the state in their struggle to escape from competition, the New Deal conspicuously failed to oblige them (despite considerable efforts by many people in the Roosevelt administration to do so).

33. BAC, "Report of Committee on the Wagner National Labor Relations Bill," April 10, 1935, Gerard Swope to W. Averill Harriman, May 6, 1937, Harriman to Daniel C. Roper, May 20, 1937, "Report of the Monetary Policy Committee of the Business Advisory Council," April 8, 1937, all in OF 3-Q, FDRL; Roswell Magill to Henry Morgenthau, October 7, 1937, Morgenthau Diaries 91.

34. White House digest of BAC report, "Statement of Policy for Amendments to the National Labor Relations Act," February 4, 1938; Daniel C. Roper to James Roosevelt, February 4, 1938; W. Averill Harriman, "Statement to the Press," January 19, 1938; all in OF 3-Q, FDRL; Robert Wood Johnson to Thomas Corcoran, May 23, 1937, June 15, July 13, November 5, November 8, 1937, all in Corcoran MSS 202; Walter Millis, "Cross Purposes in the New Deal," *Virginia Quarterly Review* 14 (Summer 1938), 359.

35. BAC Resolution, March 13, 1935; BAC, "Report of the Committee on Revision of the National Industrial Recovery Act," January 17, 1935; White House digest of BAC reports, "Underlying Causes of the Recession," and "Interim Report of the Committee on Business Legislation," February 4, 1938, Daniel Roper to James Roosevelt, February 4, 1938, Roper to FDR, January 17, 1938, Robert E. Wood to Roper, January 3, 1938, W. Averill Harriman to Roper, January 4, 1938, BAC "Resolution," October 7, 1938, all in OF 3-Q, FDRL; Johnson to Thomas Corcoran, November 8, 1937, November 23, 1937, both in Corcoran MSS 202; Johnson to FDR, June 20, 1938, PPF 3652, FDRL; "Cooperation Between Producers and Consumers," *Daily Metal Reporter*, June 3, 1939, reprint in OF 172, FDRL.

36. Donald R. Richberg, *My Hero: The Indiscreet Memoirs of an Eventful but Unheroic Life* (New York: Putnam's, 1954), pp. 26–30; Thomas E. Vadney, *The Wayward Liberal: A Political Biography of Donald Richberg* (Lexington: University of Kentucky Press, 1970), pp. 10–16, 22.

37. See ibid., pp. 48, 134, 312; Richberg to Arthur Krock, October 25, 1944, and Richberg to John S. Lord, January 21, 1946, both in Richberg MSS 2.

38. Richberg, *My Hero*, pp. 37, 42–140; Vadney, *Wayward Liberal*, p. 94; Richberg, *Tents of the Mighty* (New York: Willett, Clark & Colby, 1930), pp. 179–203, 226–32, 265.

39. Richberg, *My Hero*, pp. 149–56; Moley, *After Seven Years*, pp. 45, 188, 294.

40. Richberg, *My Hero*, pp. 163–65; Hawley, *The New Deal and the Problem of Monopoly*, pp. 25, 42.

41. Richberg, "Depression Causes and Remedies," testimony before Senate Committee on Finance, February 23, 1933, 12–15, 25, Richberg MSS 19.

42. Richberg, *My Hero*, pp. 174–76, 183, 187–88.

43. Ibid., pp. 185–87, 234–37; Vadney, *Wayward Liberal*, p. 151.

44. Harold L. Ickes, *The Secret Diary of Harold L. Ickes*, 3 vols. (New York: Simon and Schuster, 1953–54), I: 209–11, 221, 247–48.

45. Richberg to FDR, February 25, 1936, with "Memorandum as to the Future of the N.R.A. Program," OF 466–Misc., FDRL; Vadney, *Wayward Liberal*, p. 173. In 1936, Richberg published a book outlining the lessons of the NRA experience, in which he emphasized his belief in the need for "mechanisms of national cooperation." Richberg, *The Rainbow* (Garden City: Doubleday, Doran, 1936), pp. 101–21, 242–84, and passim. See also Richberg to Marvin McIntyre, January 25, March 10, 1938, Richberg MSS 2; Richberg to FDR, February 19, 1937; draft of letter to Business Advisory Council, [n.d.], 1937, memorandum, [n.d.], 1937, all in OF 1961, FDRL; Richberg, "Future Federal Regulation of Business," speech before Ohio State Bar Association, January 9, 1937, *Vital Speeches*, February 1937, pp. 238–41; "Drafting Richberg," *Business Week*, January 9, 1937, p. 5.

46. "Government and Business," Richberg speech, January 26, 1938, OF 1961, FDRL; Robert H. Jackson, unpublished autobiography, 1944, Jackson MSS 188.

47. Richberg to FDR, April 23, 1938, Richberg MSS 6; "How Sick Is Business?" Richberg speech, May 19, 1938, OF 1961, FDRL. See also Richberg, "The Monopoly Issue," *University of Pennsylvania Law Review* 87 (February 1939), 12–15; Marquis W. Childs, "Jackson versus Richberg," *Nation*, January 29, 1938, p. 119; Vadney, *Wayward Liberal*, p. 181.

48. "What Do They Mean: Monopoly?" *Fortune*, April 1938, p. 126; T.R.B., "FDR Is Just Around the Corner," *New Republic*, June 29, 1938, p. 215; Walter Millis, "Cross Purposes in the New Deal," *Virginia Quarterly Review* 14 (Summer 1938), 360–61; James Farley speech, February 6, 1940, Tumulty MSS 60.

49. Memorandum by Adolf Berle, Wayne Taylor, and Roger Ransom, April 1, 1938, Berle Diary, April 9, 1938, both in Berle MSS 210; Jordan Schwarz, *Liberal: Adolf A. Berle and the Vision of an American Era* (New York: The Free Press, 1987), pp. 119–20.

50. Rexford G. Tugwell, "The Progressive Orthodoxy of Franklin D. Roosevelt," *Ethics* 64 (1953), pp. 1–3; Raymond Moley, *The First New Deal* (New York: Harcourt, Brace & World, 1966), pp. 293–97.

51. Wallace speech, February 24, 1938, in Henry A. Wallace, *Democracy Reborn*, ed. Russell Lord (New York: Reynal & Hitchcock, 1944), pp. 142–43. See also Louis Bean, "Need for Industrial Production Program as a Basis for Sound Price Policies," *Plan Age*, July 1935, pp. 18–22.

52. Mordecai Ezekiel, *Jobs for All Through Industrial Expansion* (New York: Alfred A. Knopf, 1939), pp. xi–xii, 3–18, and passim; Ezekiel, *$2500 a Year: From Scarcity to Abundance* (New York: Harcourt, Brace, 1936), pp. 160–73; Ezekiel, "Democratic Economic Planning," *Common Sense*, July 1938, pp. 8–10; Ezekiel, "After the New Deal. VI: Over the Horizon," *New Republic*, August 23, 1939, pp. 64–66; Ezekiel, "Problems in Industrial Planning Under American Institutions," *Plan Age*, January 1939, pp. 1–7; Ezekiel to Thomas Blaisdell, February 20, 1940, Ezekiel MSS 12; Ezekiel to W. P. Chrysler, [n.d.], 1939, and "Memorandum on Discussions with Businessmen," April 6, 1939, both in Frank MSS 26.

53. Jerome Frank, *Save America First: How to Make Our Democracy Work* (New York: Harper & Brothers, 1938), pp. 290–304; "Remedies for Monopoly," *Nation*, April 15, 1939, p. 421; "Can Business and Government Work Together?," *Town Meeting*, December 11, 1939, pp. 16–21; Frank to Thomas Corcoran, November 29, 1937, Corcoran MSS 197; Frank, "Town Hall" speech, [n.d.], 1939, Frank MSS 29.

54. Gardiner Means to National Resource Planning Board, October 11, 1939, Means MSS 7.

55. Millis, "Cross Purposes in the New Deal," p. 358; James T. Flynn, "Other People's Money," *New Republic*, January 26, 1938, p. 337.

56. "National Minima for Labor," *New Republic*, December 1, 1937, p. 88; George Soule, "This Recovery: What Brought It? Will It Last?" *Harper's*, March 1937, p. 342; "Again—The Trust Problem," *New Republic*, January 19, 1938, p. 295; "A New NRA," *Nation*, March 25, 1939, p. 337; "Liberals Never Learn," *Nation*, March 18, 1939, p. 309; Robert Jackson speech, "Business Confidence and Government Policy," December 26, 1937, Clapper MSS 200.

57. George Soule, "Toward a Planned Society," *New Republic*, November 8, 1939, pp. 29–32; John W. Owens, "A Balance Sheet for Americans," *Atlantic Monthly*, July 1940, p. 43; Thurman W. Arnold, *The Folklore of Capitalism* (New Haven: Yale University Press, 1937), pp. 221, 268; Arnold, "Feathers and Prices," *Common Sense*, July 1939, p. 6; Leuchtenburg, "The New Deal and the Analogue of War," p. 135; Leon Henderson to John Chamberlain, January 29, 1938, Hopkins MSS 54. David Cushman Coyle expressed a similar argument in 1935 in writing of the failure of the NRA: "The advocates of national planning, which was to be the road out of chaos, have some explaining to do. . . . In order to get the complete regimentation that engineering operation requires, all the incompatible personalities must be banished or imprisoned or killed." Coyle, "The Twilight of National Planning," *Harper's*, October 1935, pp. 557–59. See also Hawley, *The New Deal and the Problem of Monopoly*, pp. 143–46.

## Chapter Three

1. Harold L. Ickes, *The Secret Diary of Harold L. Ickes*, 3 vols. (New York: Simon and Schuster, 1953–1954), II: 243.

2. Robert S. Allen, "Wall Street and the White House," *Nation*, October 30, 1937, p. 467; Kenneth D. Roose, *The Economics of Recession and Revival: An Interpretation of 1937–38* (New Haven: Yale University Press, 1954), pp. 143–44.

3. Michael Bernstein, *The Great Depression: Delayed Recovery and Economic Change in America, 1929–1939* (New York: Cambridge University Press, 1987), pp. 10–11; Roose, *Economics of Recession and Revival*, pp. 142–57. Contemporary economists who expressed skepticism about the "administered price" explanation include Sumner H. Slichter, "Corporate Price Policies as a Factor in the Recent Business Recession," *Proceedings of the Academy of Political Science* 18 (January 1939), pp. 142–55; Lloyd G. Reynolds, "Producers' Goods Prices in Expansion and Decline," *Journal of the American Statistical Association* 34 (March 1939), 32–40; Henry B. Arthur, "Prices of

Consumers' Goods in Expansion and Recession," ibid., pp. 41–43; Willard L. Thorp and Walter F. Crowder, "Concentration and Product Characteristics as Factors in Price-Quantity Behavior," *American Economic Review* 30 (February 1941), 407–08; Jules Backman, "Price Inflexibility and Changes in Production," ibid. 29 (September 1939), 480–86.

4. Thomas G. Corcoran to Felix Frankfurter, December 15, [1937], Corcoran MSS 198.

5. Joseph Alsop and Robert Kintner, "We Shall Make America Over: The New Dealers Move In," *Saturday Evening Post*, November 12, 1938, pp. 8–9; Samuel I. Rosenman, *Working with Roosevelt* (New York: Harper & Brothers, 1952), p. 105; Arthur M. Schlesinger, Jr., *The Politics of Upheaval* (Boston: Houghton Mifflin, 1960), pp. 578–79. Moley himself later minimized the significance of the incident, but did not deny that it had occurred. Raymond Moley, *After Seven Years* (New York: Harper & Brothers, 1939), pp. 344–46.

6. See also Stanley High, "Mr. Roosevelt and the Future," *Harper's*, September 1937, pp. 337–46, and "The Neo-New Dealers," *Saturday Evening Post*, May 22, 1937, pp. 10–11; Beverly Smith, "Corcoran and Cohen," *American Magazine*, August 1937, pp. 22–23, 125–28; and Alva Johnston, "White House Tommy," *Saturday Evening Post*, July 31, 1937, pp. 5–7, 65–66; Paul W. Ward, "Washington Weekly: Planning the Next Depression," *Nation*, March 6, 1937, pp. 258–59; T.R.B., "Washington Notes," *New Republic*, January 12, 1938, p. 281. James Rowe, a young lawyer who became increasingly active in the "liberal crowd," described the group as "the 'shock troops' of the New Deal—the men who really get the tremendous volume of work done that must be done.... They *believe* in the New Deal and are 100 per centers *only* for that reason." Rowe to Corcoran, [n.d.], 1938. Corcoran MSS 211.

7. Max Freedman, ed., *Roosevelt and Frankfurter: Their Correspondence, 1928–1945* (Boston: Atlantic Monthly Press, 1967), p. 257; Michael E. Parrish, *Felix Frankfurter: The Reform Years* (New York: The Free Press, 1982), pp. 106–08, 199–204, 220–37.

8. Felix Frankfurter, "The Young Men Go to Washington," *Fortune*, January 1936, p. 87; Frankfurter to Jerome Frank, September 29, 1933, Frank MSS 12; George N. Peek, *Why Quit Our Own* (New York: Van Nostrand, 1936), p. 20; Peter H. Irons, *The New Deal Lawyers* (Princeton: Princeton University Press, 1982), p. 10.

9. Monica L. Niznik, "Thomas G. Corcoran: The Public Service of Franklin Roosevelt's 'Tommy the Cork' " (Ph.D. Dissertation, Notre Dame University, 1981), pp. 7–9, 13–23; Joseph P. Lash, *Dreamers and Dealers* (New York: Doubleday, 1988), pp. 54–62; Jordan A. Schwarz, *The New Dealers: Power Politics in the Age of Roosevelt* (New York: Alfred A. Knopf, 1993), p. 140.

10. Niznik, "Thomas G. Corcoran," pp. 29–46; Lash, *Dreamers and Dealers*, pp. 62–75.

11. Corcoran served briefly as assistant secretary of the treasury in 1933, but remained on the RFC board of directors as the Treasury-RFC liaison; after Henry Morgenthau became secretary of the treasury late in 1933, Corcoran's position there became, in his own view, untenable, and he returned to

the RFC staff. In later years, he would occasionally serve as (in his own words) "administrative assistant to the White House," but always unofficially; his base remained the RFC. Niznik, "Thomas G. Corcoran," pp. 57–58, 64–69, 147.

12. See Corcoran to Frankfurter, January 23, 1933, September 24, October 12, 1938, and others in Corcoran MSS 198; Frankfurter, June 18, 1934, Frankfurter MSS 49; Corcoran to Lash, *Dreamers and Dealers*, p. 73.

13. Schwarz, *The New Dealers*, pp. 140–41; Katie Loucheim, ed., *The Making of the New Deal: The Insiders Speak* (Cambridge: Harvard University Press, 1983), pp. 63, 67–70.

14. Ibid., pp. 105–06; Niznik, "Thomas G. Corcoran," pp. 380–82.

15. Niznik, "Thomas G. Corcoran," pp. 130–33, 147–50, 232–36, 276–79; Moley, *After Seven Years*, pp. 343–44; Rosenman, *Working with Roosevelt*, pp. 94, 107, 114–16; Hugh Johnson, unidentified clipping, April 2, 1936, Magee MSS; Schwarz, *The New Dealers*, pp. 140–42.

16. Lash, *Dreamers and Dealers*, pp. 276–85; Ickes, *Secret Diary*, II: 508; Berle diary, April 9, July 16, 1938, February 22, 1939, Berle MSS 210; Eleanor Roosevelt to Harry Hopkins, December 6, 1944, Hopkins MSS 214; Harold Smith diary, September 4, 1939, Smith MSS 1; James A. Farley diary, January 3, 1938, Farley MSS 42; Morgenthau Presidential Diary, May 18, 1939; Corcoran to Harry Hopkins, December 15, 1937, Corcoran MSS 208.

17. Stanley High, "The White House Is Calling," *Harper's*, November 1937, p. 587; John T. Flynn, "Other People's Money," *New Republic*, August 18, 1937, p. 46; Schwarz, *The New Dealers*, pp. 143–46.

18. Hopkins to Corcoran, May 13, 1938, Corcoran MSS 200; Alsop and Kintner, "We Shall Make America Over," p. 9; Henry H. Adams, *Harry Hopkins: A Biography* (New York: Putnam's, 1977), p. 124; George McJimsey, *Harry Hopkins: Ally of the Poor and Defender of Democracy* (Cambridge: Harvard University Press, 1987), pp. 117–19.

19. Ickes, *Secret Diary*, II: 508. Hopkins joined the Cabinet as Secretary of Commerce in 1938.

20. Berle diary, July 16, 1938, Berle MSS 210; Ickes, *Secret Diary*, II: 412. "This is only another bit of evidence to show how much Henry Wallace hates me," Ickes wrote after describing a squabble at a Cabinet meeting, "but I am afraid that his feeling by this time is pretty thoroughly reciprocated."

21. High, "The Neo-New Dealers," pp. 10–11, 106–07.

22. See, for example, Jerome Frank to Thurman Arnold, February 7, 1938, Frank MSS 21; William O. Douglas to Thurman Arnold, February 8, 1938, and Arnold to Douglas, February 11, 1938, both in Douglas MSS 14; Jerome Frank to Robert Jackson, January 6, 1940, Jackson to Frank, January 17, 1940, and Jackson to Felix Frankfurter, January 24, 1939, all in Jackson MSS 13; Thomas Corcoran to Douglas, September 20, December 7, 1938, Corcoran MSS 196; Corcoran to Jackson, September 23, 1938, and Jackson to Corcoran, September 27, 1938, Corcoran MSS 201; Archibald MacLeish to Corcoran, May 2, 1942, MacLeish MSS 5; MacLeish to Frankfurter, January 26, 1940, MacLeish MSS 8; Bruce Bliven to MacLeish, November 7, 1941, MacLeish MSS 3; Benjamin Cohen to Hugo Black, February 2, 1938, Black MSS 23; Douglas to James Landis, September 4, 1935, and Landis to Frankfurter, July 6, 1936, Landis MSS

10; Ickes, *Secret Diary*, III: 173; "Summary of Discussion Between the Advisory Committee and Industrial Committee," National Resources Committee, June 17, 1938, Means MSS 7; "A New NRA," *Nation*, March 25, 1939, p. 337; High, "The Neo-New Dealers," pp. 106–07; T.R.B., "Washington Notes," *New Republic*, January 12, 1938, p. 281. Hugh Johnson took note of the emergence of these "new liberals" (whom he labeled the "Harvard Crowd") as early as 1935; see Ellis Hawley, *The New Deal and the Problem of Monopoly* (Princeton: Princeton University Press, 1966), pp. 283–84. Adolf Berle, a member of the earlier "brains trust," which had been drawn mainly from Columbia and was more committed to planning and associational ideas, referred to them scornfully as "the boys"; see Berle diary, July 16, 1938, Berle MSS 210. Hugh Heclo suggests ways in which "networks" take shape and affect the policymaking process in "Issue Networks and the Executive Establishment," in Anthony King, ed., *The New American Political System* (Washington: American Enterprise Institute, 1978), pp. 87–124.

23. See, for example, Lauchlin Currie, "Causes of the Recession," Federal Reserve memorandum, April 1, 1938, Hopkins MSS 55; Leon Henderson to John Chamberlain, January 29, 1938, Hopkins MSS 54; untitled Federal Reserve memorandum, February 16, 1938, Eccles MSS 5-8; Gardiner C. Means, "Possibilities and Limitations of Antitrust Policy," June 1938, Corcoran MSS 240; Means, "The Consumer and the New Deal," speech draft, [n.d.], Blaisdell File 40, NRPB RG 187; William Harlan Hale, "The Men Behind the President. 3. What They Think," *Common Sense*, July 1938, p. 18.

24. According to the waiter, the executives were conspiring to lay off workers as part of an "unemployment boycott" that would force Roosevelt "and his gang" to "come to terms." The FBI found no evidence to support the charge. See Vasilia N. Getz to Roosevelt, November 19, 1937, Roosevelt to Attorney General Homer Cummings, November 26, 1937, and J. Edgar Hoover to Roosevelt, December 11, 1937, all in Corcoran MSS 203.

25. Roosevelt was, in fact, not at all certain about his attitude toward monopoly late in 1937, but he did nothing to discourage the aggressive posturing by members of his administration and at times, as in the exchange with Ickes, actively encouraged it. Ickes, *Secret Diary*, II: 229, 232, 240–43, 262; diary entry, December 8, 1937, Morgenthau Diaries 101; Hawley, *New Deal and the Problem of Monopoly*, pp. 389, 391–93.

26. *New York Times*, December 31, 1937; Ickes, *Secret Diary*, II: 282–85, 305; Ferdinand Lundberg, *America's Sixty Families* (New York: Vanguard Press, 1937), p. 3; Lundberg to Ickes, January 14, February 16, 1938, Ickes to Lundberg, February 1, February 18, 1938, all in Ickes MSS 299.

27. Jackson made several speeches in New York early in 1938 designed to test the waters for a possible gubernatorial race. He evoked no discernible popular enthusiasm, and both he and Roosevelt evidently decided shortly thereafter that his future did not lie in electoral politics. James Farley diaries, December 31, 1937, January 3, February 10, 1938, Farley MSS 42; Farley to Claude G. Bowers, March 21, 1938, ibid. 6; transcript of Treasury meeting, January 11, 1938, Morgenthau Diaries 106; Berle diary, January 10, 1938, Berle MSS 210; Adams, *Harry Hopkins: A Biography*, p. 123; Jonathan Mitchell, "Jackson Democrat," *New Republic*, January 26, 1938, pp. 326–28; Eugene C.

Gerhart, *America's Advocate: Robert H. Jackson* (Indianapolis: Bobbs-Merrill, 1958), pp. 122–25, 131–32, 136–38.

28. Jackson, "Business Confidence and Government Policy," radio speech over Mutual Broadcasting System, December 26, 1937, Clapper MSS 200; Jackson, "The Menace to Free Enterprise," speech to the American Political Science Association, December 29, 1937, Jackson MSS 30. In a letter to the editor of the *New York Times*, March 3, 1939, Jackson insisted that he had not originated the phrase "capital strike." It appeared first, he claimed, in *The Annalist*, an American business magazine, which wrote in November 1937 that "the only ultimate answer to a strike on the part of labor is a strike on the part of capital." The phrase was repeated in a pamphlet published by Stanwood Menken, a "well known lawyer," and appeared again in an article in the *Yale Review* by Sir Arthur Salter—who was apparently Jackson's direct source. "The child probably has become mine by adoption," he conceded. Jackson was responding to an editorial claiming that he had borrowed the term from "a British writer," presumably Salter. *New York Times*, February 26, 1939.

29. Ickes, *Secret Diary*, II: 282–85, 305; Jackson, autobiography draft, 1944, Jackson MSS 188; Farley diary, January 3, 1938, Farley MSS 42; "The Administration Strikes Back," *New Republic*, January 5, 1938.

30. Message to Congress, January 3, 1938, in Samuel I. Rosenman, ed., *The Public Papers and Addresses of Franklin D. Roosevelt*, 4 vols. (New York: Macmillan, 1941), 1938 volume, pp. 9–11; Ickes, *Secret Diary*, II: 287–88; T.R.B., "Washington Notes," *New Republic*, January 12, 1938, p. 281; "Mr. Roosevelt's Counteroffensive," ibid., p. 268.

31. Brandeis wrote in 1933: "I am so firmly convinced that the large unit is not as efficient—I mean the very large unit—as the smaller unit, that I believe that if it were possible today to make the corporations act in accordance with what doubtless all of us would agree should be the rules of trade no huge corporation would be created, or if created, would be successful." For an important discussion of Brandeis's regulatory philosophy, see Thomas K. McCraw, *Prophets of Regulation* (Cambridge: Harvard University Press, 1984), pp. 94–109, 135–42; and McCraw, "Rethinking the Trust Question," in McCraw, ed., *Regulation in Perspective: Historical Essays* (Boston: Harvard Business School, 1981), pp. 1–55; Jerome Frank, memorandum on "Mr. Justice Brandeis," [n.d.], Frank MSS 19.

32. George C. Norris to Claude Pepper, August 28, 1939, in Corcoran MSS 208; William Borah to Dan Herrington, February 28, 1938, and Borah to Seth Burstedt, April 22, 1938, both in Borah MSS 772; Robert M. La Follette, Jr., to Alvin C. Reis, April 28, 1938, La Follette MSS C-16; La Follette speech, May 8, 1944, La Follette MSS C-22; Patrick J. Maney, *"Young Bob" La Follette: A Biography of Robert M. La Follette, Jr., 1895–1953* (Columbia: University of Missouri Press, 1978), pp. 200–04; Wright Patman to FDR, November 25, 1938, and July 3, 1940, both in OF 288, FDRL; "Again—The Trust Problem," *New Republic*, January 19, 1938, p. 295; Leon Henderson diary, March 21, 1940, Henderson MSS 36; Homer Cummings, "The Unsolved Problem of Monopoly," speech, November 29, 1937, Clapper MSS 200; John T. Flynn, "Other People's Money," *New Republic*, May 12, 1937, and "One-Man Fight," *New*

*Republic*, October 28, 1940; Max Lerner, "Propaganda's Golden Age, I," *Nation*, November 4, 1939, p. 496, and "Propaganda's Golden Age, II," *Nation*, November 11, 1939, p. 522; Alan Brinkley, *Voices of Protest: Huey Long, Father Coughlin, and the Great Depression* (New York: Alfred A. Knopf, 1982), pp. 144–59, 226–37; Michael Kazin, *The Populist Persuasion: An American History* (New York: Basic Books, 1995), chaps. 1–6.

33. Robert Jackson, draft of unpublished autobiography, 1944, Jackson MSS 188.

34. Jackson to Bruce Barton, July 15, 1937, Jackson MSS 9; Felix Frankfurter, "In Memoriam: Robert H. Jackson," reprint of essay originally published in *Columbia Law Review*, April 1955, Black MSS 60; Jonathan Mitchell, "Jackson Democrat," *New Republic*, January 26, 1938, pp. 326–28; Edward S. Mason, "Methods of Developing a Proper Control of Big Business," American Economic Association, *Readings in the Social Control of Industry* (Philadelphia: Blakiston, 1942), pp. 223–25. During his brief tenure as head of the Antitrust Division of the Justice Department, Jackson gave some support to those trying to revive enforcement of the antitrust laws; but he did not compile a record much in keeping with his populist rhetoric, leading some to wonder whether his commitment to "atomization" was more than rhetorical. See Walter Millis, "Cross Purposes in the New Deal," *Virginia Quarterly Review* 14 (Summer 1938), 363–67.

35. Saul Nelson, "What Is Monopoly?" *Harper's*, June 1938, p. 66; Joseph Edmunds, "High Finance Among Friends," *Nation*, February 13, 1937, pp. 182–84; McCraw, *Prophets of Regulation*, pp. 105–07; Jackson to Barton, July 15, 1937, Jackson MSS 9.

36. Jackson speech, "The Menace to Free Enterprise," December 29, 1937, Jackson MSS 30. See also, e.g., Joseph C. O'Mahoney radio speeches, December 8, 1936, and January 13, 1937, PPF 1200, FDRL; Nelson, "What Is Monopoly?" p. 67; Louchheim, *The Making of the New Deal*, p. 143.

37. Jackson to Barton, July 15, 1937, Jackson MSS 9; "Business and Government," *Fortune*, April 1938, p. 70.

38. Means, "The Consumer and the New Deal," [n.d.], NRPB, Thomas Blaisdell Files 35, RG187, NA; Hale, "The Men Behind the President," p. 18; Victor S. Yarros, "Again the Monopoly Issue," *The Christian Century*, July 13, 1938, pp. 869–70; T.R.B., "FDR Is Just Around the Corner," *New Republic*, June 29, 1938, pp. 215–16; "What Do They Mean: Monopoly?" *Fortune*, April 1938, p. 120; "The Attack on Monopoly," *Nation*, January 8, 1938.

39. Maury Maverick, "A Progressive Defines Monopoly: The Third Form of Government," *Common Sense*, January 1939, p. 12; "The Attack on Monopoly," p. 32; "Again—The Trust Problem," *New Republic*, p. 295.

40. Benjamin Cohen to Senator E. P. Costigan, June 7, 1934, Frank MSS 40; McCraw, *Prophets of Regulation*, pp. 210–11.

41. William O. Douglas to Karl Llewelyn, December 20, 1938, Douglas MSS 18.

42. Frankfurter, "The Young Men," p. 62; "Business Advice to the President," *New Republic*, February 2, 1938, p. 352; McCraw, *Prophets of Regulation*, p. 212; Irons, *New Deal Lawyers*, p. 296.

43. Leon Henderson memorandum, September 1937, Hopkins MSS 54.

44. "The Attack on Monopoly," pp. 32–33; Gardiner C. Means, "The Distribution of Control and Responsibility in a Modern Economy," *Political Science Quarterly* 50 (March 1935), 62–67.

45. James M. Landis, *The Administrative Process* (New Haven: Yale University Press, 1938), pp. 24–25, 28–30; W. Jett Lauck, "After the New Deal. IV: A Program for America," *New Republic*, July 5, 1939, pp. 245–46; McCraw, *Prophets of Regulation*, pp. 188, 210, 212–16.

46. "R.V.G." [otherwise unidentified] to Harry Hopkins, July 1, 1940, Jackson MS 30 (the language is from an anti-monopoly plank proposed for but not used in the 1940 Democratic platform); Leon Henderson to John Chamberlain, January 29, 1938, and Henderson to Harry Hopkins, March 23, 1938, both in Hopkins MSS 54; "Summary of Discussion Between the Advisory Committee and Industrial Committee," National Resource Committee, June 17, 1938, Means MSS 7; "The New New Deal," *New Republic*, March 2, 1938, p. 88; "Prices and Social Policy," *New Republic*, February 17, 1941, p. 244.

## Chapter Four

1. *New York Times*, December 31, 1933. Keynes sent an advance copy of the letter to Roosevelt through Felix Frankfurter. See Frankfurter to FDR, December 16, 1933, in Max Freedman, ed., *Roosevelt and Frankfurter: Their Correspondence, 1928–1945* (Boston: Little, Brown, 1967), pp. 177–83.

2. Keynes to FDR, February 1, 1938, Morgenthau Diaries 112.

3. Paul Samuelson, "The General Theory," in Seymour Harris, ed., *The New Economics: Keynes' Influence on Theory and Public Policy* (New York: Alfred A. Knopf, 1947), pp. 148–49.

4. Harold Ickes, *The Secret Diary of Harold Ickes*, 3 vols. (New York: Simon and Schuster, 1953–1954), II: 229, 317; Bernard Baruch to FDR, July 9, 1941, FDR to Baruch, July 11, 1941, both in PSF 117, FDRL; Arthur M. Schlesinger, Jr., *The Politics of Upheaval* (Boston: Houghton Mifflin, 1960), pp. 649–50.

5. Louis H. Bean to Jerome Frank, November 10, 1938, Frank MSS 21.

6. The assumption that "scarcity is a fundamental and permanent characteristic of the necessary commodities of life" and that "there never have been and never can be enough goods to go around" was, Robert S. Lynd wrote in 1936, "one of the most firmly rooted economic convictions. . . . It lives in us twentieth-century moderns with a strength bred of countless centuries of struggle. . . . [T]oday, in an age of technological plenty . . . [m]en have not stopped to examine their institutional hair shirt of Scarcity." "Democracy's Third Estate: The Consumer," *Political Science Quarterly* 51 (December 1936), 483–86.

7. Rexford G. Tugwell, "Notes on the Life and Work of Simon Nelson Patten," *Journal of Political Economy* 31 (1923), 166; Simon N. Patten, *The Theory of Social Forces* (Philadelphia: American Academy of Political and Social Science, 1896), pp. 75–87; Daniel M. Fox, *The Discovery of Abundance: Simon N. Patten and the Transformation of Social Theory* (Ithaca: Cornell University Press, 1967), p. 71; Joseph Dorfman, *The Economic Mind in Ameri-*

*can Civilization* (New York: Viking, 1949), III: 182–88. See also Kathleen Donohue, "Conceptualizing the Good Society: The Idea of the Consumer in Modern American Political Thought," Ph.D. Dissertation, University of Virginia, 1993.

8. Simon N. Patten, *The Theory of Prosperity* (New York: Macmillan, 1902), pp. 140–48, 224, 230–37.

9. Patten, *The New Basis of Civilization* (New York: Macmillan, 1910), pp. 121–27; Patten, *The Theory of Prosperity*, pp. 2–3, 60–64, 88–90, 224–27; Fox, *The Discovery of Abundance*, pp. 89–92; Arthur M. Schlesinger, Jr., *The Crisis of the Old Order* (Boston: Houghton Mifflin, 1957), pp. 136–37; "Extravagance as a Virtue," *Current Opinion*, January 1913, p. 51. Patten's identification of abundance and consumption as the central facts of modern industrial life was similar to the view of his contemporary Thorstein Veblen; but while Veblen saw consumption as a possible threat to the existence of a "good society," Patten generally welcomed it as a vehicle of social betterment and even transcendence. See Rexford G. Tugwell, "The Fourth Power," *Planning and Civic Comment*, April–June 1939, pp. 1–15; and Daniel Horowitz, "Consumption and Its Discontents: Simon N. Patten, Thortein Veblen, and George Gunton," *Journal of American History* 67 (1980), 301–17.

10. Wesley C. Mitchell, *Business Cycles: The Problem and Its Setting* (New York: National Bureau of Economic Research, 1927), pp. 35–42. "Prosperity is checked," Mitchell wrote, "by the failure of consumers' incomes to keep pace with the output of consumers' goods." Mitchell, "A Review," in President's Conference on Unemployment, *Recent Economic Changes in the United States* (New York: McGraw-Hill, 1929), II: 841, 866–67, 909; Mitchell, "Business Cycles," *The World Today*, October 1933, pp. 27–28; Rexford G. Tugwell, "Notes on the Life and Work of Simon Nelson Patten," pp. 203–08; Tugwell, *Industry's Coming of Age* (New York: Harcourt, Brace, 1927), pp. 191–95. Tugwell wrote: "There is a surprising spread of the idea that reducing wages is the easiest way to cut off an important part of the market; and lowered incomes anywhere in the community are viewed by business men with an alarm which is in great contrast with earlier attitudes. . . . [A]s businesses grow greater, it is more and more apparent that workers and consumers are identical"; p. 195. William E. Stoneman, *A History of the Economic Analysis of the Great Depression in America* (New York: Garland, 1979), pp. 9, 13–38.

11. Caroline F. Ware and Gardiner C. Means, *The Modern Economy in Action* (New York: Harcourt, Brace, 1936), pp. 133–43.

12. On the rise of consumer activism, see Horace M. Kallen, *The Decline and Rise of the Consumer* (New York: Appleton-Century, 1936), pp. 153–200; Helen Sorenson, *The Consumer Movement: What It Is and What It Means* (New York: Harper & Brothers, 1941), pp. 3–30 and passim. On the role of the advertising industry in encouraging and legitimizing consumption, see Roland Marchand, *Advertising the American Dream, 1920–1940* (Berkeley: University of California Press, 1985), pp. 25–43, 120–63, and passim; Stuart Ewen, *Captains of Consciousness: Advertising and the Social Roots of the Consumer Culture* (New York: McGraw-Hill, 1976), pp. 81–109 and passim: T. J. Jackson Lears, "From Salvation to Self-Realization: Advertising and the

Therapeutic Roots of the Consumer Culture, 1880–1930," in Lears and Richard Wightman Fox, eds., *The Culture of Consumption: Critical Essays in American History, 1880–1890* (New York: Pantheon, 1983), pp. 1–38. The growing importance of consumer activism was not lost on the Roosevelt administration. Tugwell, among others, courted consumer groups and told one of them in 1934 that "the organization of consumers' leagues in the United States has been a recognition of the inherent power of organized consumer action. Historically your organizations have endeavored to use this latent power . . . in support of numerous attempts by various groups to raise living standards for working people." Speech draft, May 1, 1934, Blaisdell File 40, NRPB, RG 187, NA.

13. Michael Bernstein, *The Great Depression: Delayed Recovery and Economic Change in America, 1929–1939* (New York: Cambridge University Press, 1987), pp. 21–40; Stanley Lebergott, *Pursuing Happiness: American Consumers in the Twentieth Century* (Princeton: Princeton University Press, 1993), pp. 69–72, 148.

14. Wesley C. Mitchell, "A Review of Findings," in President's Research Committee on Social Trends, *Recent Social Trends in the United States* (New York: McGraw-Hill, 1933), pp. xiii, xxx; Dorfman, *The Economic Mind*, III: 455–73. Mitchell is most notable for introducing to economic discourse the now familiar concept of the "business cycle." He argued that fluctuations in business activity were not aberrations from a stable norm, that fluctuation was itself the norm. "Business cycle" theory contributed both directly and indirectly to the increased interest in consumption. By challenging orthodox assumptions about a natural equilibrium in the economy, it opened the way for challenges to other orthodoxies. By identifying a recurrent cyclical pattern in business, it encouraged economists (and others) to look for tools that might counter the effects of the downward cycles of production; the stimulation of consumption was one such tool.

15. George Soule, *A Planned Society* (New York: Macmillan, 1932), pp. 232–34, 262–63.

16. Stuart Chase, *A New Deal* (New York: Macmillan, 1932), pp. 1–3, 241; Chase, *The Nemesis of American Business, and Other Essays* (New York: Macmillan, 1931), pp. 12–13, 78–79; Chase, *Prosperity: Fact or Myth?* (New York: Charles Boni, 1929), pp. 111–34, 173–88; Stoneman, *History of Economic Analysis*, pp. 78–79.

17. Samuel I. Rosenman, ed., *The Public Papers and Addresses of Franklin D. Roosevelt*, 4 vols. (New York: Random House, 1938), I: 750–52; Frank Freidel, *Franklin D. Roosevelt: The Triumph* (Boston: Little, Brown, 1956), pp. 353–56.

18. Ellis Hawley, *The New Deal and the Problem of Monopoly* (Princeton: Princeton University Press, 1966), pp. 61, 75–80, 198–204, 275–76; Persia Campbell, *Consumer Representation in the New Deal* (New York: Columbia University Press, 1940), pp. 27–87.

19. Leon Henderson, "No Recovery Without Spending," undated memorandum [1936], Lubin MSS 51.

20. George Soule, "This Recovery: What Brought It? Will It Last?" *Harper's*, March 1937, p. 343; Colston E. Warne, "Consumers on the March," *Nation*, June 5, 1937, pp. 645–46.

21. Thomas Blaisdell to Rexford G. Tugwell, May 1, 1934, Blaisdell File 40, NRPB, RG 187; "The Consumer Movement," *Business Week*, April 22, 1939, pp. 40–52; Gardiner C. Means, "The Consumer and the New Deal," *Annals of the American Academy of Political and Social Science* 173 (May 1934), 7–17; Campbell, *Consumer Representation in the New Deal*, pp. 23–25, 107–11, 163–68, 262–78; J. B. Matthews, *Guinea Pigs No More* (New York: Covici, Friede, 1936), pp. 23–27, 77–78, 189–91, 244–47, 259–64; Bertram B. Fowler, *Consumer Cooperation in America* (New York: Vanguard Press, 1936), pp. 3–8, 88–118, 294–301; Rexford G. Tugwell, ed., "Consumers and the New Deal," in Tugwell, *The Battle for Democracy* (New York: Columbia University Press, 1935), pp. 268–86. The NRA Consumers' Advisory Board had relatively little influence within the agency, but it did help raise to prominence its first director, Leon Henderson, who would later become a central figure in, among other things, consumer-oriented New Deal policies. Hawley, *The New Deal and the Problem of Monopoly*, pp. 75–78.

22. John H. Williams, "Deficit Spending," *American Economic Review* 30 (February 1941), 52. "The only fiscal attack upon the depression," Williams wrote, "was not through 'income creating' expenditures, so much discussed later on, but through what may be called 'capital repair' expenditures by the Reconstruction Finance Corporation." See also Adolf Berle to FDR (draft of letter), January [n.d.], 1938, Berle MSS 210. Berle was no ally of consumption theories, but he was a strong supporter of public investment in capital projects. He admired Jones's use of the RFC and (according to one biographer) at times hoped to emulate Hjalmar Schacht, the innovative financier who had organized Nazi Germany's early experiments in state capitalism. Jordan Schwarz, *Liberal: Adolf A. Berle and the Vision of an American Era* (New York: The Free Press, 1987), p. 119; Schwarz, *The New Dealers: Power Politics in the Age of Roosevelt* (New York: Alfred A. Knopf, 1993), pp. xi–xvii, 3–31, 59–95; Schwarz, *The Speculator: Bernard M. Baruch in Washington, 1917–1965* (Chapel Hill: University of North Carolina Press, 1981), pp. 240–45, 288–90; Donald Richberg to David Lilienthal, July 24, 1944, Richberg MSS 2; Ickes, *Secret Diary*, III: 107; James Farley diary, December 4, 1937, April 12, 1938, Farley MSS 43. Udo Sautter, "Government and Unemployment: The Use of Public Works Before the New Deal," *Journal of American History* 73 (1986), 59–86, is a good overview of some of the public spending efforts of pre–New Deal governments (federal, state, and local).

23. The federal deficits of the 1930s in fact did little more than sustain the levels of public spending of the late 1920s. That was because the increases in federal spending were offset by reductions in state and local expenditures. Only in 1931 and 1936 (years in which the federal government made large, one-time veterans' benefits payments) was the fiscal stimulus significantly larger than in 1929. E. Cary Brown, "Fiscal Policy in the Thirties: A Reappraisal," *American Economic Review* 46 (December 1956), 863–69. According to Brown, "Fiscal policy . . . seems to have been an unsuccessful recovery device in the 'thirties—not because it did not work, but because it was not tried."

24. Address to Congress, May 22, 1935, in Rosenman, ed., *Public Papers and Addresses*, 4: 182–93; message to Congress, January 24, 1936, in ibid., 5: 67. Congress sustained the President's veto in 1935 but overrode his veto of a

similar bill in January 1936. Payment of the bonus apparently contributed to the significant economic growth of 1936 and early 1937; but some economists have suggested that the rapid exhaustion of the bonus funds subsequently contributed to the economy's rapid downturn late in 1937. Kenneth D. Roose, *Economics of Recession and Revival: An Interpretation of 1937–38* (New Haven: Yale University Press, 1954), p. 79; Alvin H. Hansen, *Full Recovery or Stagnation?* (New York: Norton, 1938), p. 269.

25. Ibid., pp. 190–92; Hansen, *Fiscal Policy and Business Cycles* (New York: Norton, 1941), pp. 94, 130–34, 398–99; Melvin D. Brockie, "The Rally, Crisis, and Depression, 1937–38" (Ph.D. Dissertation, UCLA, 1948), pp. 61–62. Mark Leff, *The Limits of Symbolic Reform: The New Deal and Taxation, 1933–1939* (New York: Cambridge University Press, 1984), pp. 11–47, 285; Leff, "Taxing the 'Forgotten Man': The Politics of Social Security Finance in the New Deal," *Journal of American History* 70 (1983), 359–81; Abraham Epstein, "Away from Social Insecurity," *New Republic*, January 4, 1939, pp. 250–51; "The Job for Congress," ibid., pp. 244–45; "Amend the Social Security Act," *New Republic*, August 24, 1938, pp. 60–61; Arthur W. Gayer, "What Is Ahead," *New Republic*, February 2, 1938, p. 392.

26. Margaret Weir and Theda Skocpol, "State Structures and the Possibilities for Keynesian Responses to the Great Depression in Sweden, Britain, and the United States," in Peter B. Evans, Dietrich Rueschemeyer, and Theda Skocpol, eds., *Bringing the State Back In* (New York: Cambridge University Press, 1985), pp. 107–10, 132–33. The pressure of public opinion also worked to reduce enthusiasm for deficit spending. Gallup polls, for example, showed consistent opposition to government spending from 1935 (when such surveys began) through the end of the decade. When respondents were asked whether government spending was "too much," "too little," or "about right," a large majority answered "too much": 60 percent in October 1935, 63 percent in February 1938. In a poll conducted in February 1937, 70 percent of those sampled answered yes to the question "Should Congress balance the budget and start reducing the national debt now?" A year later, in the depths of the 1937–38 recession, Gallup asked voters to choose between reducing taxes to help business or increasing spending on relief as ways "to get us out of the depression"; 79 percent chose "help business." George H. Gallup, *The Gallup Poll: Public Opinion, 1935–1971*, 3 vols. (New York: Random House, 1972), vol. I, pp. 1, 45, 89, 134, 145; *New York Times*, March [n.d.], 1938, Thomas G. Corcoran to George Gallup, April 25, 1938, and Gallup to Corcoran, May 2, 1938, all in Corcoran MSS 239.

27. Alexander Keyssar, *Out of Work: The First Century of Unemployment in Massachusetts* (New York: Cambridge University Press, 1986), pp. 212–14; Carlos Schwantes, *Coxey's Army: An American Odyssey* (Lincoln: University of Nebraska Press, 1986).

28. Lizabeth Cohen, *Making a New Deal: Industrial Workers in Chicago, 1919–1939* (New York: Cambridge University Press, 1990), pp. 267–89; Roy Rosenzweig, "Organizing the Unemployed: The Early Years of the Great Depression, 1929–1933," *Radical America* 10 (1976), 37–56; Frances Fox Piven and Richard Cloward, *Poor People's Movements: Why They Succeed, How They Fail* (New York: Pantheon, 1977), pp. 48–92; Alan Brinkley, *Voices of*

*Protest: Huey Long, Father Coughlin, and the Great Depression* (New York: Alfred A. Knopf, 1982), pp. 165–75, 222–26; Abraham Holtzman, *The Townsend Movement: A Political Study* (New York: Bookman Associates, 1963), pp. 28–46.

29. William Trufant Foster and Waddill Catchings, *Money* (Boston: Houghton Mifflin, 1923), pp. 351–56 and passim. See also Foster, "Edison-Ford Commodity Money," *Proceedings of the American Academy of Political Science* 10 (1922–1923), 187–205, another example of conventional monetarist views.

30. Foster and Catchings, *Profits* (Boston: Houghton Mifflin, 1925), pp. v–vi, 223–46, 398–418.

31. Foster and Catchings, *Business Without a Buyer* (Boston: Houghton Mifflin, 1927), pp. v–vii; Foster and Catchings, *The Road to Plenty* (Boston: Houghton Mifflin, 1928), pp. 3–10 and passim; Schlesinger, *Crisis of the Old Order*, pp. 134–36.

32. Foster and Catchings, *Business Without a Buyer*, p. 20; Foster and Catchings, *The Road to Plenty*, pp. 24, 54–56, 100, 111; Foster and Catchings, *Progress and Plenty* (Boston: Houghton Mifflin, 1930), p. 81. For an account of the halting efforts of academic economists to consider consumptionist policies, see Walter S. Salant, "Alvin Hansen and the Fiscal Policy Seminar," *Quarterly Journal of Economics* 90 (1976), 14–23.

33. Foster and Catchings, "Must We Reduce Our Standard of Living?," *The Forum*, February 1931, p. 75.

34. Foster and Catchings, *Business Without a Buyer*, pp. 20–21; Foster and Catchings, *The Road to Plenty*, pp. 100, 156–58; Schlesinger, *The Crisis of the Old Order*, p. 135; Foster and Catchings, " 'In the Day of Adversity,' " *Atlantic Monthly*, July 1931, pp. 103–06; Alan H. Gleason, "Foster and Catchings: A Reappraisal," *Journal of Political Economy* 67 (April 1959), 156–72.

35. Otto T. Mallery, "The Long-Range Planning of Public Works," in President's Conference on Unemployment, *Business Cycles and Unemployment* (New York: McGraw-Hill, 1923), pp. 231–61; E. Jay Howenstine, Jr., "Public Works Policy in the Twenties," *Social Research* 13 (1946), 478–85, 491–500; Herbert Stein, *The Fiscal Revolution in America* (Chicago: University of Chicago Press, 1969), pp. 7–11; Dean L. May, *From New Deal to New Economics: The American Liberal Response to the Recession of 1937* (New York: Garland, 1981), pp. 69–76; Sautter, "Government and Unemployment," pp. 64–76.

36. Arthur D. Gayer, *Public Works in Prosperity and Depression* (New York: National Bureau of Economic Research, 1935), pp. 366–401; John M. Clark, *Economics of Planning Public Works* (Washington: The National Planning Board, 1935), pp. 155–59; Alan Sweezy, "The Keynesians and Government Policy, 1933–1939," *American Economic Review* 62 (May 1972), 118–19; James Harvey Rogers to Marvin McIntyre, October 28, 1937, James Roosevelt to Rogers, November 8, 1937, Rogers to Robert S. Shriver, December 9, 1937, all in Rogers MSS 21; Byrd L. Jones, "James Harvey Rogers: An Intellectual Biography" (Ph.D. Dissertation, Yale University, 1966), pp. 146, 175, 210–11, 297, 506–07.

37. Schlesinger, *Crisis of the Old Order*, p. 137.

38. Leonard J. Arrington, *David Eccles: Pioneer Western Industrialist* (Logan: Utah State University Press, 1975), pp. 5–61.

39. Shortly after Marriner's birth, David Eccles moved his new family to Baker, Oregon, where he had extensive lumbering interests. He apparently believed the relocation would protect him from prosecution under federal anti-polygamy laws. Several years later, after such prosecutions had declined, he moved the family back to Logan. The Mormon Church itself did not ban polygamy until 1890. After David Eccles's death, another woman filed suit against the estate claiming that she had married Eccles in 1898 and had borne him a son. A court ruled in her favor and awarded a settlement to the child, but Eccles's Ogden and Logan families never acknowledged this putative third family. Arrington, *David Eccles*, pp. 63–66, 71–72, 86–87, 153–58, 183.

40. Marriner S. Eccles, *Beckoning Frontiers: Public and Personal Recollections* (New York: Alfred A. Knopf, 1951), p. 27. Several scholars have suggested that the traditional communal values of the Mormons made Eccles more receptive to the idea of government responsibility for social and economic welfare. There is, however, no record of Eccles himself referring to Mormonism as a source of his later beliefs. Hamilton Gardner, "Cooperation Among the Mormons," *Quarterly Journal of Economics* 31 (1917), 461–99, and Gardner, "Communism Among the Mormons," ibid. 37 (1922), 134–74; May, *From New Deal to New Economics*, pp. 40–42; Leonard J. Arrington, Feramorz Y. Fox, and Dean L. May, *Building the City of God: Community and Cooperation Among the Mormons* (Salt Lake City: Deseret Book Company, 1976), pp. 337–52; Arrington, *Great Basin Kingdom: An Economic History of the Latter-day Saints* (Cambridge: Harvard University Press, 1958), pp. 293–322.

41. Eccles, *Beckoning Frontiers*, p. 36.

42. Sidney Hyman, *Marriner Eccles: Private Entrepreneur and Public Servant* (Stanford: Stanford University Graduate School of Business, 1976), pp. 49–67.

43. Arrington, *David Eccles*, pp. 188, 190; Eccles, *Beckoning Frontiers*, p. 37.

44. Ibid., pp. 74, 76, 81.

45. Hyman, *Marriner S. Eccles*, pp. 71–73, 93; Eccles, *Beckoning Frontiers*, p. 71; Eccles to William T. Foster, November 16, 1936; Foster to Eccles, January 15, 1936, November 16, December 17, 1936, all in Eccles MSS 44-10; Lauchlin Currie, "Comments on Pump Priming," *History of Political Economy* 10 (Winter 1978), 542–53.

46. Eccles, *Beckoning Frontiers*, p. 83.

47. Ibid., pp. 85–93, 104–16; May, *From New Deal to New Economics*, p. 45.

48. Hyman, *Marriner Eccles*, p. 123.

49. The retitling of the head of the Federal Reserve Board—from "governor" to "chairman"—was a consequence of the Banking Act of 1935.

50. Eccles, *Beckoning Frontiers*, pp. 35, 128, 199; Morgenthau memorandum, November 4, 1937, Morgenthau Diaries 94; May, *From New Deal to New Economics*, pp. 44–48.

51. Arch O. Egbert, "Marriner Eccles and the Banking Act of 1935" (Ph.D. Dissertation, Brigham Young University, 1967), pp. 71–155; Hyman, *Marriner Eccles*, pp. 167–91; William Greider, *Secrets of the Temple: How the Federal Reserve Runs the Country* (New York: Simon and Schuster, 1987), pp. 310–15;

Walter E. Spahr, *The Monetary Policies of Marriner S. Eccles* (New York: Economists' National Committee on Monetary Policy, 1951), pp. 4–11.

52. "The question naturally arises," Eccles wrote the economist James Harvey Rogers in 1937, "whether monetary action would not distract attention from the real troubles and make it appear that the authorities believe the cure does lie in such action when, in fact, it is a relatively subordinate consideration." Eccles to Rogers, December 6, 1937, Rogers MSS 21.

53. Eccles, *Beckoning Frontiers*, pp. 185–86; "A Suggested Works Program," Eccles memorandum to FDR, March 6, 1935, "Financial and Monetary Policies of the Administration," Federal Reserve Board memorandum, August 22, 1935, Eccles to FDR, December 28, 1935, all in Eccles MSS 5-5; L. Dwight Israelsen, "Marriner S. Eccles, Chairman of the Federal Reserve Board," *American Economic Review* 75 (May 1985), 357–62.

54. Eccles to Herbert E. Gaston, June 15, 1936, Eccles MSS 7-9; Eccles to Barnaby Conrad, February 7, 1936, Eccles MSS 7-1; "Public Spending as a Means to Recovery: A Statement of Chairman Eccles' Position," August 6, 1936, Eccles to Roosevelt (draft of proposed presidential address), August 1, 1936, both in Eccles MSS 7-10; Stein, *The Fiscal Revolution in America*, p. 93.

55. Foster and Catchings, *The Road to Plenty*, pp. 158, 202; May, *From New Deal to New Economics*, pp. 83–84, 129–30.

56. Eccles, *Beckoning Frontiers*, pp. 183–84.

57. Eccles to FDR, March 8, 1938, Morgenthau Diaries 113; Eccles to FDR, [n.d.], 1938, Eccles MSS 7-4.

58. Elliot Thurston to Eccles, October 31, 1937, Eccles MSS 38-2; Eccles to FDR, March 8, 1938, Morgenthau Diaries 113; transcript of Treasury meeting, November 5, 1937, ibid., 94; Federal Reserve Board memorandum, February 16, 1938 (untitled speech draft), Eccles MSS 5-8.

59. George Soule, "The Present Industrial Depression," *New Republic*, November 24, 1937, p. 62.

60. Transcript of remarks by Leon Henderson, March 20, 1937, Cohen File 3, Interior, RG 48, NA; Leon Henderson to Harry Hopkins, September [n.d.], 1937, October 12, 1937, March 23, 1938, and [n.d.], 1938, all in Hopkins MSS 54.

61. Richard N. Chapman, *Contours of Public Policy, 1939–1945* (New York: Garland, 1981), pp. 10–11; Henderson to Lubin, [n.d.], 1938, Lubin MSS 51; Henderson, "Emerging Industrio-Government Problems," November 9, 1937; Henderson to Hopkins, November 27, 1937, and Henderson to Benjamin Cohen, June 9, 1938, all in Cohen File 3, Interior, RG 48.

62. Alan Sweezy, "The Keynesians and Government Policy, 1933–1939," *American Economic Review* 62 (1972), 116–23; William O. Douglas to J. M. Keynes, July 29, 1937, Douglas to Frankfurter, June 30, 1937, both in Douglas MSS 16; H. N. Hirsch, *The Enigma of Felix Frankfurter* (New York: Basic Books, 1981), pp. 113–14; Stephen W. Baskerville, "Frankfurter, Keynes, and the Fight for Public Works, 1932–1935," *The Maryland Historian* 9 (1978), 4, 11; Harold Ickes, *Secret Diary*, II: 366 (entry of April 10, 1938); Chester Davis to Eccles, October 30, 1937, Eccles MSS 38-2.

63. Cohen, *Making a New Deal*, pp. 283–89; Steve Fraser, *Labor Will Rule: Sidney Hillman and the Rise of American Labor* (New York: The Free

Press, 1991), pp. 407–40; John Crampton, *The National Farmers Union: Ideology of a Pressure Group* (Lincoln: University of Nebraska Press, 1965), pp. 20–63; Michael Flamm, "The National Farmers Union and the Evolution of Agrarian Liberalism, 1937–1946," M.A. thesis, Columbia University, 1992, pp. 19–27; James Farley diary, March 28, 1938, Farley MSS 43; Herbert Stein, *The Fiscal Revolution in America* (Chicago: University of Chicago Press, 1969), p. 106.

64. Patrick J. Maney, *"Young Bob" La Follette: A Biography of Robert M. La Follette, Jr., 1895–1953* (Columbia: University of Missouri Press, 1978), p. 200; Sweezy, "Keynesians and Government Policy," p. 123.

65. "The President and the New Depression," *New Republic*, December 15, 1937, p. 159. See also George Soule, "The Present Industrial Depression," *New Republic*, November 24, 1937, p. 63; Soule, "What Has Happened—And Whose Fault Is It?" *New Republic*, February 2, 1938, pp. 378–82; "Economic Authorities," *New Republic*, February 2, 1938, p. 386; Arthur D. Gayer, "What Is Ahead?" *New Republic*, February 2, 1938, pp. 388–93; "Wanted: Three-Year Plan," *Nation*, January 15, 1938, p. 61.

## Chapter Five

1. Harold Ickes, *The Secret Diary of Harold Ickes*, 3 vols. (New York: Simon and Schuster, 1954–1955), II: 339–40; Dean L. May, *From New Deal to New Economics: The American Liberal Response to the Recession of 1937* (New York: Garland, 1981), p. 116; Max Freedman, ed., *Roosevelt and Frankfurter: Their Correspondence, 1928–1945* (Boston: Little, Brown, 1967), p. 439; Eccles to FDR, [n.d.], 1938, Morgenthau Diaries 113.

2. Proclamation No. 2256, October 12, 1937, and Fireside Chat, October 12, 1937, both in Samuel I. Rosenman, ed., *The Public Papers and Addresses of Franklin D. Roosevelt*, 4 vols. (New York: Macmillan, 1941), 1937 volume, pp. 428–38; "Roosevelt Over Business," *Business Week*, October 23, 1937, p. 64.

3. Message to Congress, November 15, 1937, in Rosenman, ed., *Public Papers and Addresses*, 1937 volume, p. 490; James MacGregor Burns, *Roosevelt: The Lion and the Fox* (New York: Harcourt, Brace & World, 1956), p. 321.

4. O. R. Altman, "Second and Third Sessions of the Seventy-fifth Congress, 1937–38," *American Political Science Review* 32 (December 1938), 1099–23; William E. Leuchtenburg, "Roosevelt, Norris and the 'Seven Little TVAs,'" *Journal of Politics* 14 (1952), 418–41; James T. Patterson, *Congressional Conservatism and the New Deal* (Lexington: University of Kentucky Press, 1967), pp. 189–210.

5. Robert Jackson, unpublished autobiography, 1944, Jackson MSS 188; Ickes, *Secret Diary*, II: 260; Henry Morgenthau, diary entries, November 4, December 7, 1937, Morgenthau Diaries 94, 101.

6. "President Makes a Gesture, Asks One From Business," *Newsweek*, January 10, 1938, pp. 7–8.

7. Press Conference, January 4, 1938, in Rosenman, ed., *Public Papers and Addresses*, 1938 volume, pp. 33–34; T.R.B., "Washington Notes," *New Republic*, January 19, 1938, p. 308.

8. Adolf Berle, for example, called the speeches "rather second rate demagogy" and commented, "I know too much about the two hundred corporations to make a personal devil out of them. I know too much about sixty families to think that they will amount to much." Beatrice Bishop Berle and Travis Beal Jacobs, eds., *Navigating the Rapids, 1918–1971* (New York: Harcourt Brace Jovanovich, 1973), p. 158; Jerome Frank to William O. Douglas, January 20, 1938, Frank MSS 25.

9. The meeting and its aftermath received remarkable public attention; it became, for example, the lead story in the *New York Times*, under unusually prominent banner headlines, for three days running. *New York Times*, January 12, 13, 14, 1938. Thomas E. Vadney, *Wayward Liberal: A Political Biography of Donald Richberg* (Lexington: University of Kentucky Press, 1970), pp. 178–79; Ellis Hawley, *The New Deal and the Problem of Monopoly* (Princeton: Princeton University Press, 1966), pp. 395–97. See also Donald Richberg, "A Suggestion for Revision of the Anti-Trust Laws," *University of Pennsylvania Law Review* 85 (November 1936), 1–14. Richberg gave a well-publicized speech in New York on January 26, 1938, outlining his ideas about "business self-regulation." See *New York Times*, January 27, 1938, for the transcript.

10. *New York Times*, January 14, 15, 1938; Berle, *Navigating the Rapids*, pp. 154–61; Rexford G. Tugwell, "The Fourth Power," *Planning and Civic Comment*, April–June 1939, pp. 7–25; Tugwell, "Implementing the General Interest," *Public Administration Review* 1 (August 1940), 32–49; "Advisory Committee" to FDR, January [n.d.], 1938, Berle MSS 210; Joseph P. Lash, *Dreamers and Dealers: A New Look at the New Deal* (New York: Doubleday, 1988), pp. 326–27; Hawley, *The New Deal and the Problem of Monopoly*, p. 397.

11. *New York Times*, January 20, 1938; "President Pats Business and Slaps Holding Companies," *Newsweek*, January 24, 1938, pp. 12–13; Raymond Moley, "In Again, Out Again," ibid., p. 44; "Mr. Roosevelt and Business: Conciliation Progress," *Newsweek*, January 31, 1938, pp. 12–13; Business Advisory Council, "Statement to the Press," January 19, 1938, Daniel Roper to Marvin McIntyre, January 5, 1938, McIntyre to FDR, January 7, 1938, Roper to FDR, January 17, 1938, Roper to James Roosevelt, February 4, 1938, all in OF 3Q, FDRL; press conference, January 21, 1938, in Rosenman, ed., *Public Papers and Addresses*, 1938 volume, pp. 57–58.

12. Berle diary, January 20, 25, 1938, Berle MSS 210; *New York Times*, January 22, 27, 1938.

13. Raymond Moley wrote scornfully, and largely accurately, of the effort: "Administration policy lurches back and forth according to the ascendancy of one crowd or the other. For the President is unwilling to choose between them." Moley, "Mixing, Not Blending," *Newsweek*, January 17, 1938, p. 44. "Business Advice to the President," *New Republic*, February 2, 1938, pp. 351–52; Berle and Jacobs, eds., *Navigating the Rapids*, pp. 161–63.

14. Like the meetings Richberg and others organized between the President and major industrialists, the small-business conference received major coverage in newspapers and magazines. See *New York Times*, February 1, 2, 3, 4, 5, 6, 1938; "Little Businessmen Called to Confer With Mr. Roosevelt," *Newsweek*, February 7, 1938, pp. 9–10; "The President Is Surprised: 'Little Men' Criticize New Deal," *Newsweek*, February 14, 1938, pp. 11–13; Hawley,

*The New Deal and the Problem of Monopoly,* p. 397; Press Conference, February 4, 1938, in Rosenman, ed., *Public Papers and Addresses,* 1938 volume, pp. 78–80.

15. "Washington 'conciliation,' " *Forbes* magazine wrote, "consists chiefly of the first three letters." In "Two-Line Editorials," *Forbes,* June 1, 1938, p. 4. Vadney, *Wayward Liberal,* p. 179; Raymond Clapper, "Appeasement: R. I. P.," March 22, 1939, Henderson MSS 23; Mark H. Leff, *The Limits of Symbolic Reform: The New Deal and Taxation, 1933–1939* (New York: Cambridge University Press, 1984), p. 211.

16. "Business Advice to the President," *New Republic,* February 2, 1938, p. 352; John Morton Blum, *From the Morgenthau Diaries: Years of Crisis, 1928–1938* (Boston: Houghton Mifflin, 1959), p. 415.

17. Annual Message to Congress, January 3, 1938, and Address at the Jackson Day Dinner, January 9, 1938, in Rosenman, ed., *Public Papers and Addresses,* 1938 volume, pp. 11, 41; "The Attack on Monopoly," *Nation,* January 8, 1938, p. 32; Irving Brant to Thomas Corcoran, January 5, 1938, Brant MSS 5.

18. Marquis Childs, "Jackson versus Richberg," *Nation,* January 29, 1938, p. 120; Ickes, *Secret Diary,* II: 295.

19. Ibid.: 326.

20. Ibid. Lash, *Dreamers and Dealers,* p. 323; "Report and Evaluation: The Modern Forum," [n.d.], 1938, Ickes MSS 71.

21. Robert E. Sherwood, *Roosevelt and Hopkins: An Intimate History* (New York: Harper & Brothers, 1950), pp. 92–93; Henry H. Adams, *Harry Hopkins* (New York: Putnam's, 1977), pp. 119–27; George J. McJimsey, *Harry Hopkins: Ally of the Poor and Defender of Democracy* (Cambridge: Harvard University Press, 1987), pp. 118–19.

22. Childs, "Jackson versus Richberg," p. 120; Joseph C. O'Mahoney radio address, "National Charters the Basis of Freedom," January 13, 1937, PPF 1200, FDRL; William Borah to E. E. Allen, April 22, 1938, Borah MSS 772; Gene Gressley, "Thurman Arnold, Antitrust, and the New Deal," *Business History Review* 38 (1964), 216–17.

23. William O. Douglas did apparently briefly consider calling for a federal incorporation law, and he asked members of his staff to draft one for him. But he apparently found little support for the idea within the administration and turned instead to the idea of an investigation. See Milton V. Freeman, in Katie Louchheim, ed., *The Making of the New Deal: The Insiders Speak* (Cambridge: Harvard University Press, 1983), p. 143; Douglas to J. H. Kelleghan, April 21, 1937, Douglas MSS 18; Douglas to FDR, January 20, 1938, Douglas MSS 14; "The Attack on Monopoly," p. 32.

24. Isidor Lubin to Marvin H. McIntyre, August 25, 1937, PSF 77, FDRL; Jonathan Mitchell, "What Makes Prices High?" *New Republic,* October 27, 1937, p. 331; Hawley, *The New Deal and the Problem of Monopoly,* p. 405.

25. William Borah to E. E. Allen, April 22, 1938, Borah MSS 772; Herman Oliphant, "Draft of Antitrust and Bank Holding Company Message," Wayne Taylor to FDR, March 26, 1938, Homer Cummings to FDR, April 21, 1938, Thurman Arnold memorandum, April [n.d.], 1938, Arnold to Cummings, April 13, 1938, all in OF 277 FDRL; *Fortune,* February 1938, pp. 58, 150, 152, 165–68; Hawley, *The New Deal and the Problem of Monopoly,* pp. 405–11.

26. "Little Business Revolts," *Nation*, February 12, 1938, p. 173; Harry Crowe to Small Business Review Committee, March 10, 1938, Walter M. Hoefelman to FDR, and "A Plan to Assist Small Business," February 14, 1938, all in OF 172A, FDRL; Business Advisory Council, "Interim Report of Committee on Business Legislation," January 6, 1938, and Daniel Roper to FDR, February 4, 1938, both in OF 3Q, FDRL.

27. George Haas to Morgenthau, April 8, 1938, Morgenthau Diaries 118; James Farley diary, December 4, 1937, and March 28, 1938, Farley MSS 42, 43; Berle to FDR (draft of unsent letter), January [n.d.], 1938, Berle, Wayne Taylor, and Ronald Ransom memorandum, April 1, 1938, Berle to Ransom, April 1, 1938, and Berle diary, January 10, 1939, all in Berle MSS 210.

28. Henderson, "What Has Happened to Recovery," radio address, January 1, 1938, Cohen Files 3, Interior, RG 48, NA; Henderson to Hopkins, November 27, 1937, ibid.; Alan Sweezy, "Keynesians and Government Policy, 1933–1939," *American Economic Review* 62 (May 1972), 117.

29. Lauchlin Currie, *The Supply and Control of Money in the United States* (Cambridge: Harvard University Press, 1934; New York: Russell & Russell, 1968), pp. 131, 156, 197; Currie, "The Failure of Monetary Policy to Prevent the Depression of 1929–1932," *Journal of Political Economy* 42 (April 1934), 145–47; Roger J. Sandilands, *The Life and Political Economy of Lauchlin Currie: New Dealer, Presidential Adviser, and Development Economist* (Durham: Duke University Press, 1990), pp. 18–34.

30. "Apostle of Spending," *Nation's Business*, August 1941, pp. 48–53; Currie to Eccles, November 17, 1934, Eccles MSS 43-1.

31. Ibid.; Lauchlin Currie, "Comments and Observations," *History of Political Economy* 10 (Winter 1978), 541–46; Currie, "Some Theoretical and Practical Implications of J. M. Keynes' General Theory," National Industrial Conference Board, *The Economic Doctrines of John Maynard Keynes* (Washington: NICB, 1938), pp. 15–27; Byrd L. Jones, "Lauchlin Currie, Pump Priming, and New Deal Fiscal Policy, 1934–1936," ibid., 509–19.

32. Currie, "Comments on Pump Priming," FRB memorandum, [n.d.], 1935, reprinted in *History of Political Economy* 10 (Winter 1978), 525–33; Currie and Martin Krost, "Federal Income-Increasing Expenditures," FRB memorandum, [n.d.], 1935, reprinted in ibid., 534–40; Currie to Eccles, September 30, 1936, Eccles MSS 43-1.

33. Currie to Eccles, March 11, 1937, Eccles MSS 72-11; Harry Dexter White to Morgenthau, April 8, 1938, Morgenthau Diaries 118; Henderson memorandum, June 9, 1938, Cohen File 3, Interior, RG48, NA; Henderson memorandum to Franklin D. Roosevelt Library, December 3, 1939, Henderson MSS 36; "Hopes for Public Spending," *New Republic*, April 13, 1938, p. 288; Lash, *Dreamers and Dealers*, pp. 318–19; May, *From New Deal to New Economics*, pp. 123–35; Donald T. Critchlow, "The Political Control of the Economy: Deficit Spending as a Political Belief, 1932–1952," *The Public Historian* 3 (1981), 5–22.

34. Currie to Eccles, December 16, 1936, and Currie, "The Present Status of the Recovery Movement," December 22, 1936, both in Eccles MSS 72-8; Currie, "The Rise of Prices and the Problem of Maintaining an Orderly Revival," March 11, 1937, Eccles MSS 5-7; Currie, "Fiscal Policy in the Upswing," April 2, 1937, Eccles MSS 72-11.

35. Currie, "A Tentative Program to Meet the Business Recession," October 13, 1937, Eccles MSS 73-5; Eccles to Marvin McIntyre, December 7, 1937, Eccles MSS, 7-3; Currie, "Causes of the Recession," April 1, 1938, Hopkins MSS 55; Currie, "Comments and Observations," 546–48; Sweezy, "Keynesians and Government Policy," 116–24.

36. Hadley Cantril, ed., *Public Opinion, 1935–1946* (Princeton: Princeton University Press, 1951), pp. 62–63; George H. Gallup, *The Gallup Poll: Public Opinion, 1935–1971*, 3 vols. (New York: Random House, 1972), I: 93–96; Robert Dallek, *Franklin D. Roosevelt and American Foreign Policy, 1933–1945* (New York: Oxford University Press, 1979), pp. 157–58; May, *From New Deal to New Economics*, pp. 130–31; Henry Morgenthau, Jr., "The Morgenthau Diaries: 2. The Struggle for a Program," *Collier's*, October 4, 1947, pp. 45–46; Presidential address at Gainesville, Georgia, March 23, 1938, in Rosenman, ed., *Public Papers and Addresses*, 1938 volume, pp. 164–68. "Today," Roosevelt said in Gainesville, "national progress and national prosperity are being held back chiefly because of selfishness on the part of a few. . . . [T]his nation will never permanently get on the road to recovery if we leave the methods and processes of recovery to those who owned the Government of the United States from 1921 to 1933."

37. Marriner S. Eccles, *Beckoning Frontiers: Public and Personal Recollections* (New York: Alfred A. Knopf, 1951), p. 311; Adams, *Harry Hopkins*, pp. 125–28; McJimsey, *Harry Hopkins*, pp. 118–19; Henderson to Roosevelt Library, December 3, 1959, Henderson MSS 36.

38. Sherwood, *Roosevelt and Hopkins*, p. 1; Henderson to Hopkins, March [n.d.], 1938, and Henderson to Hopkins, March 23, 1938, both in Hopkins MSS 54.

39. Hawley, *The New Deal and the Problem of Monopoly*, pp. 408–09; Eccles, "Memorandum for members of the informal discussion group," April 15, 1938, Eccles MSS 38-6; James Farley diary, April 9, 1938, Farley MSS 43; Frederic Delano to Morgenthau, April 12, 1938, Morgenthau Diaries 120; Adams, *Harry Hopkins*, pp. 128–29.

40. Blum, *From the Morgenthau Diaries*, pp. 417–19; Morgenthau, "The Struggle for a Program," p. 48; Morgenthau, "Memorandum for the President," April 10, 1938, Morgenthau Diaries 118.

41. Ibid.; diary entries, April 11, 12, 13, 1938, Morgenthau Presidential Diaries, 1.

42. Blum, *From the Morgenthau Diaries*, pp. 421–25; Message to Congress, April 14, 1938, and Fireside Chat, April 14, 1938, both in Rosenman, ed., *Public Papers and Addresses*, 1938 volume, pp. 221–48; Herbert Stein, *The Fiscal Revolution in America* (Chicago: University of Chicago Press), pp. 111–12.

43. Jonathan Mitchell, "What Makes Prices High?" *New Republic*, October 27, 1937, p. 331; Leon Henderson to Harry Hopkins, November 9, 1942, Hopkins MSS 85.

44. Ibid.; Leon Henderson diary notes, March 23, 1938, Henderson MSS 36; Cohen to Hopkins, November 10, 1942, Hopkins MSS 85; Robert Jackson, autobiography draft, Jackson MSS 188.

45. Berle, draft of anti-monopoly message, April [n.d.], 1938, Berle MSS 210; Wayne C. Taylor to FDR, and "Draft of Antitrust and Bank Holding

Company Message," March 26, 1938, Homer Cummings to FDR, and "Arnold Memorandum," April 21, 1938, Huston Thompson to Marvin McIntyre, April 25, 1938, all in OF 277, FDRL; Jackson, unpublished autobiography, Jackson MSS 188; Henry Morgenthau, diary entry, April 29, 1938, Morgenthau Presidential Diaries 1; Message to Congress, April 29, 1938, in Rosenman, ed., *Public Papers and Addresses*, 1938 volume, pp. 305–32.

46. Joint Resolution: "To Create a Temporary National Economic Committee," S. J. Res. 300, 75th Cong., 3d sess.; Cantril, *Public Opinion*, pp. 755–56; James T. Patterson, *Congressional Conservatism and the New Deal*, pp. 242–46.

47. Ibid., pp. 277–87; Sidney M. Milkis, *The President and the Parties: The Transformation of the American Party System Since the New Deal* (New York: Oxford University Press, 1993), pp. 75–97.

48. Message to Congress, April 29, 1938, pp. 308, 312; "What Do They Mean: Monopoly?" *Fortune*, April 1938, p. 75; Ickes, *Secret Diary*, II: 386; Saul Nelson, "What Is Monopoly?" *Harper's*, June 1938, pp. 66–67; Victor S. Yarros, "Again the Monopoly Issue," *The Christian Century*, July 13, 1938, pp. 869–70.

49. Raymond Moley, *After Seven Years* (New York: Harper & Brothers, 1939), p. 376; Hawley, *The New Deal and the Problem of Monopoly*, p. 419.

50. Fireside Chat, April 14, 1938, pp. 240–43; Irving Fisher to FDR, April 15, 1938, Eccles MSS 7-4; May, *From New Deal to New Economics*, p. 142; Stein, *The Fiscal Revolution in America*, pp. 109–15; Theda Skocpol and Margaret Weir, "State Structures and the Possibilities for Keynesian Responses to the Great Depression in Sweden, Britain, and the United States," in Peter B. Evans, Dietrich Rueschemeyer, and Skocpol, eds., *Bringing the State Back In* (New York: Cambridge University Press, 1985), pp. 132–36.

51. Eccles to FDR, "The Next Steps in the Recovery Program," April 27, 1938, Eccles MSS 5-8; "Roosevelt's Expansion Program," *New Republic*, April 27, 1938, p. 346; "Spending and Recovery," *Nation*, April 23, 1938, pp. 455–56; Robert Lekachman, *The Age of Keynes* (New York: Random House, 1966), pp. 138–39.

52. Currie, "Causes of the Recession," p. 36; Bruce Bliven, "Confidential: To the President," *New Republic*, April 20, 1938, p. 327; "Spending and Recovery," pp. 456–57.

## Chapter Six

1. Thurman W. Arnold, *The Folklore of Capitalism* (New Haven: Yale University Press, 1937), pp. 96, 211, 213–41.

2. Ibid., p. 96; Max Lerner, "Trust-Buster's White Paper," *New Republic*, September 16, 1940, p. 389.

3. Ibid., pp. 389–90.

4. Thurman W. Arnold, *Fair Fights and Foul: A Dissenting Lawyer's Life* (New York: Harcourt, Brace & World, 1965), pp. 3–20; Gene M. Gressley, ed., *Voltaire and the Cowboy: The Letters of Thurman Arnold* (Boulder: Colorado Associated University Press, 1977), pp. 8–9. Gressley's long introduction to

this collection of letters is the most extensive biographical study of Arnold yet to appear.

5. Arnold, *Fair Fights and Foul*, pp. 30–35; Joseph Alsop and Robert Kintner, "Trust Buster: The Folklore of Thurman Arnold," *Saturday Evening Post*, August 12, 1939, pp. 30–33; Scripps-Howard wire service profile, March 11, 1938, Clapper MSS 102.

6. Arnold to Charles Clark, October 12, 1929, March 18, 1930; Arnold to John R. Turner, December 23, 1930, both in Arnold MSS; Gressley, *Voltaire and the Cowboy*, pp. 25–30.

7. Laura Kalman, *Legal Realism at Yale, 1927–1960* (Chapel Hill: University of North Carolina Press, 1986), pp. 3–10; Jerome Frank to Leon Henderson, July 31, 1939, Frank MSS 29; Stuart Chase to Frank, June 29, 1937, Frank MSS 23.

8. Arnold, "Theories About Economic Theory," *Annals of the American Academy of Political Science* 273 (March 1934), 36; Edward N. Kearny, *Thurman Arnold, Social Critic: The Satirical Challenge to Orthodoxy* (Albuquerque: University of New Mexico Press, 1970), pp. 14–15, 31–32, 49; Douglas Ayer, "In Quest of Efficiency: The Ideological Journey of Thurman Arnold in the Interwar Period," *Stanford Law Review* 23 (June 1971), 1065–68; Arnold, "Criminal Attempts—The Rise and Fall of an Abstraction," *Yale Law Journal* 40 (1930), 53–62, 79–80.

9. Arnold, *Symbols of Government* (New Haven: Yale University Press, 1935), pp. 206, 224, 237. See also Arnold and Wesley A. Sturges, "The Progress of the New Administration," *Yale Review* 22 (1933), 656–77.

10. Arnold, *Folklore of Capitalism*, pp. 115, 185, 263–64.

11. Ibid., p. 389; Warren J. Samuels, "Legal Realism and the Burden of Symbolism: The Correspondence of Thurman Arnold," *Law and Society Review* 13 (1979), 997–1008; Kearny, *Thurman Arnold*, pp. 49, 55–56; Max Lerner, "The Shadow World of Thurman Arnold," *Yale Law Journal* 47 (March 1938), 689; Joseph Featherstone, "The Machiavelli of the New Deal," *New Republic*, August 7, 1965, pp. 22–26; Christopher Lasch, *The True and Only Heaven: Progress and Its Critics* (New York: Norton, 1991), pp. 430–32.

12. Stuart Chase to Jerome Frank, June 29, 1937, Frank MSS 23; Frank to Arnold, October 25, 1939, and Arnold to Bernard Kilgore, November 3, 1939, Arnold MSS; Peter Irons, *The New Deal Lawyers* (Princeton: Princeton University Press, 1982), pp. 7–9, 124–25.

13. Arnold, *Folklore of Capitalism*, pp. 96, 211, 213–41. Arnold's only previous commentary on the trust question was "The Restatement of the Law of Trusts," *Columbia Law Review* 31 (1931), 800–23, in which he offered a skeptical commentary on laws governing the *creation* of trusts but had virtually nothing to say about the *antitrust* laws.

14. *New York Times*, March 6, 1938; Robert Jackson, unpublished autobiography, 1944, Jackson MSS 188; Arnold to Leon Green, March 17, 1938, Arnold to Herbert F. Goodrich, March 24, 1938, both in Arnold MSS; Arnold, *Fair Fights and Foul*, pp. 135–36; Wilson D. Miscamble, "Thurman Arnold Goes to Washington: A Look at Antitrust Policy in the Later New Deal," *Business History Review* 56 (1982), 5–9.

15. Among the statements that surfaced to embarrass Arnold during his

confirmation hearings was the following: "Men like Senator Borah founded political careers on the continuance of [antitrust] crusades, which were entirely futile but enormously picturesque, and which paid big dividends in terms of personal prestige." Arnold, *Folklore of Capitalism*, p. 217.

16. Hearings before a subcommittee of the Senate Judiciary Committee, 75th Cong., 3rd sess. (March 11, 1938), pp. 4–6, Wendell Berge MSS 15; Henry Hyde to William Borah, July 6, 1938, and Walter Williams to Borah, February 23, 1939, both in Borah MSS 772; Arnold to Matthew Josephson, March 29, 1938, and Arnold to Douglas Maggs, April 22, 1937, both in Arnold MSS; Arnold to Borah, March 16, 1938, in Gressley, *Voltaire and the Cowboy*, pp. 268–69; Harold L. Ickes, *The Secret Diary of Harold L. Ickes*, 3 vols. (New York: Simon and Schuster, 1954), II: 347.

17. Arnold to Borah, March 16, 1938, Arnold MSS; Gressley, "Thurman Arnold, Antitrust, and the New Deal," *Business History Review* 38 (1964), 217–21.

18. Karl A. Boedecker, "A Critical Appraisal of the Antitrust Policy of the United States Government from 1933 to 1945" (Ph.D. Dissertation, Wisconsin, 1947), p. 223; Arnold, "An Inquiry into the Monopoly Issue," *New York Times Magazine*, August 21, 1938, pp. 1–2; "The New Deal and the Trusts," *New Republic*, December 7, 1938, p. 115; *New York Times*, July 8, 1939; "Trust Buster Benched," *Newsweek*, February 22, 1943, pp. 32–34; Harold Smith diary, November 27, 30, 1939, Smith MSS 1; Gressley, "Thurman Arnold," p. 224.

19. Arnold speech, April 28, 1938, Berge MSS 15; Arnold, *Bottlenecks of Business*, pp. 141–43, 152–54.

20. Arnold increased pressure on businesses by filing not only civil but criminal suits. Any settlement, he insisted, must be "subject to reexamination by the court at the earliest convenient time. . . . It should provide access to the corporate books and records so that examination of how the plan is working will be easy." Ibid., pp. 152–63; Milton Katz, "Consent Decrees and Antitrust Administration," *Harvard Law Review* 8 (1940), 415–47; Benjamin Cohen to Milton Katz, January 15, 1940, TNEC 58, RG 144, NA; Ellis W. Hawley, *The New Deal and the Problem of Monopoly* (Princeton: Princeton University Press, 1966), pp. 429–30; Gressley, "Thurman Arnold," pp. 222–23; Bruce Bliven, "Lower to Washington," *New Republic*, December 27, 1939, p. 278.

21. Arnold, *Bottlenecks of Business*, pp. 191–93; Alsop and Kintner, "Trust Buster," p. 7; Bliven, "Lower to Washington," pp. 278–79.

22. *New York Times*, July 8, 16, 1939; transcript of Treasury meeting, November 5, 1937, Morgenthau Diaries 94; Arnold, *Bottlenecks of Business*, pp. 37–38; Sidney Fine, *Frank Murphy: The Washington Years* (Ann Arbor: University of Michigan Press, 1984), p. 50.

23. Arnold, *Bottlenecks of Business*, pp. 38–43, 50–54; Fine, *Frank Murphy*, p. 50; Arnold to John Bainbridge, June 3, 1940, Arnold MSS. This and some other episodes in Arnold's career are discussed in more detail in Alan Brinkley, "The Antimonopoly Ideal and the Liberal State: The Case of Thurman Arnold," *Journal of American History* 80 (1993), 557–79.

24. Corwin Edwards, "Thurman Arnold and the Antitrust Laws," *Political Science Quarterly* 58 (1943), 338–55; Arnold to Robert H. Jackson, June 12,

1940, and Arnold to Richardson Wood, October 19, 1940, both in Arnold MSS; "Arnold vs. ICC," *Business Week*, August 1, 1942, pp. 23–24; "Monopoly Attacks Increasing," *Newsweek*, November 6, 1939, p. 50; I. F. Stone, "Thurman Arnold and the Railroads," *Nation*, March 6, 1943, p. 332; Burnham Carter, "The Sherman Anti-Trust Blackjack," *American Mercury*, April 1941, pp. 427–32; Arnold to William H. Grimes, November 18, 1938, Arnold to Kenneth W. Payne, August 2, 1941, Arnold to R. I. Elliott, November 14, 1938, Arnold to Edwin S. Friendly, October 21, 1940, all in Arnold MSS.

25. Arnold to Leon Henderson, March 16, 1939, TNEC, RG 144, NA; Arnold, "The Abuse of Patents," *Atlantic Monthly*, July 1942, p. 16; Arnold, "We Must Reform the Patent Law," September 1942, p. 54; Edwards, "Thurman Arnold and the Antitrust Laws," pp. 343, 353; Arnold, *Bottlenecks of Business*, p. 277.

26. The literature on anti-monopoly ideas in America is vast, and as contested as the ideas themselves. Among the works that suggest the populist and democratic underpinnings of anti-monopoly sentiment are Bruce Palmer, *"Man Over Money": The Southern Populist Critique of American Capitalism* (Chapel Hill: University of North Carolina Press, 1980), pp. 114–17; David Montgomery, *Beyond Equality: Labor and the Radical Republicans, 1862–1972* (New York: Alfred A. Knopf, 1967), pp. 335–56, 425–47; Steven L. Piott, *The Antimonopoly Persuasion: Popular Resistance to the Rise of Big Business in the Midwest* (Westport, Ct.: Greenwood Press, 1985), pp. 1–10 and passim. Among works that explore the links between consumers and anti-monopoly sentiment are H. Roger Grant, *Insurance Reform: Consumer Action in the Progressive Era* (Ames: Iowa State University Press, 1979), and David P. Thelen, *The New Citizenship: Origins of Progressivism in Wisconsin, 1885–1900* (Columbia: University of Missouri Press, 1972). Hans Thorelli, *The Federal Antitrust Policy* (Baltimore: The Johns Hopkins University Press, 1955), reviews the origins of the antitrust laws themselves.

27. Thomas K. McCraw, *Prophets of Regulation* (Cambridge: Harvard University Press, 1984), pp. 94–109, 135–42.

28. *New York Times*, July 8, 1939; Arnold, "What Is Monopoly?" *Vital Speeches*, July 1, 1938, p. 568.

29. Arnold, "The Abuse of Patents," *Atlantic Monthly*, July 1942, p. 16.

30. Arnold, *Bottlenecks of Business*, p. 4. Phillip Cullis, in as yet unpublished work, challenges at least part of this argument and argues that Arnold was, in fact, much more concerned about the size of corporate organizations than his occasional rhetorical statements to the contrary suggest. See Cullis, "Antitrust in America: The Scholarly Debate, 1910–1943" (Ph.D. Dissertation, Cambridge University, 1993).

31. Arnold to Allen C. Dibble, August 23, 1940, Arnold MSS; "Monopoly and the New Deal," transcript of University of Chicago Round Table, November 27, 1938, pp. 2–5, Berge MSS.

32. *New York Times*, November 25, 1943; "Do Monopolies Retard or Advance Business Recovery?" *Town Meeting*, January 30, 1939, pp. 11–12; Arnold, "Feathers and Prices," *Common Sense*, July 1939, p. 6; Alan R. Sweezy, "Mr. Arnold and the Trusts," *New Republic*, June 8, 1942, p. 803; Arnold to William Allen White, September 9, 1943, Arnold MSS.

33. Arnold, *Bottlenecks of Business*, p. 122; Arnold, "Feathers and Prices," pp. 5–6; Lerner, "Trust-Buster's White Paper," p. 389; Arnold, "How Far Should Government Control Business: Competition Requires a Referee," *Vital Speeches of the Day*, March 1, 1939, pp. 290–92; Leon Henderson diary, September 9, 1938, Henderson MSS 36.

34. James R. Brackett to Milton Katz, February 9, 1940, TNEC Records 58, RG 144, NA; Arnold, "An Inquiry into the Monopoly Issue," *New York Times Magazine*, August 21, 1938, pp. 2, 14; Arnold to Elliott Dunlap Smith, October 12, 1938, Arnold to E. J. Coil, September 9, 1940, Stuart Chase to Arnold, April 15, 1941, Arnold to James Landis, March 23, 1937, Arnold to William Douglas, May 7, 1937, Curtice Hitchcock to Arnold, November 1, 1938, all in Arnold MSS; Ayer, "In Quest of Efficiency," p. 1085; Lasch, *The True and Only Heaven*, pp. 432–34.

35. Arnold, *Bottlenecks of Business*, p. 274; Arnold, "Why Trustbusting?" n.d., TNEC Records 92, RG 144, NA.

36. Samuels, "Legal Realism," p. 1008.

37. Arnold, *Bottlenecks of Business*, pp. 263–81; Ayer, "In Quest of Efficiency," p. 1077; Arnold to Allen C. Dibble, August 23, 1940, Arnold MSS; Gressley, "Thurman Arnold," pp. 230–31.

38. Arnold, *Bottlenecks of Business*, pp. 9, 276–77; Arnold, "An Inquiry into the Monopoly Issue," p. 14; Arnold to Lon Fuller, January 21, 1941, Guy Martin to Arnold, February 2, 1938, both in Arnold MSS; "Prices and Social Policy," *New Republic*, February 17, 1941, p. 244; Arnold, *Folklore of Capitalism*, p. 174.

39. Arnold, *Bottlenecks of Business*; Alva Johnston, "Thurman Arnold's Biggest Case," *The New Yorker*, January 31, 1942, pp. 41–42; Arnold to Arthur Sulzberger, August 25, 1939, Carl Holderman to Arnold, December 22, 1939, Arnold to Frank Knox, June 25, 1940, J. David Stern to Robert S. Allen, December 9, 1939, all in Arnold MSS.

40. Arnold to Dorothy Thompson, November 27, 1939, Arnold MSS; Arnold, *Fair Fights and Foul*, pp. 115–16.

41. Arnold, *Folklore of Capitalism*, p. 191; Arnold to Buckley Griffin, November 7, 1940, Arnold MSS.

42. Arnold, "Labor's Hidden Holdup Men," *Reader's Digest*, 1941, clipping in Arnold MSS; A. E. Duncan to Arnold, June 20, 1941, Arnold to Richardson Wood, October 19, 1940, Arnold to Attorney General, June 21, 1940, all in ibid.; "The Folklore of Unionism," *Time*, October 18, 1943, p. 24. In his memoirs, Arnold wrote with apparent approval of the Taft-Hartley Act of 1948: "Today there is still no effective curb against the abuse by unions of their privileges, though some of the practices described have been declared unfair under the Taft-Hartley Act." *Fair Fights and Foul*, p. 119. See also *New York Times*, January 28, 1940, December 6, 1941; Elliot Thurston memorandum, October 31, 1937, Eccles MSS 38-2; Arnold to Charles J. Connick, December 4, 1941, Arnold MSS.

43. *New York Times*, November 28, 1940; "Blunderbuss," *Nation*, December 2, 1939, pp. 596–97; Robert Jackson, unpublished autobiography, 1944, Jackson MSS 188; "Arnold Anti-Labor Drive Scorned," *American Federationist*, November 1941; Leon Henderson diary, November 3, 1939, Henderson

MSS 36; Carl Holderman to Arnold, December 22, 1939, and Arnold to Holderman, January 2, 1940, both in Arnold MSS; Lizabeth Cohen, *Making a New Deal: Industrial Workers in Chicago, 1919–1939* (New York: Cambridge University Press, 1990), pp. 283–89; Gary Gerstle, *Working-Class Americanism: The Politics of Labor in a Textile City, 1914–1960* (New York: Cambridge University Press, 1989), pp. 180–87.

44. *United States* v. *Hutcheson*, 312 U.S. 219 (1941); Arnold, *Fair Fights and Foul*, p. 116; AFL, "Committee Report, Labor and the Anti-Trust Drive," [n.d.], 1941, Frey MSS 13; Gressley, *Voltaire and the Cowboy*, pp. 49–50; Arnold to Edward A. Evans, February 17, 1941, and Arnold to Reed Powell, February 21, 1941, both in Arnold MSS.

45. Richard Lee Strout, "The Folklore of Thurman Arnold," *New Republic*, April 27, 1942, p. 570; Arnold, *Folklore of Capitalism*, p. 205; Arnold, draft of unpublished article for *The Progressive*, 1944, Berge MSS. Several of Arnold's colleagues in the Antitrust Division spoke even more ominously of how the elimination of competition from German industry during World War I had helped create the fascist economic arrangements of the Nazi era. See, e.g., Heinrich Kronstein to Arnold, December 16, 1941, Arnold MSS.

46. Arnold, *Bottlenecks of Business*, p. 73; Arnold, "How Monopolies Have Hobbled Defense," *Reader's Digest*, July 1941, pp. 51, 55; Arnold, speech to the National Petroleum Association, September 13, 1939, and speech to the California Bar Association, September 19, 1941, both in Clapper MSS 102; New York *Herald Tribune*, September 14, 1939; Arnold to Frank W. Abel, June 2, 1942, and Joseph Zashin to Arnold, April 15, 1942, both in Arnold MSS; *New York Times*, April 15, 1942; Gressley, "Thurman Arnold," pp. 227–29; Eliot Janeway, *The Struggle for Survival: A Chronicle of Economic Mobilization in World War II* (New Haven: Yale University Press, 1951), p. 187.

47. Arnold radio speech, July 2, 1940, and Wilber Stammler to Avery, June 24, 1940, both in Arnold MSS.

48. Arnold, "Defense and Restraints of Trade," *New Republic*, May 19, 1941, p. 687.

49. *New York Times*, September 18, 1940; "Dinner-Table Treason," *Time*, April 6, 1942, pp. 15–16; "Blast at Standard Winds Up Antitrust Actions for the Duration," *Newsweek*, April 6, 1942, p. 42; I. F. Stone, "The Truth About Rubber," *Nation*, April 18, 1942, p. 451; "Arnold vs. Standard Oil," *Newsweek*, June 8, 1942, pp. 47–48; Arnold, "Confidence Must Replace Fear," *Vital Speeches*, July 1, 1942, pp. 558–59.

50. Jordan A. Schwarz, *The Speculator: Bernard M. Baruch in Washington, 1917–1965* (Chapel Hill: University of North Carolina Press, 1981), p. 428; Hawley, *New Deal and the Problem of Monopoly*, pp. 441–43; Stone, "Handcuffing Thurman Arnold," pp. 387–88; Johnston, "Thurman Arnold's Biggest Case," p. 40; "An Antitrust Holiday?" *Business Week*, April 4, 1942, pp. 15–17.

51. "Last Roundup," *Time*, February 22, 1943, p. 18; *New York Times*, March 10, 1943; "Trust Buster Benched," *Newsweek*, p. 34; Donald H. Riddle, "The Truman Committee: A Study in Congressional-Military Relations" (Ph.D. Dissertation, Princeton, 1956), pp. 42–43; I. F. Stone, "Thurman Arnold and the Railroads," *Nation*, March 6, 1943; Arnold, "How Cartels Affect You," *American Mercury*, March 1943, p. 321. Arnold served on the Court of Appeals

only briefly. In 1945, bored and frustrated by the judicial life, he resigned and formed a new legal partnership: Arnold, Fortas, and Porter (later Arnold and Porter), which became one of Washington's most powerful law firms. There he spent the rest of his professional life. He died in 1969, at the age of seventy-eight.

52. William G. Carleton, "The Promise of American Liberalism," *Antioch Review* 8 (Fall 1948), 341–42; Milo Perkins, "Cartels: What Shall We Do About Them?" *Harper's*, November 1944, pp. 570–78.

53. Richard Hofstadter, "What Happened to the Antitrust Movement? Notes on the Evolution of an American Creed," in Earl F. Cheit, ed., *The Business Establishment* (New York: John Wiley, 1964), p. 114.

54. The President's "monopoly" message to Congress in April 1938 suggested the official administration attitude. "[A]lthough we must recognize the inadequacies of existing laws," Roosevelt noted, "we seek to enforce them so that the public shall not be deprived of such protection as they afford. . . . But the existing anti-trust laws are inadequate—most importantly because of new financial economic conditions with which they are powerless to cope." Message to Congress, April 29, 1938, Rosenman, ed., *Public Papers and Addresses*, 1938 volume, pp. 313–15.

55. *New York Times*, May 17, 1939. The fullest account of the activities of the TNEC is David Lynch, *The Concentration of Economic Power* (New York: Columbia University Press, 1946), a semi-official history clearly sympathetic to its subject.

56. "New Trust Busters," *Nation*, July 16, 1938, pp. 59–60; Kenneth G. Crawford, "From Pump-Priming to Pumping," *Nation*, May 27, 1939, pp. 606–07; T.R.B., "FDR Is Just Around the Corner," *New Republic*, June 29, 1938, p. 215; "Monopoly Inquiry Holds," *Newsweek*, July 18, 1938, p. 34; Raymond Moley, "Monopoly Mystery," *Saturday Evening Post*, March 30, 1940, pp. 9–11.

57. Public Resolution No. 113, 75th Cong., 3d sess., "To create a temporary national economic committee," June 16, 1938; Dewey Anderson, "A Brief History of the Temporary National Economic Committee," March 31, 1941, Henderson MSS 25; Henderson memorandum, December 3, 1959, Henderson MSS 36. Henderson resigned as executive secretary in mid-1939 to accept an appointment to the Securities and Exchange Commission. He was succeeded by James Brackett and, later, Dewey Anderson. But Henderson remained active in the work of the committee until the end. Lynch, *Concentration of Economic Power*, pp. 47–49; "What Henderson Has Done," *New Republic*, May 10, 1939, p. 3.

58. O'Mahoney to Roosevelt, June 19, 1939, OF 3322, FDRL; O'Mahoney, "Final Statement Before the TNEC," March 11, 1941, Clapper MS 182; *Newsweek*, August 14, 1941, p. 84.

59. Noel Kaho, "An Analysis of Monopoly," August 1938, TNEC 57, RG 144, NA; Lynch, *Concentration of Economic Power*, pp. 35–43; "The New Trust Busters," *Nation*, July 16, 1938, p. 60; Leon Henderson diary, September 20, 1938, November 15, 1938, Henderson MSS 36; Oliver McKee, Jr., "Monopoly Investigators," *Commonweal*, November 4, 1938, pp. 35–37; Anderson, "A Brief History."

60. David A. Horowitz, "Senator Borah's Crusade to Save Small Business from the New Deal," *The Historian* 55 (1993), 693–708; Lynch, *Concentration of Economic Power*, pp. 38–43, 48–50; Kaho, "An Analysis of Monopoly"; McKee, "Monopoly Investigators," p. 35; "Monopoly Inquiry Holds," *Newsweek*, July 18, 1938, p. 32; Henderson diary, September 20, 1938, November 15, 1938, March 13, 1939, Henderson MSS 36; Henderson to FDR, March 7, 1939, Henderson MSS 25; O'Mahoney to FDR, June 19, 1939, Hopkins MSS 119.

61. That relationship deepened as the investigations continued and members of the administration began to consider ways to find a permanent bureaucratic home for some of the TNEC's activities. Harold Smith, director of the Bureau of the Budget, organized a series of meetings in 1940 to make the link between the inquiry and the NRPB official and lasting. Smith diary, January 20, 1940, Smith MSS 1.

62. Thomas Blaisdell to Benjamin Cohen, May 31, 1938, Cohen File 9, Interior, RG 48, NA; Corwin Edwards, "Summary of Industrial Committee Meeting," June 17, 1938, Gardiner Means, "Summary of June 5 Meeting," [n.d.], 1938, Mordecai Ezekiel, "Summary of Industrial Committee Meeting," [n.d.], 1938, Means to NRC Industrial Committee, June 28, 1938, all in Means MSS 7; Henderson to Ickes, September 20, 1938, TNEC 94, RG 144, NA: Ezekiel to Blaisdell, June 14, 1938, Blaisdell to Thomas Eliot et al., July 9, 1938, both in Frank MSS 22; Hawley, *New Deal and the Problem of Monopoly*, pp. 456–57; Joseph P. Lash, *Dreamers and Dealers* (New York: Doubleday, 1988), pp. 376–77.

63. Hawley, *New Deal and the Problem of Monopoly*, p. 461.

64. The standard for judging how well an economic organization "worked," Berle argued, was (1) "Does it provide an adequate supply of goods," (2) "Does it provide a maximum number of people with an opportunity to make a living," and (3) "Does it accomplish this process with due regard for the liberty and self-development of the individual?" Berle, "Memorandum of Suggestions: Investigation of Business Organization and Practices," July 12, 1938, Berle MSS 71; Berle to Stephen Early, July 15, 1938, OF 3322, FDRL; *Kiplinger Washington Letter*, August 20, 1938, Berle MSS 71; Berle diary, July 9, 1938, Berle MSS 210; Jordan Schwarz, *Liberal: Adolf A. Berle and the Vision of an American Era* (New York: The Free Press, 1987), p. 120.

65. Eccles memorandum to White House, "The Immediate Need for More Spending," June 6, 1938, Eccles MSS 5-8; Thomas Blaisdell to William O. Douglas, September 27, 1938, and Beardsley Ruml, "Compensatory Fiscal Policy," September 5, 1938, both in Frank MSS 25; Corwin Edwards, "Summary of NRC Industrial Committee Meeting," June 17, 1938, Means MSS 7.

66. U.S. Congress, Senate, Temporary National Economic Committee, "Final Report and Recommendations," 77th Cong., 1st sess., Doc. No. 35, March 31, 1941, pp. 648–87, 695–726; Summaries of TNEC hearings, Henderson MSS 22; Lynch, *Concentration of Economic Power*, pp. 70–90, 159; U.S. Congress, Senate, Temporary National Economic Committee, Monograph No. 1, *Price Behavior and Business Policy*, 76th Cong., 3d sess., 1940; idem, Monograph No. 27, *The Structure of Industry*, 76:3, 1941; Wright Patman to Roosevelt, November 25, 1938, and July 3, 1940, both in OF 288, FDRL.

67. Edward N. Stettinius, "Washington Notes," July 4, September 30, October 6, 1938, Stettinius MSS 64.

68. U.S. Congress, Senate, Temporary National Economic Committee, "Final Report of the Executive Secretary," 77th Cong., 1st sess., March 15, 1941, passim, and "Final Report and Recommendations," pp. 7, 21, 23, 35–40, and passim; M. M. Bober, "Price and Production Policies," *American Economic Review* 32 (June 1942), 23–52.

69. John T. Flynn, "For Bigger and Better Monopolies," *New Republic*, October 26, 1938, p. 333, and "Monopoly and Oligopoly," *New Republic*, May 3, 1939, pp. 377–78.

70. Dwight Macdonald, "The Monopoly Committee: A Study in Frustration," *American Scholar* 8 (1939), 307–08.

71. "Twilight of TNEC," *Time*, April 14, 1941, pp. 86–87; "The TNEC and the War," *Commonweal*, April 25, 1941, p. 4; "TNEC: Magnificent Failure," *Business Week*, March 22, 1941, pp. 22–27; Robert Brady, "Reports and Conclusions of the TNEC," *Economic Journal* 53 (1943), 415; I. F. Stone, "The TNEC Recommends—What?" *Nation*, April 19, 1941, pp. 463–64; "TNEC Squeaks," April 7, 1941, p. 453; Myron W. Watkins, "Present Position and Prospects of Antitrust Policy," *American Economic Review* 32 (June 1942), 89–118; Raymond Moley, "The Odyssey of the TNEC," *Newsweek*, August 14, 1941, p. 84; Richard N. Chapman, *Contours of Public Policy, 1939–1945* (New York: Garland, 1981), pp. 113–14.

72. Personal Statement of Isidor Lubin and Leon Henderson, in TNEC, "Final Report and Recommendations," p. 51.

73. Herbert Stein, *The Fiscal Revolution in America* (Chicago: University of Chicago Press, 1969), pp. 167–68.

74. U.S. Congress, Senate, "Hearings Before the Temporary National Economic Committee," Part I, "Economic Prologue," 75th Cong., 3d sess., December 1–3, 1938, pp. 3–80; "Behind the Monopoly Inquiry," *New Republic*, December 14, 1938, pp. 160–61; "Investigating Scarcity," *Nation*, December 10, 1938, p. 608.

75. Kenneth G. Crawford, "From Pump-Priming to Pumping," *Nation*, May 27, 1939, pp. 606–07. Some administration members of the committee were quietly engaged in trying to discredit O'Mahoney with the White House; they considered him too reflexively committed to old anti-monopolist ideas. See Jerome Frank to FDR, September 20, 1939, Henderson MSS 25. O'Mahoney, in the meantime, was himself beginning to support deficit spending as at least an interim solution to the nation's economic problems, although he continued to warn that in the long run such spending would lead to disaster and that more basic, structural remedies would be necessary. O'Mahoney to FDR, June 19, 1939, Hopkins MSS 119.

76. Mordecai Ezekiel to Thomas Blaisdell, June 14, 1938, and Blaisdell to Thomas Eliot et al., July 9, 1938, both in Frank MSS 22; FDR to O'Mahoney, May 16, 1939, Berle to FDR, May 10, 1939, both in OF 3322, FDRL; *New York Times*, May 17, 1939.

77. TNEC memo, February 10, 1939, Henderson MSS 25; Henderson diary, February 21, 1939, Henderson MSS 36; Peter R. Nehemkis to Berle, [n.d.], 1939, Berle MSS 71; "Again—The Trust Problem," *New Republic*, January 19, 1938, p. 296; "Investigating Scarcity," p. 608.

78. *New York Times*, May 17, 1939; Lauchlin Currie, "Comments on Pump Priming," *History of Political Economy* 10 (Winter 1978), 525–33; Chapman,

*Contours of Public Policy,* p. 28; Stein, *Fiscal Revolution,* p. 168; Currie to Benjamin Cohen, July 16, 1938, and Alan Sweezy, "Notes on Industrial Policy," July 15, 1938, both in Cohen File 3, Interior, RG 48, NA. Currie helped recruit Hansen to consult with the TNEC and worked with him and others on the May 1939 testimony. Along with Stuart Chase, he encouraged witnesses to use language carefully so as to make Keynesian ideas politically palatable— for example, by referring to "investment" instead of "spending." Such coaching became the source of considerable controversy when Arthur Krock of the *New York Times* published a hostile account of it in his column. Lynch, *Concentration of Economic Power,* pp. 63–64; Alfred H. Bornemann, "The Keynesian Paradigm and Economic Policy," *American Journal of Economics and Sociology* 35 (1976), 125–35; *New York Times,* June 7, 1939; U.S. Congress, Senate, "Hearings Before the Temporary National Economic Committee," Part 9, "Savings and Investment," 76th Cong., 1st sess., May 16, 1939, pp. 3520–38.

79. Richard Strout, "Hansen of Harvard," *New Republic,* December 29, 1941, pp. 888–90.

80. Leon Henderson to Jerome Frank, November 14, 1938, TNEC 99, RG 144, NA; Dewey Anderson to Hansen, August 9, 1940, TNEC 58, RG 144, NA.

81. Alvin H. Hansen, "Mr. Keynes on Underemployment Equilibrium," *Journal of Political Economy* 44 (October 1936), 667–86; Hansen, *Full Employment or Stagnation?* (New York: Norton, 1938), pp. 267–302; Robert Lekachman, *The Age of Keynes* (New York: Random House, 1966), pp. 127–37; Seymour Harris, ed., *The New Economics: Keynes's Influence on Theory and Public Policy* (New York: Alfred A. Knopf, 1947), p. 35.

82. U.S. Congress, Senate, "Hearings Before the Temporary National Economic Committee," Part 9, "Savings and Investment," 76th Cong., 1st sess., May 16, 1939, pp. 3543–44, 3546–52; *New York Times,* May 17, 1939; summary and transcript of TNEC hearings of May 16, 1939, Memo 45, May 20, 1939, Henderson MSS 22; Crawford, "From Pump-Priming to Pumping," p. 606.

83. TNEC, "Final Report of the Executive Secretary," pp. 319–81; Lubin dissent (drafted by A. F. Hinrichs), March 27, 1941, Lubin MSS 89. What particularly angered Lubin, Henderson, and others was the statement in the Final Report (presumably inserted by O'Mahoney) that "We cannot continue to rely upon government expenditures, whether by way of contribution or loan, to sustain enterprise and private employment, unless we are willing to invite eventually some form of the authoritarian state." TNEC, "Final Report and Recommendations," p. 9.

84. Ezekiel, draft of a foreword to the second edition of *Jobs For All,* [n.d.], 1939, and Ezekiel to Thomas Blaisdell, February 2, 1940, both in Ezekiel MSS 12.

85. Currie memorandum to Marriner Eccles, April 19, 1939, Eccles MSS 73-14.

86. Schwellenbach speech to Young Democrats, July 15, 1938, Schwellenbach MSS 3.

87. National Resources Committee, *The Problems of a Changing Population* (Washington, D.C.: Government Printing Office, 1938); Alvin H. Hansen, "Economic Progress and Declining Population Growth," *American Economic*

*Review* 29 (March 1939), 1–15; Philip W. Warken, *A History of the National Resources Planning Board, 1933–1943* (New York: Garland, 1979), pp. 85–86; Alvin Johnson, "Instead of the New Deal," *Yale Review* 29 (1939), p. 3; Roy Helton, "One Hundred Billion a Year: Could We Earn It: And Do We Want To?" *Harper's*, August 1938, pp. 277–79; Marriner Eccles, memorandum, June 6, 1939, Eccles MSS 5-9; Louis H. Bean to Jerome Frank, December 6, 1938, Frank MSS 21.

88. Summary of TNEC testimony, May 16, 1939, Memo 45, Henderson MSS 22; Hansen speech at the University of Cincinnati, March 15, 1940, Hansen MSS 3.10; Hansen, "Economic Progress and Declining Population Growth," *American Economic Review* 29 (1939), pp. 3–15; Robert Lekachman, *The Age of Keynes*, pp. 131–32; William E. Stoneman, *A History of the Economic Analysis of the Great Depression* (New York: Garland, 1979), pp. 110–11, 158; Joseph Schumpeter, *Business Cycles: A Theoretical, Historical, and Statistical Analysis of the Capitalist Process* (New York: McGraw-Hill, 1939), p. 908. See Michael Bernstein, *The Great Depression: Delayed Recovery and Economic Change in America, 1929–1939* (New York: Cambridge University Press, 1987), for a discussion of the slow but ultimately decisive development of new economic sectors, which filled the void left by the slowing expansion of "mature" industries.

89. Hansen, "Economic Progress and Declining Population Growth," p. 3; Helton, "One Hundred Billion a Year," pp. 274–75.

90. John T. Flynn, "Saving the System," *New Republic*, August 23, 1939, p. 74.

91. Stuart Chase, "Freedom from Want: A Postwar Budget for America," *Harper's*, October 1942, p. 468; Jerome Frank to Mordecai Ezekiel, August 28, 1939, Frank MSS 26; Max Lerner, "Economic Strategy in a Democracy," *New Republic*, June 22, 1942, p. 858; Emmet F. Connely, "Let Business Roll Its Own: The TNEC, Stuart Chase, and the New Financing," *Harper's*, May 1940, pp. 645–50; Henry Hilgard Villard, "Some Aspects of the Concept of Capacity to Produce," *The Review of Economic Statistics* 21 (February 1939), 13–20; "Technologically Fired," *New Republic*, May 6, 1940, pp. 595–96; Morris Cooke to the editor of the *New Republic*, May 3, 1940, PPF 940, FDRL; Sidney Hillman, "The Promise of American Labor," *New Republic*, November 8, 1939, p. 64.

92. Statement before the NRPB Fiscal and Monetary Advisory Board [prepared by officials of the Treasury Department], May 25, 1939, Bureau of the Budget, RG 51, 38.3.

93. Alan Sweezy, "The Keynesians and Government Policy, 1933–1939," *American Economic Review* 62 (May 1972), 116–24.

94. Hansen speech at University of Cincinnati, March 15, 1940, and Hansen to Sir Dennis H. Robertson, September 9, 1939, both in Hansen MSS 3.10.

95. Alvin H. Hansen, "Extensive Expansion and Population Growth," *Journal of Political Economy* 48 (August 1940), 583–85; Hansen speech, University of Cincinnati, March 15, 1940, J. M. Clark to Hansen, February 13, 1939, both in Hansen MSS 3.10; Crawford, "From Pump-Priming to Pumping," pp. 606–07; Hansen, *Full Recovery or Stagnation?*, pp. 322–29.

96. Leon Henderson, "Emerging Industrio-Governmental Problems," November 9, 1937, and Corwin Edwards to Henderson, April 22, 1939, both in Cohen File 9, Interior, RG 48, NA.

97. Hofstadter, "What Happened to the Antitrust Movement?," p. 113. See, e.g., Milo Perkins, "Cartels: What Shall We Do About Them?" pp. 570–78. Perkins's answer to his own question was, essentially, "nothing." "We Americans," he wrote, "have got to operate in the world as it is today and not in the fairyland of our oratory." Americans must adjust to "an era which has already gone a long way toward cartelization." See also Carleton, "The Promise of American Liberalism," pp. 331–45.

## Chapter Seven

1. Walter Lippmann, "The World Conflict in Its Relation to American Democracy," *The Annals* 72 (July 1917), 7–8.

2. Walter Lippmann, "Wake Up, America," New York *Herald Tribune*, December 9, 1941; Richard W. Resh, "Tutors to Society: Five American Intellectuals and War, 1917–1945" (Ph.D. Dissertation, University of Wisconsin, 1966), pp. 22, 42–44.

3. "Blackout for the New Deal?" *New Republic*, March 16, 1942, p. 351.

4. John B. Kirby, *Black Americans in the Roosevelt Era: Liberalism and Race* (Knoxville: University of Tennessee Press, 1980), chaps. 7–9; John Morton Blum, *V Was for Victory: Politics and American Culture During World War II* (New York: Harcourt Brace Jovanovich, 1976), chap. 6; William L. O'Neill, *A Democracy at War: America's Fight at Home & Abroad in World War II* (New York: The Free Press, 1993), chap. 11; Susan M. Hartmann, *The Home Front and Beyond: American Women in the 1940s* (Boston: Twayne, 1982), chaps. 7, 8, 10, 11; Alan Brinkley, "World War II and American Liberalism," in Lewis A. Erenberg and Susan E. Hirsch, eds., *The War in American Culture: Society and Consciousness During World War II* (University of Chicago Press, 1994).

5. Max Lerner, "War as Revolution. III," *Nation*, August 17, 1940, pp. 131–32; I. F. Stone, "A Test of Mr. Roosevelt," *Nation*, August 2, 1941, p. 87, and "The Cartel Cancer," *Nation*, February 12, 1944, p. 178; "Organizing a War Economy," *New Republic*, May 4, 1942, p. 592; Harold Strauss, "Don't Plan for Collapse. II," *Nation*, January 10, 1942, p. 36; Charles E. Noyes, "Make America Produce! The Economics of Freedom," *Nation*, December 7, 1940, pp. 555–58; George Soule, "The War in Washington," *New Republic*, September 27, 1939, pp. 204–06; Soule, "On Industry's Battle Front," *Nation*, January 17, 1942, p. 56; "On the Domestic Front," *Nation*, December 15, 1941, pp. 812–13; Felix Frankfurter to Hugo Black, November 10, 1942, Black MSS 60; Quincy Howe, "Twelve Things War Will Do to America," *Harper's*, November 1942, p. 579.

6. "What We Must Defend," *New Republic*, February 17, 1941, p. 227.

7. I. F. Stone, "One Year After Pearl Harbor," *Nation*, December 12, 1942, pp. 639–40; Harold L. Ickes, *The Secret Diary of Harold L. Ickes*, 3 vols. (New York: Simon and Schuster, 1953–1954), II: 716, III: 5.

8. Eliot Janeway, *The Struggle for Survival: A Chronicle of Economic Mobilization in World War II* (New Haven: Yale University Press, 1951), pp. 125–45, 191–99; Office of Facts and Figures, "Survey of Intelligence Materials, No. 17," April 1, 1942, MacLeish MSS 5; Richard Rovere, "Warning to the Liberals," *Common Sense*, August 11, 1942, pp. 266–68; Stephen J. Sniegoski, "Unified Democracy: An Aspect of World War II Interventionist Thought, 1939–1941," *The Maryland Historian* 9 (1978), 43; Margaret Weir, Ann Shola Orloff, and Theda Skocpol, "Understanding American Social Politics," in Weir, Orloff, and Skocpol, eds., *The Politics of Social Policy in the United States* (Princeton: Princeton University Press, 1988), pp. 19–21. On declining popular support for New Deal measures, see, e.g., George H. Gallup, *The Gallup Poll: Public Opinion, 1935–1971*, 3 vols. (New York: Random House, 1972), I: 134, 144, 150–51.

9. Gustav Stolper to Foreign Office, March 30, 1943, FO371—34213, PRO; Eliot Janeway, "Trials and Error," *Fortune*, December 1942, pp. 26, 30, 32; James Farley, Memorandum on Conversation with the President, December 28, 1938, and Memorandum on the 1938 Election Results, January 10, 1939, both in Farley MSS 43.

10. Richard N. Chapman, *Contours of Public Policy, 1939–1945* (New York: Garland, 1981), pp. 33–35, 45–53, 56–57; White to John H. Finley, August 23, 1939, White MSS 317; John Robert Moore, "The Conservative Coalition in the United States Senate, 1942–1945," *Journal of Southern History* 33 (1967), 368–73; James T. Patterson, *Congressional Conservatism and the New Deal: The Growth of the Conservative Coalition in Congress, 1933–1939* (Lexington: University of Kentucky Press, 1967), pp. 288–324; Joseph Tumulty to James Farley, February 28, 1939, Tumulty MSS 60.

11. Chapman, *Contours of Public Policy*, p. 210; Leon Henderson speech, June 29, 1943, Lubin MSS 51. David L. Porter, *Congress and the Waning of the New Deal* (Port Washington, N.Y.: Kennikat Press, 1980), provides a detailed picture of the congressional dismantling of the New Deal and the frustration of Roosevelt's initiatives after 1938.

12. James Rowe to FDR, March 29, 1943, PSF 77, FDRL; I. F. Stone, "Capital Notes," *Nation*, February 6, 1943, p. 187; Marquis W. Childs, "The President's Best Friend," *Saturday Evening Post*, April 19, 1941, p. 128; David Caute, *The Great Fear: The Anti-Communist Purge Under Truman and Eisenhower* (New York: Simon and Schuster, 1978), pp. 88–89; Chapman, *Contours of Public Policy*, pp. 211–13.

13. Henry A. Wallace, *Democracy Reborn*, ed. Russell Lord (New York: Reynal & Hitchcock, 1944), p. 238; Felix Frankfurter diary, January 16, 1943, Frankfurter MSS; "Defeatist Liberals," *New Republic*, March 6, 1944, p. 302.

14. Gallup, *The Gallup Poll*, I: 200, 203, 212, 234, 276, 284, 303, 331, 395, 447–48, 451; Leo P. Ribuffo, *The Old Christian Right: The Protestant Far Right from the Great Depression to the Cold War* (Philadelphia: Temple University Press, 1983), chaps. 4–6; Ira Katznelson, Kim Geiger, Daniel Kryder, "Limiting Liberalism: The Southern Veto in Congress, 1933–1950," *Political Science Quarterly* 108 (1993), 283–306; John Morton Blum, *V Was for Victory*, pp. 221–34.

15. Roosevelt, "Address on the State of the Union," January 7, 1943, in

Samuel Rosenman, ed., *The Public Papers and Addresses of Franklin D. Roosevelt* (New York: Russell & Russell, 1950), 12: 30–32; Roosevelt, "Address on the State of the Union," January 11, 1944, in Rosenman, ed., *Public Papers and Addresses* (New York: Harper & Row, 1950), 13: 41–42; "What We Must Defend," *New Republic*, February 17, 1941; James MacGregor Burns, *Roosevelt: The Soldier of Freedom, 1940–1945* (New York: Harcourt Brace Jovanovich, 1970), pp. 34–35, 306; Blum, *V Was for Victory*, pp. 248–49; Janeway, *Struggle for Survival*, p. 23.

16. Ickes, *Secret Diary*, III: 107; David Brody, "The New Deal and World War II," in John Braeman, Robert H. Bremner, and David Brody, eds., *The New Deal*, 2 vols. (Columbus: Ohio State University Press, 1975), I: 270–71; Gustav Stolper to Foreign Office, July 13, 1943, FO371—34213, PRO; Blum, *V Was for Victory*, pp. 244–45.

17. Ickes, *Secret Diary*, III: 295; T.R.B., "Washington Notes," *New Republic*, September 20, 1943, p. 393, and "FDR and the Conservative Trend," *New Republic*, August 23, 1943, p. 254; George Soule, "Roosevelt in 1943," *New Republic*, September 6, 1943, p. 327; Leon Henderson diary, March 13, 1945, and Henderson memorandum to Franklin D. Roosevelt Library, December 3, 1959, both in Henderson MSS 36.

18. I. F. Stone, "Capital Notes," *Nation*, January 23, 1943, p. 116.

19. "New Dealers Still Wanted," *New Republic*, January 13, 1941, p. 40; untitled clipping, *PM*, January 4, 1945, Corcoran MSS 120; T.R.B., "Washington Notes," *New Republic*, August 19, 1940, p. 244; Paul A. C. Koistinen, "The Hammer and the Sword: Labor, the Military, and Industrial Mobilization, 1920–1945" (Ph.D. Dissertation, University of California, Berkeley, 1964), pp. 804–05; I. F. Stone, "The Cartel Cancer," *Nation*, February 12, 1944, p. 178; "Mr. Berge's Antitrust," *Fortune*, August 1944, p. 141; Wendell Berge to George T. Colton, March 16, 1944, Berge MSS; Helen Fuller, "The Ring Around the President," *New Republic*, October 25, 1943, p. 564; Ickes, *Secret Diary*, III: 207; Harold Smith diary, October 9, 1941, Smith MSS 2; Henderson diary notes, February 24, 1944, Henderson MSS 36; I. F. Stone, "Capital Notes," *Nation*, February 6, 1943, p. 187; John Fischer, "Truman: A Little West of Center," *Harper's*, December 1945, pp. 486–87.

20. Henderson memorandum to the Roosevelt Library, December 3, 1959, Henderson MSS 36; Adolf Berle diary, August 24, 1939, Berle MSS 210; Henderson to Jerome Frank, November 19, 1938, Frank MSS 27; Henderson to Benjamin Cohen, May 4, June 9, December 19, 1938, all in Interior Department Records, Cohen—3, RG 48, NA.

21. W. H. Lawrence, "Tough Man With Two Jobs," *New York Times Magazine*, February 13, 1943, p. 16; "What Henderson Has Done," *New Republic*, May 10, 1939, p. 3; Michael Darrock, "What Happened to Price Control?" *Harper's*, July 1943, pp. 121–22.

22. Henderson to FDR, September 26, 1940, PSF 152, FDRL; "Report on Rationing," November 25, 1942, Henderson MSS 29; "The General Program," [n.d.], 1942, and Henderson to FDR, April 13, April 17, 1942, all in PSF 26, FDRL; Gustav Stolper to Foreign Office, January 21, 1943, FO371—34177, PRO; Darrock, "What Happened to Price Control?," pp. 121–22.

23. Bruce Catton, *The War Lords of Washington* (New York: Harcourt,

Brace, 1948), p. 41; Robert A. Taft radio address, April 25, 1941, Taft MSS 756; "SMR" to Robert A. Taft, November 18, 1942, Taft MSS 730; "Price Administrator on Spot," *Business Week*, July 5, 1941, pp. 15–16; *Kiplinger Washington Letter*, August 15, 1942; Darrock, "What Happened to Price Control?," pp. 120–21.

24. Ibid.; James Rowe to FDR, January 23, 1941, PSF 152; Henderson memorandum to Roosevelt Library, December 3, 1959, Henderson MSS 36.

25. I. F. Stone, "The Loss of Leon Henderson," *Nation*, December 26, 1942, p. 703; Michael Straight, "Why Henderson Goes," *New Republic*, December 28, 1942, p. 847; Henderson speech to UJA Appeal Rally, June 29, 1943, Lubin MSS 51.

26. Victor Reuther, "Labor in the War and After," *Antioch Review* 3 (1943), p. 318; "Mr. Wallace Walks the Plank," *New Republic*, July 26, 1943, p. 93; I. F. Stone, "Wallace Betrayed," *Nation*, July 24, 1943, pp. 89–90.

27. Chapman, *Contours of Public Policy*, pp. 83–84, 191–93.

28. The most thorough existing biography of Wallace is the two-volume work by Edward L. and Frederick H. Schapsmeier: *Henry A. Wallace of Iowa: The Agrarian Years, 1910–1940* (Ames: Iowa State University Press, 1968), and *Prophet in Politics: Henry A. Wallace and the War Years, 1940–1965* (Ames: Iowa State University Press, 1970). A good brief profile is Richard S. Kirkendall, "Henry A. Wallace," in Otis Graham and Megan Robinson Wander, eds., *Franklin D. Roosevelt: His Life and Times. An Encyclopedic View* (Boston: G. K. Hall, 1985), pp. 441–43. See also Norman D. Markowitz, *The Rise and Fall of the People's Century: Henry A. Wallace and American Liberalism* (New York: The Free Press, 1973), pp. 9–31.

29. *Kiplinger Washington Letter*, August 30, 1941, Nelson MS 2; "Model Executive," *Newsweek*, April 27, 1942, p. 42; Martin Dies to Wallace, March 28, 1942, Jones MSS 176; Schapsmeier, *Prophet in Politics*, pp. 51–54.

30. J. B. Confliffe to Louis Bean, July 17, 1942, Dewey Anderson to William T. Stone, July 16, 1942, both in Bean MSS 9; Theodore J. Kreps to Bean, July 17, 1943, Bean MSS 29; Office of Facts and Figures (OFF), "War Aims and Postwar Policies," April 1, 1942, MacLeish MSS 5; OFF, "Report to the Nation: The American Preparation for War," January 1942, MacLeish MSS 53; "Organizing for Economic War," *New Republic*, August 11, 1941, p. 176; Louis Bean, "Note to the Files," July 13, 1943, Bean MSS 34; James Wechsler, "Wallace-Jones Clash Likely on Bolivia's Labor Policy," *PM*, December 24, 1942, p. 8; Janeway, *The Struggle for Survival*, p. 342.

31. FDR to Jones, June 27, 1939, Jones MS 30; Jordan A. Schwarz, *The New Dealers: Power Politics in the Age of Roosevelt* (New York: Alfred A. Knopf, 1993), pp. 59–95; Gerald T. White, *Billions for Defense: Government Financing by the Defense Plant Corporation during World War II* (University, Ala.: The University of Alabama Press, 1980), p. 13.

32. Ickes, *Secret Diary*, III: 631; Hopkins to Jones, September 17, 1941, Jones to Hopkins, January 7, 1942, both in Jones MSS 14; Jones to Eleanor Roosevelt, December 19, 1937, Eleanor Roosevelt to Jones, December 22, 1937, both in Jones MSS 23; Jones to FDR, July 15, 1939, A. R. Clas to Gladys Mikell, October 7, 1941, Jones to FDR, [n.d.], 1941, all in Jones MSS 29; Samuel Lubell, "The New Deal's J. P. Morgan," *Saturday Evening Post*, November 30, 1940,

pp. 88–92; Chapman, *Contours of Public Policy*, pp. 37–39, 42–44; Dwight Macdonald, "Jesse Jones: Reluctant Dragon. I," *Nation*, February 7, 1942, pp. 158–60, and "Jesse Jones: Reluctant Dragon. II," *Nation*, February 14, 1942, p. 190; Jesse H. Jones, *Fifty Billion Dollars: My Thirteen Years with the RFC (1932–1945)* (New York: Macmillan, 1951), p. 262; Grace Tully, *F.D.R.: My Boss* (New York: Scribner's, 1949), p. 188–92; Eleanor Roosevelt to FDR, July 23, 1944, PSF 73, FDRL.

33. I. F. Stone, "Why Wallace Spoke Out," *Nation*, July 10, 1943, p. 35; Harold Smith, notes on conference with the President, April 8, 1942, Smith MSS 3.

34. Excerpts from Jones testimony before the Senate Banking and Currency Committee, December 2, 1942, excerpts from Wallace-Perkins Testimony, December 8, 1942, Clapper MSS 105; Perkins to FDR, March 31, 1943, PSF 73, FDRL; Jones to FDR, January 29, 1943, Jones MSS 176; Milo Perkins to Harold Ickes, December 15, 1942, Ickes MSS 157.

35. Jones, *Fifty Billion Dollars*, pp. 495–96; Jesse Jones, unsigned memorandum, February 15, 1943, "W.L.P." to Jones, February 11, 1943, G. Temple Bridgman to Will Clayton, [n.d.], 1943, all in Jones MSS 176; Harold Smith, daily record, April 27, 1942, Smith MSS 2; Helen Fuller, "The Jones-Wallace Feud," *New Republic*, July 12, 1943, pp. 43–44.

36. I. F. Stone, "The Anti-Wallace Plot," *Nation*, December 19, 1942, pp. 671–72; Wallace to Jones, June 3, 1943, and Jones to Wallace, June 3, 1943, James F. Byrnes to Jones, July 6, 1943, Jones to Byrnes, July 7, 1943, all in Jones MSS 176; Milo Perkins to Harry Hopkins, June 29, 1943, Hopkins MSS 133.

37. Milo Perkins to Carter Glass, July 5, 1943, Jones to James F. Byrnes, July 7, 1943, OF 4226, FDRL; Wallace to FDR, July [n.d.], 1945, OF 4735, FDRL; James F. Byrnes, *All in One Lifetime* (New York: Harper & Brothers, 1958), pp. 192–94; FDR to Jones, FDR to Wallace, July 15, 1943, OF 4226, FDRL.

38. Schapsmeier, *Prophet in Politics*, p. 71.

39. Wallace, *Democracy Reborn*, pp. 253–254; I. F. Stone, "Henry Wallace—A Great American," *Nation*, July 22, 1944, pp. 91–92; Freda Kirchwey, "The Battle of Chicago," *Nation*, July 29, 1944, pp. 118–20; I. F. Stone, "Wallace In, Jones Out," *Nation*, January 27, 1945, p. 89; Robert A. Taft, transcript of Senate speech, February 19, 1945, Taft MSS 752; Schapsmeier, *Prophet in Politics*, pp. 100–13, 120–26. The White House mail showed an enormous and overwhelmingly favorable response to Wallace's nomination as secretary of commerce; OF 3V, FDRL.

40. "Mr. Wallace Walks the Plank," pp. 93–95.

41. Nathan Robertson, "New Dealers Rally to Support of Wallace," *PM*, July 18, 1943, p. 2. A substantial file of letters representing public response to the dismissals of Wallace and Jones (and divided, roughly equally, into pro-Wallace and pro-Jones folders) is in OF 4226, FDRL.

42. Horace Kallen, "Fascism for the Italians," *New Republic*, January 12, 1927, p. 211; John P. Diggins, *Mussolini and Fascism: The View from America* (Princeton: Princeton University Press, 1972), pp. 204, 220–39; Diggins, "Flirtation with Fascism: American Pragmatic Liberals and Mussolini's Italy," *American Historical Review* 71 (1966), p. 495; Edward A. Purcell, Jr., *The Crisis of*

*Democratic Theory: Scientific Naturalism and the Problem of Value* (Lexington: The University Press of Kentucky, 1973), pp. 117–38; Benjamin L. Alpers, "Understanding Dictatorship and Defining Democracy in American Public Culture, 1930–1945," Ph.D. Dissertation, Princeton University, 1994, pp. 22–95.

43. David Green, *Shaping Political Consciousness: The Language of Politics in America from McKinley to Reagan* (Ithaca: Cornell University Press, 1987), p. 160; Allardyce Nicol, "American Opinions on War Aims and Post-War Problems," January 18, 1943, FO371—35367, PRO; Albert Jay Nock, "In Defense of the Individual," *Atlantic Monthly*, April 1940, pp. 834–38; Wilhelm Ropke, "Totalitarian 'Prosperity,' " *Harper's*, July 1939, pp. 165–70; Gustav Stolper, "A Partnership of Disaster," *Nation's Business*, May 1943, p. 32; Ben DuBois, "Wall Street in New Threat to Main Street," *Independent Business*, November–December 1940, pp. 8–10; David Sarnoff, "Post-War Horizons," speech before the Chamber of Commerce of the State of New York, February 4, 1943, OF 4351, FDRL.

44. Theodore Rosenof, *Patterns of Political Economy in America: The Failure to Develop a Democratic Left Synthesis, 1933–1950* (New York: Garland, 1983), pp. 222–23; Samuel T. Francis, *Power and History: The Political Thought of James Burnham* (Lanham, Md.: University Press of America, 1984), pp. 1–9; Kevin J. Smant, *How Great the Triumph: James Burnham, Anticommunism and the Conservative Movement* (Lanham, Md.: University Press of America, 1992), pp. 1–16.

45. James Burnham, *The Managerial Revolution* (New York: John Day, 1941), pp. 152–71, 206–51, and passim; Burnham, "Is Democracy Possible?," in Irving DeWitt Talmadge, ed., *Whose Revolution?* (New York: Howell, Soskin, 1941), pp. 193–201.

46. Ibid., pp. 169–70.

47. Ibid., pp. 170–71, 285; Robert L. Heilbroner, *The Worldly Philosophers*, 3d ed. (New York: Simon and Schuster, 1967), p. 271; "James Burnham," *Current Biography*, 1941, pp. 121–23. See Francis, *Power and History*, pp. 7–24, and Smant, *How Great the Triumph*, pp. 10–26, for generally sympathetic analyses of the ideas in *The Managerial Revolution*.

48. Seymour E. Harris, "Breaking a Lance With Mr. Hayek," *New York Times Book Review*, December 9, 1945, pp. 3, 14, 16. Recent scholarly discussions of Hayek's ideas include Eamonn Butler, *Hayek: His Contribution to the Political and Economic Thought of Our Time* (London: Temple Smith, 1983), a hagiographical account; Jim Tomlinson, *Hayek and the Market* (London: Pluto Press, 1990), a critique from the left; Chandran Kukathas, *Hayek and Modern Liberalism* (Oxford: Clarendon Press, 1989), a guardedly critical analysis; John N. Gray, *Hayek on Liberty* (Oxford: Basil Blackwell, 1984), a sympathetic effort to systematize Hayek's thought; Lawrence Jay Cronin, "Methodological Liberalism: The Thought of F. A. Hayek" (Ph.D. Dissertation, Ohio State University, 1985); Calvin M. Hoy, "Hayek's Philosophy of Liberty" (Ph.D. Dissertation, Columbia University, 1982); and Alan Brinkley, "The Problem of American Conservatism," *American Historical Review* 99 (1994), 415–19.

49. Hayek to Lippmann, April 6, 1937, Lippmann MSS III, 77.

50. C. Hartley Grattan, "Hayek's Hayride," *Harper's*, July 1945, pp. 48–49.

Hayek had earlier published a much briefer version of much the same argument: *Freedom and the Economic System* (Chicago: University of Chicago Press, 1939).

51. Friedrich A. Hayek, *The Road to Serfdom* (Chicago: University of Chicago Press, 1944), pp. ix, 2.

53. Hayek, *The Road to Serfdom,* pp. 92, 145–46. Theodore Rosenof, "Freedom, Planning, and Totalitarianism: The Reception of F. A. Hayek's *Road to Serfdom,*" *Canadian Review of American Studies* 5 (1974), 149–65, analyzes contemporary reaction to the book. Norman Barry et al., *Hayek's 'Serfdom' Revisited* (London: Institute of Economic Affairs, 1984), contains essays by mostly sympathetic scholars and writers re-examining the book's message on the occasion of the fortieth anniversary of its publication.

53. John D. Millett, *The Process and Organization of Government Planning* (New York: Columbia University Press, 1947), pp. 5–6; Carl J. Friedrich, "*The Road to Serfdom,*" *American Political Science Review* 39 (June 1945), 575–79.

54. Alvin H. Hansen, "The New Crusade Against Planning," *New Republic,* January 1, 1945, pp. 10–12; "Prosperity," *New Republic,* November 27, 1944, pp. 725–26. William Beveridge wrote Hansen, after reading his review of the book, that Hayek's "vogue among those who want to block everything is remarkable." Beveridge to Hansen, March 15, 1945, Beveridge MSS 3.10.

55. Reinhold Niebuhr, "The Collectivist Bogy," *Nation,* October 21, 1944, pp. 478–80; Stuart Chase, "Back to Grandfather," *Nation,* May 9, 1945, p. 566; Henry Hazlitt, "An Economist's View of Planning," *New York Times Book Review,* September 24, 1944, p. 1; Antonin Basch, "*The Road to Serfdom,*" *Political Science Quarterly* 60 (1945), 149; Hansen, "The New Crusade Against Planning," p. 12.

56. See, e.g., Michael Kazin, *The Populist Persuasion: An American History* (New York: Basic Books, 1995), chaps. 5–6; Alan Brinkley, *Voices of Protest: Huey Long, Father Coughlin, and the Great Depression* (New York: Alfred A. Knopf, 1982), chaps. 3, 5, 7.

57. Reinhold Niebuhr, *The Children of Light and the Children of Darkness* (New York: Scribner's, 1944), p. 117; Rosenof, *Patterns of Political Economy,* pp. 228–32; Rosenof, "Freedom, Planning, and Totalitarianism," pp. 150–60. Niebuhr was offering a muted echo of some of the more thoughtful conservative defenses of Hayek, among them one by the historian Louis Hacker: "Is it any wonder that Mr. Hayek is troubled by all this current talk of the return to a new Mercantilism? Central planning—governmental control over investment, the mobility of labor, prices and wages, foreign trade— must operate through the authoritarian state which substitutes for the decisions of the market place the mandates of the functionary." Louis M. Hacker, "The State vs. Liberty," *American Mercury* 62 (January 1946), 108. Hacker was writing in response to one of the harshest liberal rejoinders to Hayek (by Herman Finer); and while he took pains to disassociate himself from Hayek's absolutism, he argued that the fear of an authoritarian state expressed in *The Road to Serfdom* was neither as fanciful nor as reactionary as its critics claimed.

58. Hansen, "New Crusade Against Planning," pp. 10–12.

59. Herbert Agar et al., *The City of Man: A Declaration on World Democracy* (New York: Viking Press, 1940), pp. 25, 56, 86. Among those involved in the creation of this brief book (and in the "Committee on Europe," from which it emerged) were Van Wyck Brooks, Ada L. Comstock, William Yandell Elliott, Dorothy Canfield Fisher, Christian Gauss, Hans Kohn, Thomas Mann, Lewis Mumford, Reinhold Niebuhr, and Robert Maynard Hutchins. John Chamberlain, "Blueprints for a New Society. I: The Weakness of State Socialism," *New Republic*, September 6, 1939, pp. 122–25.

60. H. J. Res. 59, 77th Cong., 1st sess., January 10, 1941, "To establish a national unemployment commission," OF 4351, FDRL; Dean L. May, *From New Deal to New Economics: The Liberal Response to the Recession* (New York: Garland, 1981), pp. 6–7, 131.

61. Freda Kirchwey, "Old Liberties for a New World," *Nation*, February 10, 1940, pp. 145–46; Eccles to FDR, June 25, 1940, Eccles MSS 5-10; Max Lerner, "The War as Revolution. I. The Breaking of Nations," *Nation*, July 27, 1940, pp. 68–71; Lewis Corey, "Marxism Reconsidered. I," *Nation*, February 17, 1940, p. 247; Harold Strauss, "Make America Produce! Liberty Is Divisible," *Nation*, December 7, 1940, pp. 552–55; Sidney Hook, *Reason, Social Myths, and Democracy* (New York: John Day, 1940), p. 46; "Government Must Not Turn to Fascist Methods," *Labor's Monthly Survey*, July 1942, pp. 1–2.

62. Adolf Berle, "Corporations and the Modern State," in Thurman Arnold et al., *The Future of Democratic Capitalism* (Philadelphia: University of Pennsylvania Press, 1950), pp. 52–53. John T. Flynn had written similarly in the *New Republic* ten years earlier that if America "threw off so-called free capitalism now it would move beyond doubt to some American form of fascism." Flynn, "Government as Investor?," *New Republic*, January 1, 1940, p. 22.

63. Charles Merriam, "The National Resource Planning Board," in George B. Galloway, ed., *Planning for America* (New York: Holt, 1941), pp. 504–05; Marion H. Hedges, "The Search for the Democratic Man," *Atlantic Monthly*, October 1943, pp. 57–61; John Chamberlain, "Blueprints for a New Society. I: The Weakness of State Socialism," *New Republic*, September 6, 1939, p. 125; Waldo Frank, "American Inventory," *Nation*, August 31, 1940, p. 170. The defensiveness extended to the way American liberals assessed planning efforts in democratic Europe. Fritz Sternberg, for example, wrote approvingly of the increased government planning of the British economy by insisting repeatedly "that the introduction of a considerable war-economy control is by no means identical with making a step toward the creation of a totalitarian state on Hitler's pattern." Sternberg, "The Defense of a Free Nation," *New Republic*, July 1, 1940, p. 16.

64. "Mr. Henderson on Wages," *New Republic*, October 6, 1941, p. 420; Henderson to Hopkins, [n.d.], Hopkins MSS 54.

65. Wallace, *Democracy Reborn*, p. 224; James G. Patton and James Loeb, Jr., "The Challenge to Progressives," *New Republic*, February 5, 1945, pp. 187–88. The Union for Democratic Action (UDA) was the precursor of the postwar Americans for Democratic Action (ADA).

66. Nancy J. Weiss, *Farewell to the Party of Lincoln: Black Politics in the*

*Age of FDR* (Princeton: Princeton University Press, 1983), pp. 120–56; Harvard Sitkoff, *A New Deal for Blacks. The Emergence of Civil Rights as a National Issue: The Depression Decade* (New York: Oxford University Press, 1976), pp. 60–65, 77–79; Mary McLeod Bethune, "My Secret Talks with FDR," in Bernard Sternsher, ed., *The Negro in Depression and War: Prelude to Revolution, 1930–1945* (Chicago: Quadrangle Books, 1969), pp. 53–65. John B. Kirby, *Black Americans in the Roosevelt Era: Liberalism and Race* (Knoxville: University of Tennessee Press, 1980), pp. 76–96; Alfred Baker Lewis, "For Better Social Security," *The Crisis*, November 1944, pp. 347, 357. Eleanor Roosevelt's commitment to racial equality was deep and genuine. But it was also limited by some of the same assumptions that inhibited other white liberals from confronting the issue of race directly. "I have never advocated any social equality whatsoever," she wrote defensively to an Alabama woman in 1944. "In this country we are free to choose our companions and no one has any right to interfere." She sought, rather, to carve out a clearly public sphere of race relations in which she believed the government could intervene without causing chaotic social disruption, which she and many others feared a drastic assault on prejudice might produce. She advocated, she claimed, "four fundamental rights" that would, she implausibly insisted, leave basic "social relations" unthreatened: equal employment opportunities, equal educational opportunities, equal justice before the law, and the right to vote. "The Four Equalities," *Time*, September 18, 1944, p. 48. Doris Kearns Goodwin, *No Ordinary Time. Franklin and Eleanor Roosevelt: The Home Front in World War II* (New York: Simon and Schuster, 1994), pp. 369–71, 521–24.

67. Robert B. Westbrook, *John Dewey and American Democracy* (Ithaca: Cornell University Press, 1991), p. 205; David Burner, *The Politics of Provincialism: The Democratic Party in Transition, 1918–1932* (New York: W. W. Norton, 1967), pp. 244–52; Weiss, *Farewell to the Party of Lincoln*, pp. 209–35; Gary Gerstle, "The Protean Character of American Liberalism," *American Historical Review* 99 (1994), pp. 8–17, 19–21, 25–31. Gerstle argues that the revival of liberal interest in racial and cultural issues was both a cause and a result of a declining interest in the class-based issues they had emphasized in the 1930s. "By the late 1940s," he writes, "liberals were writing as though ethnicity were a repository for healthy, and rational, human sentiments; class, by contrast, was treated as a pit of irrational and dangerous passion" (p. 30).

68. Kirby, *Black Americans in the New Deal*, pp. 106–51; Frank Freidel, *F.D.R. and the South* (Baton Rouge: Louisiana State University Press, 1965), p. 86; Weiss, *Farewell to the Party of Lincoln*, pp. 96–119; Walter White, *A Man Called White: The Autobiography of Walter White* (New York: Viking, 1948), pp. 169–70. The quotation is from White's account of the meeting, published years later, and it seems likely that it is only an approximate re-creation of the President's statement.

69. Blum, *V Was for Victory*, pp. 182–220; Herbert Garfinkel, *When Negroes March: The March on Washington Movement in the Organizational Politics for FEPC* (Glencoe, Ill.: The Free Press, 1959).

70. Horace R. Cayton, "The Negro's Challenge," *Nation*, July 3, 1943, pp. 10–12; Richard Polenberg, *War and Society: The United States, 1941–1945* (Philadelphia: J. B. Lippincott, 1972), pp. 99–130.

71. "Defeat at Detroit," *Nation*, July 3, 1943, p. 4. See also Cayton, "The Negro's Challenge," pp. 10–12; "Soldiers and the Rights of Negroes," *Nation*, October 9, 1943, p. 418; "The Race Problem," *Christianity and Society* 7 (Summer 1942), pp. 3–5.

72. Alvin Johnson, "Race in the World to Come," *Yale Review* 33 (1943), p. 193; Otelia Cromwell, "Democracy and the Negro," *American Scholar* 13 (1944), pp. 149–50, 155.

73. Niebuhr, *The Children of Light and the Children of Darkness: A Vindication of Democracy and a Critique of Its Traditional Defence* (New York: Charles Scribner's Sons, 1944), pp. 140–44. See also Niebuhr, "Christian Faith and the Race Problem," *Christianity and Society* (Spring 1945), pp. 21–24.

74. Gunnar Myrdal, *An American Dilemma: The Negro Problem and Modern Democracy*, 2 vols. (New York: Harper & Row, 1944), I, lxix–lxxvii, II, 997, 1009; Walter Jackson, *Gunnar Myrdal and America's Conscience: Social Engineering and Racial Liberalism, 1938–1987* (Chapel Hill: University of North Carolina Press, 1990), pp. 150–68, 186–231; Sissela Bok, unpublished "Introductory Remarks" at a conference on "An American Dilemma Revisited: Race Relations in a Changing World," April 20, 1994, Morehouse College.

75. Jackson, *Gunnar Myrdal*, pp. 242–45; David W. Southern, *Gunnar Myrdal and Black-White Relations: The Use and Abuse of 'An American Dilemma,' 1944–1969* (Baton Rouge: Louisiana State University Press, 1987), pp. 71–99; Reinhold Niebuhr, "An American Dilemma," *Christianity and Society*, Summer 1944, p. 42; "American Dilemma," *Time*, February 7, 1944, p. 16. Among Myrdal's collaborators—not all of whom fully approved of the results—were Ruth Benedict, Franz Boas, Ralph Bunche, Franklin Frazier, Horace Cayton, Melville J. Herskovits, Charles S. Johnson, Alain Locke, Howard Odum, Robert E. Park, Arthur Raper, Rupert B. Vance, Jacob Viner, and Walter White. Myrdal, *An American Dilemma*, pp. lii–liv.

76. See, e.g., Archibald MacLeish, "The People Are Indivisible," *Nation*, October 28, 1944, p. 509.

77. Although the bulk of the growth was a result of military production, the consumer economy expanded by 12 percent during the same years. Alan S. Milward, *War, Economy and Society: 1939–1945* (Berkeley: University of California Press, 1977), pp. 63–65; Blum, *V Was for Victory*, pp. 90–93.

78. Alvin H. Hansen, "Planning Full Employment," *Nation*, October 21, 1941, p. 492; "Is There a New Frontier?" *New Republic*, November 27, 1944, pp. 708–10; "A New Bill of Rights," *Nation*, March 20, 1943, p. 402. Stein, *Fiscal Revolution*, pp. 175–77.

79. FDR to Jesse Jones, April 30, 1941, Jones MSS 30; Cyrus Eaton to FDR, July 3, 1942, PSF 10, FDRL; I. F. Stone, "Donald Nelson Has Chosen," *Nation*, March 21, 1942, p. 331; Michael Straight, "Dollar-a-Year Sabotage," *New Republic*, March 30, 1942, pp. 417–18; "Post-War Planning—Dollar-a-Year Style," *Nation*, May 23, 1942, p. 588; Harold Ickes to Lady Bird Johnson, August 13, 1942, Ickes MSS 161.

80. "Call for Business Men," *Business Week*, October 9, 1943, p. 108; Paul Hodges, "Business Skill Dons Khaki," *Nation's Business*, April 1943, p. 25; Harold Laski, "The American Myth and the Peace," *Nation*, February 12, 1944,

180; Roland N. Stromberg, "American Business and the Approach of War, 1935–1941," *Journal of Economic History* 13 (1953), 74–75; Philip H. Burch, Jr., "The NAM as an Interest Group," *Politics and Society* 4 (1973), 97–130.

81. Bradley Dewey to Bruce K. Brown, August 3, 1944, Ickes MSS 380. Dewey, a rubber industry executive, had served as rubber director in the WPB; Brown was deputy petroleum director under Ickes.

82. Gerard Swope to Louis Howe, November 2, 1933, "Report of the Business Advisory Council," April 10, 1935, "Resolution," May 2, 1935, W. A. Harriman to Daniel C. Roper, May 20, 1937, all in OF 3Q, FDRL; Robert M. Collins, "Positive Business Responses to the New Deal: The Roots of the Committee for Economic Development, 1933–1942," *Business History Review* 52 (1978), 375–83; Robert M. Collins, *The Business Response to Keynes, 1919–1964* (New York: Columbia University Press, 1981), pp. 53–112.

83. John F. Fennelly to Jesse Jones, August 28, 1944, and Jesse Jones to FDR, August 29, 1944, both in FDRL OF 5384; Washington *Daily News*, August 29, 1944; Beardsley Ruml, George Soule, Oswald W. Knauth, Alvin H. Hansen, "A Postwar National Fiscal Policy," *New Republic*, February 28, 1944, pp. 265–71; Ronald Radosh, "The Myth of the New Deal," Radosh and Murray Rothbard, eds., *A New History of the Leviathan: Essays on the Rise of the American Corporate State* (New York: Dutton, 1972), pp. 156–58.

84. Wallace, *Democracy Reborn*, p. 21; Chester Bowles to FDR, November 17, 1944, Bowles MSS I, 10; FDR to Jesse Jones, April 30, 1941, Jones MSS 30; Chapman, *Patterns of Political Economy*, pp. 251–52.

85. Arnold to William Allen White, September 9, 1943, White MSS C413. For a discussion of Henry Kaiser and his relationship to the New Deal, see Jordan Schwarz, *The New Dealers: Power Politics in the Age of Roosevelt* (New York: Alfred A. Knopf, 1993), pp. 299–303, 308–17, 324–28.

## Chapter Eight

1. Clifford Durr, "The Postwar Relationship Between Government and Business," *American Economic Review* 33 (1943), 47. See also George Soule, "The War in Washington," *New Republic*, September 27, 1939, pp. 205–06; "New Deal Plans Industry Council," *Business Week*, March 20, 1943, p. 15.

2. Robert D. Cuff, "American Mobilization for War 1917–1945: Political Culture vs. Bureaucratic Administration," in N. F. Dreisziger, ed., *Mobilization for Total War: The Canadian, American, and British Experience, 1914–1918, 1937–1945* (Waterloo, Ont.: Wilfred Laurier University Press, 1981), p. 80.

3. Richard Lee Strout, "The Folklore of Thurman Arnold," *New Republic*, April 27, 1942, p. 570; Arnold, "How Monopolies Have Hobbled Defense," *Reader's Digest*, July 1941, pp. 51, 55; Arnold, "Defense and Restraints of Trade," *New Republic*, May 19, 1941, p. 687.

4. That they had reason for such concerns is clear in, among other things, a December 1942 memorandum to Donald Nelson from the man who was then his chief deputy on the War Production Board, Ferdinand Eberstadt: "I think that the impact of concentration could be completely removed if the Anti-Trust Laws were waived during the war and for a period of six months

thereafter so that each industry could set up its own concentration program." Eberstadt to Nelson, December 5, 1942, Baruch MSS 33.

5. Donald Nelson, *Arsenal of Democracy* (New York: Harcourt, Brace, 1946), p. 87; Jordan Schwarz, *The Speculator: Bernard M. Baruch in Washington, 1917–1965* (Chapel Hill: University of North Carolina Press, 1981), pp. 358–59.

6. Henderson diary, September 28, 1939, Henderson MSS 36; Schwarz, *The Speculator*, pp. 329–31, 359. Baruch was deeply hurt by his exclusion, particularly since it came only a few months after the President had promised him the chairmanship of a similar board and then withdrawn the offer.

7. Leon Henderson diary, September 28, 1938, Henderson MSS 36; Harold Smith diary, September 4, 1939, Smith MSS 1; "Queer Dollar-a-Year Men," *New Republic*, September 20, 1939, p. 174; George Soule, "The War in Washington," *New Republic*, September 27, 1939, p. 205.

8. Adolf Berle diary, August 17, 1939, Berle MSS 210.

9. Harold Smith diary, September 7, 1939, Smith MSS 1; U.S. Congress, Senate, "Industrial Mobilization Plan Revision of 1939," 76th Cong., 2d sess., October 24, 1939, p. 7 and passim; Paul A. C. Koistinen, "Mobilizing the World War II Economy: Labor and the Industrial-Military Alliance," *Pacific Historical Review* 42 (November 1973), 446–47.

10. *Wall Street Journal*, September 27, 1939.

11. Public opinion polls showed a rise in support for aid to Britain from 55 percent in March 1940 to 80 percent in late June. George H. Gallup, *The Gallup Poll: Public Opinion, 1935–1971*, 3 vols. (New York: Random House, 1972), I: 212, 225, 230, 233, 237–38, 240. Harold Ickes, *The Secret Diary of Harold Ickes*, 3 vols. (New York: Simon and Schuster, 1953–1954), III: 194–95; Schwarz, *The Speculator*, p. 366; Henry L. Stimson and McGeorge Bundy, *On Active Service in Peace and War* (New York: Harper & Brothers, 1948), pp. 323–31. Knudsen's service on the NDAC followed a long previous association with the Roosevelt administration, through both the NRA and the Business Advisory Council.

12. Ickes, *Secret Diary*, III: 194–96, 207–09; "Industrial Mobilization for War: A History of the War Production Board and Predecessor Agencies," April 30, 1946, Nelson MSS 10; T.R.B., "The Camel's Nose," *New Republic*, June 10, 1940, pp. 790–91.

13. "Industrial Mobilization for War," April 30, 1946, Nelson MSS 10; Robert K. Murray, "Government and Labor during World War II," *Current History* 37 (September 1959), 146–47; Eliot Janeway, *The Struggle for Survival: A Chronicle of Economic Mobilization in World War II* (New Haven: Yale University Press, 1951), pp. 123–25.

14. Ferdinand Eberstadt diary, November 4, 1941, Eberstadt MSS 23; Michael Straight, "The Mirage of Production," *New Republic*, July 28, 1941, pp. 107–10; Leon Henderson diary, January 6, 16, 1941, Henderson MSS 36; Harold Smith diary, February 13, 1941, Smith MSS 2; Ickes, *Secret Diary*, III: 591; I. F. Stone, "Division in the OPM," *Nation*, March 8, 1941, p. 259, and "Heat Haze in Washington," *Nation*, July 12, 1941, p. 28; George R. Clark, "The Strange Story of the Reuther Plan," *Harper's*, May 1942, pp. 652–53.

15. "What Defense Shakeup Means," *Business Week*, September 6, 1941,

pp. 15–16; "Industrial Mobilization for War," May 24, 1946, Nelson MSS 12; "The New Defense Board," *New Republic*, September 8, 1941, p. 294; Schwarz, *The Speculator*, pp. 375–76.

16. "What Defense Shakeup Means," pp. 15–16; "The New Defense Board," p. 295; Koistinen, "Mobilizing the World War II Economy," pp. 447–48; Barton J. Bernstein, "The Automobile Industry and the Coming of the Second World War," *Southwestern Social Science Quarterly* 47 (1966), 23–33.

17. Nelson, *Arsenal of Democracy*, pp. 13–21; Roosevelt to Nelson, January 16, 1942, Nelson MSS 2; Executive Order, January 13, 1942, OF 4735, FDRL. There is some evidence that Nelson was not as surprised by the appointment as he suggested in his memoirs; Harry Hopkins claimed to have met with him earlier in the day to "prepare him for the meeting." Robert E. Sherwood, *Roosevelt and Hopkins* (New York: Harper & Brothers, 1950), pp. 475–76.

18. W. H. Lawrence, " 'Too Much, Too Soon,' " *New York Times Magazine*, January 25, 1942, p. 9; "The People Win," *Time*, January 26, 1942, p. 12; "Nelson Gets World's Biggest Single Job," *Life*, January 26, 1942, pp. 29–36; R. E. Wood to Nelson, February [n.d.], 1942, Nelson MSS 2; Schwarz, *The Speculator*, p. 389.

19. Michael Straight, "Donald Nelson Takes Over," *New Republic*, September 15, 1941, p. 329; "What Defense Shakeup Means," p. 16; J. P. McEvoy, "The Nation's Busiest Businessman," *Reader's Digest*, June 1942, p. 41; W. H. Lawrence, "A Day With Nelson," *New York Times Magazine*, February 22, 1942, p. 16; Lawrence, " 'Too Much, Too Soon,' " p. 9; Schwarz, *The Speculator*, p. 389; Baruch to Nelson, February 21, May 19, July 6, 1942, Nelson MSS 2.

20. St. Clair McKelway, "A Businessman, Sir," *The New Yorker*, March 28, 1942, p. 26; Noel Busch, "Donald Nelson," *Life*, September 15, 1941, pp. 329–30; "Don Nelson: The Man from Sears Goes to War," *Fortune*, November 1941, pp. 153–56.

21. Busch, "Donald Nelson," p. 330; "Don Nelson," *Fortune*, p. 153.

22. Ibid., p. 156; Busch, "Donald Nelson," p. 330; Robert E. Wood to Nelson, June 5, 1940, Nelson MSS 2.

23. "Industrial Mobilization for War," p. 21, Nelson MSS 10; Henderson diary, January 5, 1941, Henderson MSS 36; *Kiplinger Washington Letter*, August 30, 1941; "Don Nelson," *Fortune*, p. 150; Thurman Arnold to Nelson, August 29, 1941, Mordecai Ezekiel to Nelson, August 29, 1941, both in Nelson MSS 2; Ickes, *Secret Diary*, III: 661.

24. Harry Hopkins memo, "The Appointment of Donald Nelson," January 14, 1942, Hopkins MSS 313; " 'Post-War' Planning—Dollar-a-Year Style," *Nation*, May 23, 1942, p. 588; "Nelson, the Coordinator," *Business Week*, January 31, 1942, p. 18; Janeway, *Struggle for Survival*, pp. 7–18, 52, 228.

25. One exception was I. F. Stone. See "WPB, Alias SPAB," *Nation*, January 31, 1942, pp. 110–11.

26. Bruce Catton to Ruth Christ, May 15, 1942, Nelson MSS 2.

27. Paul A. C. Koistinen, "Warfare and Power Relations in America: Mobilizing the World War II Economy," in James Titus, ed., *The Home Front and War in the Twentieth Century: The American Experience in Comparative*

*Perspective* (Proceedings of the Tenth Military History Symposium, United States Air Force Academy and Office of Air Force History, USAF, 1984), pp. 104–05; Stimson, *On Active Service*, pp. 340–44.

28. John Fischer, "The Army Takes Over," *Harper's*, May 1945, pp. 482–83, 485; "Roll of Honor," *Time*, August 10, 1942, p. 20; Janeway, *Struggle for Survival*, p. 52; Stimson, *On Active Service*, pp. 340–44.

29. Fischer, "The Army Takes Over," p. 483; George R. Leighton, "Crisis in Washington," *Harper's*, December 1942, p. 5.

30. Leon Henderson to Roosevelt, October 14, 1940, OF 813A, FDRL; Somervell to Nelson, May 15, 1942, J. S. Knowlson to Nelson, May 19, 1942, Nelson to Somervell, May 21, 1942, both in WPB 91, RG 179, NA; Somervell to Nelson, March 30, 1942, Nelson to Somervell, March 27, 1942, both in Nelson MSS 2; "Here Comes the Army," *Time*, August 3, 1942, p. 16; Jeffrey Dorwart, *Eberstadt and Forrestal: A National Security Partnership* (College Station: Texas A&M University Press, 1991), pp. 44–48; Samuel P. Huntington, *The Soldier and the State* (Cambridge: Harvard University Press, 1957), pp. 315–44.

31. Among those urging Nelson to take charge by setting up his own industrial committees was Bernard Baruch, who began pressing the idea when Nelson was still chairing SPAB. Baruch to Nelson, September 7, November 7, 1941, Nelson MSS 2; Schwarz, *The Speculator*, p. 429. Robert E. Wood, Nelson's former employer at Sears, offered the opposite advice. Wood to Nelson, February [n.d.], 1942, Nelson MSS 2; Fischer, "The Army Takes Over," p. 486.

32. Somervell to Nelson, May 15, 1942, and Nelson to Somervell, May 21, 1942, both in WPB 91, RG 179, NA; Nelson to Robert E. Wood, February 10, 1942, Nelson MSS 2; Paul A. C. Koistinen, "The Hammer and the Sword: Labor, the Military, and Industrial Mobilization, 1920–1945" (Ph.D. Dissertation, University of California, Berkeley, 1964), pp. 639–40; "Here Comes the Army," pp. 16–17; Bruce Catton, *War Lords of Washington* (New York: Harcourt, Brace, 1948), p. 177.

33. Thomas Sancton, "Chaos in Production," *New Republic*, August 31, 1942, p. 251; I. F. Stone, "Brass-Hat Production," *Nation*, December 5, 1942, p. 607; *Kiplinger Washington Letter*, August 15, 1942, Nelson MSS 2.

34. "Palace Revolution," *Time*, August 31, 1942.

35. Nelson to Eberstadt, July 10, 1942, Eberstadt to Nelson, July 11, 1942, Nelson to Eberstadt, September 18, 1942, all in Eberstadt MSS 116; "Priorities Deflated," *Newsweek*, September 7, 1942, p. 62; "Palace Revolution," August 31, 1942; Leighton, "Crisis in Washington," p. 5; Dorwart, *Eberstadt and Forrestal*, pp. 52–55.

36. Stone, "Brass-Hat Production," *Nation*, December 5, 1942, pp. 607–08.

37. Ickes, *Secret Diary*, III: 5, 182.

38. David Brody, "The New Deal and World War II," in John Braeman, Robert H. Bremner, and Brody, eds., *The New Deal* (Columbus: Ohio State University Press, 1975), I: 288–89; Koistinen, "Hammer and Sword," p. 663; Koistinen, "Mobilizing the World War II Economy," pp. 449–50; Edwin Amenta and Theda Skocpol, "Redefining the New Deal: World War II and the Development of Social Provision in the United States," in Margaret Weir,

Ann Shola Orloff, and Skocpol, eds., *The Politics of Social Policy in the United States* (Princeton: Princeton University Press, 1988), pp. 110–11; Robert K. Murray, "Government and Labor During World War II," *Current History* 37 (September 1959), pp. 147–48; Janeway, *Struggle for Survival*, pp. 12–18; Schwarz, *The Speculator*, pp. 387–88.

39. Harold Smith, "Conference with the President," January 16, 1942, Smith MSS 3; "Dollar-a-Year Men," *Business Week*, April 12, 1941, pp. 46–47.

40. Washington *Star*, November 18, 1943; James Rowe to FDR, February 6, 1941, PSF 144, FDRL.

41. " 'Post-War' Planning—Dollar-a-Year Style," *Nation*, May 23, 1942, p. 588; Thomas Sancton, "Chaos in Production," *New Republic*, August 31, 1942, p. 252; T.R.B., "Dollar-a-Year Bunglers," *New Republic*, September 7, 1942, p. 242; I. F. Stone, "Donald Nelson Has Chosen," *Nation*, March 21, 1942, p. 332.

42. Ibid.; Stone, "Nelson and Guthrie," *Nation*, June 27, 1942, p. 731; Michael Straight, "Dollar-a-Year Sabotage," *New Republic*, March 30, 1942, p. 418; "Don Nelson's Men," *Business Week*, July 4, 1942, pp. 50–52; "The Pain and the Necessity," *Time*, June 29, 1942, p. 18; *Kiplinger Washington Letter*, August 15, 1942, Nelson MSS 2; Bruce Bliven to Max Lerner, August 24, 1942, Lerner MSS 1.

43. Henderson to FDR, January 18, 1943, Hopkins MSS 314; Truman to Nelson, February 16, 1942, Nelson MSS 2; James Mathews to Wayne Coy, November 25, 1941, Democratic National Committee MSS 1171; "Organizing a War Economy," *New Republic*, May 4, 1942, p. 591; Catton, *War Lords of Washington*, pp. 120–22; Donald H. Riddle, "The Truman Committee: A Study in Congressional-Military Relations" (unpublished Ph.D. Dissertation, Princeton University, 1956), pp. 49–50. One of the last liberal appeals for a fundamental restructuring of war mobilization came from the *New Republic* in September 1942, in a call for "a new conception of the function of the WPB and the organization of a war economy." "How to Save the WPB," *New Republic*, September 28, 1942, p. 368.

44. H. S. Person, "Postwar Control of Monopolies," *New Republic*, December 27, 1943, pp. 907–09.

45. Eberstadt to Baruch, November 1, 1942, Eberstadt MSS 23; Catton, *War Lords of Washington*, pp. 310–11; "The Priorities Crisis," *Fortune*, October 1941, p. 58; Koistinen, "Hammer and Sword," p. 640, 665–66; M. A. Adelman, "The Measurement of Industrial Concentration," *Review of Economics and Statistics*, 33 (1951), 269–96; Ernest B. Fricke, "The New Deal and the Modernization of Small Business: The Mcreary Tire & Rubber Company, 1930–1940," *Business History Review* 56 (1982), 559–76; John Morton Blum, *V Was for Victory: Politics and American Culture During World War II* (New York: Harcourt Brace Jovanovich, 1976), pp. 124–27.

46. Wright Patman to FDR, December 19, 1942, OF 3745, FDRL; Patman to James F. Byrnes, March 20, 1943, OF 4735F, FDRL; James Murray to FDR, August 24, September 15, 1942, OF 172, FDRL; Murray, "Memorandum on the Smaller War Plants Corporation," October 13, 1943, OF 4735F, FDRL; Joseph C. O'Mahoney to Eleanor Roosevelt, November 19, 1941, OF 4735F, FDRL; T.R.B., "Washington Notes," *New Republic*, October 25, 1943, p. 572; U.S. Senate, 78th Cong., 1st sess., "American Small Business," January 18, 1943, Senatorial File 63, HSTL.

47. The SWPC was not the first effort to solve the small-business problem. In 1941, Sidney Hillman, then co-chairman of OPM, had tried to institute a program (based on a comparable effort in Britain) of "farming out" parts of complex jobs to small firms. But the program came to naught. Steve Fraser, *Labor Will Rule: Sidney Hillman and the Rise of American Labor* (New York: The Free Press, 1991), pp. 481–82.

48. Spence W. Pitts to E. E. Quantrell, August 6, 1942, WPB 1042, RG 179, NA; M. L. McElroy, "Concentration as a Small-Business Measure," ibid.; "Resolution for the Federal Advisory Council," December 7, 1943, WPB 1076, RG 179, NA; "Planning Committee Recommendation Number 10," July 1, 1942, Nelson MSS 11.

49. Harry S. Truman to Lou E. Holland, February 4, 1941, and June 20, 1942, both in Senatorial File 116, HSTL; Donald J. Mrozek, "Organizing Small Business During World War II: The Experience of the Kansas City Region," *Missouri Historical Review* 81 (January 1977), 174–92.

50. Norman Pond to Donald Nelson, March 3, 1943, WPB 91, RG 179, NA; Holland to Donald Nelson, February 11, 1943, and Nelson to FDR, February 11, 1943, both in OF 4735F, FDRL; Holland to FDR, January 18, 1943, OF 4735F, FDRL; Holland to Harry S. Truman, Senatorial File 63, HSTL; Holland to Donald Nelson, February 16, 1943, Truman Senatorial File 215, HSTL; I. F. Stone, "Crumbs for Small Business," *Nation*, February 20, 1943, p. 259.

51. FDR to James F. Byrnes, December 18, 1942, and Byrnes to FDR, January 14, 1943, both in OF 4735F, FDRL.

52. James F. Byrnes to FDR, January 11, 1943, OF 4735F, FDRL; Wright Patman to FDR, December 19, 1942, OF 3745, FDRL; Patman to Byrnes, March 20, 1943, OF 4735F, FDRL; Byrnes to Marvin McIntyre, January 19, 1943, OF 4735, FDRL; Robert Wood Johnson to Truman, March 9, 1943, Senatorial File 215, HSTL; Johnson to Donald Nelson, April 10, 1943, Nelson to FDR, April 15, 1943, both in OF 4735F, FDRL; Blake O'Connor to Maurice C. Latta, October 16, 1943, OF 4735F, FDRL; Johnson to FDR, September 25, 1943, PPF 3652, FDRL.

53. Roosevelt wrote Harold Smith at the time of the Maverick appointment asking for more funds for SWPC. "A lot hinges on the improvement of their service to the small business people," he said. FDR to Smith, March 8, 1944, OF 4735F, FDRL. Koistinen, "Hammer and Sword," pp. 665–66; FDR to Harold Smith, March 8, 1944, OF 4735F, FDRL; Maverick, "Notes for Address to Congress on Little Business," [n.d.], 1944, OF 4735F, FDRL; "Final Report, Office of Small Business," [n.d.], 1945, OF 3-T, HSTL.

54. Coral Hughes, "A Maverick in Washington," *Coronet*, August 1944; Washington *Sunday Star*, March 5, 1944, OF 4735F, FDRL; Richard B. Henderson, *Maury Maverick: A Political Biography* (Austin: University of Texas Press, 1970), pp. 239–50; Maverick to J. A. Krug, February 16, 1945, OF 4735F, FDRL; Maverick to J. A. Krug, August 30, 1944, Baruch MSS 34; "Thirteenth Bimonthly Report of the SWPC," June 1, 1944, through July 31, 1944, Baruch MSS 34.

55. Harold L. Ickes to FDR, June 9, 1944, James F. Byrnes to FDR, June 14, 1944, both in OF 4735, FDRL; Samuel Lubell to Baruch, January 18, 1944, Baruch MSS 44; Baruch to Maverick, February 13, 1944, Baruch MSS 34; Blum, *V Was for Victory*, pp. 128–29.

56. "Controlled Materials Plan," WPB report, November 2, 1942, "Report to War Production Board on the Controlled Materials Plan," February 9, 1943, Eberstadt to Nelson, October 31, 1943, all in Eberstadt MSS 116; Baruch to Eberstadt, January 28, 1944, Baruch MSS 29; Schwarz, *The Speculator*, pp. 433–34; "Monopoly Bottleneck," *Nation*, January 23, 1943, p. 113; Dorwart, *Eberstadt and Forrestal*, pp. 53–58.

57. "Struggle for Power," *Time*, February 15, 1943, p. 77; Frankfurter diary, February 17, 1943, Frankfurter MSS; "The WPB: Is It?" *Fortune*, March 1943, p. 94; Catton, *War Lords of Washington*, pp. 205–07; Eberstadt to Nelson, February 5, 1943 [apparently unsent], Eberstadt MSS 163.

58. Eberstadt himself hotly denied that he was a restrictionist or an agent of the military and Wall Street, and he spoke scathingly of those liberals who he believed were trying to distort his real beliefs. There was some truth to his complaints. In fact, Eberstadt complained frequently (if not often publicly) of the shortsighted policies of the War Department in ignoring the needs of the civilian economy and refusing to permit planning for a successful peacetime reconversion. But he also spoke with some envy of the Canadian war effort, unencumbered by what he considered America's ill-begotten antitrust laws; and after his departure from government, he denounced the WPB as an agency "being set up to control business after the war." Eberstadt diary, June 15, July 21, 1943, Eberstadt memorandum, May 10, 1943, Eberstadt memorandum, "Principles of Procedure and Organization of Industrial Demobilization," November 6, 1943, all in Eberstadt MSS 23.

59. "The New WPB," *New Republic*, March 1, 1943, p. 272; Schwarz, *The Speculator*, pp. 433–35; Koistinen, "The Hammer and the Sword," pp. 700–03; Koistinen, "Warfare and Power Relations in America: Mobilizing the World War II Economy," in James Titus, ed., *The Home Front and War in the Twentieth Century: The American Experience in Comparative Perspective* (Proceedings of the Tenth Military History Symposium, United States Air Force Academy and Office of Air Force History, USAF, 1984), p. 98; Catton, *War Lords of Washington*, pp. 46, 62.

60. Ickes to Lady Bird Johnson, August 13, 1942, Ickes MSS 161.

61. Roper to Nelson, January 20, 1943, Nelson MSS 2.

62. Harold Smith, memorandum on conversation with the President, February 15, 1943, Smith MSS 3; Schwarz, *The Speculator*, pp. 435–40; Catton, *War Lords of Washington*, pp. 205–07.

63. "I deem it wise to make a change in the direction of war production," Roosevelt's letter to Baruch stated, "and I am coming back to the elder statesman for assistance. I want to appoint you as Chairman of the War Production Board with power to direct the activities of the organization." FDR to Baruch, February 5, 1943, Eberstadt MSS 23. Harold Smith, notes on conference with the President, February 15, 1943, Smith MSS 3; Baruch to Nelson, September 12, 1946, Eberstadt MSS 116; Schwarz, *The Speculator*, pp. 438–39.

64. *New York Times*, February 14, 1943; WPB press release, February 16, 1943, Eberstadt press release, February 16, 1943, both in Eberstadt MSS 116; Isidor Lubin to Leon Henderson, March 9, 1943, Lubin MSS 51; I. F. Stone, "The Charming Mr. Baruch," *Nation*, February 27, 1943, p. 299; "The New

WPB," *New Republic*, March 1, 1943, p. 272; Janeway, *The Struggle for Survival*, p. 320; Catton, *War Lords of Washington*, p. 206; Schwarz, *The Speculator*, pp. 437–38.

65. Nelson, *Arsenal of Democracy*, pp. 388–99; Catton, *War Lords of Washington*, pp. 206–07; Harold Smith, notes on conference with the President, February 15, 1943, Smith MSS 3; Charles W. Chambers to Baruch, February 18, 1943, Baruch MSS 35. Baruch made no public response to this humiliation, and he continued to play an advisory role in Washington for the rest of the war. He later claimed that he had declined the offer to head the WPB. "There is no doubt that had I desired to accept, the President would have made me Chairman of the Board," he wrote Nelson in 1946. "I have a letter to that effect." Baruch to Nelson, September 12, 1946, Eberstadt MSS 116. But much of his private conversation and correspondence over the months following the February imbroglio was suffused with a bitterness and self-pity that suggests otherwise. "I can't laugh anymore," he wrote to Eberstadt in November 1943, in response to a newspaper clipping Eberstadt had sent him. "It's too serious and my life is cracked." Eberstadt to Baruch, November 16, 1943, and Baruch to Eberstadt, [n.d.], both in Eberstadt MSS 23. See also Eberstadt diary, May 3, 1943, Eberstadt MSS 23.

66. Baruch to Leon Henderson, November 30, 1943, Baruch MSS 29; Baruch, "Confidential Memorandum," June 30, 1943, Baruch MSS 31; I. F. Stone, "The Charming Mr. Baruch," pp. 298–99; Stone, "Mr. Nelson and Complacency," *Nation*, July 17, 1943, p. 62; Stone, "Nelson vs. Wilson," *Nation*, September 22, 1944, p. 260; " 'Dear Charlie,' " *Time*, September 4, 1944, pp. 18–19; FDR to Nelson, November 2, 1944, Nelson MSS 2; Norman Pond to Donald Nelson, March 3, 1943, WPB 91, RG 179, NA; James W. Fesler, memorandum on Nelson's farewell to the WPB, October 4, 1944, WPB 148, RG 179, NA; Bernard Baruch to Donald Nelson, November 16, 1943, Nelson MSS 2; "He Went to Moscow," *Time*, November 22, 1943, pp. 20–21; Harold Ickes to Charles E. Wilson, September 6, 1944, Ickes MSS 380; "Business Loses Two Spokesmen in WPB Reconversion Shake-up," *Newsweek*, September 4, 1944, pp. 66–68.

67. "Nelson, Wilson and Krug," *New Republic*, September 4, 1944, p. 265; Helen Fuller, "Krug and Reconversion," *New Republic*, August 20, 1945, p. 219; Krug to Manly Fleischmann, November 23, 1943, Krug MSS 1; Krug to Forrest Allen, October 19, 1943, Krug MSS 1.

68. Eberstadt diary, May 31, June 15, 1943, Eberstadt MSS 23; I. F. Stone, "Enter the New OWM," *Nation*, June 5, 1943, p. 798; Robert K. Murray, "Government and Labor During World War II," *Current History* 3 (September 1959), 148; Stolper to Foreign Office [London], June 4, 1943, FO 371-34213, PRO; Schwarz, *The Speculator*, p. 447; organizational chart, [n.d.], Baruch MSS 34; David Robertson, *Sly and Able: A Political Biography of Janes F. Byrnes* (New York: W. W. Norton, 1984), chap. 12.

69. *New York Times*, September 21, 1948; New York *World Telegram and Sun*, March 10, 1950; W. M. Jeffers to Eberstadt, March 20, 1950, Eberstadt MSS 116; Eliot Janeway, "Where was Mr. Nelson?" *Saturday Review*, September 7, 1946, p. 11; Eberstadt letter to multiple correspondents, August 23, 1946, Eberstadt MSS 116. See also Brian Waddell, "Economic Mobilization for

World War II and the Transformation of the US. State," *Politics and Society* 22 (1994), 165–94, which discusses the role of industry domination of mobilization in weakening the civilian state.

70. The literature describing the origins and character of what has come to be known as the military-industrial complex is vast. C. Wright Mills was among the first scholars to describe its characteristics in *The Power Elite* (New York: Oxford University Press, 1956), pp. 171–224. William Appleman Williams, similarly, cited the "military-industrial complex" as part of "an imperial complex" that dominated American foreign policy and political economy; see *Americans in a Changing World: A History of the United States in the Twentieth Century* (New York: Harper & Row, 1978), p. 375. Daniel Yergin describes the complex as a central element of the "national-security state" in *Shattered Peace: The Origins of the Cold War and the National Security State* (Boston: Houghton Mifflin, 1977). See also Paul A. C. Koistinen, *The Military-Industrial Complex: A Historical Perspective* (New York: Praeger, 1980), and "Mobilizing the World War II Economy," *Pacific Historical Review* 42 (1973), 443–78; Bruce G. Brunton, "The Origins and Early Development of the American Military-Industrial Complex" (Ph.D. Dissertation, University of Utah, 1989), and "An Historical Perspective on the Future of the Military-Industrial Complex," *Social Science Journal* 28 (1991), 45–62; Charles A. Cannon, "The Military-Industrial Complex in American Politics, 1953–1970" (Ph.D. Dissertation, Stanford, 1975); Gregory Hooks, *Forging the Military-Industrial Complex: World War II's Battle of the Potomac* (Urbana: University of Illinois Press, 1991); Steve Fraser, *Labor Will Rule: Sidney Hillman and the Rise of American Labor* (New York: The Free Press, 1991), pp. 481–83; Gerald D. Nash, "The West and the Military-Industrial Complex," *Montana* 40 (1990), 72–75; Ben Baack and Edward Ray, "The Political Economy of the Origins of the Military-Industrial Complex in the United States," *Journal of Economic History* 45 (1985), pp. 369–75; Roger W. Lotchin, "The Political Culture of the Metropolitan-Military Complex," *Social Science History* 16 (1992), 275–99; Huntington, *The Soldier and the State*, chaps. 12–13; Gautam Sen, "The Economics of U.S. Defense: The Military Industrial Complex and Neo-Marxist Economic Theories Reconsidered," *Millennium: Journal of International Studies* 15 (1986), 179–95.

# Chapter Nine

1. Irving Bernstein, *Turbulent Years: A History of the American Worker, 1933–1941* (Boston: Houghton Mifflin, 1969), pp. 769–71; David Brody, *Workers in Industrial America* (New York: Oxford University Press, 1980), pp. 82–116, 138–46; Robert K. Murray, "Government and Labor During World War II," *Current History* 37 (September 1959), p. 152.

2. Brody, *Workers in Industrial America*, pp. 146–58; John P. Frey, "Labor's Stake in Capitalism," *Nation's Business*, September 1943, pp. 27, 70–74; Paul A. C. Koistinen, "The Hammer and the Sword: Labor, the Military, and Industrial Mobilization, 1920–1945" (Ph.D. Dissertation, University of California, Berkeley, 1964), pp. 255–56; Christopher L. Tomlins, *The State and the*

*Unions: Law, and the Organized Labor Movement in America, 1880–1960* (New York: Cambridge University Press, 1985), pp. 148, 195–96; Steve Fraser, "The Labor Question," in Fraser and Gary Gerstle, eds., *The Rise and Fall of the New Deal Order* (Princeton: Princeton University Press, 1989), pp. 55–84; Lizabeth Cohen, *Making a New Deal: Industrial Workers in Chicago, 1919–1939* (New York: Cambridge University Press, 1990), pp. 251–89.

3. Harry Hopkins, speech to Des Moines Economic Club, February 24, 1939, Clapper MSS 153; I. F. Stone, "Labor and the Long View," *Nation*, March 7, 1942, p. 276; Karl E. Klare, "Judicial Deradicalization of the Wagner Act and the Origins of Modern Legal Consciousness, 1937–1941," *Minnesota Law Review* 65 (1978), 265–339; Kenneth M. Casebeer, "Holder of the Pen: An Interview with Leon Keyserling on Drafting the Wagner Act," *University of Miami Law Review* 42 (November 1987), pp. 285–363; Christopher L. Tomlins, "The New Deal, Collective Bargaining, and the Triumph of Industrial Pluralism," *Industrial and Labor Relations Review* 39 (October 1985), 19–34; Tomlins, *The State and the Unions*, 195–96, 247; James B. Atleson, "Wartime Labor Regulation, the Industrial Pluralists, and the Law of Collective Bargaining," in Nelson Lichtenstein and Howell John Harris, eds., *Industrial Democracy in America: The Ambiguous Promise* (New York: Cambridge University Press, 1993), pp. 142–75; Koistinen, "The Hammer and the Sword," pp. 86–87, 103.

4. For discussions of the political economy of World War I, see Robert D. Cuff, *The War Industries Board: Business-Government Relations during World War I* (Baltimore: The Johns Hopkins University Press, 1973), and David M. Kennedy, *Over Here: The First World War and American Society* (New York: Oxford University Press, 1980), pp. 93–143. On Lewis, see Melvyn Dubofsky and Warren Van Tine, *John L. Lewis* (New York: Quadrangle/New York Times Book Co., 1977), pp. 339–70.

5. Morris Cooke, "Why Labor Is in Politics," *New Republic*, October 9, 1944, p. 455; Leo XIII, "On the Condition of Workers," in *Two Basic Social Encyclicals* (New York: Benziger Brothers, 1943), pp. 3–81; Pius XI, *Quadragesimo Ano/Forty Years After Reconstructing Social Order* (New York: Benziger Brothers, 1943), pp. 20–24; Neil Betten, *Catholic Activism and the Industrial Worker* (Gainesville: University Presses of Florida, 1976), pp. 10–12, 22–24, 113–15; David J. O'Brien, *American Catholics and Social Reform: The New Deal Years* (New York: Oxford University Press, 1968), pp. 17–21; George Q. Flynn, *American Catholics and Social Reform* (Lexington: University of Kentucky Press, 1968), pp. 22–35.

6. Mordecai Ezekiel, *$2500 a Year* (New York: Harcourt, Brace, 1936), pp. 68–104, 292–96.

7. Ezekiel, "Democratic Economic Planning," *Common Sense*, July 1938, pp. 8–10; Ezekiel, *Jobs for All Through Industrial Expansion* (New York: Alfred A. Knopf, 1939), pp. 11–18, 58–63, 104–11, 284–85, 290–91.

8. Alan Walker, "The CIO Goes Out for Defense," *New Republic*, October 13, 1941, pp. 467–68; John Chamberlain, "The Steelworkers," *Fortune*, February 1944, pp. 165–66, 209–28.

9. Murray to FDR, December 18, 1940, Murray to FDR, March 11, 1941, both in OF 2546, FDRL; Walker, "CIO Goes Out for Defense," p. 468; T.R.B.,

"Industry Committees," *New Republic*, December 30, 1940, p. 899; I. F. Stone, "Little Steel 'Soviets,' " *Nation*, December 28, 1940, pp. 650–51; Irwin Ross, "Labor, Capital & Co.: Unions and Management Get Together," *Harper's*, September 1941, p. 420.

10. James Robb to FDR, February 20, 1941, OF 172, FDRL; Rose M. Stein, "The Murray Plan," *Nation*, May 3, 1941, pp. 526–27; "Labor's National Emergency," *Business Week*, November 22, 1941, p. 16; David Brody, "The New Deal and World War II," in John Braeman, Robert H. Bremner, David Brody, eds., *The New Deal* (Columbus: Ohio State University Press, 1975), I, 282–83; Nelson Lichtenstein, *Labor's War at Home: The CIO in World War II* (New York: Cambridge University Press, 1982), pp. 41–42, 84–85.

11. J. Edgar Hoover to Francis Biddle, May 22, 1940, enclosing copy of letter from Victor and Walter Reuther to Melvin and Gladys Bishop, January 20, 1934, PSF 77, FDRL; Lichtenstein, *Labor's War at Home*, pp. 86–87. A recent biography is John Barnard, *Walter Reuther and the Rise of the Auto Workers* (Boston: Little, Brown, 1983).

12. George R. Clark, "The Strange Story of the Reuther Plan," *Harper's*, May 1942, pp. 645–49; I. F. Stone, "Labor's Plan: 500 Planes a Day," *Nation*, December 21, 1940, pp. 624–25; Barton J. Bernstein, "The Automobile Industry and the Coming of the Second World War," *Southwestern Social Science Quarterly* 41 (1966), 23–26; Brody, "The New Deal and World War II," pp. 281–82.

13. Clark, "The Strange Story of the Reuther Plan," pp. 647–49, 654; "Why We Are Falling Behind," *New Republic*, February 17, 1941, p. 236; Brody, "The New Deal and World War II," pp. 281–84; Bruce Catton, *War Lords of Washington* (New York: Harcourt, Brace, 1948), p. 96.

14. Max Lerner, "A Fighting Faith in Labor," *New Republic*, January 13, 1941, p. 52; Robert S. Lynd, "Not That Way, Mr. Nelson," *Nation*, April 4, 1942, p. 394; Catton, *War Lords of Washington*, pp. 92–96.

15. Clark, "The Strange Story of the Reuther Plan," pp. 648–49; "On the Domestic Front," *New Republic*, December 15, 1941, p. 812; Lichtenstein, *Labor's War at Home*, p. 87; Bernstein, "The Automobile Industry and the Coming of the Second World War," pp. 22–33; Brody, "The New Deal and World War II," p. 284.

16. "Why We Are Falling Behind," p. 236; form letter, National Small Business Men's Association, January 19, 1942, OF 172, FDRL; Brody, "The New Deal and World War II," p. 285; J. Douglas Brown to Sidney Hillman, June 25, August 4, 1941, Hillman MSS 101; Steve Fraser, *Labor Will Rule: Sidney Hillman and the Rise of American Labor* (New York: The Free Press, 1991), pp. 474–77.

17. I. F. Stone, "What Mr. Knudsen Thinks," *Nation*, March 29, 1941, p. 372; Clark, "The Strange Story of the Reuther Plan," pp. 649–50; Fraser, *Labor Will Rule*, p. 474; Catton, *War Lords of Washington*, p. 99; Lichtenstein, *Labor's War at Home*, pp. 87–89.

18. James S. Adams to Donald Nelson, January 14, 1942, Nelson MSS 2; Victor G. Reuther, "Labor in the War—and After," *Antioch Review* 3 (1943), 315; *Labor's Monthly Survey*, March 1942, p. 6; "Why We Are Falling Behind," p. 236; "New Dealers Still Wanted," *New Republic*, January 13, 1941, p. 40;

"Revive the Reuther Plan," *Nation*, July 26, 1941, p. 65; Fred DeArmond, "Move Over Managers," *Nation's Business*, February 1942, pp. 38, 64; Catton, *War Lords of Washington*, p. 106; Brody, "The New Deal and World War II," p. 287; Lichtenstein, *Labor's War at Home*, pp. 88–89; Bruno Stein, "Labor's Role in Government Agencies During World War II," *Journal of Economic History* 17 (1957), 401–02; John Chamberlain, "The Steelworkers," *Fortune*, February 1944, p. 226; Morris Cooke, "Why Labor Is in Politics," *New Republic*, October 9, 1944, p. 455.

19. William Green to FDR, December 17, 1941, AFL Press Release, December 15, 1941, FDR to Green, December 22, 1941, all in OF 142, FDRL; "The No-Strike Agreement," *Nation*, January 3, 1942, p. 5; Murray, "Government and Labor During World War II," p. 147.

20. "Army Takes Over," *Business Week*, June 14, 1941, pp. 14–15; "Labor's National Emergency," *Business Week*, November 22, 1941, pp. 15–16; "Strikes—1941 v. 1918," ibid., p. 72; Lichtenstein, *Labor's War at Home*, pp. 50–52.

21. "No Surrender," *Business Week*, December 6, 1941, p. 14; "Full Speed Ahead on Defense," *Labor's Monthly Survey*, November 1941, p. 1; "Labor Freedom the Basis of All Freedom," *Labor's Monthly Survey*, December 1941, p. 1; "NDMB Job: To Keep Talk Going," *Business Week*, June 28, 1941, p. 44; Edwin Amenta and Theda Skocpol, "Redefining the New Deal: World War II and the Development of Social Provision in the United States," in Margaret Weir, Ann Shola Orloff, and Skocpol, eds., *The Politics of Social Policy in the United States* (Princeton: Princeton University Press, 1988), p. 114; Henry L. Stimson to FDR, May 26, 1941, PPF 20, FDRL.

22. Harold Ickes to FDR, August 1, 1942, Ickes MSS 206; John E. Hamm to James Rowe, March 4, 1941, Henderson MSS 36; Koistinen, "Hammer and Sword," pp. 165–66, 178.

23. Wayne Coy to FDR, January 29, 1942, OF 2546, FDRL; Gardner Jackson to Marvin McIntyre, May 13, 1942, Jackson to FDR, May 1, 1942, FDR to Mcintyre, May 5, 1942, OF 2546, FDRL; Dubofsky and Van Tine, *John L. Lewis*, pp. 418–23; Murray, "Government and Labor During World War II," p. 149.

24. Philip Murray to FDR, November 12, 1943, OF 4735, FDRL; William Green to FDR, July 20, 1942, OF 142, FDRL; Dubofsky and Van Tine, *John L. Lewis*, p. 418.

25. John Chamberlain, "Democracy and the Closed Shop," *Fortune*, January 1942, pp. 64–65, 126–37; James MacGregor Burns, "Maintenance of Membership: A Study in Administrative Statesmanship," *Journal of Politics* 10 (1948), 110–16; Lichtenstein, *Labor's War at Home*, pp. 78–80.

26. Felix Frankfurter to FDR, March 20, 1942, PSF 151, FDRL; Wayne Coy to FDR, April 28, 1942, OF 2546, FDRL; Brody, "The New Deal and World War II," pp. 279–80; Klare, "Judicial Deradicalization," p. 318; Richard W. Resh, "Tutors to Society: Five American Intellectuals and War, 1917–1945" (Ph.D. Dissertation, University of Wisconsin, 1966), p. 119; Milton Derber, "Labor-Management in World War II," *Current History* 48 (June 1965), 343–45.

27. David Brody, "The Emergence of Mass-Production Unionism," in

John Braeman, Robert H. Bremner, and Everett Walters, eds., *Change and Continuity in Twentieth Century America* (Columbus: Ohio State University Press, 1964), 243–62; Robert S. McElvaine, *The Great Depression: America, 1929–1941* (New York: Times Books, 1984), pp. 291–97; David Montgomery, *Workers' Control in America* (New York: Cambridge University Press, 1979), pp. 153–80; Brody, *Workers in Industrial America*, pp. 120–72; Nelson Lichtenstein and Howell John Harris, "Introduction: A Century of Industrial Democracy in America," in Lichtenstein and Harris, eds., *Industrial Democracy in America*, pp. 1–19; Gary Gerstle, *Working-Class Americanism: The Politics of Labor in a Textile City, 1914–1960* (New York: Cambridge University Press, 1989), pp. 182–86, 219–25; Cohen, *Making a New Deal*, pp. 283–89, 305–13, 365–67.

28. Nelson Lichtenstein, "Great Expectations: The Promise of Industrial Jurisprudence and Its Demise, 1930–1960," in Lichtenstein and Harris, eds., *Industrial Democracy in America*, pp. 113–41; Cohen, *Making a New Deal*, pp. 301–13.

29. OWI Intelligence Reports 35 and 36, August 7, 14, 1942, MacLeish MSS 53; "Statement to the President of the United States by the Combined War Labor Board," June 3, 1943, "Memorandum Submitted by CIO Members of Combined Labor Victory Committee," [n.d.], 1943, both in OF 4735, FDRL; Polenberg, *War and Society*, p. 160; Dwight MacDonald, "The World's Biggest Union," *Common Sense*, November 1943, pp. 411–14; "What's Itching Labor," *Fortune*, November 1944, pp. 101–02, 228–36.

30. Polenberg, *War and Society*, pp. 160–61; Al Nash, "A Unionist Remembers: Militant Unionism and Political Factions," *Dissent* 24 (1977), p. 185; Hugh M. Ayer, "Hoosier Labor in the Second World War," *Indiana Magazine of History* 59 (1963), 112; Harvard Sitkoff, "Racial Militancy and Interracial Violence in the Second World War," *Journal of American History* 58 (1971), 661–81; Joshua Freeman, "Delivering the Goods: Industrial Unionism During World War II," *Labor History* 19 (1978), 570–93; Alan Winkler, "The Philadelphia Transit Strike of 1949," *Journal of American History* 59 (1972), 74–89.

31. Harold Ickes to John J. McCloy, December 30, 1943, Ickes MSS 206; Isidor Lubin to Harry Hopkins, August 11, 1944, Hopkins MSS 314; "Hope for a Free World?" *Labor's Monthly Survey*, March 1945, pp. 1–2; "Swing to Right," *Business Week*, August 16, 1941, pp. 65–66; Reuther, "Labor in the War—and After," pp. 311–27; Polenberg, *War and Society*, pp. 160–61; Lichtenstein, *Labor's War at Home*, pp. 154–55, 185–88.

32. T. C. Hannah, "Effect of Good Management on Employer and Employee Relationships: Who Is the Master?" *Vital Speeches of the Day*, July 15, 1943, pp. 593–607; "No Surrender," *Business Week*, December 6, 1941, p. 14; "The 40-Hour Week," *Time*, March 30, 1942, pp. 1–2; Merle Thorpe, "An American Resource in Jeopardy," *Nation's Business*, February 1942, p. 13; Thurman Arnold, "Labor Against Itself," *Reader's Digest*, January 1944, pp. 39–40; DeArmond, "Move Over Managers," pp. 34–38; Howell John Harris, *The Right to Manage: Industrial Relations Policies of American Business in the 1940s* (Madison: University of Wisconsin Press, 1982), pp. 116–45; Koistinen, "Hammer and Sword," pp. 251–53.

33. George H. Gallup, *The Gallup Poll: Public Opinion, 1935–1971*, 3 vols. (New York: Random House, 1972), I: 355, 365, 389, 418; Fred A. Virkus to FDR, January 19, 1942, OF 172, FDRL; Thayer Harp to FDR, April 30, 1942, OF 487, FDRL.

34. Max Lerner, "A Fighting Faith in Labor," *New Republic*, January 13, 1941, p. 52; Julius Hochman, "Let's Look at Labor. VII. The Opportunity for Leadership," *Nation*, September 11, 1943, pp. 290–94; William Allen White to Robert La Follette, April 7, 1942, White MSS C397.

35. Victor Reuther, "Labor in the War—and After," pp. 315–23; UAW-CIO Press Release, January 3, 1944, OF 2546, FDRL; Sumner H. Slichter, "The Labor Crisis," *Atlantic Monthly*, February 1944, pp. 37–41; Freeman, "Delivering the Goods," pp. 577–78; Brody, "The New Deal and World War II," pp. 279–80.

36. Polenberg, *War and Society*, pp. 161–62; Dubofsky and Van Tine, *John L. Lewis*, pp. 421–22.

37. Hadley Cantril, "Suggestions for Reversing the Adverse Trend of Public Opinion on the Administration's Conduct of Domestic Affairs," July 20, 1943, PPF 1829, FDRL; Leon Henderson, speech to UJA Appeal Rally, June 29, 1943, Lubin MSS 51; Robert Wood Johnson to FDR, July 15, 1943, OF 4735-7, FDRL; "The Miners Have a Case," *New Republic*, June 14, 1943, p. 780; "King Coal," *Economist*, May 22, 1943, p. 656; Gallup, *The Gallup Poll*, I: 389; Polenberg, *War and Society*, pp. 161–66; Murray, "Government and Labor During World War II," p. 149.

38. Harold Ickes to FDR, June 2, June 7, 1943, OF 4735, FDRL; William H. Davis to Ickes, December 31, 1943, Ickes to Davis, January 4, 1944, both in Ickes MSS 380; Dubofsky and Van Tine, *John L. Lewis*, pp. 434–39; Lichtenstein, *Labor's War at Home*, pp. 159–61.

39. Francis Biddle to FDR, June 24, 1943, with "Proposed Veto Message re S. 796," Biddle to Harold D. Smith, [n.d.], 1943, William H. Davis to FDR, July 30, 1943, all in OF 4735, FDRL; Josiah W. Bailey to James F. Byrnes, February 10, 1943, PSF 147, FDRL; Gustav Stolper to Foreign Office, May 13, 1943, FO371—34213, PRO; Roland Young, *Congressional Politics in the Second World War* (New York: Columbia University Press, 1956), pp. 63–67; Richard N. Chapman, *Contours of Public Policy, 1939–1945* (New York: Garland, 1981), pp. 229–33; Murray, "Government and Labor During World War II," p. 150; Lichtenstein, *Labor's War at Home*, pp. 167–68; Polenberg, *War and Society*, pp. 166–69; Victor Reuther, "Labor in the War—and After," p. 315.

40. This account of Hillman's early life relies heavily on Steve Fraser's excellent biography, *Labor Will Rule*. See also Matthew Josephson, *Sidney Hillman: Statesman of American Labor* (Garden City: Doubleday, 1952), and Len DeCaux, *Labor Radical: From the Wobblies to the CIO* (Boston: Beacon Press, 1970), pp. 328–44. On the "new unionism," see Fraser, "Dress Rehearsal for the New Deal: Shop-Floor Insurgents, Political Elites, and Industrial Democracy in the Amalgamated Clothing Workers," in Michael H. Frisch and Daniel Walkowitz, eds., *Working-Class America: Essays on Labor, Community, and American Society* (Urbana: University of Illinois Press, 1983), pp. 212–55; and Lichtenstein, *Labor's War at Home*, pp. 33–36.

41. Mike Davis, "The Barren Marriage of American Labor and the Demo-

cratic Party," in _Prisoners of the American Dream_ (New York: Verso, 1986), pp. 67–68; Fraser, _Labor Will Rule_, pp. 195, 230.

42. Ibid., pp. 262, 320; Ronald Radosh, "The Corporate Ideology of American Labor Leaders from Gompers to Hillman," in James Weinstein and David W. Eakins, eds., _For a New America: Essays in History and Politics from Studies on the Left, 1959–1967_ (New York: Random House, 1972), pp. 125–34, 141–49.

43. Ibid., pp. 67–69; Alan Brinkley, "The Election of 1936," in Arthur M. Schlesinger, Jr., ed., _Running for President: The Candidates and Their Images_ (New York: Simon and Schuster, 1994), pp. 187–88; Fraser, _Labor Will Rule_, p. 358.

44. Hillman, "The Promise of American Labor," _New Republic_, November 8, 1939, p. 64; Henry A. Wallace to FDR, February 21, 1939, PSF 3, FDRL; _New York Times_, February 19, 1939; Fraser, _Labor Will Rule_, pp. 448–49.

45. Hillman, "Speech to New England Conference," November 24, 1939, Hillman MSS 170-8; "CIO Convention—Atlantic City, November 18–23," unsigned memorandum, December 5, 1940, OF 2546, FDRL; Benjamin Stolberg, "Sidney Hillman: Success Story," _Saturday Evening Post_, October 19, 1940, pp. 13, 96–97; Koistinen, "Hammer and Sword," pp. 136–37; _New York Times_, July 2, 5, 6, 1938; Fraser, _Labor Will Rule_, pp. 437, 448–49.

46. J. Douglas Brown to Hillman, June 10, 11, 1941, Hillman MSS 101; "Knudsen's Coup d'État," _Nation_, April 5, 1941, pp. 396–97; "What Is Defense Labor Policy?," _Business Week_, February 8, 1941, p. 15; Catton, _War Lords of Washington_, p. 97; Koistinen, "Hammer and Sword," pp. 100–02; Fraser, _Labor Will Rule_, pp. 459, 468.

47. Catton, _War Lords of Washington_, p. 99; Leo Huberman, "Murray of the CIO," _Who_, May 1941, p. 64; Brody, "The New Deal and World War II," p. 287; Fraser, _Labor Will Rule_, pp. 430, 475.

48. FDR to Hillman, April 18, 1942, Hillman MSS 109; Hillman to FDR, May 1, 1942, Hillman MSS 83; Stein, "Labor's Role in Government Agencies During World War II," pp. 397–99; Murray, "Government and Labor During World War II," p. 150.

49. Fraser, _Labor Will Rule_, p. 490; Frankfurter to FDR, March 20, 1942, PSF 151, FDRL, and in Max Freedman, ed., _Roosevelt and Frankfurter: Their Correspondence, 1928–1945_ (Boston: Atlantic Monthly Press, 1967), pp. 652–54; Stolberg, "Sidney Hillman," p. 92; Koistinen, "Hammer and Sword," pp. 136–37; Bruno Stein, "Labor's Role in Government Agencies During World War II," _Journal of Economic History_ 17 (1957), 393, 387–99.

50. Davis, "The Barren Marriage of American Labor and the Democratic Party," pp. 83–86; Fraser, _Labor Will Rule_, pp. 503–38.

51. Ibid., pp. 503–05; Hillman, address to Massachusetts CIO Convention, April 4, 1943, Hillman MSS 171.

52. Fraser, _Labor Will Rule_, p. 506.

53. Victor Reuther, "Labor in the War and After," pp. 324–25; Walter P. Reuther, "Reuther Challenges 'Our Fear of Abundance,'" _New York Times Magazine_, September 16, 1945, p. 35; William Green, "Protecting Our American System of Freedom: If I Were an Industrial Manager," _Vital Speeches of the Day_, January 15, 1945, p. 219; Barton Bernstein, "Walter Reuther and the

General Motors Strike of 1945–1946," *Michigan History* 49 (1965), 277; Edward Cowdrick, "Labor's Goals," *Nation's Business*, June 1944, pp. 21, 70.

54. See. e.g., Davis, "The Barren Marriage of American Labor and the Democratic Party," pp. 52–101.

55. Bernstein, *Turbulent Years*, pp. 768–83.

56. Nelson Lichtenstein, "From Corporatism to Collective Bargaining: Organized Labor and the Eclipse of Social Democracy in the Postwar Era," in Fraser and Gerstle, eds., *The Rise and Fall of the New Deal Order*, pp. 122–52. Lichtenstein identifies substantial working-class efforts to broaden the movement's economic and political agenda after the war and argues, much more strongly than I do, that significant changes were still possible in those years.

## Chapter Ten

1. David Kennedy, *Over Here: The First World War in American Society* (New York: Oxford University Press, 1980), pp. 59–69; George Creel, *How We Advertised America* (New York: Harper & Brothers, 1920).

2. Allan M. Winkler, *The Politics of Propaganda: The Office of War Information, 1942–1945* (New Haven: Yale University Press, 1978), pp. 9–42. A recent biography of MacLeish is Scott Donaldson, *Archibald MacLeish: An American Life* (Boston: Houghton Mifflin, 1992). See also John Morton Blum, "Archibald MacLeish: Art for Action," in Blum, *Liberty, Justice, Order* (New York: Norton, 1993), pp. 227–60.

3. Archibald MacLeish, "The Unimagined America," *Atlantic Monthly*, June 1943, pp. 59–63.

4. See, for example, George Soule, "The Lessons of Last Time," *New Republic*, February 2, 1942, pp. 163–84.

5. See, e.g., I. F. Stone, "What F.D.R. Forgot," *Nation*, January 8, 1944, p. 35; George Soule, "War in Washington," *New Republic*, September 27, 1939, p. 204.

6. Such hopes often assumed extravagant forms. Bruce Bliven, an editor of the *New Republic*, began preparing a special issue in 1944 on the postwar economy. It was to describe "the America that might be, can be, and must be. . . . Utopia in our time." Bliven to Max Lerner, October 3, 1944, Lerner MSS 1.

7. I. F. Stone, "What F.D.R. Forgot," p. 35.

8. George Soule, "Full Employment After the War," *New Republic*, August 10, 1942, p. 167; Milo Perkins, "The Future We Fight For," *New Republic*, June 15, 1942, pp. 820–21.

9. Mel Scott, "Neighborhoods of Tomorrow," *Recreation*, September 1945, pp. 324–25; John D. Millett, *The Process and Organization of Government Planning* (New York: Columbia University Press, 1947), p. 1; George Soule, "Planning Wins," *New Republic*, June 22, 1942, p. 857; Charles E. Merriam and Frank P. Bourgin, "Jefferson as a Planner of National Resources," *Ethics*, July 1943, p. 292.

10. "Is National Planning Inevitable?" *America's Town Meeting of the Air,*

April 1, 1937, p. 11; "Economic Planning: 1938," *Common Sense*, July 1938, pp. 3–4; Lewis Mumford, "Mr. Lippmann's Heresy," *New Republic*, September 29, 1937, p. 220; Harold Strauss, "Make America Produce! Liberty Is Divisible," *Nation*, December 7, 1940, pp. 552–55; Louise S. Cobb, "Wartime Recreation Councils in Small Cities," *Recreation*, March 1944, pp. 684–86; Charles E. Merriam, "Observations on Centralization and Decentralization: The Federal System in War Time," *State Government*, January 1943, pp. 3–5, 18; Barry Karl, *Executive Reorganization and Reform in the New Deal* (Chicago: University of Chicago Press, 1963), pp. 73–79; Philip W. Warken, *A History of the National Resources Planning Board, 1933–1943* (New York: Garland, 1979), pp. 28–30.

11. Means, "The Road to Freedom," June 15, 1945, Means MSS 37.

12. Mordecai Ezekiel, *Jobs for All Through Industrial Expansion* (New York: Alfred A. Knopf, 1939); William Harlan Hale, "The Men Behind the President. 3. What They Think," *Common Sense*, July 1938, p. 19; Leo Barnes, "The Anatomy of Full Employment," *Nation*, May 26, 1945, pp. 596–97; Ezekiel, "Towards a Planned Economy," in J. Donald Kingsley and David W. Petegorsky, eds., *Strategy for Democracy* (New York: Longmans, Green, 1942), pp. 151–65.

13. Ezekiel, untitled memorandum, March 1943, Ezekiel MSS 12. See also "Can Good Living Standards Be Assured Americans After the War?" *Town Meeting*, January 28, 1943, p. 14.

14. "Enemy of Abundance," *New Republic*, February 15, 1943, p. 197. See also Stuart Chase, "Production First," *Nation*, January 13, 1945, p. 39; Chester Bowles to Walter Reuther, December 2, 1947, Bowles MSS, Part II, I, 44; Bowles, "A Plan to Prevent Depression," [n.d.], 1946, ibid., 20.

15. I. F. Stone, "On Reconversion," *Nation*, August 12, 1944, p. 176.

16. Stuart Chase, "Financing America's Future. III. 'Nothing to Fear But Fear,' " *Nation*, October 23, 1943, p. 466.

17. Seymour Harris, "The Price of Prosperity. I," *New Republic*, January 15, 1945, p. 75.

18. Redvers Opie to Alvin Hansen, May 19, 1943, Hansen MSS 3.10; Archibald MacLeish to Keynes, July 8, 1941, and October 10, 1944, MacLeish MSS 12; Felix Frankfurter to Alfred Harcourt, February 2, 1939, copy in MacLeish MSS 8; William O. Douglas to Keynes, July 29, 1937, Douglas MSS 8.

19. Paul Samuelson, "The General Theory," in Seymour Harris, ed., *The New Economics: Keynes' Influence on Theory and Public Policy* (New York: Alfred A. Knopf, 1947), p. 152; Paul Sweezy, "Keynes: The Economist," ibid., p. 107; Robert Lekachman, *The Age of Keynes* (New York: Random House, 1966), pp. 150–52.

20. Bliven to Max Lerner, August 24, 1942, Lerner MSS 1.

21. Richard Strout, "Hansen of Harvard," *New Republic*, December 29, 1941, p. 888; Alvin W. Hansen, "Wanted: Ten Million Jobs," *Atlantic Monthly*, September 1943, pp. 65–69; Hansen and Guy Greer, "The Federal Debt and the Future," *Harper's*, April 1942, p. 500; Hansen to Marriner Eccles, July 29, 1944, Eccles MSS 7-12; Hansen, "Reconversion and Postwar Needs," in CIO Political Action Committee, *Full Employment: Proceedings of the Conference on Full Employment* (New York: CIO PAC, 1944), p. 10; "Minutes of Meeting

of the Subcommittee on Employment Policies," State Department, October 14, 1943, Hansen MSS 3.10.

22. Hansen to Eccles, August 18, 1944, enclosing a copy of "Postwar Employment Program," August 17, 1944, Eccles MSS 7-12.

23. Hansen and Guy Greer, "Toward Full Use," *Fortune*, November 1942, pp. 170–72; Hansen and Greer, "The Federal Debt and the Future," *Harper's*, April 1942, pp. 489–500; Hansen to unidentified correspondent, [n.d.], 1944, Hansen MSS 3.11; Henry C. Simons, "Hansen on Fiscal Policy," *Journal of Political Economy* 50 (April 1942), 161–62; Robert Skidelsky, "Keynes and the Reconstruction of Liberalism," *Encounter* 52 (April 1979), pp. 35–36; Herbert Stein, *The Fiscal Revolution in America* (Chicago: University of Chicago Press, 1969), p. 145.

24. Chase, "Financing America's Future. III," p. 466.

25. Boris Shishkin, "The Next Depression," *American Federationist*, October 1944, pp. 3–6, 21–22; Stuart Chase, "When War Spending Stops," *Harper's*, June 1943, p. 22; George Soule, "The Post-War Depression," *New Republic*, July 20, 1942, p. 76; Harold Strauss, "Don't Plan for Collapse," *Nation*, January 3, 1942, pp. 9–12; Stanley Lebergott, "Shall We *Guarantee* Full Employment?" *Harper's*, February 1945, pp. 193–96; Thomas R. Amlie, "Jobs for All," *Nation*, November 27, 1943, pp. 625–52.

26. A Cantril poll conducted in 1943 found that over 90 percent of those asked agreed that "one of our aims should be to see that everyone in this country has a chance to get a job after the war," and that 68 percent of them thought it could be done. Oscar Cox to Harry Hopkins, February 10, 1943, Hopkins MSS 39; typescript of introduction to Hansen and Harvey S. Perloff, *State and Local Finance in the National Economy*, 1943, Hansen MSS 3.11; Hansen to Eccles, August 18, 1944, Eccles MSS 7-12.

27. Charles E. Merriam, "Planning in a Democracy," *The American City*, August 1940, p. 71.

28. I. F. Stone, "The Truman Program," *Nation*, September 15, 1945, p. 247; memorandum from "Division Labor Assistants" to Joseph Keenan and Clinton Golden, August 22, 1944, WPB 2305, RG 179, NA; Jordan Schwarz, *The Speculator: Bernard M. Baruch in Washington, 1917–1965* (Chapel Hill: University of North Carolina Press, 1981), pp. 454–56.

29. Donald Nelson, "Active Reserve Producers Plan," February 28, 1944, Nelson MSS 12; W. Y. Elliott to Nelson, August 11, 1944, Andrew Stevenson to A. H. Bunker, August 23, 1944, both in WPB 2305, RG 179, NA; Nelson to William D. Leahy, July 10, 1944, Nelson MSS 2.

30. Nelson, "Statement to the Truman Committee," July 6, 1944, Nelson to Charles Wilson, July 29, 1944, both in Nelson MSS 2; Barton J. Bernstein, "The Debate on Industrial Reconversion," *American Journal of Economics and Sociology* 26 (1967), 167–72; Schwarz, *The Speculator*, pp. 454–55.

31. Lewis Corey, "Problems of the Peace: III. Boom and Bust?" *Antioch Review* 4 (Fall 1944), 449–64.

32. William D. Leahy to Nelson, July 7, 1944, OF 4735, FDRL; Nelson to FDR, July 10, 1944, OF 4735, FDRL.

33. Charles E. Wilson to James F. Byrnes, November 4, 1943, WPB 2350,

RG 179, NA; I. F. Stone, "Nelson vs. Wilson," *Nation*, September 22, 1944, p. 260.

34. T.R.B., "Washington Notes," *New Republic*, July 3, 1944, p. 15.

35. Maverick to W. H. Forse, August 23, 1944, Maverick to Nelson, August 23, 1944, both in Nelson MSS 2; Maverick to Nelson, June 16, 1944, WPB 2305, RG 179, NA; Chester Bowles to Nelson, March 10, 1944, Bowles MSS I, 8.

36. Nelson, "Active Reserve Producers Plan," February 28, 1944, Nelson MSS 12; Stone, "Nelson vs. Wilson," p. 260; Thirteenth Bimonthly Report of the SWPC, June 1 through July 31, 1944, Baruch MSS 34; Samuel Lubell to Bernard Baruch, January 18, 1944, Baruch MSS 44.

37. *New York Times*, December 11, 1944; Norman Pond to Nelson, March 3, 1943, WPB 91, RG 179, NA.

38. Bruce Catton, *War Lords of Washington* (New York: Harcourt, Brace, 1948), pp. 247–48, T.R.B., "Washington Notes," *New Republic*, July 3, 1944, p. 15.

39. Donald Nelson, *Arsenal of Democracy* (New York: Harcourt, Brace, 1946), p. 402.

40. Nelson, "Initial Stages in the Approach to Reconversion," July 7, 1944, Nelson MSS 12.

41. John Morton Blum, *V Was for Victory: Politics and American Culture During World War II* (New York: Harcourt Brace Jovanovich, 1976), p. 128–30; Nelson, *Arsenal of Democracy*, pp. 411–16.

42. Maury Maverick to Donald Nelson, June 16, 1944, WPB 2305, RG 179, NA; "Notes for Mr. Nelson's Testimony Before the Truman Committee," June 19, 1944, Nelson MSS 12; Stone, "Nelson vs. Wilson," p. 260; Donald H. Riddle, "The Truman Committee: A Study in Congressional-Military Relations" (Ph.D. Dissertation, Princeton University, 1956), pp. 213–29, 252–53; Richard B. Henderson, *Maury Maverick: A Political Biography* (Austin: University of Texas Press, 1970), pp. 239–48; Barton J. Bernstein, "The Debate on Industrial Reconversion," *American Journal of Economics and Sociology* 26 (1967), 167–72.

43. "Please, Sir, who is going to champion the cause of the 'little guy' while Donald Nelson is away?" the president of a small St. Louis bank wrote Roosevelt after the announcement. F. R. Windegger to FDR, August 23, 1944, OF 4735, FDRL. Many other, similar protests are in the same file.

44. FDR to Nelson, November 2, 1944, Nelson MSS 2; Wilson to Byrnes, November 4, 1943, WPB 2350, RG 179, NA: Wilson to FDR, OF 4735, FDRL; "Business Loses Two Spokesmen in WPB Reconversion Shake-up," *Newsweek*, September 4, 1944, pp. 67–68; " 'Dear Charlie,' " *Time*, September 4, 1944, pp. 18–19.

45. Krug to Forrest Allen, October 19, 1943, Krug to Manly Fleischmann, November 23, 1943, both in Krug MSS 1; Krug to W. Y. Elliott, August 30, 1944, S. W. Anderson to Krug, November 30, 1944, both in WPB 2305, RG 179, NA; Helen Fuller, "Krug and Reconversion," *New Republic*, August 20, 1945, pp. 219–20; Barton J. Bernstein, "The Removal of War Production Board Controls on Business, 1944–1946," *Business History Review* 39 (1965), 246–50.

46. T.R.B., "Washington Notes," July 3, 1944, p. 15; I. F. Stone, "Nelson vs. Wilson," p. 260.

47. Gerald T. White, *Billions for Defense: Government Financing by the Defense Plant Corporation during World War II* (University, Ala.: University of Alabama Press, 1980), pp. 11–50; Jesse H. Jones, *Fifty Billion Dollars: My Thirteen Years with the RFC, 1932–1945* (New York: Macmillan, 1951), pp. 315–16; Michael Straight, "Jesse Jones, Bottleneck," *New Republic*, December 29, 1941, pp. 881–82.

48. Ibid., p. 316; Robert J. Gordon, "$45 Billion of U.S. Private Investment Has Been Mislaid," *American Economic Review* 59 (June 1969), 225–31; "New Deal Plans Industry Council," *Business Week*, March 20, 1943, pp. 15–16; David Lilienthal and Robert H. Marquis, "The Conduct of Business Enterprises by the Federal Government," *Harvard Law Review* 54 (February 1941), p. 601; White, *Billions for Defense*, pp. 67–87. Extensive records of the particular plants and projects the DPC authorized and funded are in WPB 993–94, RG 179, NA.

49. I. F. Stone, "Defense Stumbles On," *Nation*, September 20, 1941, pp. 244–45; Dwight Macdonald, "Jesse Jones: Reluctant Dragon. II," *Nation*, February 14, 1942, p. 189; Harold L. Ickes, *The Secret Diary of Harold L. Ickes*, 3 vols. (New York: Simon and Schuster, 1953–1954), III: 296; Straight, "Jesse Jones: Bottleneck," p. 882.

50. White, *Billions for Defense*, pp. 54–57; Jordan Schwarz, *The New Dealers: Power Politics in the Age of Roosevelt* (New York: Alfred A. Knopf, 1993), pp. 314–15.

51. "Defense Plant Corporation" [n.d.], WPB 2243, RG 179, NA; Clifford Durr, "The Postwar Relationship Between Government and Business," *American Economic Review* 33 (1943), 49–50.

52. "F.D.R. to Jesse Jones: An Imaginary Letter," *Nation*, February 3, 1945, p. 117; "The War Surplus Bill," *Nation*, August 26, 1944, p. 228; Lois Flanagan to Ferdinand Eberstadt (including memorandum, "Statements of Harold Ickes"), August 16, 1944, Eberstadt MSS 95; White, *Billions for Defense*, p. 91.

53. H. S. Person, "Postwar Control of Monopolies," *New Republic*, December 27, 1943, pp. 907–09; David Lilienthal, "Conduct of Business Enterprises," *Harvard Law Review* 54 (February 1941), p. 601; I. F. Stone, "Millionaires' Beveridge Plan," *Nation*, March 25, 1944, p. 35; Clifford J. Durr, "The Postwar Relationship between Government and Business," *American Economic Review* 33 (March 1943), 50; White, *Billions for Defense*, pp. 90–91.

54. Bernard Baruch and John Hancock, *Report on War and Post-War Adjustment Policies, February 15, 1944* (Washington: Government Printing Office, 1944); Harold Smith, "Notes on Conference with the President," October 20, November 2, 1943, Smith MSS 3; "War and Post-War Adjustment Policies," February 10, 1944, Baruch MSS 31; White, *Billions for Defense*, pp. 93–94; Baruch to Byrnes, August 30, 1944, Baruch MSS 31.

55. Baruch and Hancock, "War and Post-War Adjustment Policies," p. 62; White, *Billions for Defense*, p. 93.

56. Eleanor Roosevelt to Harry Hopkins, August 12, 1944, Hopkins MSS 214; "The Baruch Plan," *New Republic*, February 28, 1944, pp. 263–64; "The Baruch Plan (Continued)," *New Republic*, March 6, 1944, p. 304; Schwarz, *The Speculator*, p. 457.

57. Stone, "Millionaires' Beveridge Plan," p. 35; "Prosperity," *New Republic*, November 27, 1944, p. 716; J. Donald Kingsley, "Hell-Bent for Chaos. I. The Plans for X-Day," *New Republic*, April 24, 1944, p. 554.

58. Stone, "Millionaires' Beveridge Plan," p. 35; "The Baruch Plan (Continued)," p. 304; Arnold to Max Lerner, March [n.d.], 1944, Lerner MSS 1; White, *Billions for Defense*, pp. 94, 112.

59. In a 1933 speech about the National Planning Board, Ickes expressed the hope that "long after the necessity for stimulating industry and creating new buying power by a comprehensive system of public works shall be a thing of the past, national planning will go on as a permanent Government institution." See "City Planning Merges into National Planning," *The American City*, November 1933, p. 65.

60. "City Planning Merges into National Planning," p. 65; National Planning Board, *Final Report, 1933–1934* (Washington: Government Printing Office, 1934), p. 1; Warken, *History of the National Resources Planning Board*, p. 47; Frederic A. Delano, "Statement for National Planning Conference," May 1939, Delano MSS 24; Patrick D. Reagan, "The Architects of Modern American National Planning" (Ph.D. Dissertation, Ohio State University, 1982), pp. 39–67.

61. Barry D. Karl, *Charles E. Merriam and the Study of Politics* (Chicago: University of Chicago Press, 1974), pp. 255–57; Charles E. Merriam, "The National Resources Planning Board," *Public Administration Review* 1 (Winter 1941), 116–21; Merriam, "The National Resources Planning Board: A Chapter in American Planning Experience," *American Political Science Review* 38 (December 1944), 1075–88; Frederic S. Lee, "From Multi-industry Planning to Keynesian Planning: Gardiner Means, the American Keynesians, and National Economic Planning at the National Resources Committee," *Journal of Policy History* 2 (1990), 186–212.

62. Charles E. Merriam, "Planning Agencies in America," *American Political Science Review* 29 (April 1935), 202–07.

63. George T. Renner, "NRC—The National Planning Agency," *Social Forces*, December 1935, pp. 301–02; Warken, *History of the National Resources Planning Board*, pp. 55–105; David Cushman Coyle, "The American National Planning Board," *Political Quarterly* 16 (July/September 1945), 246–47.

64. Frederic A. Delano, "New National Resources Planning Board," *Planning and Civic Comment* 5 (July–September 1939), p. 1; John D. Millett, *The Process and Organization of Government Planning* (New York: Columbia University Press, 1947), pp. 85–93, 145–46; Warken, *History of the National Resources Planning Board*, pp. 108–09.

65. Delano to FDR, December 31, 1940, OF 1092, FDRL; Charles W. Eliot II to Alvin Hansen, March 8, 1939, Hansen MSS 3.10; Minutes of Industrial Committee meeting, January 13, 1939, Means MSS 7.

66. Washington *Post*, November 19, 1938; "A Fiscal and Monetary Advisory Board," August 10, 1938, Eccles MSS 38-7; Morgenthau to Harold D. Smith, June 23, 1939, Fiscal and Monetary Advisory Board, Records of Daniel W. Bell, Bureau of the Budget, Record Group 51, Series 38.3.

67. Fiscal and Monetary Advisory Board statement, May 25, 1939, Ruml to Daniel W. Bell, November 2, 1938, and Minutes of Conference with the President, December 19, 1938, all in ibid.; Harold Smith diary, May 12, 1939, Smith MSS 1; Millett, *Process and Organization of Government Planning*, pp. 142–43.

68. Corwin Edwards, Summary of NRC Meeting on Industrial Policy, June 5, 1938, Interior Archives, RG 48, Box 10 ("Cohen"), NA; Thomas Blaisdell to Thomas Eliot, July 9, 1938, ibid.

69. National Resources Planning Board, *The Structure of the American Economy: Part II. Toward Full Use of Resources* (Washington: U.S. Government Printing Office, 1940), pp. 1–2, 6; National Resources Committee, *The Structure of the American Economy: Part I. Basic Characteristics* (Washington: U.S. Government Printing Office, 1939). The three other NRPB reports mentioned here were all published by the Government Printing Office in 1940. For a summary of the NRPB's work in 1940, see Frederic A. Delano to FDR, November 12, 1940, OF 1092, FDRL.

70. NRPB, *The Structure of the American Economy: Part II*, pp. 3–4, 10, 16–19, 26, 33–34, 45. Implicit, and on occasion explicit, in this discussion was a rejection of Part I of *The Structure of the American Economy* for its unreflective preoccupation with older, structural ideas of reform and its lack of attention to newer, compensatory approaches. The writers of Part II referred diplomatically to the first document as a useful reference work. Harold Smith, describing an NRPB meeting in Charlottesville in the fall of 1939 to discuss Part I, referred to Part I as "a very tedious performance." Smith diary, September 17–20, 1939, Smith MSS 1. See also Delano to FDR, December 31, 1940, OF 1092, FDRL.

71. Frederic A. Delano et al., "National Resources Planning Board," *Free World*, November 1942, pp. 175–78; Delano to FDR, March 14, 1941, OF 1092, FDRL; "Proposed Messages to Congress on Post War Security," October 1, 1941, OF 1092, FDRL; Millett, *Process and Organization of Government Planning*, pp. 118–19, 142.

72. Delano to Eccles, June 16, 1939, Eccles MSS 6-1; Delano to FDR, January 30, March 14, 1941, OF 1092, FDRL; "Plan for the Future," *Time*, August 25, 1941, p. 18; George Soule, "The Bogey of Excess Capacity," *New Republic*, April 7, 1941, p. 460.

73. NRPB, "Full Employment Now and Tomorrow: An Approach to Post-Defense Planning," July 1941, OF 1092, FDRL; NRPB, "National Resources Development Report"; NRPB, "The NRPB in Wartime," *Frontiers of Democracy* 8 (February 15, 1942), 143. See also memorandum to Stephen Early (telephone summaries), February 4, 1943, OF 1092 (5), FDRL; L. B. Parker to Rep. Harry Sheppard, March 11, 1943, OF 4351 (2), FDRL; Bruce Bliven, Max Lerner, and George Soule, "Charter for America," *New Republic*, April 19, 1943, p. 528; J. Raymond Walsh, "Action for Postwar Planning," *Antioch Review* 3 (1943), 153–61; Frederic Delano et al. to FDR, August 24, 1943, OF 1092, FDRL; NRPB, "Post-War Plan and Program," February 1943, Senatorial File 43, HSTL. "National Income" is calculated differently from "Gross National Product" and is consistently slightly lower. In 1933, it had been $40 billion (less than half the 1929 figure). In 1939, the last year before the war-induced boom, it was $83 billion. Bureau of the Census, *Historical Statistics of the United States: Colonial Times to 1970*, 2 vols. (Washington: U.S. Government Printing Office, 1975), I: 216, 224.

74. The NRPB presented the report to the President a few days before Pearl Harbor, and Delano remained reluctant to push for its release for many

months after America entered the war. Only late in 1942 did he and other NRPB members begin gently prodding the President to send the report to Congress; he finally did so in March 1943, in part because the release of the Beveridge report in Britain a few months before had increased the pressure on him to act. Keith W. Olson, "The American Beveridge Plan," *Mid-America* 68 (1983), 90–92; Marion Clawson, *New Deal Planning: The National Resources Planning Board* (Baltimore: The Johns Hopkins University Press, 1981), pp. 136–43; Warken, *History of the National Resources Planning Board*, pp. 215–16, 224–26.

75. *New York Times*, January 20, 1943; Mordecai Ezekiel, "Full Employment—Beveridge Model," *Nation*, March 3, 1945, p. 253; "A New Bill of Rights," *Nation*, March 20, 1943, p. 401; Alvin Hansen, "Beveridge," *New Republic*, February 19, 1945, pp. 251–52; Richard L. Stout, "The Beveridge Report," *New Republic*, December 14, 1942, p. 785; Memorandum, Political and Economic Planning (P.E.P.) Committee, June 4, 1942, CAB.87—80, PRO; William Beveridge, memorandum to P.E.P. Committee, "The Scale of Social Insurance Benefits and Allied Services," January 16, 1942, CAB.87—79, PRO; British Press Service, "American Survey," December 4, 1942, and Office of War Information, "U.S. Newspaper Comment on Beveridge Report," December 27, 1942, both in Beveridge MSS XI, 32.

76. Eveline Burns, "Comparison of the NRPB Report with the Beveridge Report," December 26, 1942, PIN.8—167, PRO; Marriner Eccles to FDR, December 17, 1942, Eccles MSS 5-11; Louis Bean to Milo Perkins, December 21, 1942, Bean MSS 34; G. E. Millard to T. Daish, February 18, 1943, and Dash to Millard, February 27, 1943, PIN.8—167, PRO; Edwin E. Witte, "American Post-War Social Security Proposals," *American Economic Review* 33 (December 1943), 830; Alvin Hansen to Beveridge, July 3, 1943, Beveridge MSS XI, 31. David Marquand, *The Unprincipled Society: New Demands and Old Politics* (London: Jonathan Cape, 1988) is a thoughtful, unsympathetic evaluation of the postwar British regime that the Beveridge report helped shape. Paul Addison, *The Road to 1945: British Politics and the Second World War* (London: Jonathan Cape, 1975), and Elizabeth Durbin, *New Jerusalems: The Labour Party and the Economics of Democratic Socialism* (London: Routledge and Kegan Paul, 1985) describe the creation of that regime.

77. National Resources Planning Board, *Security, Work, and Relief Policies* (Washington: Government Printing Office, 1942), p. 1.

78. Ibid., pp. 1, 546–49.

79. Ibid., pp. 325–28, 341, 495, 502.

80. Ibid., pp. 2–3.

81. Alvin H. Hansen, *After the War—Full Employment* (Washington: Government Printing Office, 1942); Olson, "The American Beveridge Plan," pp. 87–88; Clawson, *New Deal Planning*, pp. 137, 182–83; Warken, *History of the National Resources Planning Board*, p. 216.

82. "A New Bill of Rights," *Nation*, March 20, 1943, p. 401; Bruce Bliven, Max Lerner, and George Soule, "Charter for America," *New Republic*, April 19, 1943, pp. 523–24; I. F. Stone, "Planning and Politics," *Nation*, March 20, 1943, p. 405; "America's Beveridge Plan," *Nation*, December 19, 1942, pp. 669–70; "A Beveridge Plan for America," *New Republic*, December 21, 1942, pp. 810–11; "Cradle to the Grave," *Christian Century*, March 24, 1943, pp. 350–51; Max

Lerner, "Problems of a Postwar World," *Proceedings of the National Council of Social Work, 1943* (New York, 1943), p. 404; "The NRPB in War-Time," *Frontiers of Democracy*, February 15, 1942, p. 143; L. B. Parker to Harry Sheppard, March 11, 1943, OF 4351 (2), FDRL; "Postwar Portent" and "Promised Land," *Newsweek*, March 22, 1943, pp. 27, 30–34; "Cradle to Grave," *Time*, March 22, 1943; Ernest K. Lindley, "How the Postwar Reports Came to Be," *Time*, March 22, 1943; Edwin E. Witte, "American Post-War Social Security Proposals," *American Economic Review* 33 (December 1943), 825–38; Chapman, *Contours of Public Policy*, pp. 255–57.

83. *New York Times*, March 14, 1943; Ralph Robey, "Postwar Bureaucratic Utopia: Part II," *Newsweek*, May 10, 1943, p. 62; "New Deal Plans Industry Council," *Business Week*, March 20, 1943, pp. 16–17; Chapman, *Contours of Public Policy*, pp. 252–54; Warken, *History of the National Resources Planning Board*, p. 227.

84. "Cradle to Grave," *Time*, March 22, 1943, p. 13; "Promised Land," *Newsweek*, March 22, 1943, pp. 30–31; Witte, "American Post-War Social Security Proposals," p. 832; John C. Cort, "Design for Planning," *Commonweal*, July 2, 1943, p. 270.

85. Wayne Coy, report on conference with the President, April 9, 1943, and Harold Smith, memorandum on conference with the President, June 3, 1943, both in Smith MSS 3; "To Save the Planning Board," *Business Week*, April 17, 1943, p. 8; Warken, *History of the National Resources Planning Board*, pp. 240–45; Clawson, *New Deal Planning*, pp. 238–41; Reagan, "Architects of Modern American National Planning," pp. 370–75.

86. Memorandum accompanying NRPB reports, from British Embassy, Washington, to Economic Reconstruction Department, Foreign Office, London, March 27, 1943, FO371—35367, PRO.

87. Frederic A. Delano to FDR, November 4, 1942, OF 1092, FDRL; George Soule, "Planning Wins," *New Republic*, March 8, 1943, p. 309; British Embassy memorandum, March 27, 1943.

88. Helen Fuller, "Look Who's Planning," *New Republic*, July 26, 1943, p. 104; Donald Worster, *Dust Bowl: The Southern Plains in the 1930s* (New York: Oxford University Press, 1979), pp. 149–63; Grant McConnell, *The Decline of Agrarian Democracy* (Berkeley: University of California Press, 1953), pp. 97–126.

89. Bruce Bliven, "Charter for America," *New Republic*, April 19, 1943, pp. 541–42; "Canning the Planners," *Commonweal*, June 11, 1943, p. 192; Charles E. Merriam, "The National Resources Planning Board: A Chapter in American Planning Experience," *American Political Science Review* 38 (December 1944), 1083–84.

90. Roosevelt issued a statement in 1942 when he signed a bill reducing the draft age in which he called for "planning in advance" to "enable the young men whose education has been interrupted to resume their schooling and afford equal opportunity for the training and education of other young men of ability after their service in the armed forces has come to an end." "Statement on Signing the Bill Reducing the Draft Age," November 13, 1942, Samuel I. Rosenman, ed., *The Public Papers and Addresses of Franklin D. Roosevelt*, 4 vols. (New York: Harper and Brothers, 1950), 1942 volume, p. 470.

91. Warken, *History of the National Resources Planning Board*, pp. 193–98;

Davis R. B. Ross, *Preparing for Ulysses: Politics and Veterans During World War II* (New York: Columbia University Press, 1969), pp. 52–64; NRPB, "The Demobilization of Men (Program for Training, Counselling, Rehabilitating, Readjustment and Placement)," June 1942, and "Preliminary Readjustment of Civilian and Military Personnel," March 1943, RG 187, NA.

92. "Fireside Chat on the Progress of the War and Plans for Peace," July 28, 1943, *Public Papers and Addresses*, 1943 volume, p. 333; Oscar Cox to Harry Hopkins, January 2, February 4, June 5, 9, 1943, Hopkins MSS 329; Draft of Address on Veterans' Readjustment, June 9, 1943, Hopkins MSS 329; Ross, *Waiting for Ulysses*, p. 64.

93. Keith W. Olson, *The G.I. Bill, the Veterans, and the Colleges* (Lexington: University Press of Kentucky, 1974), pp. 3–24; Richard Polenberg, *War and Society: The United States, 1941–1945* (Philadelphia: Lippincott, 1972), pp. 96–96; Roland Young, *Congressional Politics During the Second World War* (New York: Columbia University Press, 1956), pp. 213–17.

94. M. B. Schnapper, ed, *Going Back to Civilian Life* (Washington: Public Affairs Press, 1944), pp. 3–26; Olson, *The G.I. Bill*, chaps. 2–5; Ross, *Preparing for Ulysses*, pp. 102–21; Chapman, *Contours of Public Policy*, p. 260.

95. Rosenman, ed., *Public Papers and Addresses of Franklin D. Roosevelt*, 1942 volume, p. 470; Edwin Amenta and Theda Skocpol, "Redefining the New Deal: World War II and the Development of Social Provision in the United States," in Margaret Weir, Ann Shola Orloff, and Skocpol, eds., *The Politics of Social Policy in the United States* (Princeton: Princeton University Press, 1988), pp. 82, 108; Ross, *Preparing for Ulysses*, p. 57. For discussion of the Civil War pensions system, see Theda Skocpol, *Protecting Soldiers and Mothers: The Political Origins of Social Policy in the United States* (Cambridge: Harvard University Press, 1992), chap. 2.

96. "Message on the State of the Union," January 11, 1944, *Public Papers and Addresses*, 1944–1945 volume, pp. 41–42.

97. Stephen K. Bailey, *Congress Makes a Law: The Story Behind the Employment Act of 1946* (New York: Columbia University Press, 1950), pp. 92–96; Nelson W. Polsby, *Political Innovation in America: The Politics of Policy Initiation* (New Haven: Yale University Press, 1984), pp. 104–06; Steve Fraser, *Labor Will Rule: Sidney Hillman and the Rise of American Labor* (New York: The Free Press, 1991), pp. 507–09.

98. Alvin H. Hansen, "Planning Full Employment," *Nation*, October 21, 1944, p. 492; Hansen, "Beveridge on Full Employment," *New Republic*, February 19, 1945, pp. 250–54; Hansen, "For a Stable Market Economy," *Atlantic Monthly*, August 1945, pp. 78–81; Hansen, "Wages and Prices: The Basic Issue," *New York Times Magazine*, January 6, 1946, pp. 9, 36; Hansen, "Social Planning for Tomorrow," in Hansen et al., *The United States After War* (Ithaca: Cornell University Press, 1945), pp. 15–34.

99. Bailey, *Congress Makes a Law*, pp. 81–92; John D. Millett, *The Process and Organization of Government Planning* (New York: Columbia University Press, 1947), pp. 129–30; Steven Gillon, *Politics and Vision: The ADA and American Liberalism, 1947–1985* (New York: Oxford University Press, 1987), pp. 9–19, 64.

100. "For Full Employment," *Nation*, December 23, 1944, p. 761; James G. Patton and James Loeb, Jr., "The Challenge to Progressives," *New Republic*,

February 5, 1945, pp. 187–206. Michael W. Flamm, "The National Farmers Union and the Evolution of Agrarian Liberalism" (M.A. essay, Columbia University, 1992), pp. 55–71, describes the NFU role in the battle for the Full Employment Bill.

101. Alvin H. Hansen, "Suggested Revision of Full Employment Bill," July 28, 1945, Hansen MSS 3.10.

102. James G. Patton and James Loeb, Jr., "The Challenge to Progressives," *New Republic*, February 5, 1945, p. 188; Heinz Eulau, Mordecai Ezekiel, Alvin H. Hansen, James Loeb, Jr., and George Soule, "The Road to Freedom—Full Employment," *New Republic*, September 24, 1945, p. 414; "For Full Employment," *Nation*, December 23, 1944, pp. 761–62; Lebergott, "Shall We *Guarantee* Full Employment?," p. 200.

103. I. F. Stone, "Capitalism and Full Employment," *Nation*, September 1, 1945, pp. 198–99; Patton and Loeb, "Challenge to Progressives," p. 188; Flamm, "The National Farmers Union," p. 68.

104. Herbert Stein, *The Fiscal Revolution in America* (Chicago: University of Chicago Press, 1969), pp. 200–01.

105. Margaret Weir, "The Federal Government and Unemployment: The Frustration of Policy Innovation from the New Deal to the Great Society," in Weir, Orloff, and Skocpol, eds., *Politics of Social Policy*, p. 160; Robert M. Collins, *The Business Response to Keynes, 1929–1964* (New York: Columbia University Press, 1981), pp. 102–09; Bailey, *Congress Makes a Law*, pp. 129–49; Stein, *Fiscal Revolution*, pp. 202–04.

106. Bailey, *Congress Makes a Law*, pp. 228–32; Blum, *V Was for Victory*, pp. 329–32.

107. Eccles to Truman, March 15, 1946, Eccles to Harold Smith, February 15, 1946, both in Eccles MSS 5-12; Robert Lekachman, *The Age of Keynes* (New York: Random House, 1966), pp. 174–75; Millett, *Process and Organization*, pp. 27–28, 103–04, 133.

108. Chester Bowles, "Speech to New York chapter of Americans for Democratic Action," November 12, 1947, Lerner MSS 1; "Is It Full Employment?" *New Republic*, February 18, 1946, p. 240; Guy Greer, "More Work Than Workers," *Social Forces*, October 1946, pp. 49–51; Lekachman, *The Age of Keynes*, pp. 170–71; Theodore Rosenof, *Patterns of Political Economy in America: The Failure to Develop a Democratic Left Synthesis, 1933–1950* (New York: Garland, 1983), pp. 205–06.

## Epilogue

1. Bowles to Max Lerner, May 29, 1947, Lerner MSS 1; William E. Leuchtenburg, "Farewell to the New Deal: The Lingering of a Fable," *The New Leader*, December 11, 1948, p. 5.

2. Stuart Chase, "Production First," *Nation*, January 13, 1945, p. 39; Arthur M. Schlesinger, Jr., "The Broad Accomplishments of the New Deal," in Seymour Harris, ed., *Saving American Capitalism* (New York: Alfred A. Knopf, 1948), pp. 78, 80; Jordan A. Schwarz, *Liberal: Adolf A. Berle and the Vision of an American Era* (New York: The Free Press, 1987), pp. 354–66.

3. A revealing glimpse of Henderson's bitterness after 1942 is in a report

by Richard Miles, of the British embassy in Washington, of a dinner party he attended in late 1943 at which Henderson was a guest. During it, Henderson spoke harshly (and apparently constantly) about the abysmal state of liberal government. Redvers Opie to Gladwyn Jebb, November 30, 1943, FO 371-35368, PRO.

4. Alvin Hansen, "Suggested Revision of the Full Employment Bill," Hansen MSS, 3.10; Chester Bowles, *Tomorrow Without Fear* (New York: Simon and Schuster, 1946).

5. "Democratic Platform of 1940," reprinted in Democratic National Committee, *Democratic Campaign Handbook* (1940), pp. 84–90; "The 1944 Democratic Platform," *Democratic Digest*, August 1944, pp. 13, 27. The 1948 Democratic platform saw a temporary revival of anti-monopoly language, part of Harry Truman's effort to inject a populist theme into his troubled presidential campaign.

# Index

A NOTE ABOUT THE AUTHOR

Alan Brinkley is a professor of American history at Columbia University. His previous books include *Voices of Protest: Huey Long, Father Coughlin, and the Great
Depression*, which won the American Book Award for History, and *The Unfinished
Nation: A Concise History of the American People*. His essays, articles, and reviews
have appeared in the *American Historical Review*, the *Journal of American History*,
the *New York Times Book Review*, the *New York Review of Books*, the *Times Literary
Supplement*, the *New Republic*, and many other publications. He lives with his wife
and daughter in New York City.

A NOTE ON THE TYPE

This book was set in a typeface called Berling. This distinguished letter is a computer
version of the original type designed by the Swedish typographer Karl Erik Forsberg
(born 1914). Forsberg is also known for designing several other typefaces, including
Parad (1936), Lunda (1938), Carolus, and Ericus, but Berling—named after the
foundry that produced it, Berlingska Stilgjuteriet of Lund—is the one for which he
is best known. Berling, a roman font with the characteristics of an old face, was first
used to produce *The Rembrandt Bible* in 1954, which won an award for the most
beautiful book of the year.

Composed by ComCom, a division of Haddon Craftsmen,
Allentown, Pennsylvania
Printed and bound by R. R. Donnelley & Sons,
Harrisonburg, Virginia
Designed by Robert C. Olsson